CompTIA®

Cloud+®

Study Guide

Third Edition

CompTIA®

Cloud+®

Study Guide

Exam CV0-003

Third Edition

Ben Piper

SYBEX
A Wiley Brand

Published by John Wiley & Sons, Inc., Hoboken, New Jersey.

Published simultaneously in Canada.

ISBN: 978-1-119-81086-5

ISBN: 978-1-119-81094-0 (ebk.)

ISBN: 978-1-119-81095-7 (ebk.)

Library of Congress Control Number: 2021942883

Cover image: © Jeremy Woodhouse/Getty Images, Inc.

Cover design: Wiley

SKY10069728_031424

Acknowledgments

There are many people who work to put a book together, and it would never be published without the dedicated, hard work of the whole team at Wiley. They are truly a fantastic group to work with, and without the Wiley team this book would have never been possible. To everyone at Wiley, a big thank-you! You made the late nights and long weekends of writing and putting this book together all worthwhile.

Special thanks to Kenyon Brown, senior acquisitions editor, who was always ready to provide resources and answer questions. His experience and guidance throughout the project were critical.

Gary Schwartz, project manager, kept this book's publishing schedule on track. His edits helped make many of the technical parts of this book more readable. Thanks also to Christine O'Connor, managing editor, Pete Gaughan, content enablement manager, and Liz Welch, copy editor.

Kunal Mittal, technical editor, checked the technical content for accuracy. He also provided invaluable feedback on how to make the technical concepts more understandable.

—Ben Piper

About the Author

Ben Piper has authored multiple books, including the *AWS Certified Solutions Architect Study Guide: Associate SAA-C02 Exam* (Sybex, 2020) and *AWS Certified Cloud Practitioner Study Guide: Foundational CLF-C01 Exam* (Sybex, 2019). You can contact Ben by visiting his website `https://benpiper.com`.

About the Technical Editor

Kunal Mittal is an entrepreneur and serves on the board of directors/advisers for multiple technology startups. His strengths are product strategy, technology strategy, and execution. His passion is building high-performing teams with a passion and gumption to innovate. Apart from technology, Kunal owns a winery in Paso Robles (central California) named LXV Wine, which won an award for being the 7th best Tasting Experience in the United States by *USA Today*.

Contents at a Glance

Contents

Introduction

Welcome to the exciting world of cloud computing and CompTIA certifications! If you picked up this book because you want to improve yourself with a secure and rewarding job in the new and fast-growing cloud computing space, you have come to the right place. Whether you are striving to enter the thriving, dynamic IT sector, or you are seeking to enhance your skills in the emerging cloud computing field, being CompTIA Cloud+ certified can seriously stack the odds of success in your favor.

CompTIA certifications are powerful instruments of success that will most certainly improve your knowledge of cloud computing. As you progress throughout this book, you'll gain a broad and deep understanding of cloud computing operations that offers unprecedented exposure to this dynamic field. The knowledge and expertise that you will gain are essential for your success in all areas of the cloud computing field.

By deciding to become Cloud+ certified, you're proudly announcing to the world that you want to become an unrivaled cloud computing expert—a goal that this book will get you well on your way to achieving. Congratulations in advance on the beginning of your brilliant future!

> **NOTE** For up-to-the-minute updates covering additions or modifications to the CompTIA certification exams, as well as additional study tools, videos, practice questions, and bonus material, be sure to visit the Sybex website and forum at www.sybex.com.

Why Should You Become Certified in Cloud Technologies?

CompTIA has created the world's leading vendor-neutral family of certifications in the technology industry. CompTIA's certifications are recognized and respected worldwide for their quality and rigorous standards. They offer a broad range of certifications on a wide variety of technology topics. When you become Cloud+ certified, you have validated your skills and expertise in the implementation and ongoing support of cloud-based services. Becoming a CompTIA Cloud+ certified professional validates that you have the knowledge to be a successful cloud engineer.

The Cloud+ certification is recognized as one of the premier cloud certifications on the market today. Studying for and passing the Cloud+ exam gives engineers the set of skills to succeed in the fast-growing field of cloud computing.

Rest assured that when you pass the CompTIA Cloud+ exam, you're headed down a path to certain success!

What Does This Book Cover?

This book, consisting of 10 chapters, follows the most recent version of the CompTIA Cloud+ exam, CV0-003. The exam blueprint is divided into five sections which are explained in sufficient detail to help you become a Cloud+ certified professional.

Chapter 1: Introducing Cloud Computing Configurations and Deployments The book starts out by investigating the most common cloud components, such as applications, compute, storage, and networking. Then it discusses how to determine the correct size and scale of the systems. You will gain a basic understanding of configurations found in the cloud and learn about production, quality assurance, and development of cloud systems.

Chapter 2: Cloud Deployments In this chapter, you'll learn about deploying services in the cloud and how to execute a deployment plan; the most common service models; and the various ways that clouds are delivered, such as public, private, and community. Common cloud terminology and storage are explained.

Next, the chapter delves into the technical background and you'll learn how to determine the needs and design of an effective cloud deployment. This includes what virtualization is, its benefits, and why it's a central technology in cloud computing. You'll learn about hypervisors and virtual machines, and how to migrate from your existing operations to the cloud.

Chapter 3: Security in the Cloud This chapter covers cloud security, starting with security policies, laws, and standards. You will then learn about specific security technologies, applications, and services.

Chapter 4: Implementing Cloud Security This chapter builds on your security knowledge by explaining how to implement secure storage, networks, and compute systems. Security tools, intrusion systems, encryption, tools, techniques, and services are introduced.

Chapter 5: Maintaining Cloud Operations This chapter focuses on keeping your cloud deployment current with the latest updates, and it discusses the processes to follow. Automation is introduced, and you will learn about the importance of cloud automation and orchestration systems. The chapter concludes with a discussion of backing up your data in the cloud.

Chapter 6: Disaster Recovery, Business Continuity, and Ongoing Maintenance We'll take a step back in this chapter and cover how to go about developing a disaster recovery plan and the common models available. You will learn the importance of business survivability during a severe outage and understand the issues concerning recovery. The chapter ends by describing how to perform ongoing maintenance in your cloud environment.

Chapter 7: Cloud Management You'll now delve deeply into the operations aspects of cloud computing. This chapter begins with a discussion of monitoring the cloud, and then it moves on to look at the allocation and provisioning of resources. Then you will learn about business requirements, application life cycles, and the impact they have on managing your cloud deployment. The chapter concludes with a discussion on the security of your cloud operations with accounts, automation, authentication, and automation models.

Chapter 8: Cloud Management Baselines, Performance, and SLAs This chapter explains how to determine what is considered normal cloud operations by creating and maintaining baseline measurements. Using these measurements, you can monitor your cloud fleet for deviations from the baseline and learn the steps to take when this occurs. Service level agreements and chargeback models are also explained in this chapter.

Chapter 9: Troubleshooting This chapter goes deeply into the technical aspects, identifying and correcting cloud technical issues. Troubleshooting of new and existing deployments is covered. You will learn about common problems found in the cloud that you will need to resolve. You will learn how to identify and resolve deviations from your baselines and what to do when breakdowns in the workflow occur. Be sure to pay close attention to this chapter!

Chapter 10: Troubleshooting Networking and Security Issues and Understanding Methodologies The final chapter continues investigating troubleshooting with a focus on tools and techniques. Common troubleshooting utilities found in Linux and Windows systems are presented, and you'll learn how to perform a structured troubleshooting approach.

Appendix A: Answers to Review Questions This appendix contains answers to the book's Review Questions.

Appendix B: Answers to Written Labs This appendix contains the answers to the book's Written Labs.

Interactive Online Learning Environment and Test Bank

Wiley has put together some great online tools to help you pass the Cloud+ exam. The interactive online learning environment that accompanies the Cloud+ exam certification guide provides a test bank and study tools to help you prepare for the exam. By using these tools, you can dramatically increase your chances of passing the exam on your first try.

Sample Tests Many sample tests are provided throughout this book and online, including the assessment test at the end of this Introduction and the Review Questions at the end of each chapter. In addition, there are two exclusive online practice exams with 50 questions each. Use these questions to test your knowledge of the study guide material. The online test bank runs on multiple devices.

Flashcards The online text banks include 100 flashcards specifically written to hit you hard, so don't get discouraged if you don't ace your way through them at first! They're there to ensure that you're ready for the exam. Armed with the Review Questions, Practice Exams, and Flashcards, you'll be more than prepared when exam day comes. Questions are provided in digital flashcard format (a question followed by a single correct answer). You can use the Flashcards to reinforce your learning and provide last-minute test prep before the exam.

Other Study Tools A glossary of key terms from this book and their definitions is available as a fully searchable PDF.

NOTE: Go to www.wiley.com/go/sybextestprep to register and gain access to this interactive online learning environment and test bank with study tools.

How to Use This Book

If you want a solid foundation for the serious effort of preparing for the CompTIA CV0-003 Cloud+ exam, then look no further. Hundreds of hours have been spent putting together this book with the sole intention of helping you to pass the exam as well as to learn about the exciting field of cloud computing! The book has been completely updated and refreshed from the original to match the new version of the CompTIA Cloud+ exam, CV0-003.

This book is loaded with valuable information, and you will get the most out of your study time if you understand why the book is organized the way it is. In order to maximize your benefit from this book, I recommend the following study method:

1. Take the assessment test that's provided at the end of this Introduction. (The answers are at the end of the test.) It's okay if you don't know any of the answers; that's why you bought this book! Carefully read over the explanations for any questions that you get wrong and note the chapters in which the material relevant to them is covered. This information should help you plan your study strategy.
2. Study each chapter carefully, making sure that you fully understand the information and the test objectives listed at the beginning of each one. Pay extra-close attention to any chapter that includes material covered in questions that you missed.
3. Complete all written labs in each chapter, referring to the text of the chapter so that you understand the reason for each answer.
4. Answer all the Review Questions related to each chapter. Many of the questions are presented in a scenario format to emulate real-world tasks that you may encounter. (The answers to the Review Questions appear in Appendix A.) Note the questions that confuse you and study the topics they cover again until the concepts are crystal clear. Again, do not just skim these questions. Make sure that you fully comprehend the reason for each correct answer. Remember that these will not be the exact questions you will find on the exam, but they're written to help you understand the chapter material and ultimately pass the exam.
5. Each chapter also concludes with a fill-in-the-blank type of written lab that is designed to improve your memory and comprehension of key items that were presented in the chapter. These labs are great for test preparation. I suggest going over the questions until you are consistently able to answer them error free. (The answers appear in Appendix B.)

6. Try your hand at the practice questions that are exclusive to this book. The questions can be found at `http://www.wiley.com/go/sybextestprep`.
7. Test yourself using all of the Flashcards, which are also found at `http://www.wiley.com/go/sybextestprep`. These are new Flashcards to help you prepare for the CV0-003 Cloud+ exam.

To learn every bit of the material covered in this book, you'll have to apply yourself regularly and with discipline. Try to set aside the same time period every day to study and select a comfortable and quiet place to do so. I am confident that if you work hard, you'll be surprised at how quickly you learn this material.

If you follow these steps and study in addition to using the Review Questions, the Practice Exams, and the electronic Flashcards, it would actually be hard to fail the Cloud+ exam. But understand that studying for the CompTIA exams is a lot like getting in shape—if you do not exercise most days, it's not going to happen!

According to the CompTIA website, the Cloud+ exam details are as follows:

Exam code: CV0-003

Exam description: CompTIA Cloud+ covers competency in cloud models, virtualization, infrastructure, security, resource management, and business continuity.

Number of questions: Minimum of 90

Type of questions: Multiple choice and performance-based

Length of test: 90 minutes

Passing score: 750 (on a scale of 100–900)
Language: English

Recommended experience:

- At least 2–3 years of work experience in IT systems administration or IT networking
- CompTIA Network+ and Server+ or equivalent knowledge
- Familiarity with any major hypervisor technology for server virtualization
- Knowledge of cloud service models
- Knowledge of IT service management
- Hands-on experience with at least one public or private cloud IaaS platform

How Do You Go About Taking the Exam?

When the time comes to schedule your exam, you will need to create an account at www.comptia.org and register for your exam.

You can purchase the exam voucher on the CompTIA website at `https://certification.comptia.org/testing/buy-voucher`. The voucher is a proof of purchase and a code number that you will use to schedule the exam at `https://www.comptia.org/testing/testing-options/about-testing-options`.

When you have a voucher and have selected a testing center, you can go ahead and schedule the Cloud+ CV0-003 exam by visiting `www.pearsonvue.com/comptia`. There you can also locate a testing center or purchase vouchers if you have not already done so.

When you have registered for the Cloud+ certification exam, you will receive a confirmation email that supplies you with all the information you will need to take the exam.

Certification Exam Policies

This section explains CompTIA's exam policies and was taken from the CompTIA website. I recommend that you visit `https://certification.comptia.org/testing/test-policies` to become familiar with CompTIA's policies.

Candidate Agreement Explains the rules and regulations regarding certification, including the retake policy, the candidate conduct policy, and the candidate appeals process.

Candidate Testing Policies Includes accommodations during an exam, exam scoring, exam content, and out-of-country testing policies.

CompTIA Voucher Terms & Conditions Details the terms and conditions governing CompTIA vouchers.

Candidate ID Policy Details the acceptable forms of identification that candidates may bring to an exam.

Certification Retake Policy Details the circumstances in which a candidate can retake a certification exam.

Exam Delivery Policies Includes testing center suspensions, delivery exclusions, and beta testing policies.

Continuing Education Policies Covers certification renewal, candidate code of ethics, and audit findings as related to the Continuing Education Program.

Exam Development Explains the exam development process.

Sharing Your Exam Results Explains the exam results sharing policy.

Unauthorized Training Materials Defines unauthorized training materials and the consequences for using them.

Candidate Appeals Process Describes the process for candidates to appeal sanctions imposed due to exam security or policy violations.

CompTIA Exam Security Hotline Can be used to report security breaches, candidate misconduct, IP infringement, use of unauthorized training materials, and other exam security-related concerns.

Tips for Taking Your Cloud+ Exam

The CompTIA Cloud+ exam contains at least 90 multiple-choice questions and must be completed in 90 minutes or less. This information may change over time, so check `www.comptia.org` for the latest updates.

Many questions on the exam offer answer choices that at first glance look identical, especially the syntax questions. Remember to read through the choices carefully because close just doesn't cut it. If you get information in the wrong order or forget one measly character, you may get the question wrong. Many of the questions will be presented as a long, involved statement that is designed to confuse or misdirect you. Read these questions carefully, and make sure that you completely understand what the question is asking. It's important to filter out irrelevant statements and focus on what they are asking you to identify as the correct answer. So, to practice, do the Practice Exams and hands-on exercises from this book's chapters over and over again until they feel natural to you. Do the online sample test until you can consistently answer all the questions correctly. Relax and read the question over and over until you are 100 percent clear on what it's asking. Then you can usually eliminate a few of the obviously wrong answers.

Here are some general tips for exam success:

- Arrive early at the exam center so that you can relax and review your study materials.
- Read the questions carefully. Don't jump to conclusions. Make sure that you're clear about exactly what each question asks. "Read twice, answer once!" Scenario questions can be long and contain information that is not relevant to the answer. Take your time and understand what they are really asking you.
- Ask for a piece of paper and pencil if it's offered to take quick notes and make sketches during the exam.
- When answering multiple-choice questions that you're unsure about, use the process of elimination to get rid of the obviously incorrect answers first. Doing this greatly improves your odds if you need to make an educated guess.

After you complete an exam, you'll get immediate, online notification of your pass or fail status, a printed examination score report that indicates your pass or fail status, and your exam results by section. (The test administrator will give you the printed score report.) Test scores are automatically forwarded to CompTIA after you take the test, so you don't need to send your score to them. If you pass the exam, you'll receive confirmation from CompTIA that you are now a Cloud+ certified professional!

Cloud+ Exam Renewal

The Cloud+ certification is good for three years from the date of the exam. You can keep your certification up-to-date by following CompTIA's continuing education program outlined at `https://certification.comptia.org/continuing-education`.

CompTIA Cloud+ Study Guide: Exam CV0-003 Objective Map

The following objective map will assist you with finding where each exam objective is covered in the chapters in this book.

1.0 Cloud Architecture and Design

Exam Objective	Chapters
1.1 Compare and contrast the different types of cloud models.	1, 2

- Deployment models
  - Public
  - Private
  - Hybrid
  - Community
  - Cloud within a cloud
  - Multicloud
  - Multitenancy
- Service models
  - Infrastructure as a Service (IaaS)
  - Platform as a Service (PaaS)
  - Software as a Service (SaaS)
- Advanced cloud services
  - Internet of Things (IoT)
  - Serverless
  - Machine learning/Artificial intelligence (AI)
- Shared responsibility model

Exam Objective	Chapters
1.2 Explain the factors that contribute to capacity planning.	2, 8, 9

- Requirements
  - Hardware
  - Software
  - Budgetary
  - Business needs analysis
- Standard templates
- Licensing
  - Per-user
  - Socket-based
  - Volume-based
  - Core-based
  - Subscription
- User density
- System load
- Trend analysis
  - Baselines
  - Patterns
  - Anomalies
- Performance capacity planning

Exam Objective	Chapters
1.3 Explain the importance of high availability and scaling in cloud environments.	1, 2, 5, 7

- Hypervisors
  - Affinity
  - Anti-affinity
- Oversubscription
  - Compute
  - Network
  - Storage
- Regions and zones
- Applications
- Containers
- Clusters

Exam Objective	Chapters
▪ High availability of network functions	
▪ Switches	
▪ Routers	
▪ Load balancers	
▪ Firewalls	
▪ Avoid single points of failure	
▪ Scalability	
▪ Auto-scaling	
▪ Horizontal scaling	
▪ Vertical scaling	
▪ Cloud bursting	
1.4 Given a scenario, analyze the solution design in support of the business requirements.	1, 2, 5, 8
▪ Requirement analysis	
▪ Software	
▪ Hardware	
▪ Integration	
▪ Budgetary	
▪ Compliance	
▪ Service-level agreement (SLA)	
▪ User and business needs	
▪ Security	
▪ Network requirements	
▪ Sizing	
▪ Subnetting	
▪ Routing	
▪ Environments	
▪ Development	
▪ Quality assurance (QA)	
▪ Staging	
▪ Blue-green	
▪ Production	
▪ Disaster recovery (DR)	

Exam Objective	Chapters
▪ Testing techniques	
▪ Vulnerability testing	
▪ Penetration testing	
▪ Performance testing	
▪ Regression testing	
▪ Functional testing	
▪ Usability testing	

2.0 Security

Exam Objective	Chapters
2.1 Given a scenario, configure identity and access management.	2, 3, 4
▪ Identification and authorization	
▪ Privileged access management	
▪ Logical access management	
▪ Account life-cycle management	
▪ Provision and deprovision accounts	
▪ Access controls	
▪ Role-based	
▪ Discretionary	
▪ Non-discretionary	
▪ Mandatory	
▪ Directory services	
▪ Lightweight directory access protocol (LDAP)	
▪ Federation	
▪ Certificate management	
▪ Multifactor authentication (MFA)	
▪ Single sign-on (SSO)	
▪ Security assertion markup language (SAML)	
▪ Public key infrastructure (PKI)	
▪ Secret management	
▪ Key management	

Exam Objective	Chapters
2.2 Given a scenario, secure a network in a cloud environment	2, 3

- Network segmentation
  - Virtual LAN (VLAN)/Virtual extensible LAN (VXLAN)/Generic network virtualization encapsulation (GENEVE)
  - Micro-segmentation
  - Tiering
- Protocols
  - Domain name service (DNS)
    - DNS over HTTPS (DoH)
    - DNS over TLS (DoT)
    - DNS security (DNSSEC)
  - Network time protocol (NTP)
    - Network time security (NTS)
  - Encryption
    - IPSec
    - Transport layer security (TLS)
    - Hypertext transfer protocol secure (HTTPS)
  - Tunneling
    - Secure Shell (SSH)
    - Layer 2 tunneling protocol (L2TP)/Point-to-point tunneling protocol (PPTP)
    - Generic routing encapsulation (GRE)
- Network services
  - Firewalls
    - Stateful
    - Stateless
  - Web application firewall (WAF)
  - Application delivery controller (ADC)
  - Intrusion protection system (IPS)/Intrusion detection system (IDS)
  - Data loss prevention (DLP)
  - Network access control (NAC)
  - Packet brokers

Exam Objective	Chapters

▪ Log and event monitoring
▪ Network flows
▪ Hardening and configuration changes
  ▪ Disabling unnecessary ports and services
  ▪ Disabling weak protocols and ciphers
  ▪ Firmware upgrades
  ▪ Control ingress and egress traffic
    ▪ Whitelisting or blacklisting
    ▪ Proxy servers
  ▪ Distributed denial of service (DDoS) protection	

2.3 Given a scenario, apply the appropriate OS and application security controls.
▪ Policies
  ▪ Password complexity
  ▪ Account lockout
  ▪ Application whitelisting
  ▪ Software feature
  ▪ User/group
▪ User permissions
▪ Antivirus/anti-malware/endpoint detection and response (EDR)
▪ Host-based IDS (HIDS)/Host-based IPS (HIPS)
▪ Hardened baselines
  ▪ Single function
▪ File integrity
▪ Log and event monitoring
▪ Configuration management
▪ Builds
  ▪ Stable
  ▪ Long-term support (LTS)
  ▪ Beta
  ▪ Canary
▪ Operating system (OS) upgrades
	2, 3, 4, 5, 7

Exam Objective	Chapters
▪ Encryption	
▪ Application programming interface (API) endpoint	
▪ Application	
▪ OS	
▪ Storage	
▪ Filesystem	
▪ Mandatory access control	
▪ Software firewall	
2.4 Given a scenario, apply data security and compliance controls in cloud environments.	3, 4, 5
▪ Encryption	
▪ Integrity	
▪ Hashing algorithms	
▪ Digital signatures	
▪ File integrity monitoring (FIM)	
▪ Classification	
▪ Segmentation	
▪ Access control	
▪ Impact of laws and regulations	
▪ Legal hold	
▪ Records management	
▪ Versioning	
▪ Retention	
▪ Destruction	
▪ Write once read many	
▪ Data loss prevention (DLP)	
▪ Cloud access security broker (CASB)	

Exam Objective	Chapters
2.5 Given a scenario, implement measures to meet security requirements.	3

- Tools
  - Vulnerability scanners
  - Port scanners
- Vulnerability assessment
  - Default and common credential scans
  - Credentialed scans
  - Network-based scans
  - Agent-based scans
  - Service availabilities
- Security patches
  - Hot fixes
  - Scheduled updates
  - Virtual patches
  - Signature updates
  - Rollups
- Risk register
- Prioritization of patch application
- Deactivate default accounts
- Impacts of security tools on systems and services
- Effects of cloud service models on security implementation

2.6 Explain the importance of incident response procedures.	9

- Preparation
  - Documentation
  - Call trees
  - Training
  - Tabletops
  - Documented incident types/categories
  - Roles and responsibilities
- Incident response procedures
  - Identification
    - Scope

Exam Objective	Chapters
▪ Investigation	
▪ Containment, eradication, and recovery	
▪ Isolation	
▪ Evidence acquisition	
▪ Chain of custody	
▪ Post-incident and lessons learned	
▪ Root cause analysis	

3.0 Deployment

Exam Objective	Chapters
3.1 Given a scenario, integrate components into a cloud solution.	1, 2, 7, 8
▪ Subscription services	
▪ File subscriptions	
▪ Communications	
▪ Email	
▪ Voice over IP (VoIP)	
▪ Messaging	
▪ Collaboration	
▪ Virtual desktop infrastructure (VDI)	
▪ Directory and identity services	
▪ Cloud resources	
▪ IaaS	
▪ PaaS	
▪ SaaS	
▪ Provisioning resources	
▪ Compute	
▪ Storage	
▪ Network	

Exam Objective	Chapters
▪ Application	
▪ Serverless	
▪ Deploying virtual machines (VMs) and custom images	
▪ Templates	
▪ OS templates	
▪ Solution templates	
▪ Identity management	
▪ Containers	
▪ Configure variables	
▪ Configure secrets	
▪ Persistent storage	
▪ Auto-scaling	
▪ Post-deployment validation	
3.2 Given a scenario, provision storage in cloud environments.	2
▪ Types	
▪ Block	
▪ Storage area network (SAN)	
▪ Zoning	
▪ File	
▪ Network attached storage (NAS)	
▪ Object	
▪ Tenants	
▪ Buckets	
▪ Tiers	
▪ Flash	
▪ Hybrid	
▪ Spinning disks	
▪ Long-term	
▪ Input/output operations per second (IOPS) and read/write	

Exam Objective	Chapters
▪ Protocols	
▪ Network file system (NFS)	
▪ Common Internet file system (CIFS)	
▪ Internet small computer system interface (iSCSI)	
▪ Fibre Channel (FC)	
▪ Non-volatile memory express over fabrics (NVMe-oF)	
▪ Redundant array of inexpensive disks (RAID)	
▪ 0	
▪ 1	
▪ 5	
▪ 6	
▪ 10	
▪ Storage system features	
▪ Compression	
▪ Deduplication	
▪ Thin provisioning	
▪ Thick provisioning	
▪ Replication	
▪ User quotas	
▪ Hyperconverged	
▪ Software-defined storage (SDS)	
3.3 Given a scenario, deploy cloud networking solutions.	2
▪ Services	
▪ Dynamic host configuration protocol (DHCP)	
▪ NTP	
▪ DNS	
▪ Content delivery network (CDN)	
▪ IP address management (IPAM)	

Exam Objective	Chapters

▪ Virtual private networks (VPNs)
  ▪ Site-to-site
  ▪ Point-to-point
  ▪ Point-to-site
  ▪ IPSec
  ▪ Multiprotocol label switching (MPLS)
▪ Virtual routing
  ▪ Dynamic and static routing
  ▪ Virtual network interface controller (vNIC)
  ▪ Subnetting
▪ Network appliances
  ▪ Load balancers
  ▪ Firewalls
▪ Virtual private cloud (VPC)
  ▪ Hub and spoke
  ▪ Peering
▪ VLAN/VXLAN/GENEVE
▪ Single root input/output virtualization (SR-IOV)
▪ Software-defined network (SDN)
	2

3.4 Given a scenario, configure the appropriate compute sizing for a deployment.
▪ Virtualization
  ▪ Hypervisors
    ▪ Type 1
    ▪ Type 2
  ▪ Simultaneous multi-threading (SMT)
  ▪ Dynamic allocations
  ▪ Oversubscription
▪ Central processing unit (CPU)/virtual CPU (vCPU)
	2

Exam Objective	Chapters
▪ Graphics processing unit (GPU)	
▪ Virtual	
▪ Shared	
▪ Pass-through	
▪ Clock speed/Instructions per cycle (IPC)	
▪ Hyperconverged	
▪ Memory	
▪ Dynamic allocation	
▪ Ballooning	
3.5 Given a scenario, perform cloud migrations.	2
▪ Physical to virtual (P2V)	
▪ Virtual to virtual (V2V)	
▪ Cloud-to-cloud migrations	
▪ Vendor lock-in	
▪ PaaS or SaaS migrations	
▪ Access control lists (ACLs)	
▪ Firewalls	
▪ Storage migrations	
▪ Block	
▪ File	
▪ Object	
▪ Database migrations	
▪ Cross-service migrations	
▪ Relational	
▪ Non-relational	

4.0 Operations and Support

Exam Objective	Chapters
4.1 Given a scenario, configure logging, monitoring, and alerting to maintain operational status.	1, 7, 8

- Logging
  - Collectors
    - Simple network management protocol (SNMP)
    - Syslog
  - Analysis
  - Severity categorization
  - Audits
  - Types
    - Access/authentication
    - System
    - Application
  - Automation
  - Trending
- Monitoring
  - Baselines
  - Thresholds
  - Tagging
  - Log scrubbing
  - Performance monitoring
    - Application
    - Infrastructure components
  - Resource utilization
  - Availability
    - SLA-defined uptime requirements
  - Verification of continuous monitoring activities
  - Service management tool integration

Exam Objective	Chapters
▪ Alerting	
▪ Common messaging methods	
▪ Enable/disable alerts	
▪ Maintenance mode	
▪ Appropriate responses	
▪ Policies for categorizing and communicating alerts	
4.2 Given a scenario, maintain efficient operation of a cloud environment.	4, 5, 7, 8
▪ Confirm completion of backups	
▪ Life-cycle management	
▪ Roadmaps	
▪ Old/current/new versions	
▪ Upgrading and migrating systems	
▪ Deprecations or end of life	
▪ Change management	
▪ Asset management	
▪ Configuration management database (CMDB)	
▪ Patching	
▪ Features or enhancements	
▪ Fixes for broken or critical infrastructure or applications	
▪ Scope of cloud elements to be patched	
▪ Hypervisors	
▪ VMs	
▪ Virtual appliances	
▪ Networking components	
▪ Applications	
▪ Storage components	
▪ Firmware	
▪ Software	
▪ OS	
▪ Policies	
▪ n-1	
▪ Rollbacks	

Exam Objective	Chapters
▪ Impacts of process improvements on systems	
▪ Upgrade methods	
▪ Rolling upgrades	
▪ Blue-green	
▪ Canary	
▪ Active-passive	
▪ Development/QA/production/DR	
▪ Dashboard and reporting	
▪ Tagging	
▪ Costs	
▪ Chargebacks	
▪ Showbacks	
▪ Elasticity usage	
▪ Connectivity	
▪ Latency	
▪ Capacity	
▪ Incidents	
▪ Health	
▪ Overall utilization	
▪ Availability	
4.3 Given a scenario, optimize cloud environments.	1, 2, 7, 8
▪ Right-sizing	
▪ Auto-scaling	
▪ Horizontal scaling	
▪ Vertical scaling	
▪ Cloud bursting	
▪ Compute	
▪ CPUs	
▪ GPUs	
▪ Memory	
▪ Containers	
▪ Storage	
▪ Tiers	
▪ Adaptive optimization	
▪ IOPS	

Exam Objective	Chapters
▪ Capacity	
▪ Deduplication	
▪ Compression	
▪ Network	
▪ Bandwidth	
▪ Network interface controllers (NICs)	
▪ Latency	
▪ SDN	
▪ Edge computing	
▪ CDN	
▪ Placement	
▪ Geographical	
▪ Cluster placement	
▪ Redundancy	
▪ Colocation	
▪ Device drivers and firmware	
▪ Generic	
▪ Vendor	
▪ Open source	
4.4 Given a scenario, apply proper automation and orchestration techniques.	1, 2, 4, 5, 7
▪ Infrastructure as code	
▪ Infrastructure components and their integration	
▪ Continuous integration/ continuous deployment (CI/CD)	
▪ Version control	
▪ Configuration management	
▪ Playbook	
▪ Containers	
▪ Automation activities	
▪ Routine operations	
▪ Updates	
▪ Scaling	
▪ Shutdowns	
▪ Restarts	
▪ Create internal APIs	

Exam Objective	Chapters
▪ Secure scripting	
▪ No hardcoded passwords	
▪ Use of individual service accounts	
▪ Password vaults	
▪ Key-based authentication	
▪ Orchestration sequencing	
4.5 Given a scenario, perform appropriate backup and restore operations.	5
▪ Backup types	
▪ Incremental	
▪ Differential	
▪ Full	
▪ Synthetic full	
▪ Snapshot	
▪ Backup objects	
▪ Application-level backup	
▪ Filesystem backup	
▪ Database dumps	
▪ Configuration files	
▪ Backup targets	
▪ Tape	
▪ Disk	
▪ Object	
▪ Backup and restore policies	
▪ Retention	
▪ Schedules	
▪ Location	
▪ SLAs	
▪ Recovery time objective (RTO)	
▪ Recovery point objective (RPO)	
▪ Mean time to recovery (MTTR)	
▪ 3-2-1 rule	
▪ Three copies of data	
▪ Two different media	
▪ One copy off site	

Exam Objective	Chapters
▪ Restoration methods	
▪ In place	
▪ Alternate location	
▪ Restore files	
▪ Snapshot	
4.6 Given a scenario, perform disaster recovery tasks.	6
▪ Failovers	
▪ Failback	
▪ Restore backups	
▪ Replication	
▪ Network configurations	
▪ On-premises and cloud sites	
▪ Hot	
▪ Warm	
▪ Cold	
▪ Requirements	
▪ RPO	
▪ RTO	
▪ SLA	
▪ Corporate guidelines	
▪ Documentation	
▪ DR kit	
▪ Playbook	
▪ Network diagram	
▪ Geographical datacenter requirements	

5.0 Troubleshooting

Exam Objective	Chapters
5.1 Given a scenario, use the troubleshooting methodology to resolve cloud-related issues.	10
▪ Always consider corporate policies, procedures, and impacts before implementing changes.	

Exam Objective	Chapters
1. Identify the problem ▪ Question the user and identify user changes to the computer and perform backups before making changes ▪ Inquire regarding environmental or infrastructure changes 2. Establish a theory of probable cause (question the obvious) ▪ If necessary, conduct external or internal research based on symptoms 3. Test the theory to determine cause ▪ Once the theory is confirmed, determine the next steps to resolve the problem ▪ If the theory is not confirmed, re-establish a new theory or escalate 4. Establish a plan of action to resolve the problem and implement the solution 5. Verify full system functionality and, if applicable, implement preventive measures 6. Document the findings, actions, and outcomes throughout the process.	

5.2 Given a scenario, troubleshoot security issues.
▪ Privilege
  ▪ Missing
  ▪ Incomplete
  ▪ Escalation
  ▪ Keys
▪ Authentication
▪ Authorization
▪ Security groups
  ▪ Network security groups
  ▪ Directory security groups
	10

Exam Objective	Chapters
▪ Keys and certificates	
▪ Expired	
▪ Revoked	
▪ Trust	
▪ Compromised	
▪ Misconfigured	
▪ Misconfigured or misapplied policies	
▪ Data security issues	
▪ Unencrypted data	
▪ Data breaches	
▪ Misclassification	
▪ Lack of encryption in protocols	
▪ Insecure ciphers	
▪ Exposed endpoints	
▪ Misconfigured or failed	
▪ security appliances	
▪ IPS	
▪ IDS	
▪ NAC	
▪ WAF	
▪ Unsupported protocols	
▪ External/internal attacks	
5.3 Given a scenario, troubleshoot deployment issues.	9
▪ Connectivity issues	
▪ Cloud service provider (CSP) or Internet service provider (ISP) outages	
▪ Performance degradation	
▪ Latency	
▪ Configurations	
▪ Scripts	
▪ Applications in containers	

Exam Objective	Chapters
▪ Misconfigured templates	
▪ Missing or incorrect tags	
▪ Insufficient capacity	
▪ Scaling configurations	
▪ Compute	
▪ Storage	
▪ Bandwidth issues	
▪ Oversubscription	
▪ Licensing issues	
▪ Vendor-related issues	
▪ Migrations of vendors or platforms	
▪ Integration of vendors or platforms	
▪ API request limits	
▪ Cost or billing issues	
5.4 Given a scenario, troubleshoot connectivity issues.	10
▪ Network security group misconfigurations	
▪ ACL	
▪ Inheritance	
▪ Common networking configuration issues	
▪ Peering	
▪ Incorrect subnet	
▪ Incorrect IP address	
▪ Incorrect IP space	
▪ Routes	
▪ Default	
▪ Static	
▪ Dynamic	
▪ Firewall	
▪ Incorrectly administered micro-segmentation	

Exam Objective	Chapters
▪ Network address translation (NAT)	
▪ VPN	
▪ Source	
▪ Destination	
▪ Load balancers	
▪ Methods	
▪ Headers	
▪ Protocols	
▪ Encryption	
▪ Back ends	
▪ Front ends	
▪ DNS records	
▪ VLAN/VXLAN/GENEVE	
▪ Proxy	
▪ Maximum transmission unit (MTU)	
▪ Quality of service (QoS)	
▪ Time synchronization issues	
▪ Network troubleshooting tools	
▪ ping	
▪ tracert/traceroute	
▪ flushdns	
▪ ipconfig/ifconfig/ip	
▪ nslookup/dig	
▪ netstat/ss	
▪ route	
▪ arp	
▪ curl	
▪ Packet capture	
▪ Packet analyzer	
▪ OpenSSL client	

Exam Objective	Chapters
5.5 Given a scenario, troubleshoot common performance issues.	9

- Resource utilization
  - CPU
  - GPU
  - Memory
  - Storage
    - I/O
    - Capacity
  - Network bandwidth
  - Network latency
  - Replication
  - Scaling
- Application
  - Memory management
  - Service overload
- Incorrectly configured or failed load balancing

Exam Objective	Chapters
5.6 Given a scenario, troubleshoot automation or orchestration issues.	9

- Account mismatches
- Change management failures
- Server name changes
- IP address changes
- Location changes
- Version/feature mismatch
- Automation tool incompatibility
  - Deprecated features
  - API version incompatibility
- Job validation issue
- Patching failure

Reader Support for This Book

If you believe you've found a mistake in this book, please bring it to our attention. At John Wiley & Sons, we understand how important it is to provide our customers with accurate content, but even with our best efforts an error may occur.

To submit your possible errata, please email it to our Customer Service Team at `wileysupport@wiley.com` with the subject line "Possible Book Errata Submission."

Assessment Test

1. Bob is accessing a self-service portal in the cloud to instantly create additional servers, storage, and database instances for his firm's DevOps group. Which of the following options best describes this operation?
   - A. Bursting
   - B. Pay-as-you-grow
   - C. Multitenancy
   - D. On-demand
2. Jillian is working on a project to interconnect her company's private data center to a cloud company that offers email services and another that can provide burstable compute capacity. What type of cloud delivery model is she creating?
   - A. Public
   - B. Hybrid
   - C. Community
   - D. Private
3. Carl is learning how cloud service providers allocate physical resources into a group. These resources are then dynamically associated with cloud services as demand requires. What best describes this?
   - A. On-demand virtualization
   - B. Dynamic scaling
   - C. Resource pooling
   - D. Elasticity
4. Liza is a new Cloud+ architect for BigCo Inc. She is investigating cloud services that provide server hardware, but not applications. What cloud service is she using?
   - A. IaaS
   - B. PaaS
   - C. SaaS
   - D. CaaS
5. Harold is investigating his options to migrate his company's time and attendance application to the cloud. He wants to be responsible only for maintaining the application and would prefer that the public cloud company manage all underlying infrastructure and servers that are required to support his application. Harold calls you and asks for assistance in selecting a cloud service model that would meet his requirements. What would you suggest that he implement?
   - A. IaaS
   - B. PaaS
   - C. SaaS
   - D. CaaS

6. June is a Cloud+ architect working on a physical to virtual migration to the public cloud. She has matched VM performance levels to her established baselines. She knows that her organization may need to adjust hardware resources in the future. What cloud characteristics can she use to match cloud capacity with future growth? (Choose three.)
   - **A.** Elasticity
   - **B.** On-demand computing
   - **C.** Availability zones
   - **D.** Resiliency virtualization
   - **E.** Pay-as-you grow
   - **F.** Resource pooling
7. What are two elements that together distinguish the cloud from a traditional data center operation? (Choose two.)
   - **A.** Load balancing
   - **B.** Automation
   - **C.** Autoscaling groups
   - **D.** Virtualization
8. Dawn is interested in selecting a community cloud provider that offers a specialized financial reporting application. What type of cloud model would you recommend Dawn investigate to meet her requirements?
   - **A.** IaaS
   - **B.** PaaS
   - **C.** SaaS
   - **D.** CaaS
9. Carol is a cloud customer that your consulting company is assisting with their migration. She is asking you about the demarcation point of operations for her public PaaS service. Which of the following defines what you are responsible for and the responsibility of the provider?
   - **A.** Availability zones
   - **B.** Community
   - **C.** Shared responsibility model
   - **D.** Baselines
10. Jonathan is architecting his client's global public cloud presence for an upcoming e-commerce deployment. You have been brought on to help design the network. He asks about providing local connections in Singapore and Malaysia. What would you suggest that he investigate?
    - **A.** Regions
    - **B.** Auto-scaling groups
    - **C.** Availability zones
    - **D.** Global DNS affinity

11. Zale is working on a collaborative project that requires the implementation of a large-scale NoSQL database that will access three petabytes of historical data. He needs durable block storage in remote flash arrays. You have been tasked with designing the storage connectivity from the database to the stored data. What type of network connection would you recommend for NoSQL read/write access to the arrays?
   - **A.** Block access
   - **B.** Zoning
   - **C.** VMFS
   - **D.** SAN
12. Physical resources are virtualized and presented as resources to virtual machines running on hypervisors. What common resources does the hypervisor virtualize? (Choose three.)
   - **A.** Layer 2
   - **B.** RAM
   - **C.** Layer 3
   - **D.** CPUs
   - **E.** RAID
   - **F.** Storage
13. As a new Cloud+ professional, you have been hired by a company that operates its own data center; however, the company is calling it a cloud. What delivery model are you working with?
   - **A.** Hybrid
   - **B.** Public
   - **C.** Private
   - **D.** Community
14. Tim just logged into his cloud management dashboard to check the health monitors of his server fleet. What is the process that he completed at login?
   - **A.** Authorization
   - **B.** Accounting
   - **C.** Authentication
   - **D.** Federation
   - **E.** Identity access
15. Martha is studying SAN technologies that use the Fibre Channel protocol, and she is asking about disk configuration in the remote storage array. She asks you which type of storage she can use on her Linux servers. What storage type can she deploy? (Choose the best answer.)
   - **A.** Meta
   - **B.** Object
   - **C.** Block
   - **D.** File

16. Patesh is becoming familiar with the interfaces available for his operations team to use to access his hybrid cloud deployment. You have been asked to explain the common types of user-based interfaces available to manage cloud objects. What are the common interfaces that you would explain to Patesh? (Choose three.)

A. Web console

B. SNMP

C. API

D. PaaS

E. CLI

17. You work for a company that offers cloud services to the railroad industry. All railroads have a similar set of requirements and access the same applications. BigWest Rail has contacted you about becoming a customer and is asking what applications are shared with other rail operators. They also ask what type of cloud model your company offers. What type of cloud is this?

A. Hybrid

B. Public

C. Private

D. Community

18. Kevin is exploring a durable block storage option that offers high performance. It also needs to support striping that allows a parity bit to be used to reconstruct a volume if a single magnetic disk fails in his array. Which storage type stripes file data and performs a parity check of data over multiple disks that can recover from a single hard disk failure?

A. RAID 0

B. RAID 1

C. RAID 3

D. RAID 5

19. You are involved in a large-scale migration project that requires moving a Windows OS running on a dual-slot, eight-core server with no hypervisor in a data center to a virtual server in the public cloud. What type of migration is this?

A. vMotion

B. P2V

C. Private to public

D. V2V

E. Synchronous replication

20. You have been asked by a new customer what type of authentication systems require something that you have and something that you know. What type of authentication technology would you recommend?

    A. Single sign-on
    B. Confederations
    C. Active Directory/LDAP
    D. Multifactor

21. Beatriz stops at her bank's ATM on her way home from work. She inserts her card into the ATM and then enters her PIN on the keypad. What type of authentication is she using?

    A. SSO
    B. Two-factor
    C. LDAP
    D. User-based

22. Roman is the cloud administrator for a company that stores object-based data in a hybrid cloud. Because of the sensitivity of the data and various regulatory restrictions on allowing users access to sensitive security data, what type of access control would meet his security policies?

    A. Mandatory access control
    B. Nondiscretionary
    C. Roles
    D. Multifactor

23. William is implementing an access control rollout for a cluster of Windows SQL database servers in a hybrid cloud environment. Developers will need full read/write access to the database servers, whereas other business units will need read-only access to particular databases. What type of access control should William deploy?

    A. Mandatory access control
    B. Nondiscretionary
    C. Role-based
    D. Multifactor

24. Quentin is a defense contractor investigating server compliance requirements needed to be certified to meet the U.S. Department of Defense security requirements for contractors. What requirement would you recommend that he focus on?

    A. FedRAMP
    B. DIACAP
    C. FISMA
    D. Section 405.13 for DoD rule A286

25. Leanna wants to deploy a public cloud service that allows her to retain responsibility only for her applications and requires the cloud provider to maintain the underlying operating system and virtualized hardware. Which service model would you recommend that she implement?

   A. IaaS

   B. PaaS

   C. SaaS

   D. CaaS

26. Robert is configuring a new cloud interconnect to access his locally hosted Active Directory services. He wants to prevent his user base from having fragmented rights and no unified authorization services. You are brought in as a service consultant to assist in optimizing and controlling user access by implementing a technology that will give access to all allowed systems at the time of user authentication. What type of system are you deploying?

   A. Token-based 2FA

   B. SSO

   C. RSA

   D. Nondiscretionary

27. Cathy is preparing her company's migration plan from a private to a hybrid cloud. She wants to outline firewall and DDoS requirements. What document should she create?

   A. DIACAP

   B. Security policy

   C. Service level agreement

   D. SOC-2

28. Perry is investigating options for interconnecting a private cloud to a new public cloud region that supports analysis of customer-streamed IoT data. He is planning on implementing a tunnel across the Internet to interconnect the two locations to avoid the high costs of a dedicated interconnection. What transport protocol would you suggest that can offer a secure connection across the unsecure Internet?

   A. AES

   B. SOC-3

   C. IPsec

   D. RC5

29. Jarleen is a consultant tasked with migrating Health Med Records Inc. customer records to a cloud-based service offering a long-term archival system. Which U.S. compliance mandate must her company align with?

   A. SOC 3

   B. HIPAA

   C. MPAA

   D. ISA 2701

30. Fluentes is a security consultant for a day trading company that must implement strong encryption of data at rest for their cloud storage tiers. What is the best option that meets most security regulations for the encryption of stored data?

   A. 3DES
   B. RSA
   C. AES-256
   D. Rivest Cipher 5

31. Randy is developing a new application that will be deployed in an IaaS-based public cloud. He builds a test image and deploys a test VM in his private cloud's development zone. When he stops and restarts one of the Linux-based servers, he notices that his storage volume data is missing. What type of storage exhibits this behavior? (Choose two.)

   A. Durable
   B. RAID
   C. Ephemeral
   D. Nondurable
   E. Block
   F. Object

32. Matt has finished running some security automation scripts on three newly deployed Linux servers. After applying intrusion detection, virus, and malware protection on the Linux images, he notices an increase in which VM metric on his server management dashboard?

   A. DMA
   B. BIOS
   C. CPU
   D. IPsec
   E. I/O

33. Jill works in the operations center, and she is tasked with monitoring security operations. What cloud-based GUI can she use for a real-time overview of security operations?

   A. Puppet automation
   B. Gemalto system
   C. Dashboard
   D. Vendor-based security appliance

34. Larken is reviewing the SLA and statement of responsibility with his community cloud provider PaaS. To whom does the responsibility for stored data integrity in the cloud belong?

   A. Cloud provider
   B. Compliance agency
   C. Cloud customer
   D. Shared responsibility

35. Mindy has been tasked with developing a new QA test logging application, but she is concerned that the application must pull data from many different cloud locations and devices. What is a good interface for her to use to meet her requirements?

A. Python

B. XML

C. API

D. SNMP

E. TLS

36. What technology was instrumental in the growth of cloud services?

A. XML

B. Python

C. Automation

D. Authentication

E. Security

F. Workflow services

G. Encryption

37. Vicky is investigating multiple hacking attempts on her cloud-based e-commerce web servers. She wants to add a front-end security system that can actively deploy countermeasures that shut down the hacking attempts. What application would you suggest that Vicky deploy?

A. DMZ

B. IDS

C. IPS

D. RAID

E. HIDS

38. What options can you offer your user base for MFA tokens? (Choose two.)

A. One-time password

B. Smartphone app

C. Automation systems

D. Key fob

E. Cloud vendor management dashboard

39. Linda works in the IT security group of her firm and has been tasked with investigating options that will allow customers to access their personal records securely via the web. What is the most common in-flight e-commerce security protocol on the market?

A. MD5

B. SSL/TLS

C. IPsec

D. VPN

40. Your company has purchased a specialized intrusion prevention system that is virtualized and designed for cloud-based network micro-segmentation deployments. When reading the documentation, you notice a link to download a Java-based application to monitor and configure the IPS application. What kind of configuration program is this?

   A. CLI

   B. GIU

   C. Vendor-based

   D. API

   E. RESTful

41. Name the type of software update that is designed to address a known bug and to bring a system up-to-date with previously released fixes.

   A. Hotfix

   B. Patch

   C. Version update

   D. Rollout

42. Your employer has developed a mission-critical application for the medical industry, and there can be no downtime during maintenance. You have designed a web architecture to take this into account and that allows you to have an exact copy of your production fleet that can be brought online to replace your existing deployment for patching and maintenance. What type of model did you implement?

   A. Cluster

   B. DevOps

   C. Blue-green

   D. Rolling

43. Jill is performing a Tuesday night backup of a Tier 2 storage volume of which she already completed a full backup on Sunday night. She only wants to back up files based on changes of the source data since the last backup. What type of backup is she performing?

   A. Full

   B. Differential

   C. Incremental

   D. Online

44. What virtual machine backup method creates a file-based image of the current state of a VM, including the complete operating system and all applications that are stored on it?

   A. Full backup

   B. Snapshot

   C. Clone

   D. Replicate

45. Ronald is a Cloud+ student studying systems that abstract and hide much of the complexity of modern cloud systems. What is he learning about?

 A. Runbooks

 B. Workflow

 C. Orchestration

 D. REST/API

46. What are common automation platforms? (Choose three.)

 A. Chef

 B. Cloud-patch

 C. Ansible

 D. DevOps

 E. Puppet

 F. Cloud Deploy

47. Marlene is updating her horizontally scaled Internet-facing web servers to remediate a critical bug. Her manager has agreed to operate under reduced computing capacity during the process but stipulates that there can be no downtime. What upgrade approach should Marlene perform to meet these requirements?

 A. Orchestration

 B. Rolling

 C. Hotfix

 D. Blue-green

48. What VM backup method can be used to create a master image to be used as a template to create additional systems?

 A. Full backup

 B. Snapshot

 C. Clone

 D. Replica

49. A new application patch is being validated prior to release to the public. The developers have a release candidate, and the DevOps manager is requesting a report that shows the pass/fail data to verify that the fix does, in fact, resolve the problem. What process is the manager verifying?

 A. Rollout

 B. Orchestration

 C. Automation

 D. QA

50. Jane has found a table merge issue in her SQL database hosted in a private cloud. While reviewing the log files, the vendor requested that she install a software change designed for rapid deployment that corrects a specific and critical issue. What are they referring to?

A. Hotfix

B. Patch

C. Version update

D. Rollout

51. To meet regulatory requirements, a medical records company is required to store customer transaction records for seven years. The records will most likely never be accessed after the second year and can be stored offline to reduce expenses. What type of storage should they implement to achieve this goal?

A. File transfer

B. Archive

C. Replication

D. Data store

52. Mark is creating a disaster recovery plan based on directives from his company's executive management team. His company's business is an e-commerce website that sells children's apparel, with 85 percent of its revenue received during the holiday season. If there was a severe disruption in operations, the loss of business could put the company's ongoing financial viability in peril. Mark is creating a plan that will restore operations in the shortest amount of time possible if there is an outage. What DR model is he implementing?

A. Hot site

B. Active/active

C. Warm site

D. Active/passive

E. Cold site

F. Rollover

53. You're researching data replication options for your SQL database. You've decided to create a backup replica in a different availability zone that could become primary should the primary zone go offline. The replica is updated in near real time after the initial write operation on the primary database. What type of solution is this?

A. Synchronous

B. Asynchronous

C. Volume sync

D. Remote mirroring

E. RAID 5

54. Pierre is deploying a solution that allows data for his e-commerce operations hosted in a public cloud to be reached at remote locations worldwide with local points of presence. He wants to reduce the load on his web servers and reduce the network latency of geographically distant customers. What are these facilities called?

 A. Regions
 B. Edge locations
 C. Availability zones
 D. Replication

55. Melinda is updating her firm's disaster recovery plans, and after receiving direction from her company's board of directors, she has been instructed to create a plan that restores operations within 48 hours of a disaster. What part of the plan should she update with the new requirements?

 A. RSO
 B. RPO
 C. RTO
 D. DBO

56. Jillian is a Cloud+ consultant for an auto parts company based in central Michigan. She is putting together a disaster recovery plan that includes a remote backup site that has a SQL server instance running at that location with a synchronously refreshed data replica. Her plan calls for activating all other services in the event of a hurricane causing an outage at her primary data center. What model is Jillian going to deploy to meet the requirements?

 A. Hot site
 B. Warm site
 C. Cold site
 D. Active/passive

57. Pete has been busy updating the disaster recovery procedures for his client's business continuity plan. The DR facility will need to be ready with floor space, power, and cooling and have loading docks to unload server and equipment racks to restore service. What type of DR implementation is Pete planning on deploying?

 A. Hot site
 B. Active/active
 C. Warm site
 D. Active/passive
 E. Cold site
 F. Rollover

58. Connie has been directed by her employer's finance department that they cannot afford to lose any more than 30 minutes of data in the case of a database failure or other catastrophic event. Connie has updated her corporate business continuity and disaster recovery plans. What metric did she change?

   A. RSO

   B. RPO

   C. RTO

   D. DBO

59. Will is testing his backup DR site and using his DNS configuration to load-balance the primary and backup sites. He wants to verify that the database in the DR facility is updated in real time and remains current with the production replica in the primary data center. What type of updates should he define in his primary data center servers prior to enabling the DNS load balancing?

   A. Synchronous replication

   B. Asynchronous replication

   C. Volume sync

   D. Mirroring

   E. RAID 5

60. Leonard is creating disaster recovery documents for his company's online operations. He is documenting metrics for a measurable SLA that outlines when you can expect operations to be back online and how much data loss can be tolerated when recovering from an outage. Which metrics is he documenting? (Choose all that apply.)

   A. RSO

   B. RTO

   C. RPO

   D. DR

   E. VxRestore

61. The ability to dynamically add additional resources on demand such as storage, CPUs, memory, and even servers is referred to as what?

   A. Bursting

   B. Pooling

   C. Elasticity

   D. Orchestration

62. Margo is reviewing the maintenance responsibilities between her company and its public cloud service provider. She notices that the cloud provider takes responsibility for the operating system, and her company assumes responsibility for all applications and services running on the operating system. What type of service model is she operating under?

   A. IaaS

   B. PaaS

   C. SaaS

   D. XaaS

63. Which service model has the most lock-ins and is the most complex to migrate?

A. IaaS

B. PaaS

C. SaaS

D. XaaS

64. Joe is in the planning stages to make sure that an upcoming company promotion during a major sporting event will not overwhelm his company's cloud-based e-commerce site. He needs to determine his options to add capacity to the web server farm so that it can process the anticipated additional workload. What do you recommend as possible solutions? (Choose three.)

A. Vertical scaling

B. Horizontal scaling

C. Edge cache

D. Cloud bursting

E. Core elasticity

65. Janice manages the MySQL database back end that runs on a multi-CPU instance that has reached 100 percent utilization. The database can run on only a single server. What options does she have to support the requirements of this database?

A. Horizontal scaling

B. Vertical scaling

C. Pooling

D. Bursting

66. A popular e-commerce site is hosting its public-facing front-end web server fleet in a public cloud. You have been tasked with determining what the normal day-to-day web hit count is so that capacity plans for the upcoming holiday selling season can be assessed. You want to track incoming web requests and graph them against delayed and missed connection counts. What type of dataset are you producing?

A. Metric

B. Variance

C. Baseline

D. Smoothing

67. Eva is the network architect for her company's large cloud deployment; she has interconnected her private cloud to a community cloud in another state. She is investigating using the community cloud to supplement her private cloud workload during end-of-month processing. What operation is she going to perform?

A. Elasticity

B. Cloud bursting

C. Vertical scaling

D. Autoscaling

68. CPU utilization on a database server has consistently been at more than 80 percent utilization. The baselines show that 57 percent utilization is normal. What is this called?

A. Deviation

B. Variance

C. Triggers

D. Baseline imbalance

69. Harold will modify an NACL to adjust remote access to a cloud-based HR application. He will be submitting a plan that outlines all details of the change. What process is he following?

A. Cloud automation

B. Change advisory

C. Change management

D. Rollout

70. To increase `TipoftheHat.com`'s security posture, Alice is reviewing user accounts that access the community cloud resources. Alice notices that the summer interns have left to go back to school but their accounts are still active. She knows that they will return over the winter break. What would you suggest that Alice do with these accounts?

A. Do nothing.

B. Delete the accounts.

C. Disable the accounts.

D. Change the resource access definitions.

E. Modify the confederation settings.

F. Change the access control.

71. Object tracking can be helpful in identifying which of the following? (Choose three.)

A. Resiliency

B. Trends

C. Metrics

D. ACLs

E. Peak usage

F. Anomalies

72. Capacity and utilization reporting often contains data on which of the following objects? (Choose three.)

A. CPU

B. OS version

C. Volume tier

D. RAM

E. Network

73. What does a cloud management system monitor to collect performance metrics?

A. Database

B. Server

C. Hypervisor

D. Objects

74. Object tracking should be aligned with which of the following?

A. VPC

B. SLA

C. RDP

D. JSON

75. What is a visual representation of current cloud operations?

A. Operational matrix

B. Management console

C. Dashboard

D. Ticker

76. Hanna is monitoring performance metrics on a video server; she sees that the server is utilizing 100 percent of the available network bandwidth. What action will most likely address the problem?

A. Implement 802.1Q tagging.

B. Install a second network adapter.

C. Update the network adapter's firmware.

D. Install a network coprocessor ASIC.

77. What type of scaling includes adding servers to a pool?

A. Horizontal

B. Round robin

C. Elasticity

D. Autoscale

E. Vertical

78. What type of scaling involves replacing an existing server with another that has more capabilities?

A. Horizontal

B. Round robin

C. Elasticity

D. Autoscale

E. Vertical

79. Ichika is preparing a change management plan to increase the processing abilities of one of her middleware servers. What components can she upgrade to increase server performance? (Choose three.)

A. CPU

B. SLA

C. RAM

D. Network I/O

E. ACL

F. DNS

80. Niko is generating baseline reports for her quarterly review meeting. She is interested in a public cloud application server's memory utilization. Where does she generate these reports?

A. Hypervisor

B. Databases

C. Logging servers

D. Cloud management and monitoring application

81. SaaS orchestration systems are whose responsibility in the public cloud?

A. Customer

B. Provider

C. Automation vendor

D. DevOps

82. What type of application commonly uses batch processing?

A. DNS

B. NTP

C. Databases

D. Middleware

83. Giulia posted a new software update to her company's popular smartphone application. After announcing the release, she has been monitoring her dashboard information and has noticed a large spike in activity. What cloud resource should she focus on?

A. CPU

B. Network bandwidth

C. RAM

D. API

E. Storage

84. Cloud capacity can be measured by comparing current usage to what?

A. Orchestration

B. Automation

C. NTP

D. Baseline

E. APIs

85. Emma is modifying a publicly accessible IP subnet on her company's e-commerce site hosted in a hybrid cloud. After performing address changes for all of her public-facing web servers, she validated the change by connecting from a bastion host located offshore. She was unable to connect to the web servers. What does she need to modify to allow the remote site to connect to the web server?

A. NTP

B. STP

C. DNS

D. API

86. Maria has noticed an increase in the response time of the NoSQL application she runs in her IaaS cloud deployment. When comparing current results against her baseline measurements that she recorded when the database was originally deployed, she verified that there has been a steady increase in the number of read requests. You have been asked to evaluate the baseline variances. Where should you focus your troubleshooting efforts?

A. Memory

B. CPU

C. Storage

D. Networking

87. Derek is monitoring storage volume utilization and is preparing a company change request to add storage capacity. He has decided to automate the volume allocation size. What cloud feature can he take advantage of?

A. SaaS

B. API

C. Elasticity

D. OpenStack

88. What application tracks a process from start to finish?

A. API

B. NTP

C. Workflow

D. Orchestration

89. Common cloud resources in your deployment that may saturate over time include which of the following? (Choose three.)

   A. RAM
   B. Power
   C. CPU
   D. Storage
   E. Monitoring
   F. IaaS

90. Homer designed an application tier for his company's new e-commerce site. He decided on an IP subnet that uses the /28 IPv4 subnet. He is planning for a maximum of 14 servers. You are brought in as a cloud architect to validate his design. What other devices may be on this subnet other than the servers that would also require IP address assignments? (Choose two.)

   A. SLA
   B. Default gateway
   C. DNS
   D. NTP
   E. API
   F. SNMP

91. Elena manages user accounts for her company's cloud presence. She has a trouble ticket open with Jill to assist her in accessing an SSD storage volume in the San Paulo region of the public cloud. What kind of user issue is she investigating?

   A. Authentication
   B. Authorization
   C. Federation
   D. SSO

92. Emma is unable to reach her Linux-based web server hosted in the Singapore zone of the cloud. She is located in Austin, Texas. What command can she use to verify the connection path?

   A. `traceroute`
   B. `ipconfig`
   C. `arp`
   D. `netstat`
   E. `ping`
   F. `tcpdump`
   G. `route print`

93. After deploying a new public website, your validation steps ask you to check the domain name–to–IP address mappings. What utility can you use for validation? (Choose two.)

   A. RDP
   B. dig

C. SSH

D. nslookup

E. IPsec

F. IPS

94. Nicola is deploying a new fleet of IIS web servers on his IaaS e-commerce site. The company has elected to use a hybrid approach and wants graphical connections to the Windows bastion hosts. What traffic must he permit through the external-facing firewall to the host?

A. SSH

B. RDP

C. DNS

D. IPS

95. Martina is troubleshooting a networking problem and needs to capture network frames being sent and received from the server's network adapter. What command would she use to collect the traces?

A. `dig`

B. `netstat`

C. `tcpdump`

D. `nslookup`

96. The remote disaster recovery location follows the warm site model. To configure the network switches, routers, and firewalls remotely, Joyce will need serial port access from her company's operations center. She has 14 serial ports currently available but needs to be prepared for any unplanned expansion requirements during a disaster recovery cutover. What device would you recommend that she install at the warm site?

A. RDP

B. Telnet

C. IPsec

D. SSH

E. Terminal server

97. The cloud data center is in a large industrial park with no company signage, extensive video cameras in the parking lot, high-security fences, and biometrics at the guard shack. What type of security is the provider implementing?

A. Building

B. Device

C. Infrastructure

D. Tunneling

98. Mergie is documenting different methods that her remote operations center can use to access a fleet of servers operating in a community cloud. Which of the following are not viable methods? (Choose two.)

A. RDP

B. Telnet

C. IDS/IPS

D. Terminal server

E. DNS

F. HTTP

99. Vasile is working a support ticket that shows the connection between the Ames field office and the Kansas City cloud edge location has dropped. She confirms it's a secure Internet-based access solution. What type of connection is this?

A. Direct peering

B. IDS

C. VPN

D. AES-256

E. RDP

100. Company users are complaining that they cannot log into a cloud-based collaboration system. The operations center has been investigating and has, so far, verified that the MFA applications are operational. What user system are they troubleshooting?

A. Authentication

B. Authorization

C. Federation

D. Kerberos

Answers to Assessment Test

1. D. On-demand cloud computing allows the consumer to add and change resources dynamically with the use of an online portal.
2. B. The interconnection of multiple cloud models is referred to as a hybrid cloud.
3. C. Resource pooling is the allocation of compute resources into a group, or pool, and then these pools are made available to a multitenant cloud environment.
4. A. Infrastructure as a service offers computing hardware, storage, and networking but not applications.
5. B. Platform as a service offers computing hardware, storage, networking, and the operating systems but not the applications.
6. A, B, E. Elasticity, on-demand computing, and pay-as-you-grow are all examples of being able to expand cloud compute resources as your needs require.
7. B, D. One of the prime advantages of cloud-based computing and the automation and virtualization it offers in the background is the ability to leverage the rapid provisioning of virtual resources to allow for on-demand computing.
8. C. Software as a service offers cloud-managed applications as well as the underlying platform and infrastructure support.
9. C. The shared responsibility model outlines what services and portions of the cloud operations the cloud consumer and the provider are responsible for.
10. A. Cloud operators segment their operations into regions for customer proximity, regulatory compliance, resiliency, and survivability.
11. D. A storage area network (SAN) is a high-speed network dedicated to storage transfers across a shared network. Block access is not a networking technology. Zoning is for restricting access to LUNs in a SAN, and VMFS is a VMware filesystem.
12. B, D, F. A hypervisor will virtualize RAM, compute, and storage; the VMs operating on the hypervisor will access these pools.
13. C. A private cloud is used exclusively by a single organization.
14. C. Authentication is the term used to describe the process of determining the identity of a user or device.
15. C. Storage area networks support block-based storage.
16. A, C, E. Application programming interfaces, command-line interfaces, and GUI-based interfaces are all commonly used tools to migrate, monitor, manage, and troubleshoot cloud-based resources.

17. D. A community cloud is used by companies with similar needs such as railroad companies.
18. D. RAID 5 uses parity information that is striped across multiple drives, which allows the drive array to be rebuilt if a single drive in the array fails. The other options do not have parity data.
19. B. When migrating a server that is running on bare metal to a hypervisor-based system, you would be performing a physical-to-virtual migration.
20. D. Multifactor authentication systems use a token generator as something you have and a PIN/password as something you know.
21. B. Two-factor authentication includes something you have and something you know.
22. A. The mandatory access control approach is implemented in high-security environments where access to sensitive data needs to be highly controlled. Using the mandatory access control approach, a user will authenticate, or log into, a system. Based on the user's identity and security levels of the individual, access rights will be determined by comparing that data against the security properties of the system being accessed.
23. C. The question outlines the function of a role-based access control approach.
24. B. The Department of Defense Information Assurance Certification and Accreditation Process (DIACAP) is the process for computer systems' IT security. DIACAP compliance is required to be certified to meet the U.S. Department of Defense security requirements for contractors.
25. B. The platform-as-a-service model offers operating system maintenance to be provided by the service provider.
26. B. Single sign-on allows a user to log in one time and be granted access to multiple systems without having to authenticate to each one individually.
27. B. The security policy outlines all aspects of your cloud security posture.
28. C. IPsec implementations are found in routers and firewalls with VPN services to provide a secure connection over an insecure network such as the Internet.
29. B. The Health Insurance Portability and Accountability Act defines the standards for protecting medical data.
30. C. Advanced Encryption Standard is a symmetrical block cipher that has options to use three lengths, including 128, 192, and 256 bits. AES 256 is a very secure standard, and it would take an extremely long time and a lot of processing power to come even close to breaking the code.
31. C, D. Temporary storage volumes that are destroyed when the VM is stopped are referred to as ephemeral or nondurable storage.
32. C. Applying security applications on a virtual server will cause an increase in CPU usage.
33. C. A dashboard is a graphical portal that provides updates and an overview of operations.

34. C. Ultimately the responsibility for data in the cloud belongs to the organization that owns the data.

35. C. An application programming interface (API) offers programmatic access, control, and configuration of a device between different and discrete software components.

36. C. Automation of cloud deployments was instrumental in the growth of cloud-based services.

37. C. Intrusion prevention systems monitor for malicious activity and actively take countermeasures to eliminate or reduce the effects of the intrusion.

38. B, D. One-time numerical tokens are generated on key fob hardware devices or smartphone soft-token applications.

39. B. SSL/TLS is most commonly used with web and smartphone applications. MD5 is a hash algorithm. IPsec is used to create VPNs over a public network, but VPNs are not as common as SSL/TLS for the scenario given.

40. C. Based on the information given, the description is for a vendor-based management application.

41. B. A patch is a piece of software that updates an application or operating system, to add a feature, fix a bug, or improve performance.

42. C. Blue-green is a software deployment model that uses two configurations for production that are identical to each other. These deployments can alternate between each other, with one active and the other inactive.

43. C. Incremental backups are operations based on changes of the source data since the last incremental backup was performed.

44. B. A snapshot is a file-based image of the current state of a VM, including the complete operating system and all applications stored on it. The snapshot will record the data on the disk and optionally its memory contents at that instant in time.

45. C. Orchestration systems enable large-scale cloud deployments by automating operations.

46. A, C, E. Common automation offerings are Chef, Puppet, and Ansible.

47. B. A rolling configuration will sequentially upgrade the web servers without causing a complete outage and would meet the requirements outlined in the question.

48. C. Cloning takes the master image and clones it to be used as another separate and independent VM. Important components of a server are changed to prevent address conflicts; these include the UUID and MAC addresses of the cloned server.

49. D. The manager is requesting data on the results of the quality assurance testing on the release.

50. A. A hotfix is a software update type that is intended to fix an immediate and specific problem.

51. B. Moving inactive data to a separate storage facility for long-term storage is called archiving.

52. A. The hot site model is the most viable option given the requirements. A hot site is a fully functional backup site that can assume operations immediately should the primary location fail or go offline.

53. B. Asynchronous replication is when data is written to the primary first, and then later a copy is written to the remote site on a scheduled arrangement or in near real time.

54. B. Edge locations are not complete cloud data centers. There are cloud connection points located in major cities and offer local caching of data for reduced response times.

55. C. The recovery time objective is the amount of time a system can be offline during a disaster; it's the amount of time it takes to get a service online and available after a failure.

56. B. A warm site approach to recovering from a primary data center outage is when the remote backup of the site is offline except for critical data storage, which is usually a database.

57. E. A cold site is a backup data center provisioned to take over operations in the event of a primary data center failure, but the servers and infrastructure are not deployed or operational until needed.

58. B. The restore point objective is the point in time that data can be recovered.

59. A. Synchronous replication offerings write data to both the primary storage system and the replica simultaneously to ensure that the remote data is current with local replicas.

60. B, C. The restore point and restore time objectives are the measurements for the amount of data lost and the time needed to get back online after an outage.

61. C. Cloud automation systems offer the ability to add and remove resources dynamically as needed; this is referred to as elasticity.

62. B. With the PaaS model, the cloud provider will maintain the operating system and all supporting infrastructure.

63. C. The higher up the services stack you go, from IaaS to PaaS to SaaS, the more difficult it will be to migrate. With IaaS, most of the cloud operations are under your direct control, which gives you the most flexibility to migrate. However, if the cloud provider controls the application, you may not have many migration options.

64. A, B, D. Cloud computing operates with a utility business model that charges you only for the resources that you consume. This model enables you to scale your cloud fleet to meet its current workload and be able to add and remove capacity as needed. There are many options to use elasticity to scale cloud operations, including vertical and horizontal scaling and bursting.

65. B. Scaling up, or vertical scaling, will add resources such as CPU instances or more RAM. When you scale up, you are increasing your compute, network, or storage capabilities.

66. C. The establishment of average usage over time is the data that gets collected for a baseline report.

67. B. Cloud bursting allows for adding capacity from another cloud service during times when additional resources are needed.

68. B. The measurement of the difference between a current reading and the baseline value is referred to as the variance.

69. C. Change management includes recording the change, planning for the change, testing the documentation, getting approvals, evaluating and validating, writing instructions for backing out the change if needed, and doing post-change review if desired.

70. C. The ability to disable an account can be helpful in situations where the account will need to be reactivated at a future date and does not need to be deleted.

71. B, E, F. Trends, usage, and deficiencies are all management report outputs that can be identified using object tracking.

72. A, D, E. CPU, RAM, and network utilization are all important objects to manage for capacity and utilization tracking. Storage volume tiers and OS versions do not apply to this scenario.

73. D. Objects are queried to gather metric data.

74. B. Tracking object performance data should match with the guaranteed levels outlined in the service level agreement.

75. C. A dashboard is a configurable graphical representation of current operational data.

76. B. If a server is using all of its network bandwidth, then the most logical solution is to increase the network adapters' bandwidth or add a second adapter and create a teaming configuration.

77. A. Horizontal scaling is the process of adding servers to a pool for increased capacity. Round-robin is a load-balancing metric and does not apply. Elasticity is the ability to add and remove resources, autoscaling is the automated process of adding and removing capacity, and vertical scaling is expanding a server.

78. E. Vertical scaling is the process of upgrading or replacing a server with one that has greater capabilities.

79. A, C, D. Server performance can be increased by adding CPU processing, memory, and network capacity. SLA, ACL, and DNS are not related to increasing server capacity.

80. D. Cloud reports are formatted collections of data contained in the management or monitoring applications.

81. B. The cloud service provider owns its automation and orchestration systems, and they cannot be directly accessed by the customer.

82. C. It's common for batch processing to be performed on database applications.

83. B. A large number of users downloading a new application would cause an increase in network bandwidth usage.

84. D. A baseline measurement is used as a reference to determine cloud capacity increases and decreases.

85. C. The Domain Name System records need to be changed to reflect the new IP address mapped to the domain name.

86. C. Databases read and write requests utilize storage I/O and should be the focus for troubleshooting.

87. C. Elasticity allows for cloud services to expand and contract based on actual usage and would be applicable to increasing storage capacity.

88. C. Workflow applications track a process from start to finish and sequence the applications that are required to complete the process.

89. A, C, D. Resources such as the amount of RAM needed, CPU cycles, and storage capacity are common systems that may become saturated as your cloud compute requirements grow.

90. B, C. In addition to the web servers, IP addresses may be required for the DNS server and the default gateway.

91. B. The question is asking about being able to access a specific cloud service. This would concern Jill having the authorization to access the storage volume. Authentication and SSO are login systems and not rights to services. A federation links user databases.

92. A. The `tracert` and `traceroute` commands are useful for network path troubleshooting. These commands show the routed path a packet of data takes from source to destination. You can use them to determine whether routing is working as expected or whether there is a route failure in the path. The other options are all incorrect because they do not provide network path data.

93. B, D. The Windows command-line utility nslookup resolves domain names to IP addressing. The Linux equivalent is the `dig` command. The other options are not valid for the solution required in the question.

94. B. The Windows Remote Desktop Protocol allows for remote connections to a Windows graphical user desktop.

95. C. The tcpdump utility allows a Linux system to capture live network traffic, and it is useful in monitoring and troubleshooting. Think of tcpdump as a command-line network analyzer. The `dig` and `nslookup` commands show DNS resolution but do not display the actual packets going across the wire. `netstat` shows connection information and is not DNS-related.

96. E. In a data center, terminal servers are deployed and have several serial ports, each cabled to a console port on a device that is being managed. This allows you to make an SSH or a Telnet connection to the terminal server and then use the serial interfaces to access the console ports on the devices to which you want to connect. The other options do not provide serial port connections.

97. C. Infrastructure security is the hardening of the facility and includes the steps outlined in the question, including nondescript facilities, video surveillance, and biometric access.

98. C, E. Common remote access tools include RDP, SSH, and terminal servers. IDSs/IPSs are for intrusion detection, and DNS is for domain name–to–IP address mappings and is not a utility for remote access.

99. C. A secure Internet-based connection would be a VPN.

100. A. Logging into systems is referred to as authentication. Also, the question references multi-factor authentication (MFA) as part of the system.

Chapter 1

Introducing Cloud Computing Configurations and Deployments

THE FOLLOWING COMPTIA CLOUD+ EXAM OBJECTIVES ARE COVERED IN THIS CHAPTER:

✓ **1.1 Compare and contrast the different types of cloud models.**

- Deployment models
  - Public
  - Private
  - Hybrid
  - Community
  - Cloud within a cloud
  - Multicloud
  - Multitenancy
- Service models
  - Infrastructure as a service (IaaS)
  - Platform as a service (PaaS)
  - Software as a service (SaaS)
- Advanced cloud services
  - Internet of Things (IoT)
  - Serverless
  - Machine learning/Artificial intelligence (AI)
- Shared responsibility model

✓ **1.3 Explain the importance of high availability and scaling in cloud environments.**

- Hypervisors
  - Affinity
  - Anti-affinity
- Regions and zones
- High availability of network functions
  - Switches
  - Routers
  - Load balancers
  - Firewalls
- Scalability
  - Auto-scaling

✓ **1.4 Given a scenario, analyze the solution design in support of the business requirements.**

- Environments
  - Development
  - Quality assurance (QA)
  - Staging
  - Production
- Testing techniques
  - Vulnerability testing
  - Penetration testing
  - Performance testing
  - Regression testing
  - Functional testing
  - Usability testing

✓ **3.1 Given a scenario, integrate components into a cloud solution.**

- Application
  - Serverless

✓ **4.1 Given a scenario, configure logging, monitoring, and alerting to maintain operational status.**

- Monitoring
  - Baselines
  - Thresholds

✓ **4.3 Given a scenario, optimize cloud environments.**

- Placement
  - Geographical
  - Cluster placement
  - Redundancy
  - Colocation

✓ **4.4 Given a scenario, apply proper automation and orchestration techniques.**

- Automation activities
  - Routine operations
  - Updates
  - Scaling

Introducing Cloud Computing

You'll begin your CompTIA Cloud+ (CV0-003) certification exam journey with a general overview of cloud computing. With a strong understanding of cloud terminology and architectures, you'll better understand the details of the cloud, which in turn means that you'll be better prepared for the Cloud+ exam and be effective when planning, deploying, and supporting cloud environments.

Let's start by briefly looking at where cloud sits in the broader scope of the IT world. Before cloud computing, organizations had to acquire the IT infrastructure needed to run their applications. Such infrastructure included servers, storage arrays, and networking equipment like routers and firewalls.

Options for where to locate this infrastructure were limited. An organization with an ample budget might build an expensive *data center* consisting of the following:

- Racks to hold servers and networking equipment
- Redundant power sources and backup batteries or generators
- Massive cooling and ventilation systems to keep the equipment from overheating
- Network connectivity within the data center and to outside networks such as the Internet

Organizations that are less fiscally blessed might rent physical space from a *colocation* (colo) facility, which is just a data center that leases rack space to the general public. Because colo customers lease only as much space as they need—be it a few rack units, an entire rack, or even multiple racks—this option is much cheaper than building and maintaining a data center from scratch. Customer organizations just have to deal with their own IT equipment and software. To put it in marketing terms, think of a colocation facility as "data center as a service."

Cloud computing takes the concept of a colocation facility and abstracts it even further. Instead of acquiring your *own* IT equipment and leasing space for it from a colo, an organization can simply use a *cloud service provider*. In addition to providing and managing the data center infrastructure, a cloud service provider (or just provider for short) *also* handles the IT hardware infrastructure—namely servers, storage, and networking. The *consumer* of the cloud services pays fees to use the provider's equipment, and such fees are typically based on usage and billed monthly. In this chapter, we'll dive further into the details of how cloud computing works and how an organization might use the cloud instead of—or in addition to—a traditional data center or colo model.

Related to the data center versus cloud distinction, there are two terms that you need to know. *On-premises* (on-prem) hosting refers to an organization hosting its own hardware, be it in a data center or a colo. In contrast, cloud computing is an example of *off-premises* (off-prem) hosting, as the hardware resources are *not* controlled by the organization that uses them. To make this distinction easy to remember, just equate on-prem with data center and off-prem with cloud.

This book will reference the National Institute of Standards (NIST) SP 800-145 publication (`https://doi.org/10.6028/NIST.SP.800-145`) as the main source of cloud computing definitions. NIST defines cloud computing as follows:

> . . . a model for enabling convenient, on-demand network access to a shared pool of configurable computing resources (e.g., networks, servers, storage, applications, and services) that can be rapidly provisioned and released with minimal management effort or service provider interaction.

Pay close attention to that last sentence. The reference to "minimal management effort or service provider interaction" is code for automation. Unlike a traditional data center or colocation facility, using the cloud doesn't require someone to physically go to a facility to install servers or plug in cables. There's no need for "remote hands" because cloud providers offer self-service management consoles that do the provisioning for you. When you think about it, cloud providers are really just providing automation-powered managed services for nearly every conceivable IT need.

In this study guide, you'll take a close look at all aspects of cloud computing as you progress on your journey to obtaining the Cloud+ certification. As an analogy to cloud computing, think of the services you get in your home through utilities, such as electricity and water services. You are probably not involved in the details of how these services are created and delivered; you turn the water faucet on and off, and pay only for what you use. Cloud computing follows the same principle, albeit applied to a variety of IT services.

Traditionally, computing did not follow this model. Instead, an organization would purchase all the hardware and software necessary to meet their needs. Adding to the cost, they needed to maintain a staff of specialized engineers to operate and maintain the systems. And they'd have to purchase more equipment than they needed to leave room for growth. This meant high capital outlays without a corresponding immediate payoff. As I mentioned earlier, organizations had to build and secure data centers to host, power, and cool the equipment.

Like utilities, cloud computing follows a pay-as-you-go model, where a provider sells computing resources that you consume as needed. This allows organizations to pay only for what they use, and it has many additional advantages that you'll explore throughout this book.

The market and adoption of the cloud computing business has exploded worldwide. In just the past decade, cloud computing has gone from a novelty for early adopters to a dominant position in the marketplace today. Although there are many statistics and measurements of the size, it is generally agreed that the market has been growing at least 15 percent annually worldwide. Current forecasts estimate the total cloud market worldwide will be more than $800 billion by the year 2025. What is clear is that the economics and business advantages of cloud computing are compelling companies to move more and more applications to the cloud, fueling additional growth well into the future.

There are many advantages to moving to the cloud, but three stand out as compelling business and operations alternatives to hosting computing resources internally in your own data center or in a colocation facility:

- In the past when computing resources were initially needed, there was often a long delay of procuring, installing, and configuring all the pieces needed to host an application. With a cloud solution, the equipment is already running in a cloud provider's data center, and you can begin hosting your application in record time, sometimes as short as in a few minutes.
- From a financial perspective, a company's capital expenditures can be reduced as cloud computing avoids the large up-front costs of purchasing the needed computing equipment and ongoing support expenses associated with maintaining it. Cloud computing, with its pay-as-you-go billing model, frees up a company's cash flow for other needs.
- As your computing or storage needs grow, a cloud computing model can expand almost immediately. Contrast this with the data center model in which you have to procure, install, and configure new equipment or software—a process that can take days if not weeks.

In-house computing requires a data center with the computing gear needed to support the organization's operations. The organization must hire engineers to tend to the operating systems, applications, storage, and networks. As illustrated in Figure 1.1, all computing is owned and operated by a single entity.

FIGURE 1.1 In-house computing

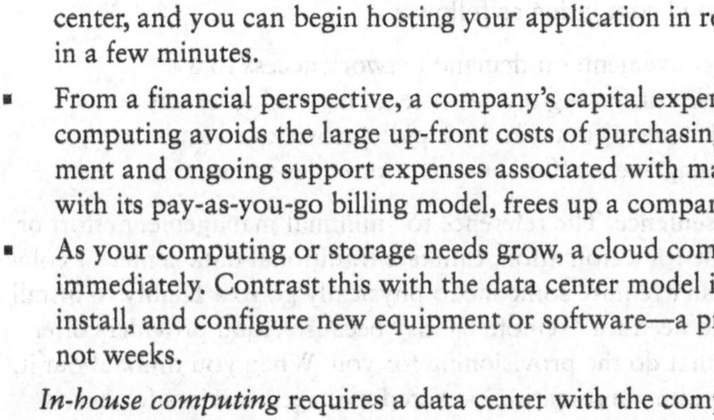

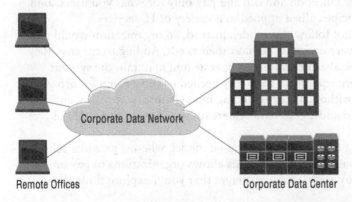

When moving to the cloud, you outsource many of these data center operations to a cloud service provider, as shown in Figure 1.2.

FIGURE 1.2 Cloud computing model

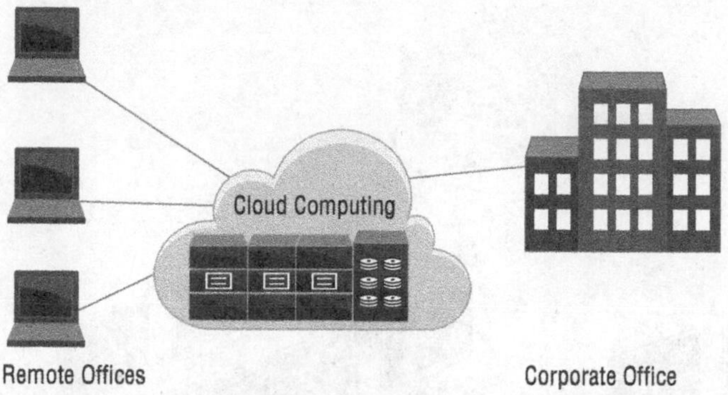

It's important to understand that the organization's data center does not actually move into the cloud, nor does the cloud provider take over the operations of the organization's data center. Instead, the cloud provider has its *own* data centers that already contain all the equipment that you need to host your applications and other IT services. The cloud provider can reach economies of scale by sharing its physical IT resources with many companies. This sounds similar to a colocation facility, but there's one big exception: you do not have physical access to the cloud provider's data center. The only way that you can use their computing resources is via the management interfaces—typically web consoles or application programming interfaces (APIs)—that they provide. There's a trade-off here: you give up control of the physical IT infrastructure in exchange for the convenience of a pay-as-you-go billing model.

In the distant past, computing was the realm of large *mainframe computers*, with a staff of highly specialized engineers and teams of programmers and administrators to manage and run the operations. Figure 1.3 shows a typical mainframe architecture. Mainframe computing was a highly capital-intensive operation that was needed to supply computing resources to a corporation.

As computers became smaller and more powerful, the client-server architecture shown in Figure 1.4 grew prevalent, and we saw the rise in departmental computing that was distributed throughout a company's operations.

Virtualization

Virtualization is what makes cloud computing possible. Simply put, *virtualization* is the ability to take physical data center resources such as servers, storage, and networking and abstract them as services that can be delivered as cloud offerings. A key benefit of virtualization is that it allows different customers to share the same physical IT infrastructure. Without this ability, cloud computing wouldn't be possible.

FIGURE 1.3 Mainframe computing

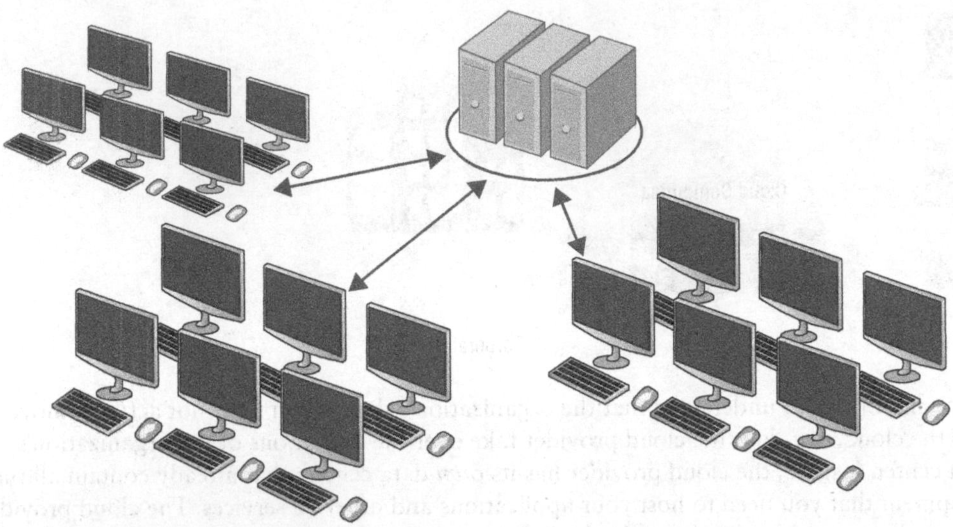

FIGURE 1.4 Client-server computing

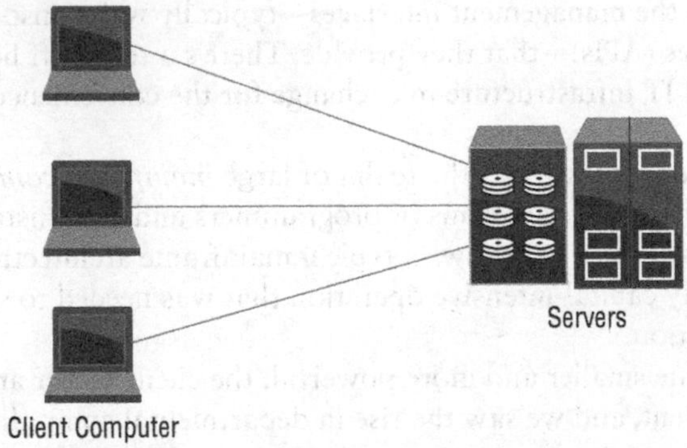

The topic of virtualization can be confusing because people use the term in wildly different ways. In its most basic interpretation, "virtual" can mean anything not purely physical—not a very helpful distinction. Hence, it helps to break virtualization down into two different categories:

- Machine virtualization
- Network virtualization

These distinctions aren't particularly important in the context of cloud computing, but because it's easy to apply the "virtual" moniker to anything and everything, we need to draw some boundaries around when the designation is appropriate.

Machine Virtualization

Machine virtualization—also called server virtualization—involves abstracting the resources of a single physical server into multiple virtual machines (VMs). Essentially, a VM is a software-emulated computer consisting of *virtual CPUs* (vCPUs), memory, storage, and networking. Like a real computer, a VM runs an operating system (OS) called a guest OS. The software that creates virtual machines and performs this abstraction is called a *hypervisor*. The hypervisor also defines the properties of a VM, including the following:

- The number of virtual CPUs
- The amount of random access memory (RAM)
- The type and amount of storage
- Virtual network interfaces and how they're connected

We'll discuss hypervisors in more detail in Chapter 2, "Cloud Deployments." Virtualization not only allows for more efficient use of hardware resources, but also reduces power consumption, cooling, and the server footprint in data centers. This is illustrated in Figure 1.5, where many VMs share common hardware platforms.

NOTE A physical server that runs VMs is called a virtualized host.

FIGURE 1.5 Virtualized computing

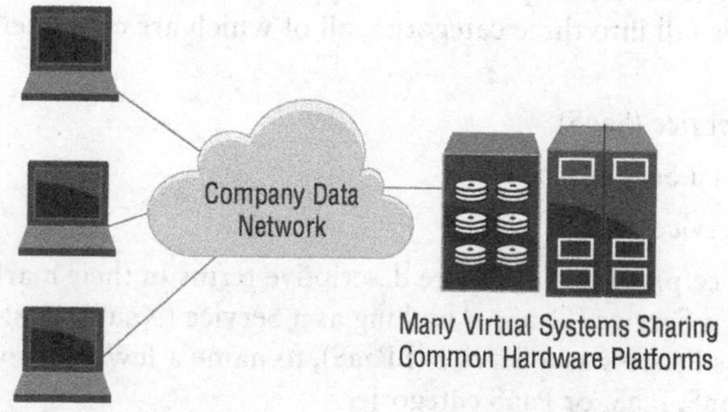

The proliferation of Internet-capable devices, such as smartphones and tablets, means an increased strain on IT infrastructure. Organizations that want to offer services to these customers can benefit greatly from the cloud's utility-like service model (see Figure 1.6). The cloud supports instant access in an always-on environment.

FIGURE 1.6 Cloud computing

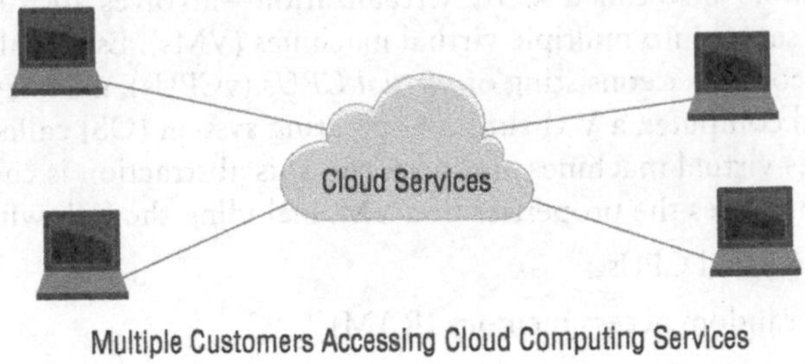

Network Virtualization

By definition, computer networks are already virtual because they're just an abstraction of physical connections. But in the context of cloud computing, *network virtualization* refers to virtual private clouds (VPCs)—isolated private networks within the cloud that allow connectivity among virtual machines and other cloud resources. There's some overlap with machine virtualization here, because VMs have virtual network interfaces that connect to these virtual private clouds.

Cloud Service Models

If a cloud provider controls all the hardware aspects of your IT infrastructure, what do you get to control? The answer depends on the type of *cloud service model* you choose. Cloud service models fall into three categories, all of which are characterized by the term as a service:

- Software as a Service (SaaS)
- Infrastructure as a Service (IaaS)
- Platform as a Service (PaaS)

Many cloud service providers use more descriptive terms in their marketing, including Communications as a Service (CaaS), Anything as a Service (XaaS), Desktop as a Service (DaaS), and Business Process as a Service (BPaaS), to name a few. However, all of these clever names fit into the SaaS, IaaS, or PaaS categories.

Software as a Service

Software as a Service (SaaS) most closely aligns with what used to be called a managed software service. For example, in the early days of the cloud, hosting companies would offer a hosted version of a certain popular, brand-name enterprise email system. Instead of having to buy, configure, and maintain this email system on your own servers, the hosting company would do it for you on its own servers. All you had to do was configure your client machines to connect to the appropriate server to send and receive email. NIST formalizes this concept in the following description of Software as a Service:

> The capability provided to the consumer is to use the provider's applications running on a cloud infrastructure. The applications are accessible from various client devices through a thin client interface such as a web browser (e.g., web-based e-mail), or a program interface. The consumer does not manage or control the underlying cloud infrastructure including network, servers, operating systems, storage, or even individual application capabilities, with the possible exception of limited user-specific application configuration settings.

The Software as a Service model is where the customer of the service accesses the application software that is owned and controlled by the cloud company, which has complete responsibility for the management and support of the application, as shown in Figure 1.7. You, on the other hand, have limited control over the operation and configuration of the software itself. Sticking to the earlier example, you can create and delete email inboxes and control how inbound and outbound emails are processed. But you can't upgrade the software to a newer version.

FIGURE 1.7 SaaS

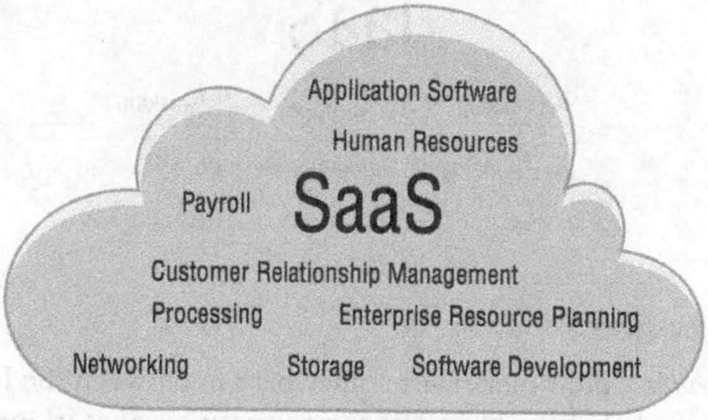

Business applications are good examples of SaaS and can include customer relationship management, enterprise resource planning, human resources, payroll, and software development applications. Hosted applications such as email or calendars that are accessible from a browser or email client are examples of SaaS.

Infrastructure as a Service

The *Infrastructure as a Service (IaaS)* model lets you create VMs and virtual networks in the cloud according to your desired specifications regarding processing power, memory, storage, and networking. The IaaS model is probably the easiest to understand because it most closely mirrors the virtualized server environments in modern data centers. NIST describes it as follows:

> The capability provided to the consumer is to provision processing, storage, networks, and other fundamental computing resources where the consumer is able to deploy and run arbitrary software, which can include operating systems and applications. The consumer does not manage or control the underlying cloud infrastructure but has control over operating systems, storage, deployed applications; and possibly limited control of select networking components (e.g., host firewalls).

IaaS is really just a server and network virtualization environment offered as a service. Because of this, it offers the customer the most flexibility of any of the e-service models. You can provision to your specifications any number of VMs, on which you can run the software of your choice. Also, some IaaS offerings even allow you to choose the virtualized host on which your VMs run, giving you the ability to spread VMs across multiple hosts for resiliency.

IaaS (shown in Figure 1.8) allows the company's data center equipment to be replaced by the cloud equivalent but retains the ability to build software infrastructure on top of the hardware as can be done in a private data center.

FIGURE 1.8 IaaS

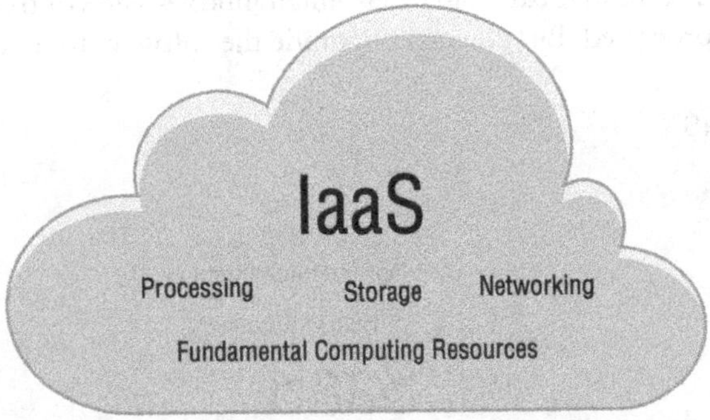

Platform as a Service

The *Platform as a Service (PaaS)* model sits somewhere in between the IaaS and SaaS models, and conceptually it is probably the most difficult to grasp because it doesn't have a clear analog in the data center. Essentially, PaaS gives you a preconfigured computing environment on which to install and run the software of your choice. You have little to no control over the configuration of the OS and VMs on which your application runs. NIST describes it thusly:

> The capability provided to the consumer is to deploy onto the cloud infrastructure consumer-created or acquired applications created using programming languages and tools supported by the provider. The consumer does not manage or control the underlying cloud infrastructure including network, servers, operating systems, or storage, but has control over the deployed applications and possibly application hosting environment configurations.

A strange but accurate way of saying it is that PaaS offers an operating system as a service on which customers can install their applications, as shown in Figure 1.9. The cloud provider takes responsibility up to and including the operating system, including all hardware and virtualized resources.

FIGURE 1.9 PaaS

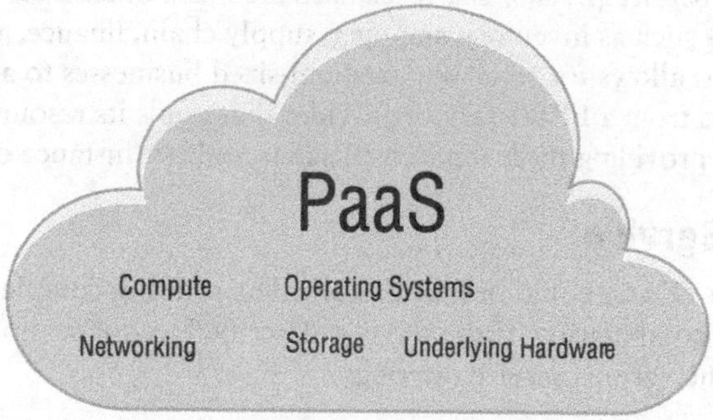

Not surprisingly, PaaS is a popular model with software developers because they can deploy their applications quickly without having to mess with provisioning VMs and keeping up with OS maintenance.

Communications as a Service

Communications as a Service (CaaS) is a particular instance of SaaS that includes hosted voice, videoconferencing, instant messaging, email, collaboration, and all other communication services that are hosted in the cloud. These outsourced corporate communication services can support on-premises or mobile users accessing the applications hosted in the cloud.

The CaaS model allows even small to medium-sized businesses to implement advanced technologies at a reasonable metered cost. There is no need for a staff to manage these communication services since the CaaS cloud provider takes responsibility. Another common term for this service is *Unified Communications as a Service (UCaaS)*.

Database as a Service

Database as a Service (DBaaS) is a manifestation of SaaS in which the cloud provider gives you a turnkey database management system on which you can create your own databases. The provider takes care of the hardware and virtual infrastructure, the operating system, and the database software itself. You need concern yourself only with the databases that you create.

Desktop as a Service

Desktop as a Service (DaaS) provides virtual desktops that consumers can access remotely via desktop or laptop computers, mobile devices, or thin clients. This solution is sometimes called *virtual desktop infrastructure (VDI)*. All desktop applications are hosted in the cloud and can consist of any type of application, such as spreadsheets, word processing, and any other common application. You choose what software to install. The DaaS provider manages all maintenance and configurations as well as licensing and version updates. DaaS is an example of the PaaS model.

Business Process as a Service

Business Process as a Service (BPaaS) is a specialized area that outsources many of a company's day-to-day operations such as inventory, shipping, supply chain, finance, and many other services to the cloud. This allows for small and medium-sized businesses to access sometimes very expensive applications from a BPaaS service provider that pools its resources and allows for economies of scale in providing these services. BPaaS is another instance of the SaaS model.

Anything as a Service

Anything as a Service (XaaS) could best be described as offering complete IT services as a package. XaaS is the combination of the services described in this section. It is a broad term that is a catchall of the various service offerings.

Cloud Reference Designs and Delivery Models

The cloud computing industry has created *reference designs* and *delivery models* to help differentiate between cloud offerings in the marketplace. By understanding the types of models, you can get the big-picture overview of the overall scope of cloud computing. This section will introduce the cloud models, and then in Chapter 2, I will expand on each one. These are the four primary cloud delivery models:

- Public
- Private
- Community
- Hybrid

Public Cloud

The primary focus of the Cloud+ certification is the *public cloud*, which is the most common delivery model deployed. The public cloud is designed for use by the general public. This is the utility-based pay-as-you-go model. Figure 1.10 illustrates a basic public cloud deployment.

FIGURE 1.10 Public cloud

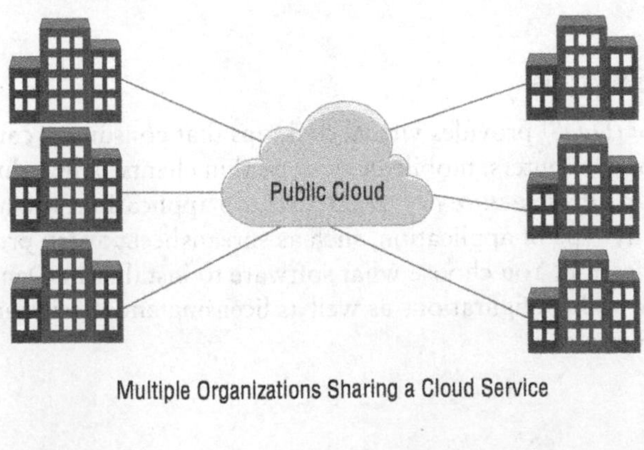

Private Cloud

A *private cloud* is for the exclusive use of a single organization, but it may be used by many units or entities inside a company. Figure 1.11 illustrates a basic private cloud deployment.

FIGURE 1.11 Private cloud

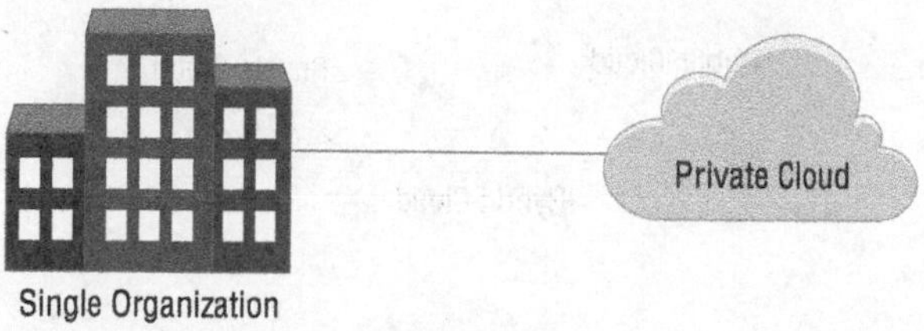

Some people have misappropriated the term *private cloud* to apply to a data center, but this is incorrect. In order to be a private cloud, it has to have the same sort of automation-powered self-service facilities as a public cloud. A traditional data center is not a cloud.

Community Cloud

Community clouds are offered for a specific community of interest and shared by companies with similar requirements for regulatory compliance, security, or policy. Examples include clouds designed for medical, financial, or government organizations that all share common use cases or require standardized architectures. Figure 1.12 shows an example of a common community cloud deployments.

FIGURE 1.12 Community cloud

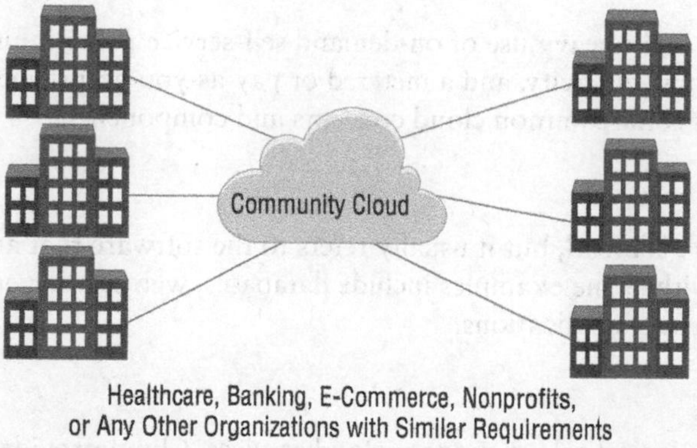

Hybrid Cloud

A *hybrid cloud* is what you get when you connect multiple cloud infrastructures that may or may not be of the same type (public, private, or community). For example, a dentist's office may use the public cloud for its email and office applications but also connect to a community cloud shared by other dentists to access an application for storing patient records. Figure 1.13 shows examples of hybrid computing.

FIGURE 1.13 Hybrid cloud

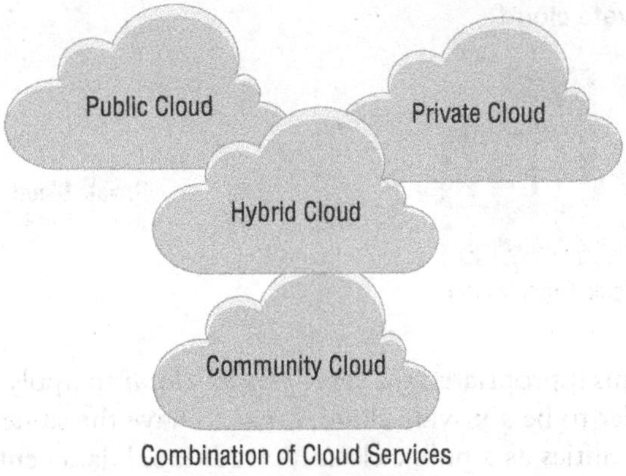

When you use multiple cloud providers redundantly, it's called a multicloud deployment. Multicloud deployments are common when there's a need to avoid the unlikely failure of an entire provider, or to avoid cloud provider lock-in.

Colloquially, a hybrid cloud may also refer to connecting cloud-based resources to a data center or office. Although technically this isn't a hybrid cloud, understand that this is actually what most people mean when they use the term.

Introducing Cloud Concepts and Components

Cloud deployments make heavy use of on-demand self-service provisioning, resource pooling via virtualization, rapid elasticity, and a metered or pay-as-you-go pricing model. In this section, we will discuss some common cloud concepts and components.

Applications

The term *application* is broad, but it usually refers to the software that an organization's end users interact with. Some examples include databases, web servers, email, big data, and line-of-business software applications.

Automation

Automation plays a critical role in modern cloud services. Cloud providers employ proprietary automation software that automates the deployment and monitoring of cloud resources, including network, storage, and compute. Automation makes rapid deployment and teardown possible, and it gives users granular control over their cloud usage.

Compute

Simply put, the cloud services that run your applications fall under the category of *compute*. People often think of compute as just virtual machines running in the cloud, but this is only half the story. Compute may refer to one of two things: IaaS virtual machines, or so-called serverless computing.

IaaS Compute may refer to an IaaS service that lets you provision virtual machines, storage, and networking resources in the cloud.

Serverless/FaaS Compute can also refer to what the marketers call *serverless* computing and what the technophiles call *function-as-a-service* (FaaS). In this model, the cloud provider hands you a slick interface into which you can upload your own application code written in a variety of programming languages, and the cloud provider executes it on compute infrastructure that they fully manage. This model obviates the need to provision virtual machines. Instead, the cloud provider handles the compute infrastructure, so all you have to do is deal with the application code. FaaS is a type of PaaS offering.

NOTE I've never figured out why it's called *compute* instead of the more familiar *computing*. My best guess, however, is that it's to distinguish the cloud model from the data center model. The term *compute* is used almost exclusively of cloud infrastructure.

Networking

Cloud providers offer most of the traditional networking functionality that you would find in a data center. The difference is that in the cloud, the networking functions provided by traditional firewalls, routers, switches, and load balancers are implemented in the provider's proprietary software. The upside of this approach is that it allows the provider to achieve high availability for these core networking functions.

In the IaaS model, cloud providers also offer Domain Name System (DNS), Dynamic Host Configuration Protocol (DHCP), and virtual private cloud networks as part of the service, so you don't have to spin up your own DNS or DHCP servers as you would in a data center environment.

Security

Just as security is a critical component in private and corporate data centers, so is it in the cloud. Cloud service providers offer many security services, including firewalls, access control, intrusion detection and prevention systems, and encryption services.

Storage

Large storage arrays and storage area networks exist in the cloud for use by cloud service consumers. Common storage media are solid-state drives (SSDs) and magnetic physical drives. Storage types include object-based, block-based, and filesystem-based systems. Some storage is optimized for high availability and durability, and others are less expensive and offer long-term archival storage.

Connecting the Cloud to the Outside World

Cloud providers give you complete control over how open or closed your cloud resources are to the rest of the world. If you want to offer a service that's available to anyone anywhere in the world, you can do that. *Ubiquitous access* refers to the ability to access cloud resources from anywhere in the network from a variety of devices such as laptops, tables, smartphones, and thin or thick clients. On the other hand, if you want to restrict access only to those within a particular office, you can do that as well. Because most cloud providers are security-conscious, they prohibit access to your cloud resources by default. You have to explicitly allow access.

Deciding Whether to Move to the Cloud

Organizations that blindly decide to move some of their IT infrastructure to the cloud are sometimes met with an unpleasant surprise when they find out how difficult and expensive it can be. It's not necessarily that the cloud is prohibitively expensive. The surprise comes from failing to understand the dependencies that exist among different IT resources in the data center. When one IT resource moves from the data center to the cloud, it usually has to drag a few other resources with it. For example, moving a database-backed application probably requires moving the database, which might be quite large. Naturally, whoever manages that database is going to have to back it up, so backups will have to be stored in the cloud as well.

Hence, you must have a very clear and detailed understanding of what it is that you are actually moving. This means having updated documentation that reflects all aspects of your operations. To perform a migration, you must know exactly which applications you are running, their dependencies, along with any storage, network, operating system, processing, memory, and any other relevant requirements. The more detailed assessment of your current operations, the better equipped you are to decide whether it makes sense to move to a cloud-based model.

Selecting Cloud Compute Resources

Let's talk about some considerations for migrating on-premises compute resources into the cloud. In the data center, you have virtual machines. It's often possible to migrate a virtual machine directly to the cloud, but the better approach is usually to create a new virtual machine in the cloud and configure it from scratch. One reason for this is that a virtual machine running in your data center will have drivers and other software specific to the virtualization platform that you're using, which will undoubtedly be different than what the cloud provider is using. Performing a "lift and shift" migration to the cloud is asking for trouble.

The sizing of virtual machines—processor power, memory, and storage—should mirror that of your data center VMs. VMs in the cloud are fundamentally no different than the

VMs in your data center. There is no "cloud magic" that makes cloud-based VMs more resource efficient. For example, an application that requires 16 GB of memory in the data center will require just as much memory when it's running in the cloud. Make sure that there is ample input/output (I/O) and low latency for storage access, and that there is enough processing and memory allocated to ensure the proper level of performance expected.

One final word on migrating machines to the cloud. Prior to machine virtualization, each physical server ran a single operating system on *bare metal*. This often meant that one server could host only a handful of applications. Nowadays, machine virtualization is the norm, both in the data center and in the cloud. However, you may occasionally run across an old application that for whatever reason has to run on a bare-metal server. Such applications generally aren't good candidates for moving to the cloud. If you're not sure, you can sometimes smoke out such legacy applications by looking for servers that have been exempted from operating system updates.

Hypervisor Affinity Rules

Another consideration involves the *physical* placement of your data center VMs. To ensure resiliency in the event of a virtualization host failure, organizations often use *hypervisor affinity* rules to ensure that redundant VMs never run on the same hardware. For example, you may have primary and secondary SQL database servers, each running on a different VM host. If the host running the primary SQL VM fails, the secondary VM running on a different host can take over. If both are running on the same host, then both VMs fail, defeating the point of redundant VMs in the first place!

Cloud providers offer the ability to enforce hypervisor affinity rules, although they may use more user-friendly terminology, such as VM-host affinity. As you plan a cloud migration, take note of VMs that are redundant or that appear to serve the same purpose. Chances are that you have hypervisor affinity rules in place that you'll want to re-create in the cloud.

Validating and Preparing for the Move to the Cloud

To perform a successful migration to the cloud, it is important to bring together all the interested parties and stakeholders. The traditional IT groups such as development, operations, OSs, storage, networking, and security will be integral parts of the migration teams. Non-IT groups, such as finance and legal, will need to be involved, because cloud computing can significantly change the cost and accounting models of departments and possibly the entire organization. In the data center model, a healthy portion of the budget goes to the up-front expenses of purchasing physical infrastructure such as servers and networking equipment. Accountants call these capital expenditures (capex for short). When moving to the cloud, these huge capital outlays aren't necessary. Instead of spending hundreds of thousands or more on IT infrastructure, you pay the cloud provider a monthly fee based on usage. This expense is ongoing for as long as you use the services, but the amount you have to fork over up front is much less. This is called an operational expenditure (opex) model. In essence, instead of buying or leasing your own equipment, you're leasing the *use* of the cloud provider's equipment.

If the company does not have the in-house expertise with cloud migrations, it may be advised to enlist the skills of companies specializing in assisting companies moving to the cloud. Also, especially with larger projects, a project manager should be assigned to track and manage the undertaking.

Once you identify the pieces that need to move to the cloud, you need to decide what cloud delivery model you want to use. If you're hosting applications on-prem, do you continue to host the same applications in the cloud using an IaaS model? Or do you offload some of the responsibility to the cloud provider by using a PaaS model? For example, you may have a custom application written in Python. You can continue to run it in VMs as you always have, but just in the cloud using an IaaS model. Or you may instead run it in the cloud without having to bother with the VMs—the PaaS model.

Also, you may decide that now's a good time to ditch some of your current applications and use an SaaS model where the cloud provider manages the back-end IT infrastructure. With this information, you can evaluate the many different cloud company's service offerings in the marketplace.

A common practice is to determine what less critical or low-risk applications could be good candidates to move to the cloud. These applications can be used as a validation or proof-of-concept project for your company.

As part of the preparation, keep the finance group involved from the start of the project. IT expenses and budgeting often are a significant expense for any company, from the smallest local mom-and-pop shop to multibillion conglomerates. The cloud computing pay-as-you-go utility cost models shift the expenses away from the large up-front capital expenditures of equipment, services, and software. Cloud computing requires little, if any, up-front capital costs, and costs are operational based on usage.

Choosing Elements and Objects in the Cloud

Before making plans to migrate anything to the cloud, it's important to decide whether you want to use the IaaS, PaaS, or SaaS model, or any combination thereof. The model you use will determine the specific cloud building blocks you'll have to put together. As you already know, IaaS leaves much of the work in your hands, making migrations more flexible but more complicated. On the other end of the spectrum, the SaaS model makes migrations quicker and easier, but at the cost of giving up control over the infrastructure.

Once you decide on the model, identify what services and capabilities are available in the cloud that fit your needs and requirements. As service providers have expanded their offerings and capabilities, understanding all your options has become almost overwhelming. Some of the largest public cloud companies have more than a thousand objects and services to choose from, with more being added regularly.

To give you an idea of the plethora of options, let's start with the IaaS model. When it comes to virtual servers, there are a variety of prebuilt OSs to choose from. On the virtual hardware side, you can choose CPU and GPU power, memory, storage volumes, and network I/O. On the network side, you have load balancing, DNS and DHCP services, routing, firewalls, network address translation (NAT), and more. For storage, most cloud companies offer block, object, and file storage.

When it comes to PaaS and SaaS models, your options are naturally more limited because the provider takes on more responsibility for the back-end infrastructure. However, it's not unusual for a provider to offer different services that seem to be very similar to one another. For example, cloud providers offer a variety of managed database services for different types of databases. Likewise, they may offer messaging or email services that are compatible with different on-prem solutions. And of course, PaaS services and tools for developing and deploying applications are limited only by the vast number of programming languages out there.

Internet of Things

The ubiquitous access and elasticity enabled by the cloud has birthed a phenomenon called the *Internet of Things (IoT)*. IoT describes the explosion of small, purpose-built devices that typically collect data and send it to a central location for processing. Some examples of IoT devices include temperature sensors, remote-controlled thermostats, and electronic buttons you push to order a new bag of kitty litter effortlessly. Some cloud providers sell such devices that you can program and integrate with the provider's IoT services.

Machine Learning/Artificial Intelligence (AI)

Machine learning/artificial intelligence (ML/AI) is fundamentally concerned with finding patterns in data. The popularity of ML/AI is growing rapidly because of its ability to make predictions and classify or label data in datasets that are too large to work with manually.

With all of the hype surrounding ML/AI, it's important to understand what it *can't* do. It can't autonomously write a coherent novel. It can't predict tomorrow's winning lottery numbers. In fact, the applications of ML/AI are much more limited than many assume. The capabilities of ML/AI are limited to three things:

- Making predictions—for example, forecasting the weather or calculating the arrival time to a destination
- Identifying patterns—Recognizing objects in images and classifying them according to their contents
- Identifying anomalies—Detecting fraud or hacking attempts

ML/AI requires significant human input, and some applications require more human input than others. In fact, ML/AI is broken down into learning models based on the degree of human input required for them to operate—supervised and unsupervised.

Supervised Learning

Supervised learning applications include predictions and image or voice recognition. It requires creating or "training" an ML/AI model by feeding sample data into it. For example, if you want to create an application that identifies your voice in an audio file, you'd train the model using some quality samples of your voice. Subsequently, the model should be able to identify your voice accurately most of the time.

The accuracy of models depends on the size and quality of the training dataset. In terms of percentage, accuracy can be as high as the upper 90s, but rarely higher.

Unsupervised Learning

Unsupervised learning applications include anomaly detection and automatic classification. Unlike the supervised learning model, the unsupervised learning model requires no manual training. Instead, unsupervised learning automatically finds patterns in a dataset and creates groupings or clusters based on those patterns. For example, given a collection of potato pictures, an unsupervised ML/AI algorithm might classify them based on size, color, and the presence or absence of eyes.

It's important to understand the limitations of this approach. The algorithm doesn't know that it's looking at potatoes, so it might classify a bean as a potato if they look similar enough. All that the algorithm does is to label the pictures based on similarities. If you want your application to be able to take a collection of random images and identify all the potatoes, you'll have to use a supervised learning model.

Another interesting unsupervised learning application is fraud detection. If you have a credit or debit card, there's a good chance that your financial institution is using ML/AI for this purpose. It works by analyzing how you normally use your card—purchase amounts, the types of merchandise or services you purchase, and so on—to establish a baseline pattern. If your purchase activity deviates too much from this pattern, the algorithm registers it as an anomaly, probably generating a call from your financial institution.

If this sounds similar to the supervised learning model, it's because it is, but with one big difference—the model is always retraining itself with new data. To better understand this, imagine that you frequent a particular coffee shop and use your card to buy coffee. One day, the coffee shop closes its doors for good, and you end up going to another shop. This may initially register as a slight anomaly, but as you continue visiting the new coffee shop, that becomes your new baseline. The model is continually retraining itself on what your normal card usage looks like.

To put a finer point on it, in supervised learning the algorithm is looking for things it *does* recognize. In unsupervised learning, the algorithm is looking for things it *doesn't* recognize.

Creating and Validating a Cloud Deployment

In this section, I will go deeper into the technology architectures and processes that you'll find in the world of cloud computing. It is important to see how much of an effect virtualization has had in the creation of cloud computing and to understand the process of taking physical hardware resources, virtualizing them, and then assigning these resources to systems and services running in the virtualized data center.

The Cloud Shared Resource Pooling Model

Every cloud service depends on resource pooling. *Resource pooling* is when the cloud service provider virtualizes physical resources into a group, or pool, and makes these pooled resources available to customers. The underlying physical resources are then dynamically allocated and reallocated as the demand requires. Recall the NIST definition of cloud computing as "a model for enabling convenient, on-demand network access to a shared pool of configurable computing resources . . ." Resource pooling is a defining feature of the cloud.

Resource pooling hides the physical hardware from the customer and allows many customers to share resources such as storage, compute power, and network bandwidth. This concept is also called multitenancy. We'll look at some examples of these pooled resources in the following sections.

Compute Pools

In the cloud provider's data center, there are numerous physical servers that each run a hypervisor. When you provision a VM in the cloud, the provider's cloud *orchestration platform* selects an available physical server to host your VM. The important point here is that it doesn't matter which particular host you get. Your VM will run the same regardless of the host. In fact, if you were to stop a running VM and then restart it, it would likely run on a completely different host, and you wouldn't be able to tell the difference. The physical servers that the provider offers up for your VMs to run on are part of a singular *compute pool*. By pooling physical servers in this way, cloud providers can flexibly dispense computing power to multiple customers. As more customers enter the cloud, the provider just has to add more servers to keep up with demand.

Drilling down a bit into the technical details, the hypervisor on each host will virtualize the physical server resources and make them available to the VM for consumption. Multiple VMs can run on a single physical host, so one of the hypervisor's jobs is to allow the VMs to share the host's resources while remaining isolated from one another so that one VM can't read the memory used by another VM, for instance. Figure 1.14 shows this relationship between the virtual machines and the hardware resources.

FIGURE 1.14 Shared resource pooling

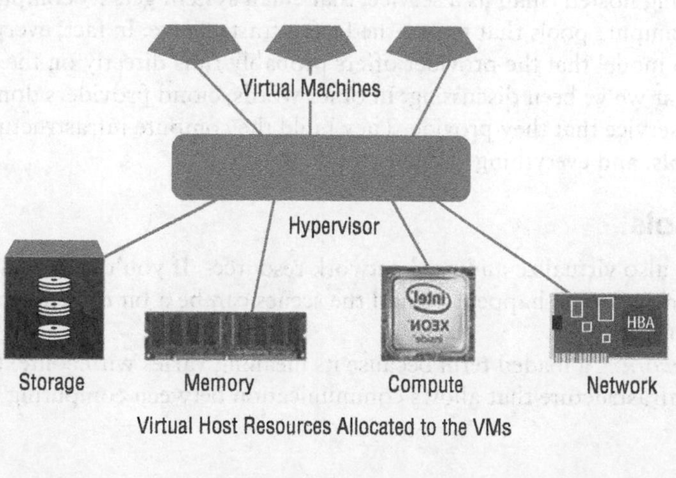

The hypervisor's job is to virtualize the host's CPUs, memory, network interfaces, and—if applicable—storage (more on storage in a moment). Let's briefly go over how the hypervisor virtualizes CPU, memory, and network interfaces.

On any given host, there's a good chance that the number of VMs will greatly outnumber the host's physical CPU cores. Therefore, the hypervisor must coordinate or schedule the various threads run by each VM on the host. If the VMs all need to use the processor simultaneously, the hypervisor will figure out how to dole out the scarce CPU resources to the VMs contending for it. This process is automatic, and you'll probably never have to think about it. But you should know about another "affinity" term that's easy to confuse with hypervisor affinity: CPU affinity. *CPU affinity* is the ability to assign a processing thread to a core instead of having the hypervisor dynamically allocate it. A VM can have CPU affinity enabled, and when a processing thread is received by the hypervisor, it will be assigned to the CPU it originally ran on. You're not likely to see it come up on the exam, but just be aware that CPU affinity can and often does result in suboptimal performance, so it's generally best to disable it. A particular CPU assigned to a VM can have a very high utilization rate while another CPU might be sitting idle; affinity will override the hypervisor's CPU selection algorithms and be forced to use the saturated CPU instead of the underutilized one.

Now let's talk about random access memory (RAM). Just as there are a limited number of CPU cores, so there is a finite amount of RAM installed in the physical server. This RAM is virtualized by the hypervisor software into *memory pools* and allocated to virtual machines. When you provision a VM, you choose the amount of RAM to allocate to it. Unlike the CPU, which is shared, RAM is not. Whatever RAM you allocate to a VM is dedicated to that VM, and no other VM can access it. When a VM consumes all of its allocated RAM, it will begin to swap the contents of some of its RAM to storage. This *swap file*, as it is called, will be used as virtual RAM. When configuring a VM, be sure to allocate enough storage space for the swap file, and keep in mind that the storage latency of the swap file will have a negative impact on the performance of the VM.

Thus far, we've discussed compute pools from the perspective of an IaaS model. But how do compute pools work with PaaS or SaaS models? Behind the scenes, almost everything's the same. What's different is that in the PaaS and SaaS models, the cloud provider runs a user-friendly interface atop the underlying compute infrastructure. For example, if the cloud provider is offering hosted email as a service, that email system gets its computing power from the same compute pools that power the IaaS infrastructure. In fact, every service under the PaaS or SaaS model that the provider offers probably runs directly on the same IaaS infrastructure that we've been discussing. In other words, cloud providers don't reinvent the wheel for every service that they provide. They build the compute infrastructure to provide the compute pools, and everything else uses those.

Network Pools

Cloud providers also virtualize and pool network resources. If you're not familiar with the details of networking, what happens behind the scenes can be a bit difficult to grasp, so we'll start in familiar territory.

The term *network* is a loaded term because its meaning varies with context. Generally, a *network* is the infrastructure that allows communication between computing resources, such as two servers or an end user and a server. That much you already know, but here's where it gets complicated. In the cloud, there are two different levels of networking:

The Underlay The underlying network (or *underlay*) consists of the physical network infrastructure that the cloud provider completely manages. This is transparent to you, and you have no visibility into it whatsoever.

The Overlay The cloud provider allows customers to create and manage virtual networks that run atop the provider's underlying network. These are sometimes called *overlay* networks or virtual private clouds (VPCs). Virtual networks are what you'll actually work with and connect your cloud resources to. In simple terms, a VPC is a private, software-defined network that exists in the cloud.

A virtual network consists of, at a minimum, a block of private IP addresses to be assigned to VMs and other network resources, such as DNS and DHCP servers. A virtual network can span multiple physical hosts—a VM running on one host can communicate with another VM running on a different host, as if they were on the same subnet. Naturally, you can connect a virtual network to an external network such as the Internet or a corporate network via a VPN.

It's important to understand that networking in the cloud operates quite differently than what you'll find in a traditional data center. In a data center, a VM's ***virtual network interface card (vNIC)*** typically connects to a ***virtual switch*** (vSwitch) that's associated with one or more physical network interfaces on the host. Each VM can be connected to a different virtual LAN (VLAN) for traffic segmentation. In this virtual switching paradigm, configuring VM networks is a mostly manual task, so the network configuration remains relatively fixed. Without getting into too many details, this inflexibility is due to the limitations of Ethernet. Additionally, such networks are limited to a maximum of about 1 million devices, which is more than enough for a data center but woefully lacking for a cloud provider that may need to support hundreds of millions of VMs.

NOTE

If you have an application that depends on Ethernet broadcast functionality, it probably won't work in the cloud. Ethernet broadcasts pose a hindrance to scalability in the cloud, so cloud providers generally don't support them.

When you create a virtual network in the cloud, the cloud provider's orchestration platform handles the details of the behind-the-scenes connectivity. For example, suppose that you're running two VMs connected to the same virtual network. These VMs may be on different physical hosts and even in different geographic locations, but they can still communicate. The important point here is that you don't need to know anything about the underlying network infrastructure. All you have to do is to create and configure a virtual network and connect your resources to it, and you're good to go. Just as the provider's proprietary orchestration software automatically picks what server to run your VMs on, so too it dynamically handles connectivity among devices on your virtual networks. This is another example of that "minimal management effort or service provider interaction" qualification that defines cloud computing.

Storage Pools

When you think of the term *storage*, you might think of files on a drive. That's one example of storage that most people are familiar with because it's how our daily-use computers store files. But in the cloud, you'll encounter three different types of storage:

- Block storage
- Object/file storage
- Filesystem storage

Regardless of the storage type, in the cloud data is redundantly replicated across multiple physical devices that compose a *storage pool*. Having data distributed across a storage pool allows the cloud provider to achieve exceptionally high read and write speeds.

Block Storage *Block storage* is designed to mimic a drive by storing data in the same way that a drive does. The virtual disks' (vDisks) VMs used to store data are backed up by block storage. In the data center, a *storage area network (SAN)* device is what provides block storage. A SAN consists of a collection of redundant drives (either spinning disks or SSDs) that store data in blocks, hence the term *block storage*. Even the drive in your personal computer stores data in this way.

In the cloud, because VMs may move from host to host, the VM's persistent storage is not attached to the host. In cloud provider terminology, block storage may be called *elastic block storage* or *block blob storage*. Notice how the terminology hints at the flexible and abstract nature of the storage.

To allocate space from a block storage pool, you create a volume that you can then attach to a VM as a virtual disk. Just as when you provision a VM and the cloud provider dynamically and automatically finds a host to run it on, so too the provider selects some SANs from the storage pool to hold the volume. One big advantage of storage pooling is that your data is stored redundantly on multiple physical SANs; if one fails, your VM can keep on running with no loss of data.

As you gain experience with the cloud, you'll notice that as a general rule, the more block storage you allocate to a vDisk, the better the performance you get. The reason for this is that allocating more storage means that storage is spread across more physical drives operating in parallel.

Although block storage is typically thought of as an IaaS analog to the SAN, it does come into play in some PaaS services. Some managed SQL database services make use of block storage. Although in most cases the cloud provider manages it, you still may get to choose some aspects of the volume such as speed and size.

NOTE

Although the storage systems are generally external from the physical servers themselves, some cloud providers do let your VM use locally attached drives for temporary storage, like swap files or caching.

Object/File Storage As the name suggests, *object/file storage* is designed just to store files. You can use object storage to store any file of virtually any size. It's often used for file backups, but it can also be used to store web assets such as images, video, HTML files, and PDF documents. Object/file storage is intended to store files that don't change frequently, so although you can use it to store a database backup, it's not appropriate for storing a live database that's regularly written to.

The cloud provider will usually offer multiple interfaces to upload or download files. For example, they may allow you to transfer files via a web interface, command-line tool, or API. They may allow you to use HTTP to download files, effectively letting you use the object store as a static web server.

One particularly important use of object storage is storing snapshots of elastic block storage volumes. When you take a snapshot of a VM's volume for backup or cloning, it may be stored in object storage, depending on the cloud provider.

Filesystem Storage Filesystem storage is similar to object/file storage in that both are for storing files. However, *filesystem storage* is meant for files that change frequently, like a live database. Filesystem storage is a popular choice for applications that need shared read/write access to the same files.

The way that you interact with filesystem storage differs from object storage. You access filesystem storage via standardized network filesystem protocols, such as Network File System (NFS) or Server Message Block (SMB). To do this, you must configure your OS to mount the networked filesystem as a volume. The OS can then read and write files, just as it would on any other attached filesystem.

In the data center environment, it's common to have file servers dedicated to offering file storage via SMB or NFS, typically for storing user documents. You could still build your own file servers in the cloud, but most cloud providers offer this as a service under the SaaS model.

Organizational Uses of the Cloud

In the cloud, just as in the data center, you don't simply deploy your applications and forget about them. Applications have to be updated or reconfigured, and you'll probably end up adding or retiring applications over time. These operations always carry the risk of breaking working things, something that can be detrimental to your organization. Therefore, it's a best practice to test changes before rolling them out and committing to them. To achieve this, it's common to separate operations into four isolated sections of the cloud:

- Production
- Quality assurance/test
- Staging
- Development

As we walk through these categories, keep in mind that they can be broken down differently according to the needs of the organization. The point here is to protect the organization from data loss and downtime caused by changes.

Production

Production environments host the live applications that the organization uses in its normal course of business. These include email, customer-facing services, and any other line-of-business applications.

The use of multiple production environments can become important during the rollout of updates. Depending on the application, you may want to release updates only to a portion of users. For example, if you're adding a new feature to a web application, you can use load balancing to direct a small portion of users (say 10 percent) to the updated version while everyone else uses the old version. If there's an unforeseen problem with the updated version, it impacts only a fraction of your users.

Of course, this is a simple example, and this approach won't necessarily work in more complex cases. If the application update causes irreversible changes to a huge database, a more cautious approach is needed. This is where it may be necessary to replicate the full production environment and test the update there. If all goes well, you cut everyone over to the updated environment. If things don't go so well, your existing production environment remains intact and functional.

Quality Assurance/Test

Quality assurance (QA)/test environments are used for the testing of software updates or new applications. QA/test environments may closely mirror production environments to ensure the accuracy of test results. To achieve this parity, you may need to copy over production data to the QA/test environment, but the environments still remain carefully separated. We'll discuss some testing methods later in the chapter.

When sensitive data exists in the production environment, doing a verbatim copy to QA/test may not be feasible. It may be necessary to use dummy data that mimics the production data.

Staging

Staging environments are used for building out a system prior to releasing it to production. In reality, a staging environment is just a preproduction environment.

Development

Development environments are typically used by software developers for creating new applications. Organizations that don't develop their own software may not need a dedicated development environment.

Scaling and Architecting Cloud Systems Based on Requirements

One of the prime advantages of cloud computing is that it enables *on-demand computing*, allowing you to deploy and pay for the computing capacity that you are actually using. This is an attractive alternative to having to absorb the costs of servers sitting on standby to address any bursts or cyclical higher compute requirements, such as end-of-month processing or holiday sales loads if, for example, you are a retailer.

Autoscaling is a cloud feature that automatically adds and removes resources based on demand. By paying only for what you need when you need it, you can take advantage of the immense computing power of the cloud without having to pay for servers that are just sitting idle during times of low demand.

For example, let's look at a small sporting goods retailer that uses a public cloud provider to host its e-commerce website. During normal operations, the retailer runs and pays for three web servers. During times of high demand, autoscaling will provision additional web servers to match the increased load. For example, the retailer may decide to run a TV commercial on a Saturday afternoon televised game. After the commercial airs, the website experiences a huge traffic spike and an increase of online orders. Once the load subsides to normal levels, autoscaling terminates the additional web servers so that the retailer doesn't have to keep paying for them when they're not needed. This works well because the retailer can match the load on the website with the needed amount of computing, memory, storage, and other back-end resources in the cloud. Combining this pay-as-you-go model with autoscaling maximizes cost efficiency because you don't have to expend money to purchase the hardware for any peak loads or future growth. Autoscaling will just provision more capacity when needed. With automation and rapid provisioning, adding capacity can be as simple as a few clicks in a console, and the resources are immediately deployed!

Contrast this scenario with what would happen without autoscaling. If the retailer were stuck with only three web servers, during the traffic spike the servers might slow down or crash. Adding more servers would be a manual, expensive, and time-consuming process that even in a best-case scenario would take several minutes to complete. By that time, the damage would have already been done.

Understanding Cloud Performance

Cloud performance encompasses all of the individual capabilities of the various components as well as how they interoperate. The performance you are able to achieve with your deployment is a combination of the capabilities and architecture of the cloud service provider and how you design and implement your operations.

Ongoing network monitoring and management allow you to measure and view an almost unlimited number of cloud objects. If any parameter extends beyond your predefined boundaries, alarms can be generated to alert operations and even to run automated scripts to remedy the issue. Here are just a few of the things you may want to monitor:

- Database performance
- Bandwidth usage

- Network latency
- Storage I/O operations per second (IOPS)
- Memory utilization

Delivering High Availability Operations

By implementing a well-architected network using best design practices, and by selecting a capable cloud service provider, you can achieve high availability operations. You and the cloud provider share responsibility for achieving high availability for your applications running in the cloud.

The cloud provider must engineer its data centers for redundant power, cooling, and network systems, and create an architecture for rapid failover if a data center goes offline for whatever reason. As we discussed with computing, network, and storage pools, the cloud provider is responsible for ensuring high availability of these pools, which means that they're also responsible for ensuring redundancy of the physical components that compose these pools.

It's your responsibility as the cloud customer to engineer and deploy your applications with the appropriate levels of availability based on your requirements and budgetary constraints. This means using different regions and availability zones to eliminate any single point of failure. It also means taking advantage of load balancing and autoscaling to route around and recover from individual component failures, like an application server or database server going offline.

Managing and Connecting to Your Cloud Resources

By definition, your cloud resources are off-premises. This raises the question of how to connect to the remote cloud data center in a way that is both reliable and secure. You'll look at this question in this chapter. Finally, you'll learn about firewalls, a mainstay of network security, and you'll see the role of firewalls in cloud management deployments.

Managing Your Cloud Resources

It's instructive to note the distinction between managing your cloud resources and using them. Managing your cloud resources includes provisioning VMs, deploying an application, or subscribing to an SaaS service such as hosted email. You'll typically manage your cloud services in one of three ways:

- Web management interface
- Command-line interface (CLI)
- APIs and SDKs

Web Management Interface

When getting started with the cloud, one of the first ways you'll manage your cloud resources is via a web interface the cloud provider offers. You'll securely access the *web* management interface over the Internet. Here are a few examples of what you can do with a typical cloud provider web interface:

IaaS: Provision VMs, create elastic block storage volumes, create virtual networks

PaaS: Upload and execute an application written in Python, deploy a web application from a Git repository

SaaS: Send and receive email, create and collaborate on documents

Note that when it comes to the PaaS and SaaS side of things, there's considerable overlap between managing a service and using it.

Command-Line Interface, APIs, and SDKs

Cloud providers offer one or more command-line interfaces to allow scripted/programmatic management of your cloud resources. The command-line interface is geared toward sysadmins who want to perform routine management tasks without having to log in and click around a web interface.

Command-line interfaces work by using the cloud provider's APIs. In simple terms, the API allows you to manage your cloud resources programmatically. In contrast to a web management interface, in which you're clicking and typing, an API endpoint is a web service that listens for specially structured requests. Cloud provider API endpoints are usually open to the Internet, encrypted using Transport Layer Security (TLS), and require some form of authentication.

Cloud providers offer *software development kits (SDKs)* for software developers who want to write applications that integrate with the cloud. SDKs take care of the details of communicating with the API endpoints so that developers can focus on writing their application.

Connecting to Your Cloud Resources

How you connect to your cloud resources depends on how you set them up. As I alluded to earlier, cloud resources that you create are not necessarily reachable via the Internet by default. There are three ways that you can connect to your resources:

- Internet
- VPN access
- Dedicated private connections

Internet

If you're hosting an application that needs to be reachable anytime and anywhere, you'll likely open it up to the Internet. If a resource is open to the Internet, it will have a publicly routable Internet IP address. This is typically going to be a web application, but it doesn't have to be. Although anywhere, anytime access can be a great benefit, keep in mind that traffic traversing the Internet is subject to high, unpredictable latency.

VPN Access

A *virtual private network (VPN)* allows for secure and usually encrypted connections over an insecure network (like the Internet), as shown in Figure 1.15. Usually, a VPN connection is set up between a customer-owned device deployment and the cloud. VPNs are appropriate for applications that do not need anywhere, anytime access. Organizations often use VPNs to connect cloud resources to offices and data centers.

FIGURE 1.15 Remote VPN access to a data center

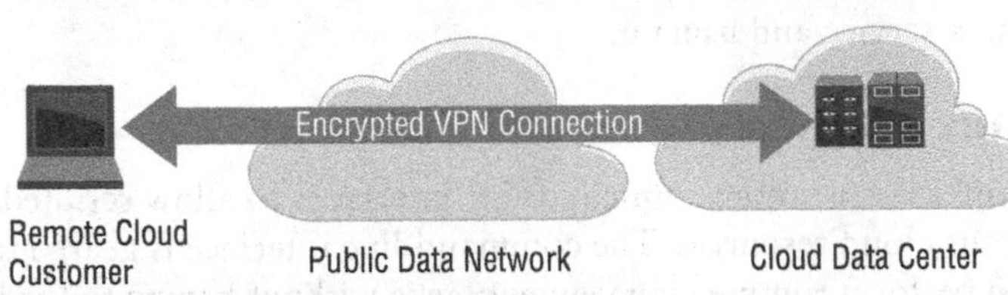

Dedicated Private Connections

Cloud providers offer connections to their data centers via private leased lines instead of the Internet. These connections offer dedicated bandwidth and predictable latency—something you can't get with Internet or VPN access. *Dedicated private connections* do not traverse the Internet, nor do they offer built-in encryption. Keep in mind that dedicated connections don't usually provide Internet access. For that, you'll need a separate Internet connection.

Is My Data Safe? (Replication and Synchronization)

Replication is the transfer and synchronization of data between computing or storage resources, and typically between multiple regions or data centers, as illustrated in Figure 1.16. For disaster recovery purposes and data security, your data must be transferred, or replicated, between data centers. Remote copies of data have traditionally been implemented with storage backup applications. However, with the virtualization of servers in the cloud, you can easily replicate complete VM instances, which allows you to replicate complete server instances, with all of the applications, service packs, and content, to a remote facility.

FIGURE 1.16 Site-to-site replication of data

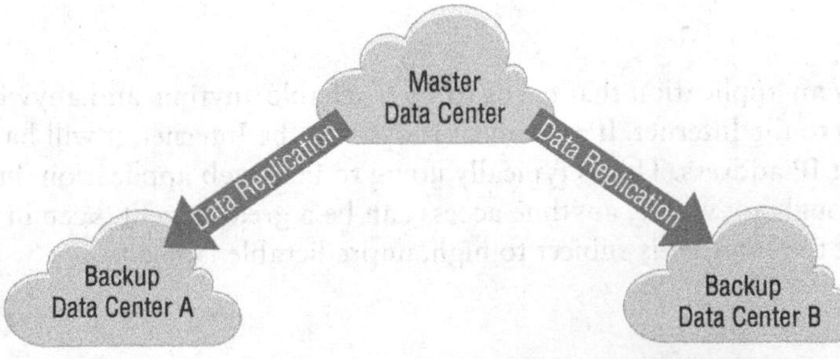

Applications such as databases have built-in replication processes that can be utilized based on your requirements. Also, many cloud service offerings can include data replication as a built-in feature or as a chargeable option.

Synchronous replication is the process of replicating data in real time from the primary storage system to a remote facility, as shown in Figure 1.17. Synchronous replication allows you to store current data at a remote location from the primary data center that can be brought online with a short recovery time and limited loss of data. Relational database systems offer synchronous replication along with automatic failover to achieve high availability.

FIGURE 1.17 Synchronous replication

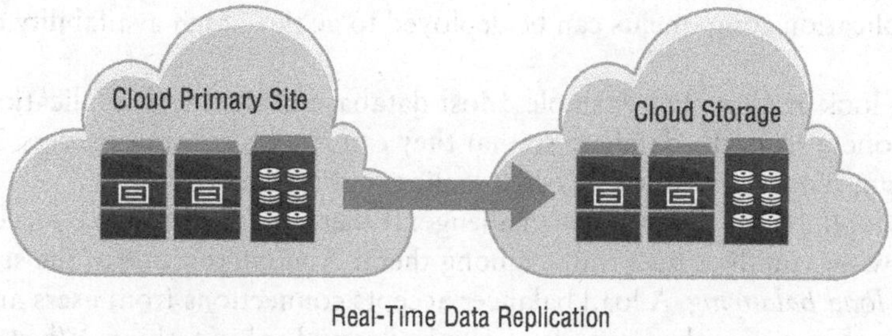

With *asynchronous replication*, the data is first written to the primary storage system in the primary storage facility or cloud location. After the data is stored, it is then copied to a remote location on a delayed or scheduled basis, as shown in Figure 1.18.

FIGURE 1.18 Asynchronous replication

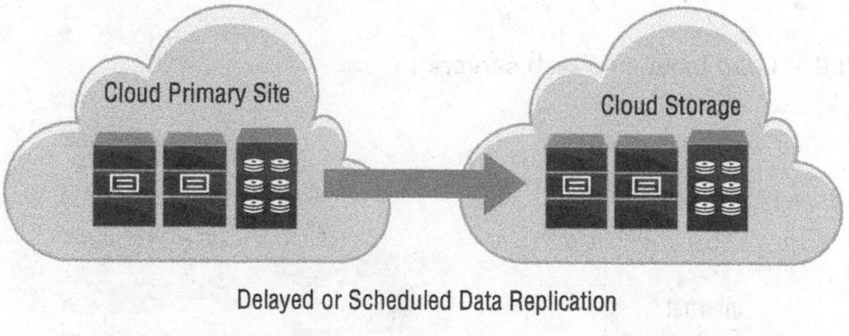

One common use case for asynchronous replication involves taking scheduled snapshots of VM storage volumes and storing those snapshots offline. The snapshots may also be replicated to a remote location for safekeeping. If you ever need to restore the VM, you can do so from the snapshot.

Another example of asynchronous replication is the creation of database read replicas. When an organization needs to run intensive, complex reports against a database, it can tax the database server and slow it down. Rather than taxing the primary database server, which might be performing critical business functions, you can asynchronously replicate the data to a read replica and then run your reports against the replica.

Asynchronous replication can be more cost effective than implementing a synchronous replication offering. Cloud providers often charge for data transfer between regions or availability zones. Because asynchronous replication is not in real time, there's typically less data to transfer.

Understanding Load Balancers

Loose coupling (also called decoupling) is a design principle in which application components are broken up in such a way that they can run on different servers. With this approach, redundant application components can be deployed to achieve high availability and scalability.

Let's take a look at a familiar example. Most database-backed web applications decouple the web component from the database so that they can run on separate servers. This makes it possible to run redundant web servers for scaling and high availability.

But loose coupling introduces a new challenge: If there are multiple web servers that users can access, how do you distribute traffic among them? And what if one of the servers fails? The answer is *load balancing*. A load balancer accepts connections from users and distributes those connections to web servers, typically in a round-robin fashion. When a load balancer sits in front of web servers, users connect to an IP address of the load balancer instead of an IP address of one of the web servers.

Other load balancing functions may include SSL/TLS termination, compression, and session tracking. Load balancers can integrate with autoscaling and server health checks so that if a web server becomes unreachable, the load balancer will detect the failure and trigger an automatic replacement or recovery action. With load balancing, you can effortlessly achieve redundancy and scalability, as shown in Figure 1.19.

FIGURE 1.19 Load balancing web servers

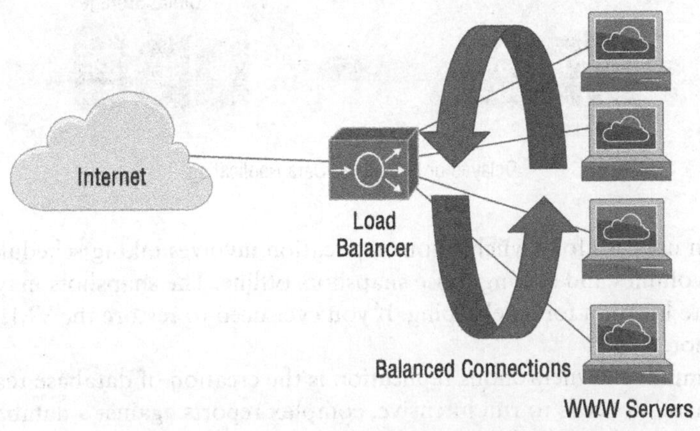

Cloud Testing

As you progress through this book, I will include information on the testing and validations that are required to ensure that changes and ongoing operations are valid and working as expected. In this chapter, you'll be introduced to three validations. Vulnerability and penetration tests are security-related, and I will expand my discussion of them throughout this book. You'll be introduced to load testing to ensure that your application works as expected when it is deployed into a heavily used production network.

Vulnerability Testing

Vulnerability testing is used to find objects in your cloud deployment that can be exploited or that are potential security threats. The *vulnerability scanner* is an application that has a database of known exploits and runs them against your deployment to see whether your cloud deployment may be susceptible or have security holes that need to be remediated. The scanner will detect and report on weaknesses in your cloud deployment. For example, if you're running an older version of a content management system (CMS) that's easily hacked, a vulnerability scan can alert you to this before you become a victim.

Penetration Testing

Penetration testing is the process of trying to exploit vulnerabilities that exist in your infrastructure. Pentesting is usually performed from outside your cloud deployment to assess the ability to access systems into your cloud from, for example, the Internet. Cloud providers have strict rules for how and when you can perform penetration testing, typically requiring advance permission and coordination with the provider. Some examples of penetration testing include trying default or easy-to-guess usernames and passwords and looking for open Transmission Control Protocol/User Datagram Protocol (TCP/UDP) ports.

Performance Testing

Performance testing (sometimes called *load testing*) puts a demand or load on your application or compute system and measures the response. By performing load testing, you can determine how your applications and cloud deployment can be expected to perform in times of heavy production usage. Load testing helps you determine a system's behavior under both normal and anticipated peak load conditions. All systems will fail at some point when under heavy loads, and by performing tests, you can identify and rectify any issues on your design.

Regression Testing

Frequent software updates are a part of the IT landscape. When you upgrade software to a new version, there's always a chance that a previously working function will break. This phenomenon is called a *regression*. *Regression testing* is designed to identify these regressions so that you can decide whether or not to update.

There was a time when organizations would postpone software updates because they would routinely break things and create troubleshooting headaches for everyone. Although this isn't as much of a problem anymore, it does happen from time to time, so it's important to perform regression testing in a controlled test environment prior to rolling out major software updates.

Functional Testing

Functional testing checks the functionality of software against a set of specifications that defines what the software must (or must not) do. In short, functional testing checks whether the software is capable of doing what you want it to do.

Usability Testing

Usability testing considers how easy or difficult it is for end users to use a system. A piece of software might pass all other tests, but the user may still find it difficult, confusing, or frustrating. Such flaws are usually not technical flaws in the code or architecture of a system, but rather flaws in the user interface or a process the user has to follow. Usability testing is designed to catch such flaws early.

In its simplest form, usability testing consists of having a user attempt to complete a specified task. Usability testing is, in a sense, a more subjective version of functional testing. Functional testing is designed to test whether the *software* performs a specified function. Usability testing tests whether the *user* can use the software.

Verifying System Requirements

After you have completed your assessments and needs analysis, you'll have then defined your requirements and which cloud service and deployment models best meet them. The next step is to select a pilot application to migrate to the cloud from your existing data center.

Prior to performing the migration, the engineering team should sit down and review the complete design, from the application, configuration, hardware, and networking to the storage and security. As part of this verification, it is helpful to stage the system in the cloud as a proof-of-concept design. This allows everyone to test the systems and configuration in a cloud environment prior to going live.

Correct Scaling for Your Requirements

The ability of the cloud to scale resources up or down rapidly to match demand is called *elasticity*. For IaaS services, this can be done automatically as needed using autoscaling. This allows cloud consumers to scale up automatically as their workload increases and then have the cloud remove the services after the workload subsides. For SaaS and PaaS services, dynamic allocation of resources occurs automatically and is handled by the cloud provider. (Later in the chapter, we'll discuss the division of responsibilities between you and the provider.) With elastic computing, there is no longer any need to deploy servers and storage systems designed to handle peak loads—servers and systems that may otherwise sit idle during normal operations. Now you can scale the cloud infrastructure to the normal load and automatically expand as needed when the occasion arises.

On-demand cloud services allow the cloud customer to create instantly additional servers, storage, processing power, or any other services as required. On-demand allows customers to consume cloud services only as needed and scale back when they are no longer required. For example, if a developer needs to provision a database and application server for testing, they can quickly provision these servers and deprovision them once they're no longer needed. This is also referred to as a *just-in-time* service because it allows cloud services to be added and removed as needed.

Pay as you grow (PAYG) is like a basic utility, such as power or water, where you pay for only what you use. This is very cost effective because there are minimal up-front costs, and the ongoing costs track your actual consumption of the service. The elasticity of the cloud lets you add resources on-demand, so there's no need to overprovision for future growth. With a normal data center operation, the computing must be overprovisioned to take into account peak usage or future requirements that may never be needed.

Making Sure the Cloud Is Always Available

In this section, you'll become familiar with common deployment architectures used by many of the leading cloud providers to address availability, survivability, and resilience in their services offerings.

Regions

Major cloud providers partition their operations into regions for fault tolerance and to offer localized performance advantages. A *region* is not a monolithic data center but rather a geographical area of presence that usually falls within a defined political boundary, such as a state or country. For example, a cloud company may offer regions throughout the world, as shown in Figure 1.20. They may have regions in Sydney and Tokyo in the Asia Pacific region, and in Europe there may be regions called London and Oslo. In North America there could be regions in Boston, Ottawa, Austin, and San Jose.

FIGURE 1.20 Cloud regions

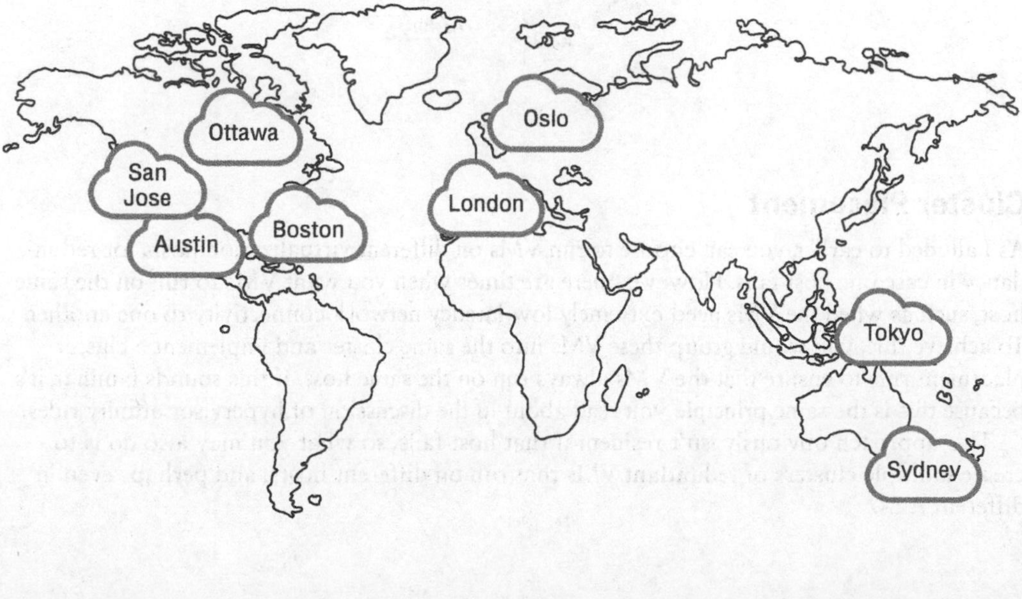

All of the regions are interconnected to each other and the Internet with high-speed optical networks but are isolated from each other, so if there is an outage in one region, it should not affect the operations of other regions.

Generally, data and resources in one region aren't replicated to any other regions unless you specifically configure such replication to occur. One of the reasons for this is to address regulatory and compliance issues that require data to remain in its country of origin.

When you deploy your cloud operations, you'll be given a choice of what region you want to use. Also, for a global presence and to reduce network delays, the cloud customer can choose to replicate operations in multiple regions around the world.

Availability Zones

Regions are divided into one or more *availability zones (AZs)*. Each region will usually have two or more availability zones for fault tolerance. AZs almost always correspond to individual data centers. Each AZ has its own redundant power and network connections. Within a region, AZs may be located a greater distance apart, especially if the region is in an area prone to natural disasters such as hurricanes or earthquakes. When running redundant VMs in the cloud, it's a best practice to spread them across AZs to take advantage of the resiliency that they provide. Figure 1.21 illustrates the concept of availability zones.

FIGURE 1.21 Availability zones

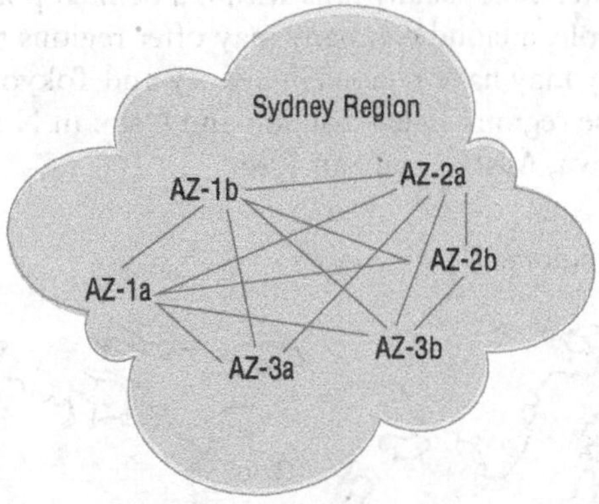

Cluster Placement

As I alluded to earlier, you can choose to run VMs on different virtualization hosts for redundancy in case one host fails. However, there are times when you want VMs to run on the same host, such as when the VMs need extremely low-latency network connectivity to one another. To achieve this, you would group these VMs into the same cluster and implement a cluster placement rule to ensure that the VMs always run on the same host. If this sounds familiar, it's because this is the same principle you read about in the discussion of hypervisor affinity rules.

This approach obviously isn't resilient if that host fails, so what you may also do is to create multiple clusters of redundant VMs that run on different hosts, and perhaps even in different AZs.

Remote Management of VMs

In this section, you'll learn about remote access techniques and look at what tools are available to manage and monitor your VMs. Remember that you don't have physical access to the cloud provider's data centers, so remote access is your only option for managing your servers. Furthermore, the cloud provider will not give you direct access to the hypervisor, which is typically going to be proprietary. This is unlike a traditional data center environment in which you can install a hypervisor management application on a workstation and fully configure and manage the hypervisor, as Figure 1.22 and Figure 1.23 illustrate.

FIGURE 1.22 Local computer running the hypervisor management application

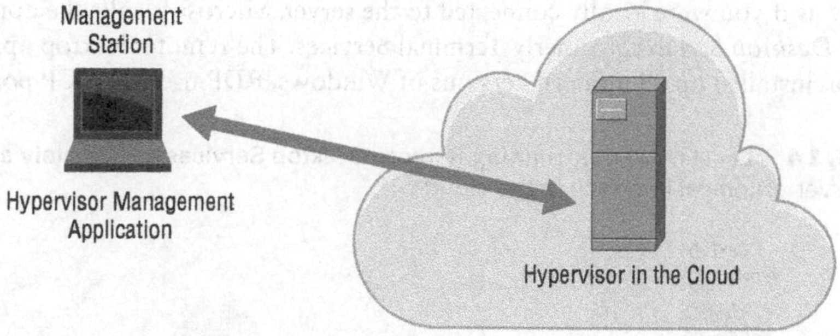

FIGURE 1.23 Remote hypervisor management application

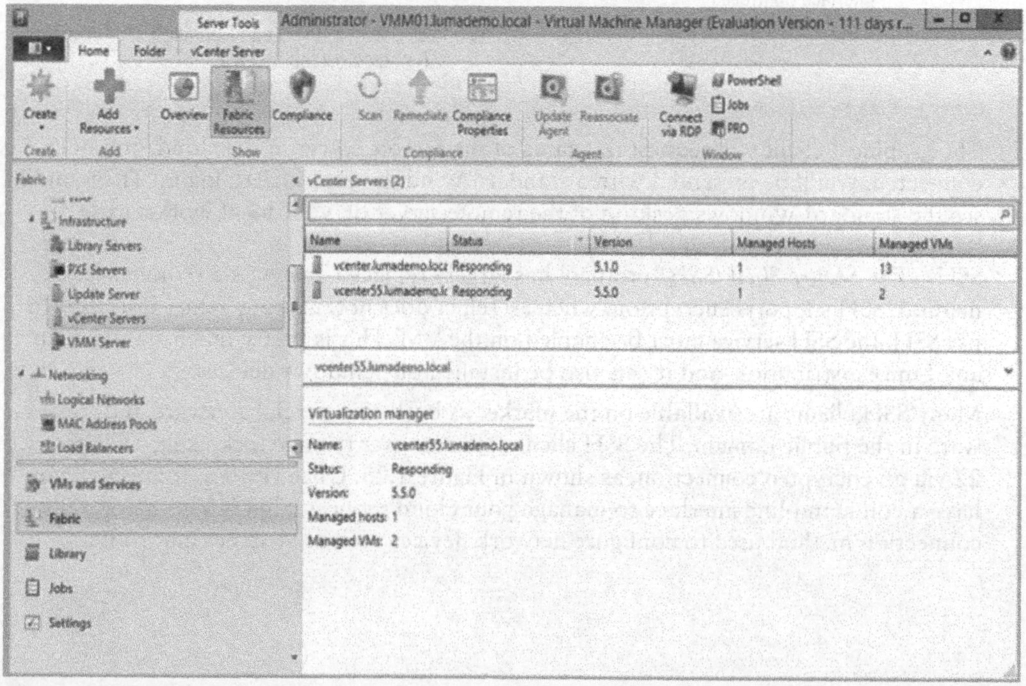

As we've discussed, your options for managing your VMs and other cloud resources are limited to the web management interface, command-line tools, and APIs that the provider gives you. But once you provision a VM, managing the OS and applications running on it is a much more familiar task. You'll manage them in almost the exact same way as you would in a data center. In fact, the whole reason providers offer IaaS services is to replicate the data center infrastructure closely enough that you can take your existing VMs and migrate them to the cloud with minimal fuss. Let's revisit some of these management options with which you're probably already familiar.

RDP *Remote Desktop Protocol (RDP)* is a proprietary protocol developed by Microsoft to allow remote access to Windows devices, as illustrated in Figure 1.24. RDP is invaluable for managing remote Windows virtual machines, since it allows you to work remotely as if you were locally connected to the server. Microsoft calls the application *Remote Desktop Services*, formerly Terminal Services. The remote desktop application comes preinstalled on all modern versions of Windows. RDP uses the TCP port 3389.

FIGURE 1.24 Local computer running Remote Desktop Services to remotely access a Windows server graphical interface in the cloud

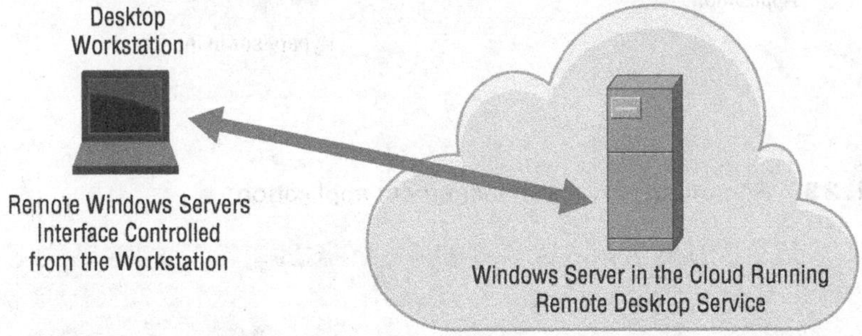

The graphical client will request the name of the remote server in the cloud, and once it's connected, you'll be presented with a standard Windows interface to log in. Then you'll see the standard Windows desktop of the remote server on your local workstation.

SSH The *Secure Shell (SSH)* protocol has largely replaced Telnet as a remote access method. SSH supports encryption, whereas Telnet does not, making Telnet insecure. To use SSH, the SSH service must be enabled on the VM. This is pretty much standard on any Linux distribution, and it can also be installed on Windows devices.

Many SSH clients are available on the market as both commercial software and freeware in the public domain. The SSH client connects over the network using TCP port 22 via an encrypted connection, as shown in Figure 1.25. Once you are connected, you have a command-line interface to manage your cloud services. SSH is a common remote connection method used to configure network devices such as switches and routers.

FIGURE 1.25 Secure Shell encrypted remote access

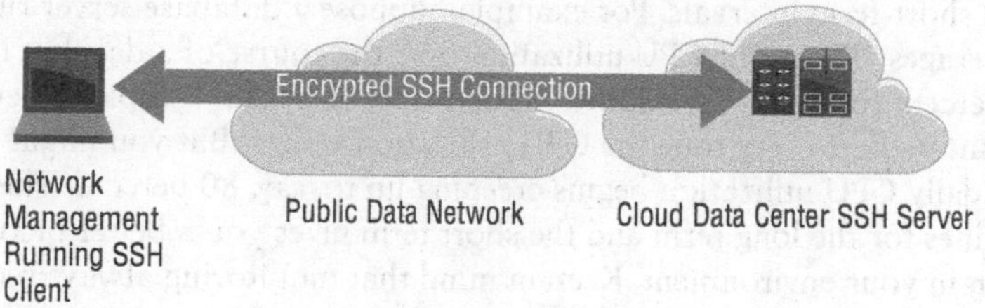

Monitoring Your Cloud Resources

Just because you have created an operational cloud deployment doesn't mean your work is over! You must continually monitor performance and also make sure that there are no interruptions to services. Fortunately, this function has largely been automated. As you'll learn in later chapters, cloud providers offer ways to collect and analyze performance and health metrics. You can also configure automated responses to various events, such as increased application response time or a VM going down. Also, alerts such as text messages, emails, or calls to other applicators can be defined and sent in response to such events.

Monitoring and *automation* go hand in hand in the cloud. For example, you can use autoscaling to add additional virtual CPUs to a VM if utilization has, for example, exceeded 98 percent for more than 10 minutes. And just like everything else in the cloud, you can configure this automation quickly and adjust it to meet changing requirements.

Writing It All Down (Documentation)

Documentation should be created by the many different teams involved in the cloud deployment, such as the server, virtualization, storage, networking, developer, security, and management teams, as well as the cloud provider.

Once the document is complete, it should be readily accessible, and the procedures to maintain consistency should be clear. A corporate compliance group may be formed to monitor and maintain adherence to the standardization process. Also, since the operations and deployment are constantly evolving and changing, the documentation will need to be constantly modified and updated.

Creating Baselines

Before migrating to the cloud, you should establish *baselines* for various aspects of your current infrastructure. Baselines to collect include CPU, memory, storage utilization, and database query times. Establishing baselines helps you determine how to size your cloud resources. Baselines also help you tune your monitoring. Use your baseline statistics as a reference, and if a metric goes significantly above or below that value, you can configure an alert to fire or autoscaling to add more capacity. The deviation of a metric from a baseline is called *variance*.

Because the metrics you'll be monitoring will likely change quickly, minute by minute, as well as slowly over longer periods of time, you'll want to take baseline samplings for both long-term and short-term intervals. For example, suppose a database server running in your data center averages 70 percent CPU utilization over the course of a day, but it occasionally spikes to 90 percent for about 15 minutes when someone runs a complex query. You don't necessarily want to alert every time the CPU utilization spikes. But you might want to know if the average daily CPU utilization begins creeping up to, say, 80 percent. Therefore, having separate baselines for the long term and the short term gives you a better picture of what's really going on in your environment. Keep in mind that monitoring always requires trial and error.

Your baselines help you form a starting point for determining what the normal metrics are for your environment, but they're not to be taken as gospel, since they will change over time. Also, given the huge number of cloud resources available, there are even more metrics that you can monitor. The key is to focus only on the most impactful metrics.

Shared Responsibility Model

Cloud providers operate under what's called a ***shared responsibility model*** that defines what you are responsible for and what the provider is responsible for. The model will vary depending on what you are contracting to use and the offerings of the service provider. Let's look at how the division of responsibilities changes with different service models.

IaaS

As the "I" in IaaS suggests, the cloud provider is responsible for the underlying infrastructure they provide as a service—all of the hardware, hypervisors, block storage, and networking. If you're running VMs, you would have responsibility for the operating system and applications, as well as configuration of your virtual network, which includes network access controls and IP routing.

NOTE **To make it easier to get started, a cloud provider may provide you with a default virtual network for your IaaS resources. Even though such a default network should work right out of the gate, it's still your responsibility to make sure that it's configured properly.**

PaaS

With a PaaS service, you're responsible for the applications you choose to run on the service, and the cloud provider would take responsibility for almost everything your application depends on—namely the VMs, OS, and storage. When it comes to the networking, the division of responsibilities may vary. The cloud provider may offer to configure networking for you automatically, giving you unique public and private IP addresses and corresponding DNS entries, or you may provide your own network configuration parameters.

SaaS

When offering Software as a Service, the cloud provider assumes full responsibility for everything, including the software itself. Your responsibility is limited to how you configure and use the software.

Summary

In this introductory chapter, you explored the big picture of cloud computing. You investigated the many types of service models offered in the marketplace today. The core models include IaaS, which strives to emulate the core components of a traditional data center and offer them as a service to facilitate migrations to the cloud. The PaaS and SaaS models extend the benefits of elasticity and pay-as-you-go pricing without the commitment and expertise required to pull off an IaaS deployment. In these models, the cloud provider handles the compute, storage, and network infrastructure.

Cloud delivery models are important to understand for the exam. You looked at the various types of models, including private, public, community, and hybrid clouds, and what the general use cases and differences are for each type of delivery model.

You also learned about the fundamental characteristics of cloud computing. The cloud offers on-demand, self-service provisioning of elastic resources that you pay for on a metered basis. The chapter discussed resource pooling and virtualization of resources such as storage, CPU, memory, storage, and networking.

The chapter also covered how to prepare to migrate your operations to the cloud and how it's important to test systems in the cloud—including sizing, performance, availability, connectivity, data integrity, and others—and that you document the results.

As you read the rest of the book, keep these fundamental concepts in mind, because they provide a structure that you'll build on as you progress on your journey to become Cloud+ certified.

Exam Essentials

Know that cloud computing is similar in operation to a utility. Cloud computing follows the utilities model where a provider will sell computing resources using an as-needed or as-consumed model. This allows a company or individual to pay for only what they use.

Know what cloud computing is. Cloud computing is a model for enabling convenient, on-demand network access to a shared pool of configurable computing resources (for example, networks, servers, storage, applications, and services) that can be rapidly provisioned and released with minimal management effort or service provider interaction. This cloud model is composed of five essential characteristics, three service models, and four deployment models.

Understand the different cloud service models and how to differentiate between them. Cloud service models are characterized by the phrase *as a service* and are accessed by many types of devices, including web browsers, thin clients, and mobile devices. There are three primary service types. Software as a Service, Infrastructure as a Service, and Platform as a Service are the core service offerings. Many cloud service providers offer more descriptive terms in their marketing and sales offerings, including Communications as a Service, Anything as a Service, and Desktop as a Service. However, all of these newer terms fit into the SaaS, IaaS, or PaaS service model. Study the service models and know the differences among IaaS, PaaS, and SaaS as well as the other service models.

Know the primary cloud delivery models. The four primary cloud delivery models are public, private, community, and hybrid clouds. Know what each one is and its function. It is critical that you understand the way cloud services are delivered in the market today and what they offer.

Be able to identify and explain cloud components. Common cloud components include applications, automation, compute, networking, security, and storage.

Know the cloud shared resource pooling model and how it is used. Resource pooling is when the cloud service provider abstracts its physical compute, storage, and networking resources into a group, or pool. The resources from these pools are dynamically allocated to customers on-demand. Resource pooling hides the underlying physical hardware from the customers in such a way that different customers share the underlying infrastructure while their cloud resources remain isolated from each other.

Understand cloud performance components. The performance you are able to achieve with your deployment is a combination of the capabilities and architecture of the cloud service provider and how you design and implement your operations. Some metrics that you'll want to consider are bandwidth usage, network latency, storage I/O operations per second (IOPS), and memory utilization.

Be able to explain how autoscaling works. The ability to automatically and dynamically add additional resources such as storage, CPUs, memory, and even servers is referred to as elasticity. Using autoscaling, this can be done "on the fly" as needed or on a scheduled basis. This allows for cloud consumers to scale up automatically as their workload increases and then have the cloud remove the services after the workload subsides. On-demand cloud services allow the cloud customer to access a self-service portal and instantly create additional servers, storage, processing power, or any other services as required. If the computing workload increases, then additional cloud resources can be created and applied as needed. On-demand allows customers to consume cloud services only as needed and scale back when they are no longer required.

Know what regions and availability zones are. Large cloud operations partition operations into geographical regions for fault tolerance and to offer localized performance advantages. A region is not a monolithic data center but rather a geographical area of presence. The actual data centers in each region are availability zones. Each region will usually have two or more availability zones for fault tolerance. The AZs are isolated locations within cloud data center regions that public cloud providers originate and operate. Each availability zone is a physically separate data center with its own redundant power and network connections.

Written Lab

Fill in the blanks for the questions provided in the written lab. You can find the answers to the written labs in Appendix B.

1. With the ________________ as a Service model, the cloud provider owns and manages all levels of the computing environment.
2. With the ________________ as a Service model, the cloud provider owns and manages the computing hardware but not the operating systems or the applications.
3. With the ________________ as a Service model, the cloud provider owns and manages the hardware and operating system but not the application software.
4. ________________ refers to the ability to access the cloud resources from anywhere in the network from a variety of devices such as laptops, tables, smartphones, and thin or thick clients.
5. ________________ is the ability to take physical data center resources such as RAM, CPU, storage, and networking and create a software representation of those resources that enables large-scale cloud offerings.
6. Private, low-latency network interconnectivity between your corporate data center and your cloud operations is accomplished using ________________.
7. ________________ is the transfer and synchronization of data between computing or storage resources.
8. ________________ addresses the issues found when cloud workloads and connections increase to the point where a single server can no longer handle the workload by spreading the workload across multiple cloud computing resources.
9. Common remote access protocols used to manage servers in the cloud include ________________ and ________________.
10. Establishing ________________ helps you determine how to size your cloud resources.

Review Questions

The following questions are designed to test your understanding of this chapter's material. You can find the answers in Appendix A. For more information on how to obtain additional questions, please see this book's Introduction.

1. What cloud model gives you complete control of the operating system?
   - **A.** IaaS
   - **B.** PaaS
   - **C.** SaaS
   - **D.** CaaS
2. A cloud service provider allocates resources into a group. These resources are then dynamically allocated and reallocated as the demand requires. What is this referred to as?
   - **A.** On-demand virtualization
   - **B.** Dynamic scaling
   - **C.** Resource pooling
   - **D.** Elasticity
3. What are three examples of IaaS elements you can provision in the cloud? (Choose three.)
   - **A.** CPU
   - **B.** OS ACLs
   - **C.** Memory
   - **D.** Storage
   - **E.** Scalability
   - **F.** SSH
4. Which of the following is not a valid pooled resource?
   - **A.** Memory
   - **B.** Storage
   - **C.** Security
   - **D.** Networking
   - **E.** CPU
5. What technologies are used to enable on-demand computing? (Choose two.)
   - **A.** Load balancing
   - **B.** Automation
   - **C.** Autoscaling groups
   - **D.** Virtualization

6. When you migrate your operations to the cloud and you decide to match computing resources with your current requirements, what can you take advantage of to expand your compute capacity in the future? (Choose three.)
   - **A.** Elasticity
   - **B.** On-demand computing
   - **C.** Availability zones
   - **D.** Resiliency virtualization
   - **E.** Pay as you grow
   - **F.** Regions
7. Your company has decided to use one cloud provider for a production application while using a different cloud provider for storing backups. What type of cloud delivery model is this?
   - **A.** Public
   - **B.** Hybrid
   - **C.** Community
   - **D.** Private
8. In a traditional virtualized data center, what shared network resource do VMs on the same host use to communicate with each other?
   - **A.** Virtual NIC
   - **B.** Region
   - **C.** Virtual switch
   - **D.** LAN
9. Which cloud characteristic allows you to pay for only the services used?
   - **A.** Bursting
   - **B.** Pay as you grow
   - **C.** Chargeback
   - **D.** Autoscaling
10. When migrating an application from the data center to the cloud, which of the following is a best practice?
    - **A.** Deploy to a test environment to validate functionality and performance.
    - **B.** Deploy directly to production so that end users can immediately report any problems.
    - **C.** Clone the VM running the application and upload it to the cloud.
    - **D.** Copy the application files to a fresh VM running in the cloud.

11. Which cloud characteristic allows you to access a self-service portal to create additional servers, storage, or other services instantly?
    - A. Bursting
    - B. Pay as you grow
    - C. Multitenancy
    - D. On-demand

12. In which cloud service model does the provider handle everything up to and including the application?
    - A. IaaS
    - B. PaaS
    - C. SaaS
    - D. ZaaS

13. Which of the following metrics can you typically monitor in the cloud? (Choose two.)
    - A. Network latency
    - B. Physical CPU host utilization
    - C. The number of available physical virtualization hosts
    - D. Inter-availability zone latency
    - E. Storage I/O operations per second

14. Cloud service providers will often segment their operations to allow for resiliency, geographic proximity, and data protection regulations. What are these geographical segmentations referred to as?
    - A. Regions
    - B. Autoscaling groups
    - C. Availability zones
    - D. Global DNS affinity

15. What are critical steps to take prior to performing a migration to the cloud? (Choose three.)
    - A. Baselines
    - B. Capacity requirements
    - C. Variance measurements
    - D. Documentation
    - E. Automation rollout

16. Cloud operations are the responsibility of both your organization and the cloud service provider. What is this model called?
    - A. Availability zone model
    - B. Community model
    - C. Shared responsibility model
    - D. Shared regional model

17. What is the process of testing your cloud access to determine whether there is any vulnerability that an attacker could exploit?

   A. Elasticity

   B. Vulnerability testing

   C. Penetration testing

   D. Load testing

18. A hospital wants to use a medical records application but must minimize its capital expenditure, minimize ongoing maintenance, and comply with various regulations. What type of cloud service model and cloud delivery model would you recommend that they use? (Choose two.)

   A. Public

   B. SaaS

   C. Community

   D. Private

   E. IaaS

19. What systems do cloud providers implement for rapid deployment of customer-requested services?

   A. RDMS

   B. Orchestration

   C. On-demand provisions

   D. Service catalogs

20. In which cloud service model does the provider manage everything except the application?

   A. IaaS

   B. PaaS

   C. SaaS

   D. CaaS

Chapter 2

Cloud Deployments

THE FOLLOWING COMPTIA CLOUD+ EXAM OBJECTIVES ARE COVERED IN THIS CHAPTER:

✓ **1.1 Compare and contrast the different types of cloud models.**

- Deployment models
    - Public
    - Private
    - Hybrid
    - Community
    - Cloud within a cloud
    - Multicloud
    - Multitenancy

✓ **1.2 Explain the factors that contribute to capacity planning.**

- Requirements
    - Hardware
    - Software
    - Budgetary
    - Business needs analysis

✓ **1.3 Explain the importance of high availability and scaling in cloud environments.**

- Containers

✓ **1.4 Given a scenario, analyze the solution design in support of the business requirements.**

- Requirement Analysis

✓ **2.1 Given a scenario, configure identity and access management.**

- Identification and authorization

- Directory services
    - Lightweight directory access protocol (LDAP)
- Federation
- Multifactor authentication (MFA)
- Single sign-on (SSO)
    - Security assertion markup language (SAML)

✓ **2.2 Given a scenario, secure a network in a cloud environment.**

- Network segmentation
    - Virtual LAN (VLAN)/Virtual extensible LAN (VXLAN)/Generic network virtualization encapsulation (GENEVE)
    - Micro-segmentation
    - Tiering
- Protocols
    - Domain name service (DNS)
        - DNS over HTTPS (DoH)/DNS over TLS (DoT)
        - DNS security (DNSSEC)
    - Encryption
        - IPSec
        - Transport Layer Security (TLS)
        - Hypertext transfer protocol secure (HTTPS)
    - Tunneling
        - Secure Shell (SSH)
    - Network services
    - Firewalls
        - Stateful
        - Stateless
    - Web application firewall (WAF)
    - Application delivery controller (ADC)
    - Intrusion protection system (IPS)/Intrusion detection system (IDS)
    - Data loss prevention (DLP)

    - Network access control (NAC)
    - Packet brokers

✓ **2.3 Given a scenario, apply the appropriate OS and application security controls.**

- Encryption

✓ **3.1 Given a scenario, integrate components into a cloud solution.**

- Subscription services
    - File subscriptions
    - Communications
        - Email
        - Voice over I (VoIP)
        - Messaging
    - Collaboration
    - Virtual desktop infrastructure (VDI)
    - Directory and identity services
    - Cloud resources
        - IaaS
        - PaaS
        - SaaS
- Provisioning resources
    - Compute
    - Storage
    - Network
- Deploying virtual machines (VMs) and custom images
- Templates
    - OS templates
    - Solution templates
- Identity management
- Containers
    - Configure variables

- Configure secrets
- Persistent storage

✓ 3.2 Given a scenario, provision storage in cloud environments.

- Types
  - Block
    - Storage area network (SAN)
    - Zoning
  - File
    - Network attached storage (NAS)
  - Object
    - Tenants
    - Buckets
- Tiers
  - Flash
  - Hybrid
  - Spinning disks
  - Long-term
- Input/output operations per second (IOPS) and read/write
- Protocols
  - Network file system (NFS)
  - Common Internet file system (CIFS)
  - Internet small computer system interface (iSCSI)
  - Fibre Channel (FC)
  - Non-volatile memory express over fabrics (NVMe-oF)
- Redundant array of inexpensive disks (RAID)
  - 0
  - 1
  - 5
  - 6
  - 10

- Storage system features
  - Compression
  - Deduplication
  - Thin provisioning
  - Thick provisioning
  - Replication
- User quotas
- Hyperconverged
- Software-defined storage (SDS)

✓ 3.3 Given a scenario, deploy cloud networking solutions.

- Services
  - Dynamic host configuration protocol (DHCP)
  - NTP
  - DNS
  - Content delivery network (CDN)
  - IP address management (IPAM)
- Virtual private networks (VPNs)
  - Site-to-site
  - Point-to-point
  - IPSec
  - Multiprotocol label switching (MPLS)
- Virtual routing
  - Dynamic and static routing
  - Virtual network interface controller (VNIC)
  - Subnetting
- Network appliances
  - Load balancers
  - Firewalls

- Virtual private cloud (VPC)
  - Hub and spoke
  - Peering
- VLAN/VXLAN/GENEVE
- Single root input/output virtualization (SR-IOV)
- Software-defined network (SDN)

✓ **3.4 Given a scenario, configure the appropriate compute sizing for a deployment.**

- Virtualization
  - Hypervisors
    - Type 1
    - Type 2
  - Simultaneous multi-threating (SMT)
  - Dynamic allocations
  - Oversubscription
- Central processing unit (CPU)/virtual CPU (vCPU)
- Graphics processing unit (GPU)
  - Virtual
    - Shared
  - Pass-through
- Clock speed/instructions per cycle (IPC)
- Hyperconverged
- Memory
  - Dynamic allocation
  - Ballooning

✓ **3.5 Given a scenario, perform cloud migrations.**

- Physical to virtual (P2V)
- Virtual to virtual (V2V)
- Cloud-to-cloud migrations
  - Vendor lock-in
  - PaaS or SaaS migrations

- Access control lists (ACLs)
- Firewalls
- Storage migrations
  - Block
  - File
  - Object
- Database migrations
  - Cross-service migrations
  - Relational
  - Non-relational

✓ **4.3 Given a scenario, optimize cloud environments.**

- Storage
  - Tiers
    - Adaptive optimization
  - IOPS
  - Capacity
  - Deduplication
  - Compression
- Network
  - Bandwidth
  - Network interface controllers (NICs)
  - Latency
  - SDN
  - Edge computing
    - CDN
- Device drivers and firmware
  - Generic
  - Vendor
  - Open source

✓ **4.4 Given a scenario, apply proper automation and orchestration techniques.**

- Containers

In Chapter 1, "Introducing Cloud Computing Configurations and Deployments," you learned about cloud computing and were introduced to the basic terminology and concepts used. The various components and architectures were explored, and you began to see how these components and subsystems come together to make a fully functioning deployment of your operations in the cloud.

In this chapter, the focus will be on deploying your computing resources in the cloud. The chapter will begin by discussing many of the business and nontechnical aspects, including project-based issues and the various cloud deployment models that must be considered. The second part of this chapter will discuss the technical issues that must be understood for a successful migration, including the compute, data format conversions, recovery, storage, security, and networking functions.

This is an important chapter that covers many of the core concepts on the CompTIA Cloud+ (CV0-003) certification exam. It also creates a foundation that you can build on in future chapters.

Executing a Cloud Deployment

For a successful migration to cloud-based computing from the legacy data center approach, you must understand all that's involved in executing a cloud deployment. This section covers the Cloud+ objectives for planning, meeting your business needs, knowing what to document, and the workflows used during the process.

To make sure that we start off on the right foot, let's briefly clarify what the terms *deployment* and *migration* mean practically. A *cloud deployment* is simply placing resources in the cloud. For example, if you spin up a few virtual machines and a load balancer to deliver an application, that's a deployment. But a deployment doesn't have to be complex. Even if you just back up some files to object storage in the cloud, that's a deployment, too—a small deployment, but a deployment nonetheless.

A *cloud migration*, on the other hand, involves "moving" *existing* resources into the cloud. These existing resources may exist in your data center or with another cloud provider. However, moving resources doesn't mean literally moving hardware—and it may not even mean moving virtual machines. In fact, most migrations entail deploying *new* resources to the cloud to mimic the existing resources and then copying the data over to complete the process. For example, suppose that you have a large database VM running in a data center. To migrate this to the cloud, you probably won't transfer the VM itself. Instead, you'll build a new database VM in the cloud with similar or superior specs and then copy the database files over. In the end, you actually end up with *two* database servers—a new one in the cloud and the existing one in your data center. Of course, you only use the new one. Furthermore, there's a really good chance that you'll retain a copy of the databases in your data center just in case. So rather than truly migrating your database server, you've simply re-created it.

The key takeaway is that a migration is rarely a "lift and shift" from one location to another. Instead, it's a process of re-creating your existing environment in the cloud. And because there are significant differences between the cloud and the data center, you may have to make some significant changes to your systems during migration.

Cloud vs. Data Center Operations

I want to share with you a real-life example. I inherited a fleet of on-premises servers that used a peculiar software-based load-balancing method that required layer 2 multicast. It was a kludge, but it worked. Cloud providers, however, do not support layer 2 multicast or broadcast, so just migrating these VMs to the cloud wouldn't have worked. It would have required rearchitecting the system to use an external load balancer. This is just one simple example, but it illustrates the point: the cloud operates differently than your data center. Keep that in mind as you read this chapter.

Understanding Deployment and Change Management

In this section, you'll learn about the process of deploying your operations into the cloud. The various steps required will be discussed. As you read this section, keep in mind that deployment and change management don't apply only to first-time deployments to the cloud. These topics come into play any time that you make a change or deploy new cloud resources.

Change Management

Change management is the process of managing all aspects of ongoing upgrades, repairs, and reconfigurations of your cloud services. The end goal is to minimize any disruptions of service. If you've worked in IT, you're probably already familiar with change management, so consider this section more of a review.

Each organization defines its own change management process, which typically includes making a change request, developing a plan to implement the change, creating a backout plan in case the change is unsuccessful, getting approvals, and finally making and testing the change. The process may also include updating documentation and conducting post-change reviews. Change management is a standard process in the operations of the cloud or enterprise data center.

With the need to gather baseline information and to ensure that your cloud architecture meets your immediate and future needs, the marketing hype of how easy it is to move to the cloud can sometimes be overstated. Managing the deployment and ongoing changes is critical to a successful cloud operation, and it is far from a trivial undertaking. That's why you should consider employing a change management process for a successful project implementation and to limit disruptions to ongoing operations.

What change management looks like depends on the requirements of your organization. Generally, the smaller the organization, the easier and quicker change management is (if it exists at all). In larger organizations, change management can be a tedious and frustrating process. A detailed change management procedure usually includes the name of the requester, a description of the change, and the reason for it. More onerous change management policies may require developing a testing and backout plan, as well as detailing the risks involved. You must also outline what resources will be needed and coordinate the activities of the various groups involved in the change. A list of individuals responsible for the various aspects of the change, including the design, configuration, deployment, and validation steps, must be prepared. There also needs to be an investigation into other changes that are taking place to make sure that no conflicts exist between those changes and yours. Also, if one change requires another change to take place before it can be implemented, the change sequences will have to be coordinated.

IT professionals often view change management as a hindrance to progress. It's worth remembering that the primary purpose of change management is to prevent problems—*not* just to get things done. Whether strict change management procedures make sense depends on the risks involved. Many times, if you can effectively argue that the risk of a proposed change is minimal, you can bypass "required" change management procedures with proper management approval.

Obtaining Buy-In from All Involved Parties

As part of the migration plan, it is important to keep all interested parties up-to-date on the plans and progress. This will include all timelines and any changes that have the potential to impact existing operations within your organization. This may include groups that are outside of IT operations, such as finance, production, human resources, and any others that may need ongoing updates on the migration projects.

In most medium to large organizations, a formal *change review group* meets to manage and approve all pending changes. This committee often consists of managers, architects, and representatives of all the project stakeholders. (Sometimes this group is called a *change advisory board*.)

The change review group's responsibility is to manage risk and to ensure that no conflicting changes are scheduled for the same maintenance window. One advantage of having multiple eyes on a single proposed change is to catch issues that you might not have considered. The following are questions that you can expect:

- What do you expect to gain from making the change?
- What are the risks involved when implementing or not implementing the change?
- What functional departments are going to be involved in implementing the change?
- How long will it take to implement the change and to validate that the change is performing as expected?
- How long will it take to back out the change if necessary?

The change review group may consider the impact that the change may have on ongoing operations, service level agreements with your customers, and the cost if the change causes an unforeseen outage. Each change request will be approved, denied, or returned for further investigation by the change review team.

Setting a Realistic Migration Timeline

As part of the planning and implementation process, timelines must be established for migrating resources to the cloud. Performing migrations incrementally can reduce the risk of an outage or having to back out the migration because of unforeseen issues.

For example, consider a two-tier web application consisting of a web front end and a database on the back end, with both tiers running in a data center. It may be feasible to migrate the front end to the cloud while leaving the back-end database in place. If users access the application in the typical way via a domain name, the migration can be as simple as building new front-end servers in the cloud and pointing the domain name to them. If something goes wrong, reverting the change may be as simple as changing some DNS records. This incremental approach has the advantage of letting you "test in production" with real users.

Following the "start small and deploy over time" field of thought, it is best to begin your migrations with small, easy-to-implement, noncritical systems as candidates to migrate to the cloud. This will give you experience in the migration process and better allow you to determine what realistic time frames will need to be arranged for migrations.

Even relatively safe migrations should take place during a *maintenance window*, which is a scheduled time that maintenance can be performed and outages are planned for ongoing support of operations. I can't tell you how many times I've witnessed outages caused by changes that weren't supposed to have a visible effect.

Assuming that the migration project team has done ample planning, the actual time window is determined by allocating time for all of the processes that need to occur sequentially during the migration. There must be time for testing and validation after the migration where all stakeholders can test and verify that the systems are working as planned after the migration. Time must be allocated in the event that a backout is required and that the original site or installation must come back online. As you can see, all of this must be condensed into your maintenance window, and it is a good idea to extend the amount of time allocated for each phase as a buffer in case of unforeseen issues.

Documenting and Following Procedures

Complete documentation is a critical component of a successful migration. You must know exactly what you are starting with, so the current documentation should be reviewed and updated as required. All systems should be accurately diagrammed, and you must make sure that you have up-to-date backups of the systems being migrated. Sources for collecting information to create documents include network monitoring and management systems, downloads of device configurations, and vendor support documents.

It's extremely important to understand that after the migration, your documentation is going to change drastically. As we discussed earlier, there is not always a one-to-one correlation between data center components and cloud components. For instance, in a data center you might have virtual LANs (VLANs), whereas in the cloud you generally will not. Even if you're migrating from one cloud provider to another, there may be subtle differences between the provider's architectures that require you to make some changes. The bottom line is that you'll end up with two sets of documentation: before migration and after migration.

Proper documentation is critical for the ongoing support of the cloud deployment. This documentation should include internal and public IP addresses, routing information, where firewalls are to be placed in the network, and what ports and protocols are allowed. Don't forget to include VPNs, load balancers, or application firewalls if you're using any. Documentation may need to be updated on a regular basis to make sure that all information is current.

Now's a good time to point out that in Chapter 5, "Maintaining Cloud Operations," we'll cover a concept called *infrastructure-as-code (IaC)*. The IaC approach lets you programmatically define and deploy your cloud infrastructure using templates, and those templates can function as de facto documentation. The nice thing about the IaC approach is that you don't have to go back after deployment and update your existing documentation. The IaC templates effectively serve as prewritten documentation! Of course, you'll still need to update diagrams and any manual changes.

Network planning and documentation should start early in the planning process and be performed in collaboration with the cloud service provider. This collaboration will allow for the correct selection and procurement of all needed networking hardware and software that may not be included by the cloud provider. In addition, this process includes ordering data circuits for the service provider to interconnect locations.

The network core should have detailed explanations and drawings of the network showing IP subnets and firewall rules. A section detailing redundancy and configuration scripts will be invaluable when performing the initial installation and for ongoing maintenance and troubleshooting. As you can imagine, it can be very time-consuming and frustrating when troubleshooting a network if there is no map to show what the big picture looks like and how the small details are implemented. Having proper documentation can help you to avoid wasting time when troubleshooting an issue.

The network documentation should also include sections on the access and distribution networks in the cloud. The access network diagrams will show all wide area networking connections, including VPN links, routing tables, access control lists, the connection to the cloud provider's network, and links to the corporate office and all data centers. Include a network management section that provides a map for the network operations center and illustrates how the network management systems are connected to the network and what devices they are monitoring.

A services section in the documentation will detail all network services information such as caching systems, Domain Name Systems, logging, load balancers, network optimization servers, IDS/IPS information, and any network analyzers.

Some cloud-based companies offer applications that can automate the network discovery after the network has been deployed into a production environment. Network mapping applications can provide detailed diagrams and configuration documents. They constantly monitor and record changes in the network and automatically update the drawings. Off-the-shelf applications are also available.

A detailed network diagram and IP addressing plan should always be created in the design phase of your cloud deployment. It is critical to identify any potential issues and provide remediation before they occur. Accurate documentation can help you meet that goal. The documentation benefits both the cloud provider and the consumer by detailing how all of the associated networks are interconnected and interoperate. During the implementation phase, detailed documentation acts as a road map, and during ongoing operations of the cloud deployment, the networking documentation is an invaluable troubleshooting tool. When you are performing capacity planning for network growth, network diagrams can serve as a starting place to plan additions and expansions in your cloud deployment.

What Is a Cloud Workflow?

Cloud service offerings include workflow architectures that manage the state of a project. Today's applications often require multiple steps in a process that can, and often do, include the interoperation of many different components and applications in the cloud. A *cloud workflow* is defined as a series of steps or activities that are required to complete a task.

For example, if your site includes an e-commerce offering, there will be many steps that are required to complete the online transaction. This will include the shopping cart, checkout, financial transaction, warehousing, and shipping functions, to name just a few. Each step has a specific set of requirements before and after its process where an outside event usually occurs to start the process. A cloud workflow service will manage the steps to complete a process that could include human processes, parallel steps, and sequential steps. Think of workflow as a state tracking and coordination system in the cloud.

This same analytical processing can be used when undertaking the cloud migration process, with the project management team designing and implementing a workflow-based approach to the migration.

Setting Up Your Cloud for Automation

Cloud automation is a fundamental characteristic of the virtualized data center. Automation in the public cloud infrastructure is provided by the cloud service provider and offered to the customers as a web dashboard, API, SDK, or command-line interface. Global cloud management systems are offered by a variety of vendors and service providers that allow hybrid cloud deployments to be centrally managed with automation systems that connect to multiple clouds simultaneously.

As you can imagine, automation is a complex and detailed topic with details beyond the scope of the Cloud+ exam. However, I'll be giving examples of automation systems used in the cloud deployment models.

What Are Cloud Tools and Management Systems?

Managing and monitoring the entire deployment is a critical part of successfully implementing and operating your cloud environment. Once the applications are deployed and fully operational, ongoing monitoring will ensure that all components of the cloud deployment are operating within defined ranges and that all the performance metrics are being met. Monitoring helps ensure that your systems are configured correctly, secure, and meet performance agreements.

There are many data points in a cloud deployment that can be monitored and managed to ensure complete coverage of the hosted applications. This can include the CPU, memory, and disk usage on servers; network interface statistics; and application logging. Thousands of objects can be monitored, and you should take care to make sure that you are monitoring what is important to your ongoing operations. Cloud providers offer monitoring capabilities that integrate with their orchestration platform, allowing you to configure automated responses to various metrics. For example, if the CPU utilization on a fleet of web servers exceeds a threshold due to increased load, you can have the provider automatically provision more instances to compensate.

Of course, you're not limited to using monitoring tools provided by the cloud provider. Traditional network management tools have been extended for cloud-based services, and at the same time, many new products and services have been introduced that specifically address this new and fast-growing market. In addition to the traditional information technology management providers, a lot of investments have been made in startup companies developing products and services for this market.

The term *network management* is very broad, so let's drill down and look at the components that encompass a complete network management solution. The basic architecture consists of one or more network management operations centers housing systems that monitor and collect information from the devices hosted in a private or public data center, as shown in Figure 2.1.

FIGURE 2.1 Managing your cloud deployment

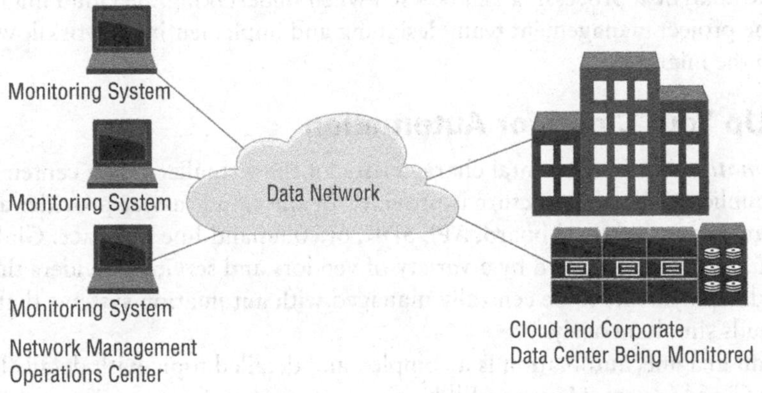

The acronym FCAPS is commonly used to cover the main areas under the management umbrella. It is broken down into the following areas: fault, configuration, accounting, performance, and security, as illustrated in Figure 2.2.

The basic architecture of a managed service operation consists of servers running specialized monitoring applications that poll or request metrics and measurements from the endpoint devices. Management systems collect logs from servers, network equipment, storage systems, and many other devices, such as load balancers, VPN concentrators, and firewalls.

FIGURE 2.2 The FCAPS management umbrella

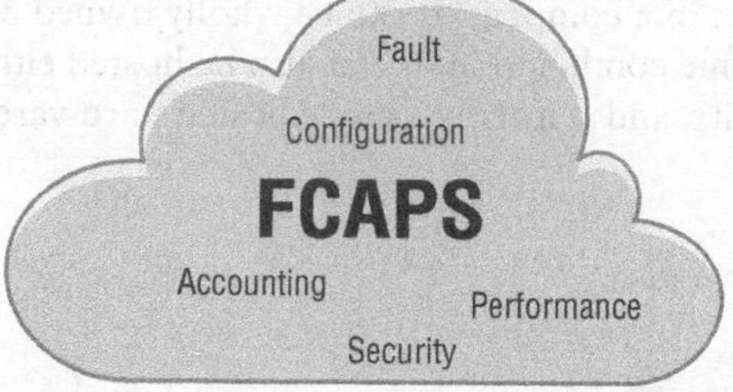

There are many applications, tools, services, and approaches to managing your data center to meet compliance requirements, protect your data, and deal with ongoing maintenance and problem resolution. However, the nature of a cloud service being remote from your operations center and hosted in a shared cloud environment can greatly add to the complexity of cloud management.

Cloud Deployment Models

In this section, you'll take a look at the various models used to deliver cloud services. As you've seen with the service models discussed earlier, it can be common to find combinations of the various deployment models offered to the market.

Public

A *public cloud* delivery model is infrastructure designed for use by the general public. Private corporations, government organizations, and academia offer public clouds. In the public delivery model, the provider hosts the service in data centers that they control, and it uses shared hardware, as shown in Figure 2.3.

FIGURE 2.3 Public cloud

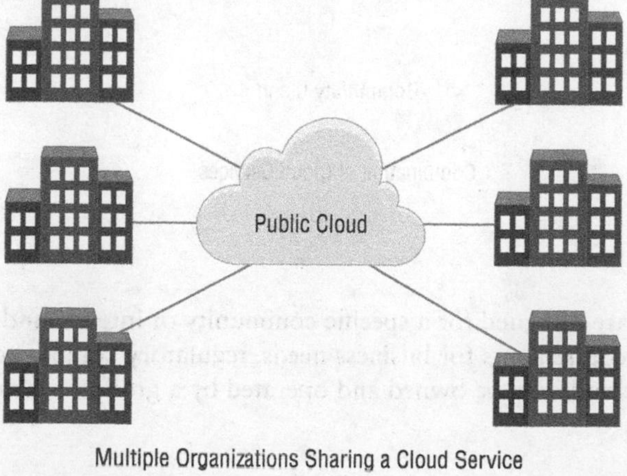

Private

A *private cloud* model is for use by a single organization, as shown in Figure 2.4, but it may be used by many units of a company. It can be wholly owned by the organization, a third-party provider, or some combination. It can also be hosted either on-premises or off-premises at a hosting facility, and it usually uses dedicated hardware rather than a shared hardware design.

FIGURE 2.4 Private cloud

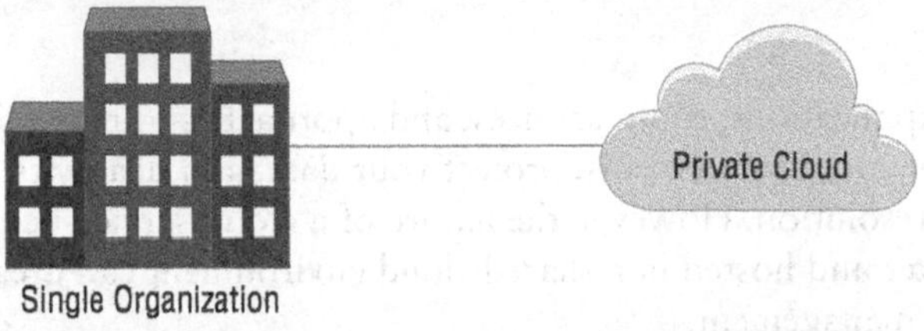

Hybrid

A *hybrid cloud* is a combination of two or more delivery models such as private, community, or public. Examples of a hybrid model include cloud bursting to handle peak processing loads or balancing the load between delivery models, as shown in Figure 2.5.

FIGURE 2.5 Hybrid cloud

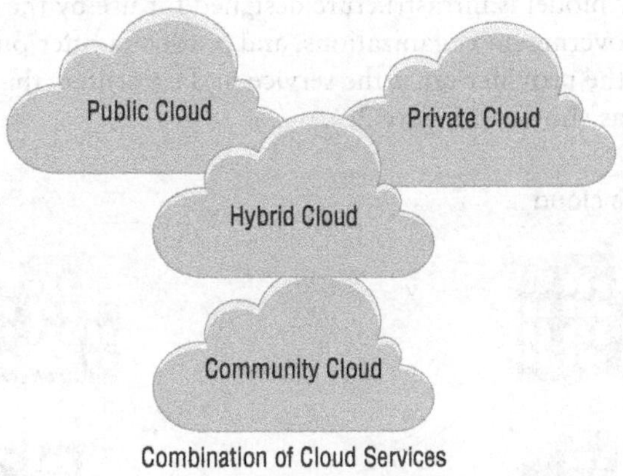

Community

Community clouds are designed for a specific community of interest and shared by companies with similar requirements for business needs, regulatory compliance, security, or policy. Community clouds can be owned and operated by a group of companies, a specialized cloud provider, or other interested parties, as illustrated in Figure 2.6. They can exist in or outside of a company's data center or hosting facility.

FIGURE 2.6 Community cloud

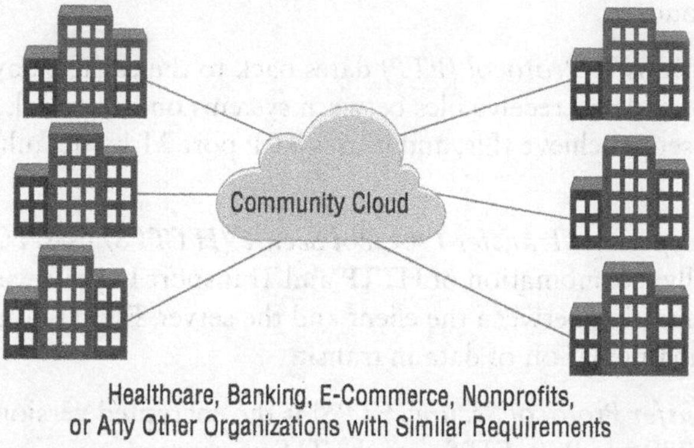

Network Deployment Considerations

Networking is a whole study area in itself, so we'll cover the topic broadly enough to give you a fundamental understanding of the concepts. This will help you when deploying networks in the cloud, and it will also serve as knowledge to build upon.

In this section, you'll be introduced to the common network protocols that are used, some basic configurations, and virtual private networks. Then you'll look at IP addressing; some services, such as intrusion detection and prevention; and the concept of the demilitarized zone in the cloud.

One of the biggest differences between the data center and the cloud is networking. As I've noted, certain network devices that you'll find in the data center do not exist in the cloud as discrete resources that you can manage. Most of the functions provided by networking devices, such as switches, routers, and firewalls, are available in the cloud, but they're either invisible or accessible only through the cloud provider's interface.

We'll look at some specific networking examples in this section, but here's one to give you an idea. In the cloud, your servers aren't connected to a virtual switch that you can log in to and manage. The functionality of the traditional switch is abstracted away from your view, and it's 100 percent under the cloud provider's purview. Therefore, the configuration specifics of your data center switches are going to have limited relevance to your cloud deployment. As you read, take note of the sometimes subtle differences between cloud networks and on-premises networks.

Network Protocols

In most modern networks, there are dozens of protocols in use. I'll describe a few here so that you are familiar with not only well-known port numbers but also the applications they represent. Understanding these common protocols and their default port numbers can help when you're configuring and validating your firewall rules.

HTTP The *Hypertext Transfer Protocol (HTTP)* uses TCP port 80 by default. HTTP is a common application protocol used by web browsers to access World Wide Web servers in the cloud.

FTP The *File Transfer Protocol (FTP)* dates back to the earliest days of networking, and it is used to send and receive files between systems on a network. FTP has a standard command set to achieve this, and it uses TCP port 21 by default but may also use port 20.

HTTPS The *Hypertext Transfer Protocol Secure (HTTPS)* uses TCP port 443. HTTPS is actually a combination of HTTP and Transport Layer Security (TLS), which encrypts the connection between the client and the server. Encryption helps prevent the interception or manipulation of data in transit.

FTPS *File Transfer Protocol Secure (FTPS)* is the encrypted version of the FTP, and it uses TCP ports 989 and 990. FTPS uses the TLS encryption.

SSH *Secure Shell (SSH)* is the encrypted version of the Telnet protocol, and it is used to access remote devices using a command-line interface. SSH uses TCP port 22.

SFTP *Secure File Transfer Protocol (SFTP)* is similar to FTPS, except that SFTP tunnels FTP over SSH; hence, SFTP uses TCP port number 22 for secure file transfers. SFTP does not use TLS.

DNS The *Domain Name System (DNS)* is most well known for mapping a human readable domain name (like `example.com`) to one or more IP address. More generally, however, DNS functions as a database of services provided by a particular domain. For example, DNS stores the mail exchanger (MX) records that specify the mail servers for a domain. DNS uses TCP and User Datagram Protocol (UDP) ports 53.

DHCP The *Dynamic Host Configuration Protocol (DHCP)* allows for automatic assignment of IP addressing information to devices on a network. This eliminates the need to configure addressing information statically when you connect to a network. DHCP listens on UDP port number 68.

SMTP The *Simple Mail Transfer Protocol (SMTP)* is used to send email messages between mail servers and uses TCP port 25.

NTP The *Network Time Protocol (NTP)* automatically configures the time of a system based on an authoritative reference clock. NTP plays a crucial role in security and logging. Some authentication mechanisms depend on accurate time synchronization. Incorrect timestamps in log files make it difficult to correlate events. NTP uses UDP port 123.

Network Ports

Many applications are assigned their own unique port number. These are often referred to as *well-known port numbers*. When an application needs to access a service on the remote end, a field inside the TCP or UDP header will contain the well-known port number in its destination port. For example, when you browse to a website using HTTPS, your browser encapsulates an HTTPS packet inside a TCP/IP packet addressed to port 443. When that packet arrives at the remote server, the server will look at the destination port and forward the data to the correct application for processing—in this case, a web server application such as Apache or Nginx.

For example, if you enter in your browser `https://www.comptia.org`, the browser will see that the `https` section specifies the HTTPS protocol, which uses the well-known TCP port number 443. The TCP/IP header will have a destination port number of 443 inserted into it and then transmitted to the remote web server.

Thousands of well-known ports are reserved; here are a few of the most common found in the cloud:

TCP Port 80 Port 80 is reserved for HTTP, which is used for World Wide Web traffic.

TCP Port 21 Port 21 is reserved for FTP applications, and the FTP server listens on port 21 for incoming client connection requests.

TCP Port 22 The SSH command-line interface, Secure Copy (SCP), and SFTP use port 22 for communications.

TCP Port 25 The protocol that routes mail between email servers is SMTP. This protocol is assigned port 25.

TCP and UDP Port 53 DNS and the domain name lookup use TCP port 53.

TCP Port 443 When you type **`https`** in your web browser, you are requesting a secure World Wide Web connection. HTTPS uses port 443 to set up an encrypted connection from the browser to a secure web server in the cloud using the SSL/TLS protocols.

UDP Ports 67, 68, 546, and 547 Devices on a TCP/IP network that do not have statically defined IP configurations rely on DHCP to assign their network configurations automatically. DHCP for I Pv4 uses UDP ports 67 and 68, and DHCP for IPv6 uses ports 546 and 547.

Network Configurations

The cloud service provider will own the networks inside its data centers. However, most cloud providers let you configure your own virtual private clouds atop the provider's networks. As with other cloud resources, this is usually done via a web-based interface, APIs, SDKs, or a command-line interface. Network configuration options include routes, access control lists, security groups, and IP address assignment. Other network services that can be configured include load balancers, application (layer 7) firewalls, content delivery, caching systems, and DNS services.

Virtual Private Networks

Virtual private networks (VPNs) allow for a secure encrypted connection over an insecure network such as the Internet, as shown in Figure 2.7. VPNs are commonly used for encrypted access to cloud services from a remote location, such as a home. This is called a point-to-site or remote access VPN. VPNs can also be site-to-site (also known as point-to-point) connections that use a public network and save the expense of a private dedicated circuit between sites. Point-to-point VPNs tend to be fixed, whereas point-to-site VPNs are usually established on demand and as needed.

FIGURE 2.7 A VPN creates a secure tunnel over an insecure network such as the Internet.

There are many types of VPN implementations, ranging from software running on a client computer to VPN services on a firewall or router to standalone dedicated VPN concentrators. The configuration of a VPN solution can be quite complex, and it involves a bewildering array of options that are beyond the scope of the Cloud+ exam.

Firewalls and Microsegmentation

One thing that throws off a lot of people who are new to cloud networking is the apparent absence of firewalls. As they explore their new cloud environment, they see the obvious parallels between the cloud and the data center—VMs, network interfaces, storage volumes—but can't seem to find any firewalls!

The apparent absence of firewalls marks a significant difference between the cloud and the data center. In the data center, a firewall isolates different portions of the network and restricts the types of traffic that can pass between subnets. For example, you may have one subnet for certain database servers and another subnet for application servers, and both subnets are separated by a firewall. By defining rules on the firewall, you can allow only the traffic that you want to pass between the application subnet and database subnet. This configuration provides some isolation, but it falls short in one important way: devices *within* the same subnet have unrestricted access to each other. The firewall can't see that intra-subnet traffic, let alone restrict it.

Cloud networks overcome this limitation by using a concept called *microsegmentation*. In the cloud, you can configure and apply packet filtering rules at the network interface level, not just the subnet level. Essentially, you configure firewall rules and choose where to apply them. This eliminates blind spots and gives you granular control over how your cloud resources communicate. This approach makes security more scalable by letting you apply rules to VMs according to their role, rather than what subnet they reside in. In the cloud you can, for example, apply a particular set of rules to all of your database VMs, regardless of what host they're on or what subnet they're in.

The terminology around firewall rules is fluid and somewhat interchangeable between cloud providers. This can be confusing, so rather than starting with terms, we'll focus on the two main places where you'll apply firewall rules in the cloud.

Interface Rules applied to the network interface of a VM are often called *security groups*. These rules allow or deny traffic to and from a VM's network interface. This is somewhat analogous to an access control list (ACL) applied to a switchport in the data center.

Network Rules applied to an entire virtual network (or subnet) are sometimes called ACLs or—confusingly—network security groups. This is analogous to an ACL applied to an entire VLAN in the data center.

The primary function provided by firewalls—namely packet filtering—is abstracted behind a friendly management interface. In other words, there is no discrete firewall device that you can place at the "edge" of your cloud, nor can you place a group of VMs "behind" a firewall device. Instead, you just create firewall rules and tell the provider where to apply them. One big advantage of microsegmentation is that the firewall rules move with the resource to which they're bound. For instance, if you apply a firewall rule to a VM's interface, that rule will remain in effect even if you move the VM to a different host.

At a minimum, firewall rules consist of four elements:

Direction: Inbound or outbound

Source: One or more IP addresses

Protocol: For example, TCP, UDP, or ICMP

Port: The TCP or UDP port (if applicable)

Firewall rules always include an implicit deny, causing them to deny all traffic by default. Therefore, the cloud provider will likely add a few rules to allow common traffic. For example, when you create a new VM, the provider will probably create a rule to allow outbound IPv4 network access to any address. Without this rule, the instance would be unable to reach out to the Internet to get updates, for example.

When creating your firewall rules, you must understand whether the firewall you're dealing with is stateful or stateless, because this will impact the rules that you need to create.

Stateful *Stateful* means that when traffic is allowed to pass in one direction, the firewall intelligently allows return traffic in the opposite direction. For example, when a VM reaches out to a server on the Internet to download updates, the firewall allows return traffic from that server. Stateful firewalls use connection tracking to identify return traffic and distinguish it from unsolicited traffic.

Stateless A *stateless* firewall doesn't automatically allow return traffic, so you must create an explicit rule to allow it. This is similar to an ACL on a traditional switch.

Consequently, stateless firewall rules tend to be broader and less restrictive than stateful firewall rules.

NOTE In the cloud, you can create a VM that runs a firewall appliance and configure your cloud network in such a way that traffic must pass through it. Understand that this is different than the native firewall functionality offered by the cloud provider.

Web Application Firewalls

A *web application firewall (WAF)* is a specialized type of firewall that monitors HTTP(S) requests to your web application, looking for exploits that might be used to gain unauthorized access or perform a denial-of-service (DoS) attack. Whereas firewalls typically allow or deny access based on information in the layer 3 (IP) or layer 4 (TCP or UDP) header, a WAF can inspect application traffic for things like injection of malicious scripts, SQL scripts used in injection attacks, and abnormal query strings. A WAF blocks such suspicious requests before they reach your application. A WAF may also offer more advanced features such as blocking traffic based on geographic location or a list of known malicious IP addresses.

Cloud providers typically offer a WAF as a managed service. There are WAF appliances that you can spin up in a VM and place in front of your application. Whether you need a WAF depends on how secure your application is to begin with. Ideally, any application you're running would be 100 percent secure and immune to any attacks. But the reality is that vulnerable applications are the norm, and you continually have to patch to plug holes as they're found. A WAF can shield your application against newly discovered vulnerabilities that you might not have had a chance to patch.

Application Delivery Controllers

An *application delivery controller (ADC)* combines some of the features of a load balancer, WAF, and firewall. These devices typically work in concert to enable access to a single application. For example, consider how you'd have to configure these devices to allow access to a secure web application. A firewall would filter incoming traffic to allow only HTTPS traffic on TCP port 443. The firewall forwards the traffic to a WAF that performs deep packet inspection to look for any suspicious requests. The WAF then directs the traffic to a load balancer that sends it along to a web server. The success of the application thus depends on each step in the process executing perfectly, and a single configuration error on any of these devices can take down the entire application.

An ADC is designed to be a one-size-fits-all network device that can streamline network management by making it unnecessary to configure and manage multiple appliances separately. Instead, because the ADC provides all the necessary functions in one device, you have fewer points of failure and don't have to worry about connectivity between as many devices.

Watching Out for the Bad Guys: Understanding IDSs/IPSs

Intrusion detection systems (IDSs) and *intrusion prevention systems (IPSs)* monitor traffic looking for patterns that could indicate a network-based attack or invasion. Both solutions can detect, in real time, suspicious activity on a network. An IDS/IPS monitors traffic looking for network activity that indicates an intrusion based on signatures that are kept up-to-date by the vendor. The intrusion detection system will alert a management system, or it can be configured to send out emails or text notifications if an attack is discovered, as shown in Figure 2.8. An intrusion detection system will not take action to remedy the situation—it only monitors and reports.

FIGURE 2.8 Intrusion detection systems monitor incoming network traffic for suspicious activity and generate alerts.

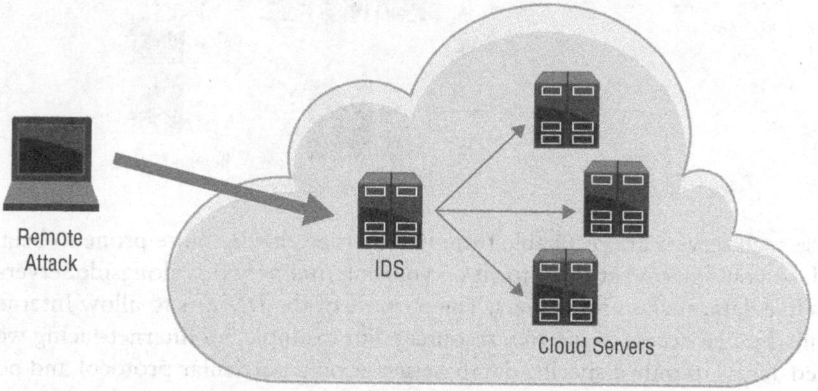

An intrusion prevention system, as shown in Figure 2.9, takes the IDS concept a step further and can actively take measures to mitigate the attack with configuration scripts and methods to stop the attack that is underway. The IPS communicates with network devices such as routers and firewalls to apply rules to block the effects of the attack.

FIGURE 2.9 Intrusion prevention systems monitor activity and prevent network attacks.

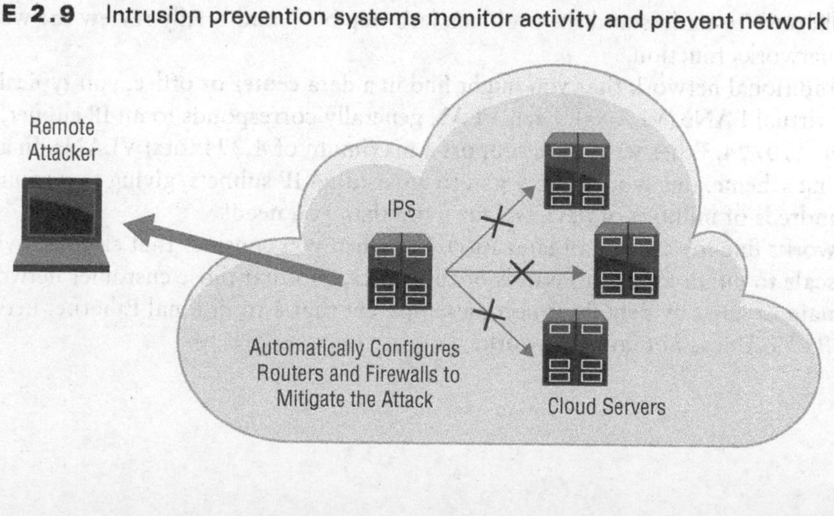

Demilitarized Zone

A *demilitarized zone (DMZ)* is a section of the network that hosts servers which need to be reachable via the Internet as well as internally (see Figure 2.10). Servers that might be placed inside a DMZ include mail, DNS, FTP, or web servers.

FIGURE 2.10 DMZ servers are accessed by the outside world via the Internet and also internally.

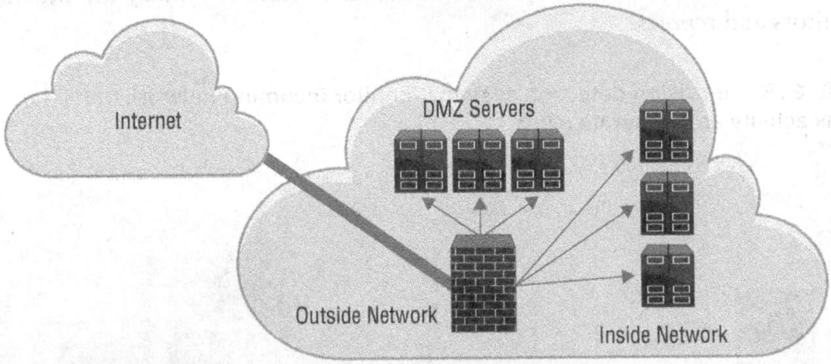

Because such servers are reachable from the Internet, they're more prone to being compromised, so you don't want them to sit on your internal network alongside servers that hold sensitive data, such as file servers. The purpose of the DMZ is to allow Internet-facing servers only limited access to internal resources. For example, an Internet-facing web server might need access to only a specific database server on a particular protocol and port. If the web server is compromised, the attacker will not be able to get to any other resources in the internal network. Also, there will be extensive policies configured on the firewall to limit access to the DMZ servers for only their intended purpose.

VXLAN Deployments

Virtual extensible LAN (VXLAN) was designed to overcome the size limitations of traditional Ethernet. To understand the problem, let's step back and briefly review the way that modern networks function.

In a traditional network that you might find in a data center or office, you typically have multiple virtual LANs (VLANs). Each VLAN generally corresponds to an IP subnet, such as `192.168.1.0/24`. Ethernet frames support a maximum of 4,094 total VLANs. In a typical networking scheme, this would allow you to have 4,094 IP subnets, giving you room for literally hundreds of millions of devices—far more than you need!

This works fine for a single organization. But when you consider that cloud providers need to scale to hundreds of thousands of customers, and that those customer networks must remain isolated by default, it becomes apparent that a traditional Ethernet network with 4,094 VLANs is not going to work.

VXLAN was designed as a solution to this problem. It's an encapsulation method that takes an Ethernet frame and encapsulates it in an IP/UDP packet destined to port 4789. (Another name for this is MAC-in-IP encapsulation.) A VXLAN header sits between the encapsulated Ethernet frame and the IP header. The VXLAN header is 8 bytes (64 bits) in length and contains a *VXLAN Network Identifier (VNI)* that differentiates Ethernet frames belonging to different virtual networks. To understand how this works, consider two different cloud customers, both using an IP subnet of `10.1.0.0/16`. How can the cloud provider ensure that their traffic doesn't get mixed together? It achieves this by assigning each customer its own VNI. A VNI is a 24-bit field that allows for more than 16 million virtual networks!

Although the primary purpose of VXLAN is to overcome the scaling limitations of Ethernet, it's often used in another way. VXLAN makes it possible to create layer 2 tunnels across IP networks, making it easier to create "stretched" VLANs that span separate geographic locations. The main reason why people do this is to allow VMs in the same subnet to move from one data center to another without having to change the IP address. This is a bad practice, leading to "split-brain" scenarios, network issues that are hard to troubleshoot, and even data loss. To be clear, there are safe ways to implement VM mobility that include VXLAN, but they do not entail stretching a VLAN across different sites.

GENEVE

One aspect of VXLAN that confuses people has to do with two things that network professionals call the data plane and the control plane. In short, the *data plane* is concerned with how data is encapsulated and formatted as it moves across the network. As you just learned, VXLAN defines a particular packet format for encapsulating Ethernet frames. The *control plane*, on the other hand, is concerned with *how* data gets to its destination—in other words, routing and forwarding. VXLAN also prescribes *how* VXLAN packets should traverse a network, using a flood-and-learn approach. Imagine that you have a dozen virtualization hosts in a data center and you're using VXLAN for transport. Now consider two VMs in the same virtual network, each running on a different host. If one VM sends a packet to the other, that packet would initially get flooded to all of the virtualization hosts because that's the way VXLAN works by default. As you might expect, this flood-and-learn approach doesn't scale. The flood-and-learn behavior is the default with VXLAN, but it isn't required. It can be used with other control plane protocols such as Ethernet VPN (EVPN) with the Border Gateway Protocol (BGP), which is highly scalable.

Generic Network Virtualization Encapsulation (GENEVE) is an alternative to VXLAN that also allows transporting Ethernet frames over an IP network. A major difference is that it defines only a packet format, but it does not prescribe how those packets should be transported. This means it's up to you to decide on the control plane. GENEVE uses UDP port 6081.

IP Address Management

When planning your cloud migration, you should have a clear picture of what IP addresses you're going to assign to the various devices in your networks—both in your data center and the cloud. You'll commonly use IP address blocks from the private, or non-Internet routable, address blocks set aside in RFC 1918, as shown in Table 2.1.

TABLE 2.1 Private IP address blocks

RFC1918 name	IP address range	Number of addresses
24-bit block	10.0.0.0 to 10.255.255.255	16,777,216
20-bit block	172.16.0.0 to 172.31.255.255	1,048,576
16-bit block	192.168.0.0 to 192.168.255.255	65,536

The purpose of private IP addresses is to preserve the limited public IP addresses that are available. Based on a cloud provider's policies, you may be able to select an address block of your choosing, or the cloud provider may assign address blocks for you to use. It is common for the cloud provider to let you choose one large block of IP addresses for your VPC and then segment this block into smaller subnetworks. It is advantageous to create as many subnets as you require and to group applications or network segments into each subnet. By creating multiple subnets, you can use network security resources such as access control lists, security groups, and firewalls to control the flow of traffic into and out of each subnet. The important thing to keep in mind when choosing addresses is not to choose addresses that are already in use by your organization. Even if the plan is to migrate from the data center to the cloud, resist the temptation to reuse the same IP addresses in the cloud. Odds are high that you'll need to connect your cloud to your data center or other network, and conflicting IP addresses are sure to put a damper on things!

Be careful not to confuse private IP addresses with public ones. Every cloud service provider owns public IP addresses that are reachable from the Internet. Depending on your needs, you may allocate a limited number of these addresses to your cloud resources for reachability from the Internet. For example, if you have a web server running on a VM, you may want to assign it a public IP address. Likewise, if you're using a load balancer to front a fleet of web servers, you would assign a public IP address to the load balancer. Public IP addresses that can be reserved and reallocated to cloud resources are sometimes called *elastic IP addresses*.

NOTE

If your cloud resources need to communicate only with internal resources, such as those within your cloud or data center, they do not need a public IP address.

Network Packet Brokers

Some organizations require packet-level analysis of traffic to and from each and every device on the network. In traditional networks, this used to be done by configuring the switched port analyzer (SPAN) feature on a switch and connecting a network monitoring tool to capture and analyze the packets. Some reasons for this can include looking for signs of malware or malicious hackers, or leakage of sensitive data. But as networks have grown larger and faster, it's become challenging to copy every single packet on the network and send it to a single device. A *network packet broker* is a specialized security appliance designed to solve this problem.

A packet broker collects and aggregates packets captured from various devices that you want to monitor, such as switches, routers, and firewalls. Packet brokers can buffer and deduplicate packets, filter them to remove unnecessary or sensitive information, and send them along to one or more network monitoring tools.

Packet brokers offer a centralized collection point for packets, something especially useful if you're running in both the cloud and on-premises. Most public cloud providers offer the ability to sniff VM traffic and send it to another VM running a network monitoring tool or virtual packet broker appliance. Alternatively, on each VM you can install an agent that forwards a copy of each packet to your packet broker for processing.

Content Delivery Networks

A *content delivery network (CDN)* is a highly available service that delivers static and dynamic content—such as web pages or streaming video—to users as fast as possible. A CDN consists of numerous points of presence or edge locations around the world, strategically positioned to be close to end users. When a user requests content stored in the CDN, the CDN determines which edge location will give them the best performance. (Usually, it's the one physically closest to them.) The CDN then routes the request to that edge location for servicing. For example, if a user in Asia browses a website stored on a CDN, they'll be served the website from a location close to Asia. If a user in Mexico hits the same website, they'll be routed to a CDN somewhere in the Americas. This reduces the amount of data that has to traverse the globe, resulting in a faster experience.

By storing redundant copies of the content in different edge locations, CDNs ensure that the content is available even if one location goes offline. All of the major public cloud providers offer a CDN, and several companies are dedicated to providing CDN services.

Service Level Agreements

Each service a cloud provider offers falls under the terms of the service level agreement for that service. The *service level agreement* (SLA) is a document that outlines specific metrics and the minimum performance or availability level and defines the penalties for failing to meet the metrics. The SLA will outline who owns the data as well as the rights and responsibilities of the customer and the provider.

Cloud providers operate on a *shared responsibility model*. The provider is responsible for the infrastructure that supports the cloud, whereas you are responsible for the resources that you create in the cloud. In short, if you have control over a resource, that resource is your responsibility. If you create a VM in the cloud, its configuration and every bit of data on it is your responsibility. If you use a managed database service, the cloud provider is responsible for the database server and underlying hardware, but you're responsible for the databases that you create on it

As you can tell, the demarcation of responsibility moves depending on the service model (IaaS, SaaS, or PaaS). How much responsibility the customer is willing to take on often drives the choice of service model. A large organization with an ample team might choose the IaaS model, which places most of the responsibility in the customer's hands. A small startup with each person doing three different jobs will likely choose an SaaS model, where the bulk of the responsibility falls to the cloud provider. Naturally, responsibility isn't cheap, and the more you offload to the provider, the more you're going to pay. Yes, the classic time/money trade-off applies to the cloud, too!

Matching Data Center Resources to Cloud Resources

Although many similarities exist between the cloud and a traditional data center, there are significant differences as well. So, before migrating, you need to understand how to translate your data center resources to cloud resources. Most things will be obvious. For starters, hardware and software requirements that are driven by your application are likely going to be the same in the cloud as in the data center—things such as OS versions, storage and memory capacity, and processing power. Other requirements, however, don't translate as cleanly. For example, if you're backing up servers to tape in the data center, your backup procedures are going to have to change for the cloud. In this section, you'll learn how to evaluate and scale your cloud compute resources to meet your needs.

What Are Available and Proposed Hardware Resources?

Cloud service providers will offer a wide range of VM configurations that are designed for different requirements, such as general compute, graphics processing units (GPUs), and heavy I/O needs such as a database application; there are also options for CPU and memory-centric configurations. These are generally referred to as instance types or flavors, "instance" being an oft-used cloud term for a VM. Each instance type defines the number of vCPUs, amount of RAM, network and storage I/O performance, and many other parameters that vary by cloud service provider. In the following sections, you'll learn about the virtualization of the hardware resources and how they are allocated to the VMs running on the cloud servers.

Physical and Virtual Processors

With advancements made in chip fabrication capabilities, CPU densities and capabilities have dramatically increased with the introduction of multicore processors. The physical server will supply the processing power to the VMs, and as such, there must be ample processing capabilities on the physical server to support a large number of VMs running on top of it. Just as with the process of determining the amount of RAM required, the CPU requirements of all the VMs hosted in the server must be calculated and then the server must be configured to meet their total requirements. The servers' motherboards will contain multiple slots for the insertion of CPUs, and each CPU may contain many processing cores. A single-server platform can be scaled to meet the processing needs of hundreds of VMs running on it.

Depending on the cloud provider, a VM host may be oversubscribed—that is, it may have more VMs than it's able to adequately support. Hence, even though you might be expecting your VM to get 2 GHz of processing power, there may be times when it's only able to eke out 1 GHz. To avoid this situation, you can usually request a dedicated VM host that's not simultaneously shared with other customers. That way, you can control how many VMs you run on each host and avoid contention for the CPU.

Physical and Virtual Memory

Virtual machines will consume *RAM* on the host server. The amount of memory required will depend on the number of virtual machines and how they are individually configured. Care must be taken by the cloud provider when implementing the servers that adequate memory is installed on the server for the VMs that are being hosted. Additional memory should also be installed to accommodate for future growth and also for what is needed for the hypervisor. Modern server designs can accommodate ever-increasing memory density. In addition to memory sizes, other parameters considered are access speeds and error correction capabilities.

Overcommitting Your Memory Resources

The hypervisors used in cloud server virtualization have a feature called *overcommitting*, which enables a virtual machine running on that hypervisor to use more memory than is physically installed on the server's motherboard. As an example, the server's physical RAM installed on the motherboard may be 64 GB, and the 32 VMs running on that server are all configured for 4 GB of RAM each; this would be a 2:1 overcommitment, with 128 GB allocated and with 64 GB physically available.

The concept of overcommitting is based on the assumption that not all servers will use the memory assigned to them. This unused memory is dynamically allocated to the other VMs that require additional RAM for operations.

Bursting and Ballooning—How Memory Is Handled

When memory is overcommitted, hypervisors employ a clever little trick to reclaim any memory that running VMs aren't using. *Memory ballooning* is a hypervisor function that allows the hypervisor to reclaim unused memory from a VM running on top of the hypervisor and to allocate that memory for other uses. By being able to reuse unused memory on the VMs, the hypervisor can optimize the RAM installed on the system.

Here's how it works. Suppose that a VM host is oversubscribed on memory and is running low. The hypervisor needs to reclaim any memory unused by any running VMs.

The hypervisor doesn't actually know what memory each VM is actively using (that's handled by the OS running in the VM). But running on each VM are special virtualization tools that integrate and communicate with the hypervisor. The hypervisor sends a signal to what's called the *balloon driver* that prompts each VM's OS to allocate any unused memory. The OS marks off this unused section of memory and reserves it, preventing other running processes from using it. The balloon driver, knowing which section of memory is free, tells the hypervisor, allowing it to reclaim the unused memory to use elsewhere. This trick comes with a cost. When the balloon driver allocates memory, it may prompt the VM's OS to move or swap some of its memory to disk—resulting in a substantial slowdown.

Understanding Hyperthreading in a CPU

Hyperthreading allows a single microprocessor core to act as if it were two separate CPUs to the operating system. Each logical or virtual processor can be started, stopped, and controlled independently from the other. The technology shares the same silicon resources on the CPU chip for command executions.

Hyperthreading is transparent to the operating system or hypervisor accessing the CPU, and the virtual machines see two cores when there is only one that is simulating two. The hypervisor or operating system must support symmetrical multiprocessing to take advantage of hyperthreading.

Hypervisor CPU Optimization with AMD-V and Intel VT-x

When hypervisor and server virtualization technologies were introduced to the marketplace, emulation software was used to enhance the capabilities and functionality of the CPUs supporting the hypervisor's virtualized servers. VM performance suffered with the software emulation approach, and both Intel and AMD moved this functionality to silicon and added microcode specifically to support virtualization. With this support, hypervisor and VM performance was greatly increased.

AMD-Virtualization (AMD-V) is the microcode and silicon extensions used to support virtualization and is now a common feature on AMD's CPU releases. Intel's answer to enhanced hardware virtualization support in its CPU products is called *Intel Virtualization Technology (Intel VT-x)*. With any virtualized system, it is important that this feature be enabled in the system BIOS to increase the performance of the servers. In modern server hardware, these features are enabled by default.

CPU Overcommitment Ratios

As you have learned, the cloud server hypervisors overcommit RAM resources; the same is true for CPU resources. The CPU overcommitment ratio is also called the virtual CPU-(vCPU)-to-physical CPU (pCPU) ratio. Overcommitting is based on the assumption that not all servers will use the CPU resources allocated to them, and those cycles can be dynamically reassigned to VMs that require the allocated compute resources.

Overcommitments are largely determined by the applications running on the virtual machines. If they are CPU intensive, a low ratio may be required. However, if the applications are not CPU bound and present a light load on the physical CPUs, a higher overcommitment ratio can be implemented. By overcommitting physical resources to the virtual services, the allocation and usage of the physical resources can be maximized, resulting in a lower cost of operations.

CPU wait time is the time that a process or thread has to wait to access a CPU for processing. With a hypervisor supporting many virtual machines running on it, the VMs may, at times, have to wait for the finite physical CPU resources to become available. The hypervisors will present each VM with a configurable amount of virtual CPU resources and control access to the actual physical resources. When there is contention, the VM may be paused from accessing the CPU to allow other virtual machines equitable access to the CPU. Hypervisor and monitoring tools can collect and display CPU wait statistics for performance tuning and capacity planning of processing requirements.

Single Root I/O Virtualization

Single-root I/O virtualization (SR-IOV) allows multiple VMs to share the same physical network interface card (NIC) on a VM host. SR-IOV effectively virtualizes a single NIC as multiple virtual NICs, each of which can connect to a different VM. This allows rapid, direct communication between the VM and the physical NIC without the need for the hypervisor to perform any virtual switching.

Templates and Images

Most cloud deployments will involve a lot of repetition. You may need multiple redundant VMs that are all running the same OS and software. As we discussed in the previous chapter, you might even need to replicate your production environments for testing. To avoid unnecessary work, you can use a template. There are a couple of different kinds of templates.

VM templates are disk images that have at a minimum a preinstalled OS. VM templates are often just called images. VM images may also have other software already installed, saving you the trouble of having to do it yourself. Many software vendors offer prebuilt templates to make it easy to deploy their particular solution. In fact, this is exactly what virtual appliances are—ready-made VM templates with preconfigured software.

If you need redundant VMs with a particular configuration or specific software, you can create your own custom reusable template. Just configure a VM the way you need it and then use that image to create your other VMs. Also, custom images go hand in hand with autoscaling. Create a custom template image with your application already installed, and as the workload increases, autoscaling can provision new, preconfigured VMs from your template.

Another type of template is used with the infrastructure-as-code (IaC) approach. IaC templates are simply text files that describe the cloud resources to create and how to configure them. IaC templates are useful for repeatedly provisioning complex cloud environments. For example, from the same IaC template, you can deploy your production environment and an identical testing environment. Because both environments are based on the same template, you can trust that they're identical.

Each cloud provider offers its own proprietary templating language, so there's a learning curve with this approach. Also, it means that if you use multiple cloud providers, you'll have to learn multiple templating languages. However, third-party tools are available that are designed to deploy to multiple cloud providers using a "one-size-fits-all" templating language.

Regardless of how you go about deploying your cloud resources, you'll have to learn the specifics of the cloud architecture and how the various pieces fit together. Although most providers have certain things in common—for example, a VM always has a network interface and usually attaches to some sort of elastic block storage—terminology and implementation can differ drastically among different cloud providers. For instance, one provider might call a virtual network a virtual network, whereas another will call it a VPC. These semantic differences can make it challenging to compare different cloud offerings.

Physical Resource High Availability

Data centers implement high availability using redundant systems configured in active/active or active/standby configurations, where one or more systems are active, and another may be on standby with a current configuration ready for immediate promotion to the master should there be a failure. High availability applies not only to computing systems but also to power, networking, and cooling. Critical systems can benefit from high availability to prevent a single point of failure from causing a large-scale outage.

Cloud providers are responsible for ensuring that their infrastructure follows the same high availability principles that you would find in traditional data centers. This is similar to the colocation model discussed in Chapter 1, but when it comes to the cloud, the cloud provider is also responsible for the computing, storage, and networking infrastructure that underpins their service offerings.

Introducing Disaster Recovery

We're going to cover disaster recovery (DR) options and techniques in detail later in this book, but it's important to get a big picture understanding of the possibilities up front. Backups and DR are critical components of any deployment, and they mustn't be an afterthought or a later add-on.

Let's start with the good news. DR is much easier to implement in the cloud than it is in the data center. In the data center, you're responsible for ensuring that backups occur, are stored properly (this usually means off-site), and retained for as long as required. When you think about it, the most difficult part of backups is the hardware. In the cloud, because the infrastructure is already in place and managed by the provider, configuring backups is relatively quick and straightforward.

Let's take a few examples. Backing up VM storage volumes may be as easy scheduling regular snapshots that are stored in a different region (satisfying the off-site requirement). If you're using a managed database service, the provider can automatically back up the database and transaction logs. If you're keeping important files in object storage, you can use versioning and replication to retain easily recoverable copies as long as you need them.

Recovery in the cloud, although sadly not as easy as backing up, is markedly easier than its data center counterpart. Once again, because the underlying hardware infrastructure already exists and is ready for use, recovery in the worst case amounts to performing another deployment. If your budget allows for it, the best case is to have redundant components already provisioned and ready to take over *before* a failure occurs.

Physical Hardware Performance Benchmarks

Earlier we discussed collecting performance baselines prior to migration to compare with your new cloud deployment as part of the migration validation process. This includes collecting hardware performance benchmarks to establish baselines.

All operating systems log metrics, such as disk I/O operations, network throughput, link utilization, and errors. Statistics can be collected for RAM and storage as well. It is important to collect and document these benchmarks to have a reference and, from that reference point, track deviations. Benchmarks can also alert you to the need to add capacity for CPU, memory, storage, and networking, for example, since you now have the data to perform trending analysis. It should be noted that most cloud management and monitoring tools can collect and analyze this data as part of the cloud provider's service offerings.

Cost Savings When Using the Cloud

Cloud economics can be compelling to a company's finance and budget groups. The primary advantage is that cloud computing offers the pay-as-you-grow model discussed in Chapter 1. There are no up-front capital expenses for servers, storage, networking, and so on. With the requirements for massive capital expenses removed from a company for computing and data center operations, that money can be better allocated elsewhere in the organization. Also, there is no requirement to purchase capacity for peak usage; with cloud computing and with resiliency and scaling, adding any needed additional capacity can be enabled in the cloud in a short time frame that is often measured in minutes.

Although the cost savings in cloud computing over owning and managing a private data center can be significant, you must take care to manage your resources effectively. Many cloud billing models are based on hours of usage. If you launch hundreds of servers and forget to shut them down or have autoscaling scale up and then fail to scale back down when the workload subsides, you may get a very large bill from your cloud company for resources that were provisioned but unused. Be sure to configure billing alerts to notify you when your resource usage is on track to exceed your budget.

Now suppose that you have a personal account with a cloud provider, and you're okay spending up to $50 a month for learning and experimenting in the cloud. You'd be wise to configure an alert for when your monthly bill hits $25. That way, if you accidentally leave some VMs running, you'll find out before your costs get out of hand. Remember, it's your responsibility to delete resources that you're not using!

Energy Savings in the Cloud

Many cloud data centers were constructed in the past 10 years or so and implement up-to-date energy-saving technologies and procedures. All other things being equal, the more energy efficient a cloud data center is, the lower the cost of operations.

Energy savings can also be realized with the higher utilization ratios found in cloud computing as compared to enterprise data centers that do not benefit from the shared service model and often have servers sitting idle or with low utilization that are still powered up and consuming energy. Modern management systems can power off servers, storage, and other systems that are not being used and can reenable them as needed.

Shared vs. Dedicated Hardware Resources in a Cloud Data Center

The primary economic cost advantages of cloud computing are based on shared virtualized resources. Virtualized storage, networking, and, of course, compute compose the vast majority of a cloud data center's operations. However, there may be times where a dedicated server is your only option. This is usually because of security regulations or application restrictions and special hardware requirements that limit you to a bare-metal server dedicated to one customer.

Although the shared model is the most common and most cost-effective, most cloud service providers offer dedicated servers at a much higher cost because of the need to allocate a complete server to one customer.

Microservices

The advent of cloud computing has prompted software developers to consider how they can rearchitect applications to take advantage of the cloud's elastic nature. To understand how this works, think of a traditional e-commerce application that must handle various functions, including a web interface, shopping carts, checkout, financial transactions, and shipping. Software developers would naturally package all these functions together in an application that would have to run on one server. The application itself may consist of multiple executables, but these components must all run on the same server in order for the various functions to coordinate and communicate. This is called a *monolithic application* because all the application components run on one server.

Monolithic applications are convenient because they're more or less self-contained. They are also fast, because they're relatively simple to deploy, and interprocess communication is instant since the components are on the same server. But monolithic applications have some drawbacks. Because all the functions run on the same server, that server becomes a single point of failure. If it goes down, every function of the application goes down with it. Also, the functions can't scale independently. If, for example, the web interface is especially slammed because of high traffic, the excess load could slow down the other functions, resulting in errors, timeouts, and perhaps even crashes. To put it in technical terms, the various functions of the application are tightly coupled together.

Containers

The obvious solution then is to break this tight coupling so that the application components can run on separate servers, allowing them to be scaled independently. A nice side effect of breaking apart or decoupling the components is that they can be deployed redundantly for high availability. This architecture of decoupling an application's components and distributing them across multiple servers is called a *microservices architecture*. The individual components are themselves called *microservices*.

You might be thinking that this architecture sounds complicated, and it is. Because each microservice can be scaled independently, you have to decide *how* to distribute them and scale them. Do you dedicate six servers for the web interface and shopping cart microservices, and three servers for everything else? Or can you put everything on six servers, except the warehousing and shipping microservices, which can reside on just two servers? And, just as important, what if you need to change the arrangement on the fly in response to increased workloads?

It becomes clear that installing and uninstalling microservices individually is not workable. They may be able to scale, but it's not worth it if you have to spend all your time playing musical chairs with them! This is where containers come in. Instead of deploying microservices natively by installing an executable on each VM where it's required, you can deploy the microservices in lightweight virtual machines called containers. A *container* is simply a lightweight VM in which you can run a Linux executable, keeping it isolated from other processes on the host. For example, on a single VM you could run multiple containers each running the web interface microservice. This gives you some redundancy such that if the process in one container crashes, the other one still remains available. Contrast this with simply running one web interface process directly on a VM. If the process crashes, the web interface is completely down on that VM. Containers are advantageous from a cost perspective because you can run multiple containers on a single VM. It's like getting multiple VMs for the price of one!

Containers make it trivial to launch, terminate, and move microservices around as needed. There are also container orchestration services such as Kubernetes to manage this process for you. Major cloud providers also offer Kubernetes as a service as well as their own container management services. It's a best practice to use some orchestration platform to manage your containers, rather than manually deploying them.

Working with Containers

Now let's talk about the technical details of implementing containers. Docker is the most popular container platform—so popular, in fact, that when you hear the words "container" and "cloud" used in the same sentence, it's almost certain that it's a reference to Docker containers. Although we won't cover Docker specifics, there are some basic aspects of containers that you need to know.

Containers work much like regular VMs. With containers, you're essentially doing nested virtualization, creating a VM within a VM. Before you can create a container, you have to build an image that holds the necessary application files. There's no need to install an OS because containers "borrow" the Linux kernel from the host VM and boot from that. Once you create your image, you can launch a container from it, specifying storage mappings, network configurations, memory, and CPU options. Keep in mind that when you map storage to a container, you're actually mapping it to a folder or storage device on the host VM. In order for containers running on different hosts to have access to shared storage, you'll need to employ a shared filesystem, which your cloud provider is happy to provide to you as a highly available service. Likewise, when you map a network interface into a container, you're virtualizing the host VM's virtual network interface.

Secrets

When you deploy an application, you have to configure it either manually or automatically. Such configuration might include database connection strings, authentication keys, usernames, passwords, IP addresses, DNS hostnames, and so on. Some configuration parameters, such as hostnames and IP addresses, will necessarily vary, so it's not feasible to hard-code them in the container image. You can pass in configuration items as environment variables when launching a container. However, it's a bad idea to store or transmit sensitive configuration items in the clear. That's why container orchestration platforms offer the ability to store such secrets securely. For instance, suppose a particular microservice requires a database connection string. When the container for that microservice launches, it can request the string from the secrets manager over a secure connection. The secrets manager decrypts the data on the fly and passes it to the container. The string is never sent in the clear, and it's not stored in the container.

NOTE There's some debate as to whether containers are actually VMs. A container virtualizes storage, memory, and CPU—the three criteria for a computing machine. And you can start, stop, and suspend it. If that's not a VM, I don't know what is!

Configuring and Deploying Storage

One thing cloud and data center computing environments have in common is that the storage systems are decoupled from the servers that use them. Each server will usually not have a large array of hard or solid-state drives installed locally inside for use by the VMs running on that specific server. In fact, many servers may not contain any hard drives at all. Instead, the servers use large storage systems that are external to the servers and interconnected over a storage area network (SAN).

Identifying Storage Configurations

Storage is a core infrastructure component found in any cloud data center. As we discussed in Chapter 1, there are three types of storage:

- Block storage
- Object/file storage
- Filesystem storage

Now let's talk about how these are commonly implemented in the cloud.

Network Attached Storage

Network-attached storage (NAS) offers network access to a shared filesystem. For example, a file server sitting on an Ethernet-based LAN and hosting shared directories is a type of NAS. The filesystem where the files are stored actually resides on the NAS server, and it handles the details of storing those files on disk. The clients that access the files—in our case, VMs running in the cloud—access the files on the NAS server using standard protocols such as Network File System (NFS) or Server Message Block/Common Internet File System (SMB/CIFS) (see Figure 2.11). SMB and CIFS use TCP port 445. The clients typically do not persistently store copies of the data locally, although they might temporarily cache files that they have open.

FIGURE 2.11 Network-attached storage

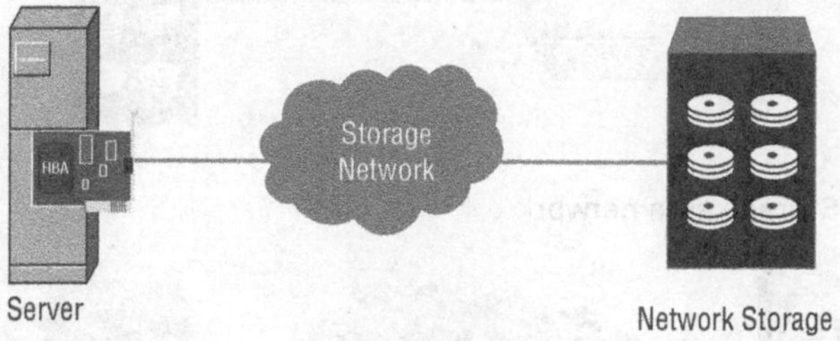

Direct-Attached Storage

In home and small business environments, *direct-attached storage (DAS)* is common and the easiest method to implement. Just as the name implies, a computer, laptop, or other computing device that has its own storage directly connected is considered to be direct-attached storage, as shown in Figure 2.12. These devices can be hard drives, solid-state drives, flash drives, or any other type of storage that is connected to the computer and not over a network. The connection used is commonly an ATA, SATA, or SCSI interface connecting the storage media to the motherboard of the computer.

Direct-attached storage does exist in the cloud, and it usually consists of disks that are offered for high-speed, temporary storage. For instance, if your application needs a temporary cache location to hold files for processing, a locally attached drive might be a good option. The data is not stored persistently and is subject to loss, but for temporary storage, this may be perfectly acceptable. Cloud providers that offer such storage may call it *ephemeral storage.*

Storage Area Networks

In large computing environments, storage systems are decoupled from the servers. These storage arrays are connected to networks dedicated to storage traffic and are separate from the networks that carry your normal VM traffic. A *storage area network (SAN)* offers high-speed, redundant, and scalable storage, as illustrated in Figure 2.13.

FIGURE 2.12 Direct-attached storage

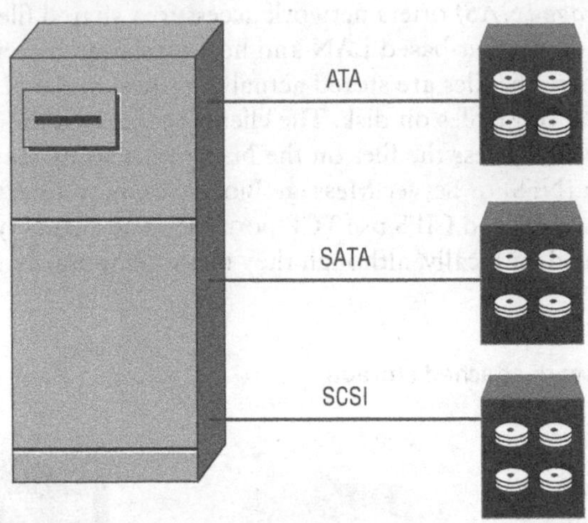

FIGURE 2.13 Storage area network

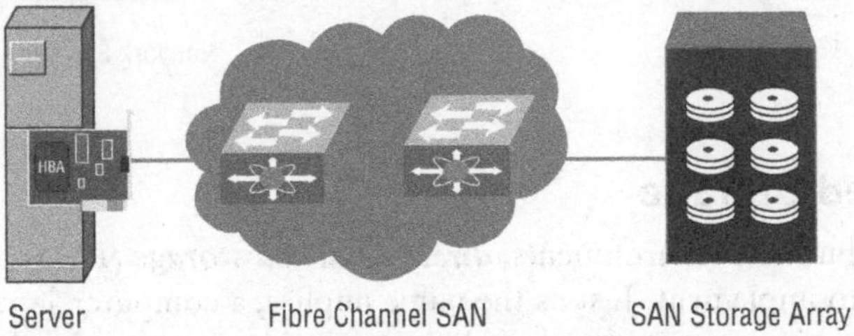

The design of the SAN and storage arrays is critical for server and application performance. If there is a high read or write latency on the drives or contention over the storage network, performance will suffer. To avoid performance issues, cloud providers implement enterprise-grade storage systems with solid-state drives (SSDs), or magnetic hard drives with disks that spin at a high RPM. For the storage network, they use high-speed interfaces to connect the servers to the SANs. The most common dedicated interface for SANs is Fibre Channel, which offers incredibly high speed and reliability.

If your storage controller supports non-volatile memory express (NVMe) drives, you might be using a newer and faster host-to-SAN technology called NVMe over fabrics (NVMeOF). As you consider migration options to cloud storage, keep in mind that high speed requirements will likely translate to higher costs in the cloud to attain those speeds. On the other hand, if you're using the slower Internet Small Computer Systems Interface (iSCSI) protocol, speed is probably not a big concern. iSCSI lets a host use an Ethernet network adapter to connect to a SAN. iSCSI uses TCP port 3260.

In addition to scalability, another advantage of decoupling storage from the servers is the ability to move VMs from one host to another seamlessly. The VM will move and continue to access its storage over the storage network. This can even be accomplished with stateful moves, where an application on a VM will continue to operate even as it is being moved between physical servers. Centralized storage is an enabler of this technology, and it is useful for maintenance, cloud bursting, fault tolerance, and disaster recovery purposes.

Object/File Storage

Cloud object storage provides a highly scalable, reliable way to store files. (Recall from Chapter 1 that the terms "file" and "object" can be used interchangeably.) Although this may sound like a NAS, it differs in some key ways. You access object storage via HTTPS or the cloud provider's proprietary API, rather than standardized networked filesystem protocols such as NFS or SMB. In other words, object storage isn't designed to be mounted like a normal filesystem, nor can it be used to store raw blocks of data. Object storage stores files and that's it. And because object storage stores only files, there are no hierarchical folder or directory structures, as found in traditional filesystems.

Redundancy in object storage is achieved simply by storing files in multiple locations. If you upload a file, that file might be stored on three different physical devices—perhaps even in three different data centers. If you then upload a second file, its three copies will likely be stored on different devices than the first file. In other words, the files that you keep in object storage won't necessarily be stored physically close together.

To understand this better, contrast object storage with a filesystem. In a filesystem, all of the files are bound together. For example, if you destroy a filesystem, you necessarily destroy all the files on it. Likewise, if you delete a folder on a filesystem, you delete all the files inside that folder. Object storage isn't like that. Files kept in object storage are not bound together, and there are no folders, so the worst that you can do is delete individual files.

Object storage sorts files into containers or buckets. For example, if you need to store image assets for two different websites, you'd have a separate bucket for each website. Understand that buckets are not like folders. They can't be nested, and you can't delete all the files in a bucket by just deleting the bucket. You first have to delete all the files in the bucket before you can delete the bucket itself.

Let's consider a fundamental difference between object storage and block storage. Recall that block storage is designed to mimic a physical disk. An OS can create its own filesystem atop block storage. In this case, it's possible for the OS to modify only a portion of a file because it has access to the individual blocks. Object storage is different. With object storage, you're limited to reading and writing files in their entirety. This means that if you want to modify even just one character in a text file on object storage, you have to reupload the entire file. To put it another way, you can't edit files on object storage. You can only replace them.

Files in object storage are addressed by their object IDs, which is analogous to a filename. An *object ID* is a pointer to a stored piece of data, and it is a globally unique identifier for the stored data. The object ID is used to locate the data or metadata in the filesystem of the cloud storage arrays.

Metadata is part of a file or sector header in a storage system that is used to identify the contents of the data. It is used in big data applications to index and search for data inside the file. Metadata can consist of many different types of information, such as the type of data or application and the security level. Object storage allows administrators to define any type of information in metadata and associate it with a file.

Extended metadata includes a long list of data that can be attached to a data file. Examples include the author, authentication type, username, password, certificates, encoding, or any other type of user-defined attribute. User-defined information about the files, its access, and its usage enables the creation of specific and sophisticated index schemes.

Software-Defined Storage

Software-defined storage (SDS) isn't a new type of storage, but rather a new way of using existing storage technologies. SDS allows you to take multiple storage systems and virtualize them as a single virtual storage system.

Whenever you're dealing with storage in the cloud, you're interacting with an SDS system. One of the most familiar applications of SDS is elastic block storage. When you provision a storage volume for a VM, you're not actually interfacing directly with a SAN. Instead, you're interacting with an SDS system that provisions the SAN resources on your behalf.

One hallmark of SDS is that it moves the locus of control from the SAN administrator to the person provisioning the VM. In traditional data centers, if you needed some block storage for a VM host, you would have to convince your SAN administrator to quickly provision a section of physical storage for you—called a logical unit number (LUN)—on the SAN. If you ran out of space, the SAN administrator would have to resize the LUN. Furthermore, if you needed to enable or disable particular SAN features, such as deduplication, encryption, or compression, the SAN administrator would have to do that for you.

SDS was designed to avoid the need to bug a SAN administrator every time that you wanted to make changes to storage. One of the earliest manifestations of SDS was the *virtual SAN (vSAN)*. A vSAN consists of multiple VMs on different physical hosts for redundancy. The vSAN can utilize local storage on these physical hosts, as well as SAN storage. The vSAN combines the available space on all of these storage systems, allowing you to provision what you need. And if you run out of space, rather than having the SAN administrator resize a LUN, you can simply request a new LUN to add to the vSAN. In addition, the vSAN may offer features such as encryption, deduplication, compression, and replication.

Storage Provisioning

When creating a cloud presence, the storage systems are as important as managing the compute resources. In this section, you'll be introduced to the creation, or *provisioning*, of storage resources in the cloud. Storage provisioning consists of creating and assigning storage, usually as volumes that are mounted or accessed from a server or remote user. In the enterprise data center, storage provisioning is a complex process that requires a dedicated team of storage engineers to implement, monitor, and manage. Storage area networks must be installed and configured, LUNs and vSANs must be created, and all of the security and everything that entails must be applied. These new storage volumes must be mounted on the VM hosts using host bus adapters. These are just the high-level topics with storage because many ongoing operational tasks are required for storage redundancy, security, and backup operations, for example.

Cloud operations have automated this process and greatly simplified the provisioning of storage for cloud consumers. It is often as simple as accessing the cloud management console with a web browser and clicking the options that you desire for storage such as replications, backups, volume size, storage type, encryption, service levels or tiers, and security parameters. Once the desired options are selected, provisioning storage is as simple as clicking the Create button and in several minutes the storage system has been created and deployed.

Thick Provisioning

When deploying a new storage system in the cloud, the automation systems can either allocate all of the storage capacity at the time of the volume creation or start with a smaller volume size and add storage capacity as needed.

Thick provisioning is the allocation of all the requested storage capacity at the time the disk is created. For example, when creating a virtual disk in the cloud, you request a capacity of 100 GB for your volume. With thick provisioning, all 100 GB will be allocated when the disk is created.

Thin Provisioning

Thin provisioning refers to storage capacity that is allocated on an as-needed basis. This prevents wasting storage capacity if it is unused. When the volume is created, it will not reserve all of the capacity requested. Instead, a smaller amount is allocated, and then additional capacity is added up to the maximum volume size as required.

Keep in mind that the volume *appears* to have the requested size. But the actual amount of storage reserved on the back-end storage will be substantially less. For example, if you create a 100 GB thinly provisioned volume for a VM, that VM will see a 100 GB volume, but the actual amount of reserved space might be only 10 GB. When the amount of used space approaches the actual amount of reserved storage, the back-end storage will have to dynamically reserve more space. When this expansion occurs, it can cause a temporary increase in read/write latency. Therefore, if speed is a concern, opt for thick provisioning.

Storage Overcommitment

Overcommitting storage resources allows you to allocate more storage space that is physically available. To achieve this, you'll need to configure the storage volumes to be thin provisioned so that the actual disk reservation for each VM starts small and expands as required. Overcommitting storage allows for more efficient use of your storage pools since storage is allocated to virtual resources on the fly.

Since overcommitting means allocating more storage than is actually available, you'll need to monitor your storage usage closely in order to avoid consuming all available storage space. If this occurs, attempts to write to storage will fail, potentially causing the abrupt failure of any resources that are using that storage. For systems that can't tolerate such outages, it's a best practice to avoid overcommitting storage.

Physical to Physical

Some legacy applications that need to be migrated may be running directly on server hardware in the data center. You may find some of these applications that are not able to be virtualized and require that the cloud provider offer actual physical machines to accommodate this need. Although this is uncommon, many cloud providers offer physical or "bare-metal" servers to accommodate this requirement. This can be expensive because it requires dedicating server hardware to a single customer.

To migrate from your source physical server to the target physical server, you must either do a completely new installation of the operating system and the application or perform a migration. The *physical-to-physical (P2P) migration* will move the application and operating system to the cloud. A P2P migration requires conversion utilities to perform the migration and take into consideration device drivers and differences in the hardware platforms. These utilities are often provided by the cloud provider or by third-party software companies. If you have a lot of data to migrate, you can ship physical drives to the cloud provider, who will perform the migration for you.

Encrypting Your Data at Rest

Data at rest is data that's kept on a storage medium such as a drive. Contrast this with *data in-transit* that passes over a network. Some regulations require encrypting data at rest, which not surprisingly is called *encryption at rest.*

In encryption at rest, the data is encrypted *before* it's written to storage. This ensures that no traces of unencrypted data are left on the storage medium. Encryption keys are used to encrypt and decrypt the files, and these keys can be managed either by the cloud service provider or the end user depending on feature offerings. Encryption at rest is broken down into two categories depending on who is responsible for managing the encryption process.

Server-Side Encryption When the cloud provider handles encryption, the actual encryption process is transparent. The provider manages the encryption keys and performs encryption and decryption on the fly. This also means that the cloud provider can decrypt the data whenever it wants to, giving them access to your data. This can happen in cases where the provider is legally compelled to turn over a customer's data to the authorities.

Client-Side Encryption The customer encrypts the data prior to sending it to the provider. This also means that the customer is responsible for managing the encryption keys. If the customer loses the encryption key, their encrypted data is inaccessible. Organizations with strict security requirements may use client-side encryption to ensure that not even the cloud provider can read their sensitive data.

Token Models

One method of securing access to storage resources is to use tokens. A *token* is a temporary credential that grants access to a resource for a limited period of time. Cloud providers use tokens to grant access to cloud resources including files in object storage, VMs, and PaaS or SaaS applications.

Tokens are used in cloud operations to authenticate APIs or command-line access to cloud servers, storage, and other services when creating a dedicated username and password isn't appropriate. For example, suppose that you run an e-commerce website where users can purchase and download software. You store the software on cloud object storage, but you don't want to leave it open where anyone can just willy-nilly download the software for free. However, it's not feasible to create a separate username and password with your cloud provider for each person who purchases from you. Instead, when a user purchases software, you can have the website generate a token that will give them temporary access to object storage to download the software. The website generates a special URL that contains the location of the software file on object storage and a token that gives time-limited read access. When the user visits the URL, the cloud provider authorizes the user to access the object based on their token. The token has a limited lifespan, so even if the URL gets out, it won't do a software pirate much good. You may also be able to configure the token to be good for one use, so that once the user downloads the software, nobody else can use the same URL to download the software again.

Input/Output Operations per Second

Storage performance is measured in *input/output operations per second (IOPS)*. An input/output (IO) operation is either a write to or a read from storage. The higher the IOPS, the faster you can store and retrieve data. Cloud providers often let you choose a guaranteed number of IOPS for block storage. Generally, there's a relationship between the amount of storage that you provision and the number of IOPS that you can request. For example, a 20 GB volume might give you only 60 IOPS, whereas a 100 GB volume would get you 300 IOPS. The reason for this is that the more storage you allocate, the more disks your data is spread across, allowing for more parallel reads and writes.

Compression and Deduplication

To make efficient use of disk space, storage systems can employ compression and deduplication. Both are remarkably similar but differ in scope. You're probably familiar with file-level compression, where redundant information in a file is stored only once, and wherever that information appears in a file, there's a pointer pointing to the location of the data.

As an illustration, think of this book as a file. The word "the" appears numerous times in the book, representing redundant information. To compress or deduplicate this information, you could replace every instance of the word "the" with a particular non-alphanumeric symbol. Whenever you see the symbol, you just mentally replace it with the word "the." Doing this would reduce the size of the book without actually losing the information.

Deduplication works the same way, except instead of replacing information only in a single file, the storage system looks for redundant information across every bit of data it stores. In the case of a SAN performing deduplication, it would seek out and deduplicate redundant information stored in every LUN. This allows for tremendous efficiency when you have hundreds of virtual disks all containing the same OS. Assuming the OS alone consumes 8 GB, deduplication could potentially free up terabytes of space!

Compression and deduplication come at a cost. In computer science, there's a concept called *time-memory trade-off*, which says that an inverse relationship exists between processing time and the amount of storage you use. Hence, compression/deduplication reduces your storage footprint but requires processing power, which means reads and writes are slower. Use compression and deduplication judiciously.

It's wise to organize your data according to speed requirements. Data that requires extremely low latency shouldn't be deduplicated or compressed. Highly redundant data that doesn't need high I/O can probably be compressed/deduplicated with minimal impact.

Storage Priorities: Understanding Storage Tiers

Data can have different requirements, such as how critical it is, how often it needs to be accessed, geographical placement, encryption, and security requirements. Certain applications may need high read or write speeds for better performance. Some types of data, such as transactional databases, may need to be accessed frequently, whereas other types of data, like old corporate records, may need to be accessed only every once in a great while. Treating data differently according to how it's used is called *storage tiering*. Different storage tiers can be defined and assigned to best meet the levels of storage the cloud customer may require.

Tier 1

Tier 1 storage is used for the most critical or frequently accessed data and is generally stored on the fastest, most redundant, or highest-quality media available. We'll cover storage arrays later in this chapter, but for now know that with Tier 1 it is important to use a storage configuration that will allow one or more disks to fail with no data being lost and access still available. Tier 1 storage arrays have the greatest manageability and monitoring capabilities and the highest I/O performance, and they are designed to have the most trustworthy reliability and durability ratings.

Tier 2

Tier 2 is a notch below and is generally used for data that does not have fast read or write performance requirements or for data that is accessed infrequently. Tier 2 data can use less expensive storage devices and can even be accessed over a remote storage network. Some examples of Tier 2 data are email storage, file sharing, or web servers where performance is important but less expensive solutions can be used.

Tier 3

Data that is often at rest and rarely accessed, or backups of Tier 1 and Tier 2 data, can be stored at the Tier 3 level. Examples of Tier 3 media are DVD, tape, or other less expensive media types. Tier 3 offers low cost for large amounts of capacity. The trade-off is that it may take hours to access the stored data for retrieval.

There can be many different tiers in a storage design in the cloud. More than three tiers can be implemented based on the complexity and the requirements of the storage system's performance. With the use of automation and scripting, data can be migrated from one tier to the other over time to meet your data retention policies.

The lower the tier number, the more critical the data is considered to be and the more the design focuses on faster performance, redundancy, and availability. For example, a Tier 1 dataset would generally offer better performance than a Tier 2 dataset, which in turn would have higher performance than a Tier 3 dataset. This is by design; for example, a Tier 3 dataset or higher may be accessed only infrequently and have no need to offer the performance of a Tier 1 dataset. By properly classifying the data needs in a multitiered cloud storage system, you can realize significant cost savings by not paying for more than what you require in your cloud design.

A company can establish storage policies and assign data requirements to the needs of the organization, thereby assigning data to be stored in the proper tier. This can result in cost savings because the organization will pay only for what is required during the data storage life cycle. For example, for regulatory purposes some data may need to be retained for a period of time. Current email may be stored and accessed as Tier 1 or 2 data, whereas infrequently accessed email archives may be moved to Tier 3. If the organization is required to retain the email files for long periods of time, the data may be stored offline since it will be classified as a higher tier than the online requirements.

Managing and Protecting Your Stored Data

The cloud provider is responsible for the availability and reliability of the storage infrastructure. One concept you'll hear about is that of *durability*, which is a measurement of how well a storage system preserves the data you store on it. For example, an annual durability of 100 percent means that the storage system is guaranteed not to lose a single bit of data over the course of a year. Of course, no cloud provider offers such amazing durability because they know that some data loss is inevitable.

Ultimately, you're responsible for ensuring the integrity and availability of your data in the cloud. Regardless of the promises a cloud provider makes regarding replication, durability, or availability, the onus is on you to protect your data. In the following sections we'll cover some strategies for doing just that.

High Availability and Failover

High availability is the ability of a system to quickly and automatically recover after a failure of one of its components. Naturally, this requires having redundant components configured in such a way that if one fails, its counterpart will take over. During a failure, there may be a delay as the redundant component takes over. Cloud providers build their infrastructure to be highly available, but outages do occasionally occur, and storage is no exception. Remember, high availability does not mean always available!

Fault tolerance refers to the ability of a system to remain continuously operational even after a component failure. A fault-tolerant system can maintain functionality because of its highly resilient design that takes into account the possibility of system failures, and it works to mitigate or work around any failures to maintain operations. A simple example of fault tolerance is redundant power supplies in a server. Even if one power supply fails, the server will remain powered on because the functioning power supply can provide ample power to the server.

Cross-Region Replication

Data replication is the process of placing copies of stored data on more than one system for disaster recovery and resiliency purposes. If all of your data is contained in one availability zone and that zone becomes unavailable, your data will be inaccessible until the cloud provider has restored operations. Worse, if the zone is destroyed by some catastrophic event such as a natural disaster, your data could be gone for good! Obviously, this is not a good arrangement. Cloud providers typically replicate storage across multiple zones, helping to improve availability. For example, a block storage volume purchased from the provider may include automatically copying the data to more than one availability zone. If a zone fails, the VMs in that zone will also fail, but the data on the block storage volume will still be intact.

However, data corruption can still occur, and such corruption can also be replicated. It's thus a best practice to replicate and retain backups of your data to satisfy your data retention and availability requirements. For especially valuable data, it's not uncommon to replicate data across different regions. Cloud providers usually offer the ability to configure automatic cross-region replication.

Replication Types: Understanding Synchronous and Asynchronous Replications

When it comes to cross-region replication for files in object storage, the process is pretty straightforward: every time a file is uploaded to object storage, replicate it to a different region. Simple!

However, it's important not to oversimplify the process of replication. This is especially true when dealing with data that's changing frequently, such as a busy transactional database. If a database failure occurs before newly written data has been backed up, you could lose a substantial amount of data. Therefore, it's crucial to decide how frequently to replicate your data.

If you can't afford to lose any data, synchronous replication is the way to go. *Synchronous replication* works by writing the data to the primary and secondary storage systems at the same time and acknowledging to the host a successful operation only after both sites have completed the transaction. This approach ensures that both copies are always synchronized. Synchronous replication is used to support high-end transactional databases that need consistent data and instantaneous failover capabilities. By using synchronous replications, you can achieve a very fast recovery time objective (RTO) in the event of a failover. So why doesn't everyone use synchronous replication? For busy databases, it could entail significant cross-region network transit costs.

A cheaper alternative is asynchronous replication. With *asynchronous replication*, there will be a delay as the data is copied to the backup site. It provides eventual consistency since it uses a store-and-forward design. Asynchronous replication is appropriate for databases that don't see frequent write activity.

Using Mirrors in Cloud-Based Storage Systems

For organizations that have stringent availability requirements, they may choose to deploy redundant resources in multiple regions, allowing for continuous operation even in the event of an entire region failure. This configuration is called a site *mirror*. A mirror can be configured in one of two ways.

One way is in an active-standby or hot-standby configuration, where one region functions as the primary or active region and all data is continuously and immediately replicated to the secondary or standby region. In case of a primary site failure, the mirror can assume processing. The other way is an active-active configuration, where both regions are actively used simultaneously.

Cloning Your Stored Data

Cloud providers offer the ability to replicate data kept on block storage volumes, although the process usually involves multiple steps. If you need to replicate a block storage volume, you can automatically take a snapshot every few hours and replicate the snapshot to a different region. You can accomplish this by using a custom script, or some cloud providers offer this as native functionality that's part of the elastic block storage system. If you need to recover the data, you can use the snapshot to provision another storage volume and attach it to a VM.

Using RAID for Redundancy

If you've worked with servers, you're no doubt familiar with the term *RAID* (Redundant Array of Inexpensive Disks). RAID lets you combine drives together to achieve performance gains, attain storage redundancy, and achieve large storage densities. By combining drives, you can achieve fault tolerance without having to sacrifice performance. The groupings of many disks can be used to create very large volumes. When a storage logical unit spans multiple hard drives, increases in performance, speed, and volume size can be achieved.

In the cloud, you won't be dealing much with RAID because that falls under the provider's purview of handling the storage infrastructure. The configuration and operation of RAID arrays takes place on hardware cards called *RAID controllers*. However, you can still configure something called *software RAID*, which lets you combine elastic block storage volumes and treat them as a single drive. These are different RAID configurations referred to as *RAID levels*, and we'll explore them to see where they are best used and discover the differences between the various levels.

RAID 0

RAID 0 (pronounced "RAID zero") is where you take a block of data to be stored and split it across two or more disks. This process is called *striping*—the file is stored across more than one hard drive. You break a file into blocks of data and then stripe the blocks across disks in the system. For example, if you have two disks in your RAID 0 array and you write a file to it, half of the file is on one drive and the other half of the file is on the other disk!

Although RAID 0 is simple, it provides no redundancy or error detection, so if one of the drives in a RAID 0 array fails, all data in lost. Despite the obvious lack of "R," it's still considered a RAID level. Because RAID 0 allows for parallel read and write operations, it's fast, making it a good option for a caching drive to store dispensable data. Figure 2.14 shows striping across multiple disks in RAID 0.

FIGURE 2.14 RAID level 0

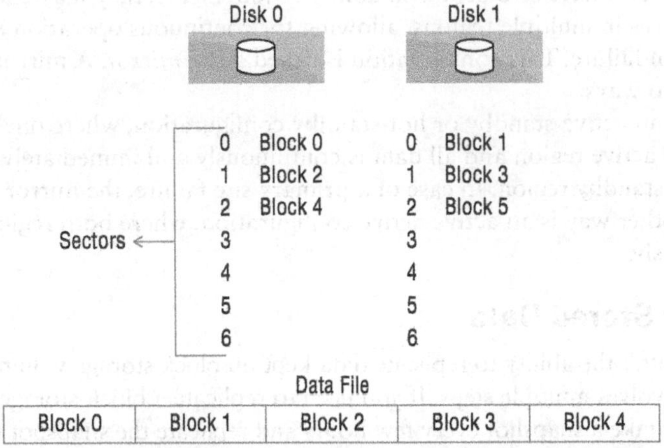

RAID 1

With *RAID 1*, all data is stored on multiple disks. RAID 1 is more commonly called *mirroring*. By storing the data on two or more separate disks, complete data redundancy is achieved. Another advantage of RAID 1 is that the data can be read off two or more disks at the same time, which allows for an improvement of read times over reading off a single disk because the data can be read in parallel. However, there isn't a comparable improvement in write performance because the data needs to be written twice.

RAID 1 is the most expensive RAID implementation since 50 percent of the storage space is for redundancy and doesn't go toward increasing storage capacity. Figure 2.15 illustrates how RAID 1 works.

FIGURE 2.15 RAID level 1

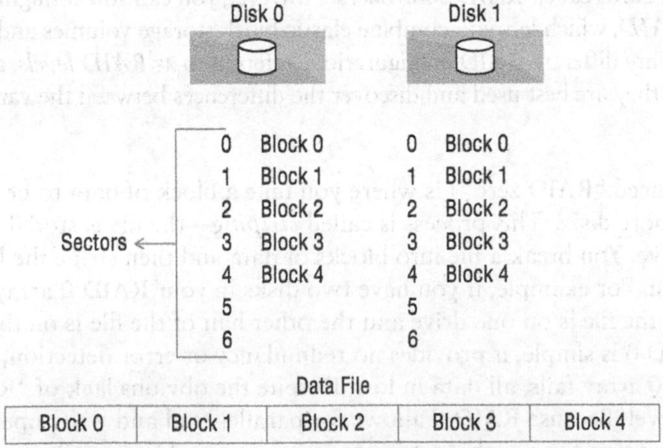

RAID 1+0

RAID levels can be combined in various ways. One common method is to create two separate RAID 1 arrays and then use RAID 0 to mirror them. This is confusingly referred to as RAID 10 or RAID 1+0 (see Figure 2.16). With *RAID 1+0,* the data is mirrored using two or more drives and then the mirrors are striped. This configuration offers both redundancy and higher performance than RAID 1, but the trade-off is a higher cost.

FIGURE 2.16 RAID level 1+0

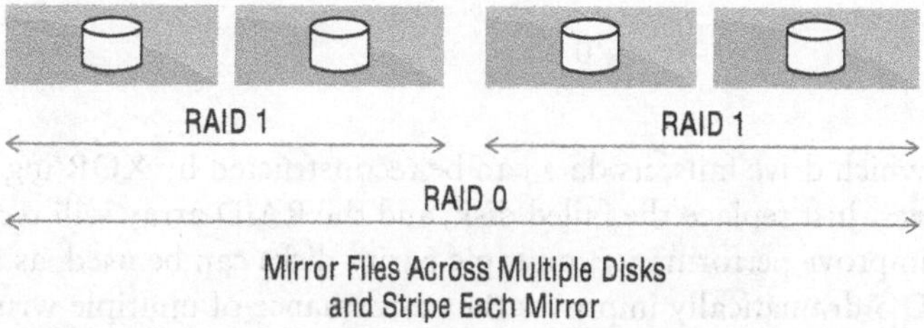

RAID 0+1

Just when you thought this couldn't get any more confusing, along comes *RAID 0+1*. This is the inverse of RAID 1+0. With RAID 0+1, the stripe is created first and then the stripe is written to the mirror, as shown in Figure 2.17.

FIGURE 2.17 RAID level 0+1

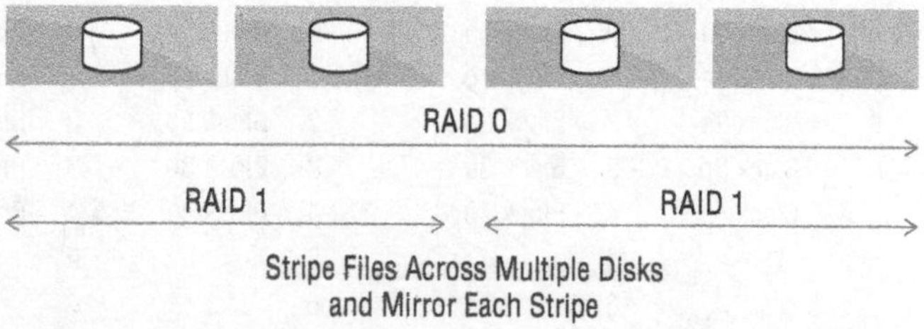

RAID 5

RAID 5 is called striping with parity, so named because it uses a stripe like RAID 0 but adds one or more parity disks. The logic of RAID 5 can be difficult to grasp if you're not familiar with binary math. To simplify it, imagine a RAID 5 array with three drives—two for striping and one for parity. Now suppose that you write the binary bits `10`. Bit `1` is written to the first drive in the stripe, and bit `0` is written to the second drive. What's written to the parity drive is the result of performing an exclusive OR (XOR) operation on the two bits, `1` and `0`. The operation `1` XOR `0` results in `1`, so a `1` is written to the parity disk. What's the point of this? This binary magic makes it possible to reconstruct the data on any single drive that fails. For example, if the second disk in the stripe fails, by XOR'ing the bits in the first disk and the parity disk, the RAID array can reconstruct the data. To see how this works, look at the following sample values for this simple striping with parity configuration:

Drive 1	Drive 2	Parity bit
1	0	1
0	1	1
1	1	0
0	0	0

Regardless of which drive fails, its data can be reconstructed by XOR'ing the bits of the other two drives. Just replace the failed disk, and the RAID array will reconstruct the missing data. To improve performance, multiple parity disks can be used, as shown in Figure 2.18. RAID 5 dramatically improves the performance of multiple writes since they are now done in parallel. With disk reads, there is a slight improvement since one more disk is used for reading.

FIGURE 2.18 RAID level 5

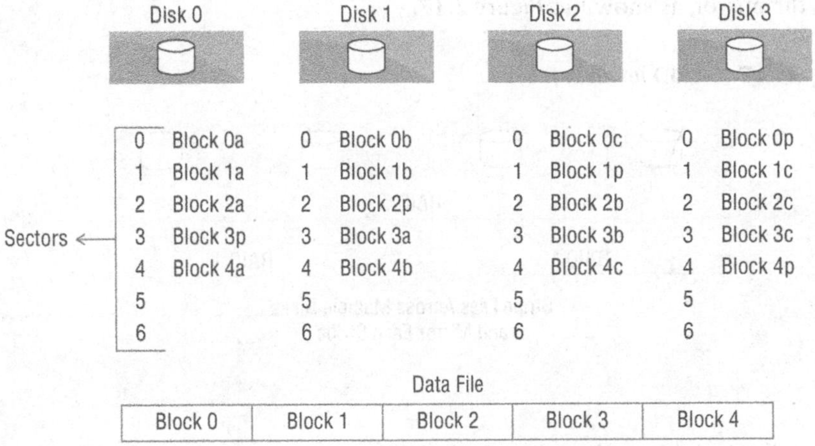

The minimum number of disks in a RAID 5 array is three, but I suggest that you use at least five or more disks to realize higher performance. RAID 5 has read and write performance close to that of RAID 1. However, RAID 5 requires much less disk space compared to other RAID levels and is a popular drive redundancy implementation found in cloud data centers.

The drawback of using RAID 5 arrays is that they may be a poor choice for use in write-intensive applications because of the performance slowdown with writing parity information. Also, when a single disk in a RAID 5 array fails, it can take a long time to rebuild a RAID 5 array, during which time performance will suffer. Also, a RAID 5 array will fail if multiple drives fail simultaneously. That's where RAID 6 comes in.

RAID 6

RAID 6 is an extension of the capabilities of RAID 5. The added capability offered in the RAID 6 configuration is that a second parity disk is added, as shown in Figure 2.19. The advantage of adding the second parity arrangement is that RAID 6 can suffer two simultaneous hard drive failures and not lose any data. However, there is a performance penalty with this configuration: the disk write performance is slower than with RAID 5 because of the need to write the second parity stripe. RAID 6 is also called striping with double parity.

FIGURE 2.19 RAID level 6

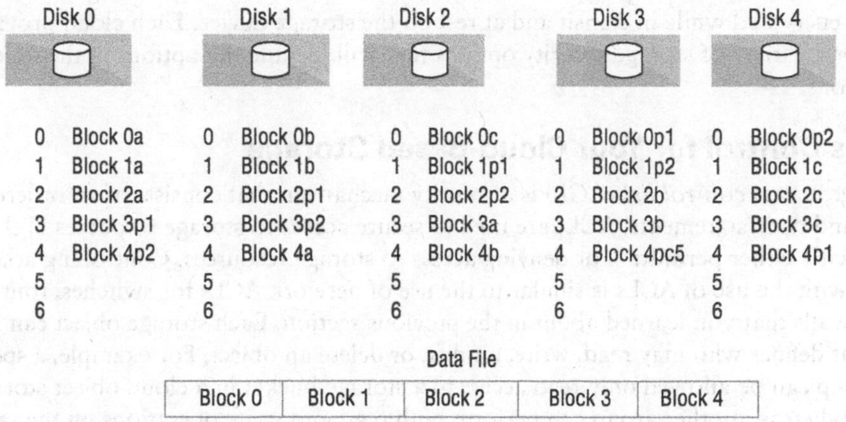

Quotas and Expiration

One of the advantages of cloud storage is its seemingly unlimited capacity. Of course, with that comes potentially unlimited costs. If you're using cloud storage that automatically expands—object storage and file level storage fall in this category—there are a couple of tools that can help you keep storage costs under control.

The first tool is *quotas*, which let you limit the amount of data you allow to be stored on your system. Quotas are typically used with filesystem storage to prevent a single user from hogging all the space. This is particularly pertinent when giving non-IT users access to a shared filesystem. In this case, the filesystem is delivered via NFS or SMB and mapped to a drive on the user's computer. Some prodigious users might figure out that they can download and store their entire music library on this amazing limitless drive! Quotas can help put a stop to that. Depending on the cloud provider, you may be able to define quotas for object storage as well.

The second tool is *object expiration*. This generally will be available only with object storage, and it lets you tell the provider to delete files automatically that are past a certain age. Alternatively, you can have the provider move the data to a different tier of storage and then optionally delete it after a period of time. Object expiration is great for things like logs that you want to keep around for a while but not forever.

What about block storage? Block storage is usually allocated up front before or simultaneously with configuring a VM, and it doesn't expand automatically. Therefore, there's no need for quotas or object expiration for block storage. Keep in mind that you can *manually* resize block storage volumes.

Storage Security Considerations

This section takes a look at security as it applies to storage. The whole point of information security is to protect your data, and one of the places your data spends most of its time is on storage. Also, there are many regulatory statutes concerning privacy of data that may apply. For example, local laws may require that data be stored in its country of origin, or that it must be encrypted while in transit and at rest on the storage device. Each cloud provider will offer a variety of storage security options that will include the options in the following sections.

Access Control for Your Cloud-Based Storage

A storage *access control list (ACL)* is a security mechanism that consists of an ordered list of permit and deny statements. ACLs are used to secure access to storage resources in the cloud by explicitly either permitting or denying access to storage resources. Controlling access to storage with the use of ACLs is similar to the use of network ACLs for switches, routers, and firewalls that you learned about in the previous section. Each storage object can have an ACL that defines who may read, write, modify, or delete an object. For example, a specific user group can be allowed only read access to a storage bucket in a cloud object storage system, whereas another group can perform both read and write operations on the same bucket. Groups can be defined as everyone, authenticated users, anonymous users, administrators, or whatever your organization requires. These groups are then filtered using an ACL to control access to storage system objects.

Hearkening back to an earlier example, a customer who purchases software from your website gets a token that grants them read-only permission to download the file containing their software. This token, however, doesn't grant them any other privileges such as deleting the file. The ACL attached to the file is what actually controls this. It contains an access control entry (ACE) that specifies that any token holder can download the file, but nothing else. To expound on the example some more, suppose that a developer needs access to modify the file. You'd add another ACE to the ACL granting that developer's cloud account permission to modify the file as well as to download it.

Understanding Obfuscation

Obfuscation is a technique to make information difficult to understand. One example of obfuscation is using random strings for usernames instead of obvious names like "admin." Using obfuscation can make it difficult for malicious hackers or hijackers to understand or use stolen data. Of course, obfuscation can also be used for nefarious purposes. Malicious actors hide malware in web pages by obfuscating the code so that it looks benign.

Storage Area Networking, Zoning, and LUN Masking

When considering how to migrate to the cloud, you should fully understand the storage configurations in your data center. When it comes to servers that used SAN-backed storage, knowing what data resides where can be a challenge. In this section, we'll briefly cover the way that SAN storage works so that you can ask the right questions of your storage admins and ensure that you don't leave important data out of your migration plan.

By default, Ethernet switches allow open communication; hosts in a subnet can communicate with each other without restriction. Fibre Channel switches take a completely different approach; by default, the SAN ports are not allowed to communicate with each other until you configure zoning on the SAN network fabric switches. *Zoning* is a SAN network security process that restricts storage access between initiators and targets. For example, when configuring zoning on a SAN network, you define what storage volumes each individual server can access. In a data center, storage is usually centralized in large storage arrays and accessed by a large number of virtual machines over a SAN. The process of zoning allows you to define what storage volumes each individual virtual machine can access, as shown in Figure 2.20.

FIGURE 2.20 Zoning filters access to storage resources on the SAN switching fabric.

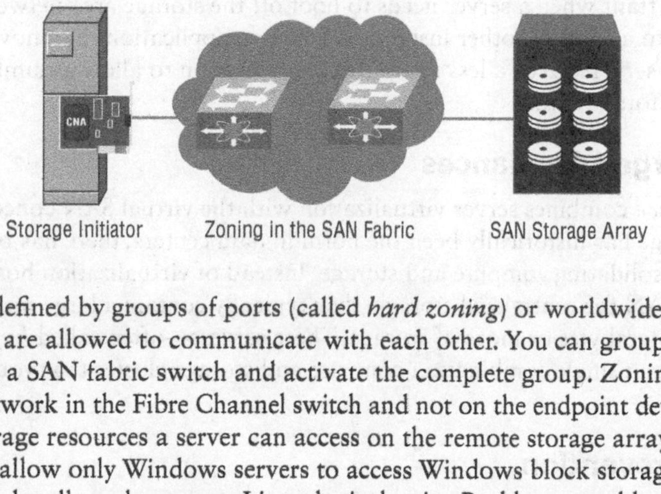

Each zone is defined by groups of ports (called *hard zoning*) or worldwide names (called *soft zoning*) that are allowed to communicate with each other. You can group multiple zones into zone sets on a SAN fabric switch and activate the complete group. Zoning is performed in the storage network in the Fibre Channel switch and not on the endpoint devices. Zoning defines what storage resources a server can access on the remote storage array. A practical application is to allow only Windows servers to access Windows block storage LUNs and for Linux only to be allowed to access Linux logical units. Problems would arise if, for example, a Linux system attempted to access a Windows filesystem. This would lead to the filesystems becoming corrupted and unusable. Also, another practical example of zoning is for each virtual machine to boot from a SAN and not use any local storage on the service on which it resides. By implementing zoning, you can ensure that each VM mounts its correct storage volumes.

LUN masking is similar to zoning, but instead of being defined at the SAN switch level, LUN masking is configured at the storage controller level, as shown in Figure 2.21. LUN masking defines the access rights between the LUNs and individual VMs or bare-metal servers. LUN masking is access control for the initiators on the SAN to the targets.

FIGURE 2.21 LUN masking filters initiator access to storage volumes on the storage controller.

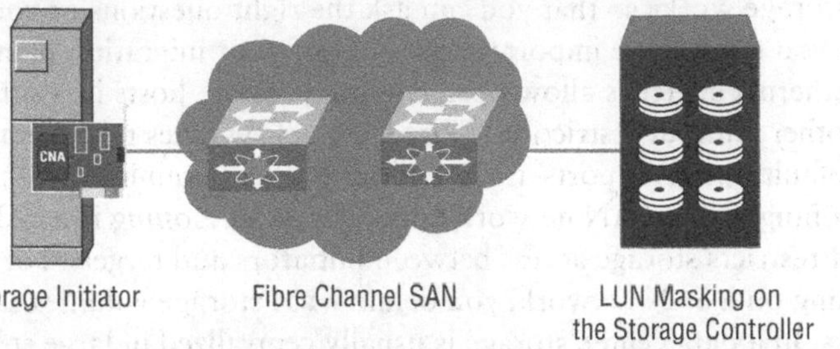

In a data center, a storage array will host a large number of LUNs. It is not secure or desirable to have these LUNs accessible to all servers on the network. With LUN masking, you can restrict the storage resources to the specific servers that require access to them. There are many configuration options, which can include a single server accessing a LUN or a group of servers in a cluster all accessing the same storage resources. The configuration options are important when a server needs to boot off the storage area network and requires exclusive access to a LUN. Another instance is when an application that moves VMs between bare-metal servers needs a less restrictive configuration to allow a number of VMs to access a central storage area.

Hyperconverged Appliances

Hyperconvergence combines server virtualization with the virtual SAN concept. Although centralized storage has historically been the norm in data centers, there has been a recent shift toward consolidating compute and storage. Instead of virtualization hosts being connected to a SAN for centralized storage, they typically contain a large number of drives providing terabytes or more of storage. These servers—often called *hyperconverged appliances*—form a single combination compute and storage cluster that you can manage as a single unit.

Data Loss Prevention

Data loss prevention (DLP) describes using methods to detect and control *how* data is used. Whereas access control methods operate using a binary allow/deny paradigm, DLP takes into consideration other factors, such as the nature or classification of the data, the medium the data is being written to or read from, how much data is being accessed, and even the time of day.

Recall from the last chapter that unsupervised machine learning can be used to detect anomalies. DLP can use similar methods to determine whether there's something suspicious about how data is moving around in your environment. For example, if a user begins copying gigabytes of documents from a file server, DLP may flag that activity as suspicious if it's not something that user normally does. Likewise, DLP can use machine learning to classify data automatically and restrict it accordingly. For example, data that appears to have Social Security numbers will be classified as sensitive and restricted accordingly. DLP may also monitor outbound network traffic to look for things that should never be transmitted, such as credit card numbers.

DLP can also be used to enforce encryption, such as automatically encrypting an external drive whenever it's plugged in. This way, if someone copies sensitive data to the drive, then later loses it in the parking lot, the data won't fall into the wrong hands. You define granular DLP policies to determine exactly how data and devices are classified and protected.

Accessing Your Storage in the Cloud

For hosting services in the cloud that utilize virtual machines, there will be storage volumes created in the cloud and these volumes will be mounted locally as disks on the VMs. Cloud vendors offer remote access to your cloud-based storage that uses special client software that synchronizes files stored on your local device to the cloud and then replicates the files to other devices connected to the same account using services such as Google Drive, Dropbox, and OneDrive. Other offerings such as Amazon S3 use a standard browser. Other common storage access methods include software API calls and CLI access and are specific to the various cloud storage offerings.

Performing a Server Migration

With the cloud being a predominantly virtualized environment, you should understand how to take your existing servers and applications and migrate them to the world of the cloud. In this section, you'll learn about this process.

As previously discussed, to establish the specifications for your VMs, you must know the CPU, memory, storage, and network specs of your existing servers. You also should collect the baseline performance information for these metrics so that you know whether the current specs are sufficient or if you need to bump it up to allow for improved growth or performance. The performance metrics will vary as to what types of applications the servers are running and the time-of-day CPU, disk, or I/O workload increases that may need to be taken into consideration. Once the baseline requirements have been collected, you can use that valuable information to scale and configure the new VM's hardware profile.

When you are migrating to the cloud, some downtime may be required. You can schedule standard data center maintenance windows for the changes to be implemented. It is common to create an implementation document that covers all the required steps to be taken during the change and how to back out those changes if a change goes bad and needs to be restored before the maintenance window closes. The implementation document should also cover in detail all the steps to be taken to validate that the migration is working as expected.

When undertaking a migration project, the implementation team will take into consideration any existing server performance issues and work to mitigate them on the new cloud computing platform. Performance issues can be identified from the collected baseline information and include such areas as CPU, storage, memory, or network bottlenecks. Based on this data, changes can be made during the migration to mitigate issues. When the migration is complete, a prepared testing plan should be followed to validate that the changes made are operating as expected. It can be a detailed and time-consuming process to test and verify all the various components in the new VM. After the migration, you should perform another baseline. The baseline data can be compared with the original information to see whether the new server is performing as expected.

Different Types of Server Migrations

As discussed earlier, you may choose to start fresh in the cloud by provisioning new VMs with a clean OS, installing your applications, and migrating data as necessary. This process is likely to go smoothly and result in fewer problems, but it can be cumbersome and time-consuming. As an alternative, you can migrate your existing machines to the cloud. If you go this route, you'll need to convert your existing machines into a format that is compatible with your cloud service provider. Major cloud service providers offer software to automate much of this process. In this section, we'll cover the different types of data center–to-cloud migrations.

NOTE Most cloud providers offer the ability to install the operating systems directly on a bare-metal server for specialized use cases where your application does not support virtualization.

Physical to Virtual

A *physical-to-virtual (P2V) migration* means taking a non-virtualized physical server that is running an operating system and applications and then migrating it to a VM running on a virtual host (see Figure 2.22). A P2V migration entails copying all the data on the existing server to a virtual disk. The copy mechanism can be done at the block level, where each block of data on each physical drive is copied verbatim to a virtual disk. This yields an exact replica of the original disk. Alternatively, a file-level copy only copies the individual files to an already-formatted virtual disk. Generally, the only time you'll use a file-level copy is if you need to change filesystem formats or if you're moving to a smaller disk size. Many companies offer software utilities, such as VMware vCenter Converter and Microsoft's Virtual Machine Manager, that can perform the conversion. Several third-party software companies and cloud providers offer fully automated P2V utilities.

FIGURE 2.22 Physical-to-virtual migration

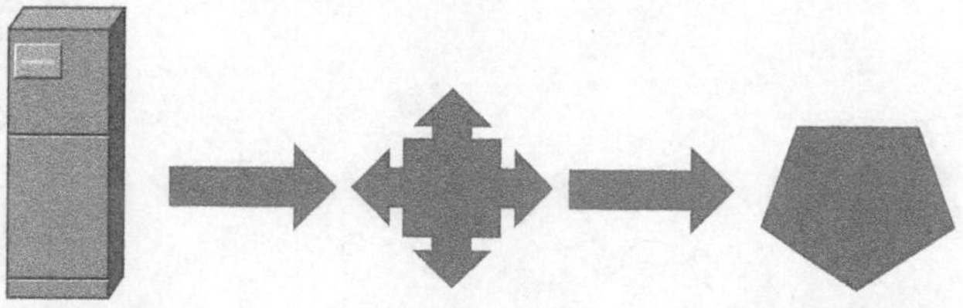

Virtual to Virtual

A *virtual-to-virtual (V2V) migration* is much more straightforward than a P2V migration. Generally, a V2V migration involves taking an existing VM's virtual disk and converting it to a format that's compatible with the cloud provider. You then use that converted image to launch a VM in the cloud, as shown in Figure 2.23.

FIGURE 2.23 Virtual-to-virtual migration

Each hypervisor model and cloud service provider may have unique VM file formats that need to be considered when migrating to the cloud. The disk file formats for the VM that is being imported must be supported by the cloud provider. Common formats include VDI from Oracle, which is VirtualBox's disk image; VMware's VMDK (Virtual Machine Disk); Microsoft's VHD (Virtual Hard Disk); and Amazon's AMI (Amazon Machine Image).

Virtual to Physical

You can perform a *virtual-to-physical (V2P) migration*, converting a virtual server to a physical server, as shown in Figure 2.24, although this technique is not as common. A use case for this type of migration would be if a particular application vendor didn't support running the application in a VM. Virtual-to-physical conversions have lots of details that must be sorted through based on the hardware and virtualization software being used. It may be that a fresh installation of the operating system and application will be required. This type of migration would need to be researched and the options explored based on each migration's unique requirements.

FIGURE 2.24 Virtual-to-physical migration

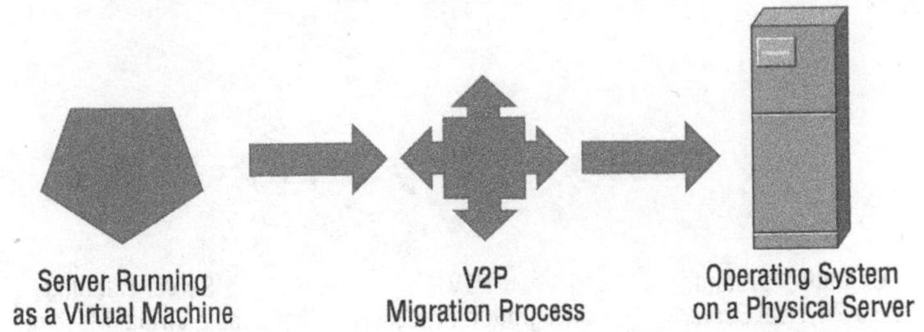

Online or Offline

Online migrations are often preferable to offline migrations because they are performed in a much shorter period of time. One restriction of an online migration is the amount of networking bandwidth that is available between the data center, where the existing server resides, and the cloud data center, where the new VM will be migrated to. If there is insufficient bandwidth to perform the migration in a reasonable amount of time, an *offline migration* should be your backup choice. In an offline migration, the disk images are stored on storage media and shipped to the cloud provider to be installed. Shipping the data on physical media introduces a delay in the migration. In addition, it will take time for the cloud provider to import the images to cloud storage and make them available to you to use in provisioning your new VMs.

Migrating Your Storage Data

Whether you rebuild from scratch in the cloud or use one of the P2V, V2V, or V2P migration methods, chances are that you'll still need to migrate data separately that's sitting on centralized storage, such as a SAN or network-attached storage (NAS) device. In most cases, what you'll actually be migrating are files, so the migration process will entail copying these files over the network to your cloud environment. The cloud service provider will work with you to make the transition to the cloud. This will vary based on the cloud provider's storage offerings and infrastructure (see Figure 2.25).

FIGURE 2.25 Storage migration

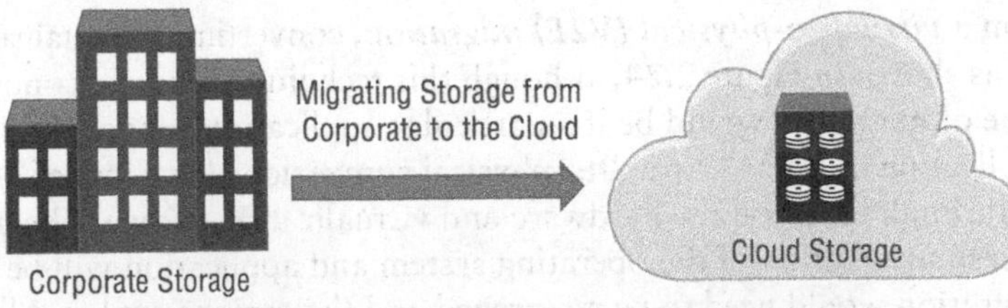

When planning the storage migration, take into account the amount of bandwidth and how long it will take to upload the data to the cloud. For example, if you are accessing the cloud over the Internet with a relatively slow connection, it may not be feasible to upload the data to the cloud. With petabyte-scale storage arrays, it could literally take weeks or months to transfer the data over a network. Many workarounds have been developed, including appliances that can be shipped to the private data center and directly connected to the storage network for a local transfer of stored data. Then the appliance can be shipped to the cloud service provider and the data directly transferred to the cloud storage service. There are options to use these appliances as local data stores in the private data center, with them performing the upload to the cloud as a background process. Each provider has unique offerings to mitigate the delays encountered when transferring such large amounts of data, including shipping container-sized storage systems that are shipped between your data center and the cloud provider.

Addressing Application Portability

Application portability is the ability to move applications from one cloud provider to another without changing the application's architecture. Application portability enables the customer to migrate their applications from one provider to another and avoid a situation where they are locked into a cloud vendor because of dependence on proprietary cloud services. It is important to consider portability as part of your migration plans to enable you to move operations to another provider if there is a breach in the service level agreement; extended outages; or geographical, regulatory, or pricing issues that arise.

To understand application portability, you need to know the difference between traditional and cloud-native applications. Traditional applications are written to use the capabilities of your run-of-the-mill Linux or Windows servers. Traditional applications are a good fit for the IaaS service model, since they just require the analogs of your basic data center resources: compute, storage, and networking. Traditional applications are the easiest to move from one cloud provider to another. The biggest issue that you're likely to face porting your traditional applications is having to perform V2V conversions or rebuilding new VMs from scratch.

Cloud-native applications, on the other hand, are written to make use of proprietary services that are only offered on a specific cloud platform. You can easily identify such services; they tend to carry the "managed" or "elastic" designations. Object storage and managed relational and nonrelational databases are some common examples. Cloud-native applications are the most difficult to migrate between cloud providers because they require rearchitecting the application, which may even include changing its source code! For example, if your application will use a managed database service, moving to another cloud provider will require changing database connection strings. Or, if your app will use the cloud provider's object storage service, it will likely do so using the provider's proprietary API or SDK. Moving to a new provider, then, will require reworking the application to use that new provider's tools to access their object storage service.

Workload Migration Common Procedures

Workload migrations require extensive planning and preparation prior to the move. Applications that are selected as candidates to run in a cloud-based infrastructure should be tested and evaluated for interoperability. It is desirable to set up a test environment to validate that the application is working as expected before moving the application into production mode. When performing validations, check for performance, service levels/uptime, serviceability, compliance, and security, and be sure to evaluate any trade-offs from hosting internally in your private data center or in the cloud.

Migrations should be performed under the guidance of a project manager and as a collaborative effort of all interested groups in your organization. Current best practices should be followed to ensure a smooth transition.

Examining Infrastructure Capable of Supporting a Migration

In this section, you'll learn about the underlying infrastructure and potential issues that should be examined and mitigated prior to the migration. For example, it is important to investigate the delays of transferring data, the downtime needed, any regulatory or legal concerns that may need to be addressed, and a good time to schedule the migration.

Available Network Capacity

As you learned earlier in the chapter when I discussed whether to perform your migration offline or online, the amount of network bandwidth may be a limiting factor. If you have a large amount to data to transfer and limited network capacity to the cloud, there may be an excessive time window required to perform the migration. This may require you to add Internet bandwidth before the migration or consider an offline migration.

As part of the planning process for your migration, the project team must determine the amount of data that needs to be transferred to the cloud and calculate the time needed when using an online migration with existing network capacity.

Downtime During the Migration

It is a given that there will be a certain amount of downtime to perform a migration. Reducing the amount of downtime during a migration is one reason to build out your cloud infrastructure from scratch rather than trying to migrate VMs using one of the earlier discussed methods. This allows you to prototype your cloud deployment to smoke out and resolve unforeseen issues before the migration.

It is important to plan for the unexpected and to allocate additional downtime as a buffer in case the migration does not go as expected. Plan for the time required to roll back to the original pre-migration state in case the cutover is not successful.

Selecting a time window to migrate workloads will be dependent on your organization's local policies and requirements. It is logical that the migration window should be performed during times that there is an anticipated light workload where downtime would have a limited impact on your operations.

Legal Questions About Migrating to the Cloud

Any legal issues, such as legal compliance requirements, must be fully investigated prior to the migration taking place. In fact, this should be an integral part of the project management team's pre-migration planning process. Any legal or compliance requirements must be included in the initial design phase of the project in order to ensure that the cloud architecture meets all legal restrictions.

Local Time Zones and Follow-the-Sun Migration Constraints

Care should be taken when performing migrations across multiple time zones to prevent any more additional downtime impact than is necessary. Take into account the local times of the data centers into which you are migrating servers and make sure that the migration takes place during periods of low usage in those local times. For instance, if you are working in Europe performing migrations in Asia, make sure that you are not impacting Asian operations in the middle of their production hours. All time zone constraints should be identified and managed as part of your migration plan.

A common support model for not only cloud computing, but also for all information technology disciplines, is the *follow-the-sun support model*. This is where a support operation is active in the part of the world that is traditionally open for business. For example, a global operation will have multiple worldwide support centers that are open and cloud-based centered around the time of day. A site in one time zone closes and hands-off operations at the end of the work shift to the next site to the west that picks up operations.

Managing User Identities and Roles

You need to protect access to your cloud resources from unauthorized access, but you also don't want to lock everything down so hard that legitimate users run into difficulty. User access control requires striking a fine balance between security and usability. User access control consists of two elements. The first element is *authentication*—that is, identifying yourself and somehow proving that you are who you claim to be. The second element is *authorization*—that is, determining what the user is permitted to do once authenticated. The access rights assigned to a user define what they are allowed to do.

In this section, you'll learn about granting rights based on an administrative user's role on the network. Then you'll learn about the differences between mandatory and discretionary access controls. To add security, you must use several steps to log into a network; this is referred to as *multifactor authentication*, which will also be covered. Finally, you'll learn about the concept of federations.

RBAC: Identifying Users and What Their Roles Are

Role-based access control (RBAC) is a method in which access rights are granted to, or restricted from, users based on which roles they perform in an organization. A *role* is essentially a collection of permissions that define what activity is allowed or denied and against what resources. For example, a role may contain a permission that allows creating a new VM but does not allow deleting one. As another example, database administrators can be given full access to manage a database application but be restricted from performing VM or storage operations. Once the roles are defined, users are then assigned to the roles. Based on the permissions of the roles, the users will inherit those rights.

There aren't any hard-and-fast rules around how you define your roles, but it's common for them to be based on job duties. For example, there may be one role for developers, another for network administrators, and another for human resources. Some examples are shown in Table 2.2; these are just examples, and you may have a long list of roles based on your organization's needs.

TABLE 2.2 Role-based access control

Organizational role	Role description
Administrator	The administrative account that has full control over the cloud environment
Guest	Usually given limited rights such as read-only access. May be used for allowing public access to resources without authentication
Auditor	Rights granted for auditing purposes, such as resources consumed, license usage, or access to corporate compliance data
Sustaining/patch management	Rights are granted to allow members of this group to access the systems for the purpose of upgrades and software patch management.
Storage administrator	Group rights are assigned here for the storage management role in monitoring and maintaining the cloud-based storage.

The scope of role-based administration should be broad enough to cover all systems that the user must access to perform their assigned tasks, but not too broad as to grant access to systems that the users in the role may not need to access.

Roles aren't just for people. You can define roles for applications to grant them programmatic access to cloud resources. For example, VMs running an image processing application could be placed into a role that grants access to a bucket in the cloud provider's object storage service.

What Happens When You Authenticate?

Authentication is the process of identifying a user and confirming that they're who they claim to be. By authenticating the user, you learn the identity of that user and can then grant permissions to cloud resources based on the user's permissions.

User authentication usually consists of a username and password combination or some variation of that, such as a token or biometric access method. Cookies can be used for web access to identify and authenticate a user connecting to your website. For example, a visitor to your e-commerce site may be prompted initially for a username and password through their browser. Once authentication is completed, a cookie is stored in the user's browser with an identity token that will subsequently be used to identify them. Applications may also need to authenticate with cloud services. This is typically done by using the cloud provider's API and authenticating with a security token that's attached to a role granting the appropriate access.

Understanding Federation

Federation allows you to use a third-party identity management system to authenticate to your cloud resources. A common example of this is using Microsoft's Active Directory for access to both corporate and cloud resources. Federation can ease your migration to the cloud because users who already have a corporate login don't have to be assigned separate credentials to access cloud resources.

The federated approach is based on industry standards such as the Security Assertion Markup Language (SAML) that allow for the needed interoperability between different organizations' systems. The approach is common in cloud-based e-commerce sites. You log into the site with your web browser, and the cloud application may be in a federation with banks and payment systems. Using the federated approach, you'll not be required to log into each system to shop, check out, arrange shipping, and purchase warranties since all these elements are integrated.

Single Sign-On Systems

Single sign-on (SSO) is an approach that reduces the need to sign into multiple systems for access. SSO allows a user to log in just one time and be granted access rights to multiple systems. Using SSO, you can centralize authentication of multiple systems into just one area, easing user administration significantly.

For example, a web server administrator may need to manage multiple web servers in the cloud simultaneously. Since all these web servers are under the administrator's control, you can create an SSO group called "web administrators," and when they log into the servers, they are granted access to all servers in the group without having to log into each one individually.

Directory servers using the Lightweight Directory Access Protocol (LDAP) are an example of SSO systems. You log into the directory services one time, and based on your rights, you are allowed to access systems on the network without any additional login requirements.

Single sign-on eliminates the need to remember multiple username and password combinations and saves the time of having to enter your authentication information over and over as you log into different systems. SSO is also effective when terminating a session. When you log off, the directory services will log out, or disconnect you from the multiple systems you had accessed.

Understanding Infrastructure Services

Networking services are applications that fall under the realm of networking and include the management of IP addressing, load balancing, network security devices such as firewalls, intrusion and prevention systems, security services, and DNS services.

Domain Name System

To resolve a name to an IP address that the IP protocol uses to connect to a remote device, the server or workstation will perform a DNS server lookup. The DNS server will have the domain name to IP address mapping and reply with the correct IP address for any given domain name. Think of this as a phone book where you know the name of a business but not the number; the phone book provides the name-to-number lookup function. DNS uses well-known TCP and UDP port 53.

Because DNS is insecure by default, it's prone to man-in-the-middle attacks that allow an attacker to intercept a DNS query and return a forged response, perhaps an IP address pointing to a website containing infectious malware. DNS Security Extensions (DNSSEC) add authentication and data integrity checks to prevent such attacks. Although DNSSEC does not prove encryption—anyone intercepting your traffic can still see your queries—it does offer data integrity by detecting whether the query or response has been changed in transit. Another security feature that was added to DNS is DNS over HTTPS (DoH), which provides authentication, data integrity, *and* encryption.

Dynamic Host Configuration Protocol

The *Dynamic Host Configuration Protocol (DHCP)* allows for automatic assignment of IP addressing information to clients on a network. This eliminates the need to statically configure addressing information when you connect to a network. In addition to providing an IP address to a device, DHCP can provide default gateway information, DNS information, and more. DHCP clients listen on UDP port 68.

Certificate Services

Most cloud providers offer their customers the ability to outsource the creation, management, and deployment of *Transport Layer Security (TLS)* digital security certificates that are used for authenticating websites and encrypting traffic between the website and the client. You can usually import a TLS certificate from a third party into the cloud provider's certificate management service. You can also have the provider's certificate service function as a *certification authority (CA)* that issues new certificates that you can then use with other cloud services such as load balancers and *content distribution networks (CDNs)*. TLS certificates have an expiration date by design. Because the certificate service fully manages the life cycle of the certificate they issue, it can automatically renew the certificate before it expires.

Load Balancing

When a single server isn't enough to handle the workload you throw at it, you need a way to distribute the workload across more servers. *Load balancing* addresses this issue by distributing incoming connections to target servers. Load-balancer functions can also alleviate load on the servers in other ways, such as offloading encryption, compression, and TCP handshakes. With load balancing, you can configure the cloud for many servers working together and sharing the load. Therefore, redundancy and scalability can be achieved, as shown in Figure 2.26.

FIGURE 2.26 Load-balancing web servers

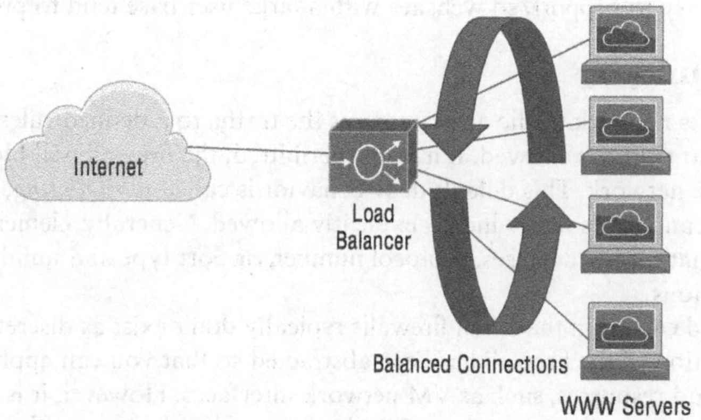

A load balancer is commonly found in front of web servers. The domain name that users use to reach the website resolves to an IP address, but it's not the address of any of the servers hosting the website. Instead, it's the IP address of an interface on the load balancer. The load balancer allocates the traffic by distributing the connections to one of many servers connected to it. Load balancing allows a website to scale by allocating many servers in the cloud to handle the workload. Also, a load balancer can check the health of each server and stop routing connections to it if there's a problem with that particular server.

Multifactor Authentication

Multifactor authentication (MFA) adds an additional layer of authentication by adding token-based systems in addition to the traditional username and password authentication model. MFA works by requiring you to provide two or more of the following in order to authenticate:

- Something you have
- Something you know
- Something you are

For example, when you go to the bank down the street to use the ATM, to authenticate you'll need to possess the ATM card (something you have) and enter a PIN (something you know) to withdraw money. Other MFA examples include presenting your ID and fingerprints to gain access to a secure data center.

When applied to information systems, MFA typically requires you to provide a one-time token, which is a string that changes at regular intervals. The string might be numeric or alphanumeric. To make the string hard to guess, it's nonsequential and usually consists of four or more characters. The token has a short life span and must be entered into your regular login as you authenticate.

Where you get the one-time token depends on the system. Many cloud providers let you use a physical key fob or virtual MFA smartphone app that can provide the code. This is pretty secure, but if you lose your phone or key fob, you're locked out of your account and have to contact the cloud provider to recover access.

For more lax security requirements, you might be able to obtain a one-time token via email or a text message. These latter methods are more prone to compromise, but they're convenient and easy to support, so websites with a large user base tend to prefer them.

Firewall Security

A *firewall* inspects network traffic and compares the traffic to a defined rules list to determine whether that traffic is allowed. If it is not permitted, the firewall will block the traffic from entering the network. This default deny behavior is called *whitelisting*, because the only traffic that can pass is that which is explicitly allowed. Generally, elements such as source and destination IP addresses, protocol number, or port type and number are used to make these decisions.

As you learned earlier, in the cloud firewalls typically don't exist as discrete devices. Instead, the function of the firewall has been abstracted so that you can apply firewall rules to individual cloud resources, such as VM network interfaces. However, it is possible to provision a virtual firewall appliance as a VM in the cloud and force traffic to pass through it to reach your cloud resources. In this way, you can have a firewall sitting at the edge of your cloud network. A benefit of this arrangement is that the firewall is in a position to log information about every packet that ingresses or egresses your cloud network. Also, you can configure your firewall to provide secure, encrypted access via a VPN. In a hybrid cloud environment, you may even integrate your cloud-based firewall appliance with your on-premises firewall management platform to make management and monitoring of your entire network easier. Standard firewall deployments are shown in Figure 2.27 and Figure 2.28.

FIGURE 2.27 Network firewall for security

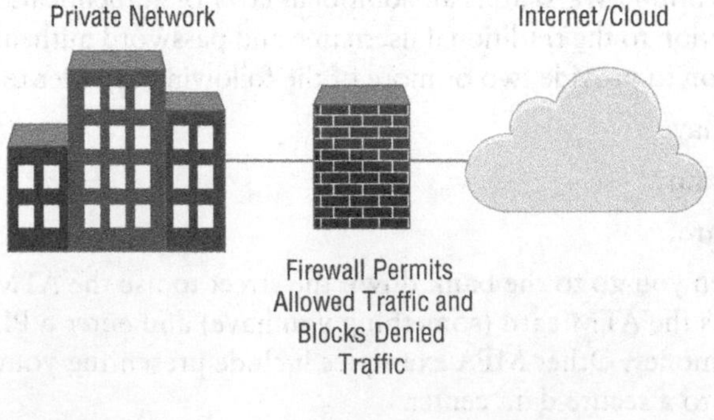

FIGURE 2.28 Firewalls define what traffic is allowed in and out of the network.

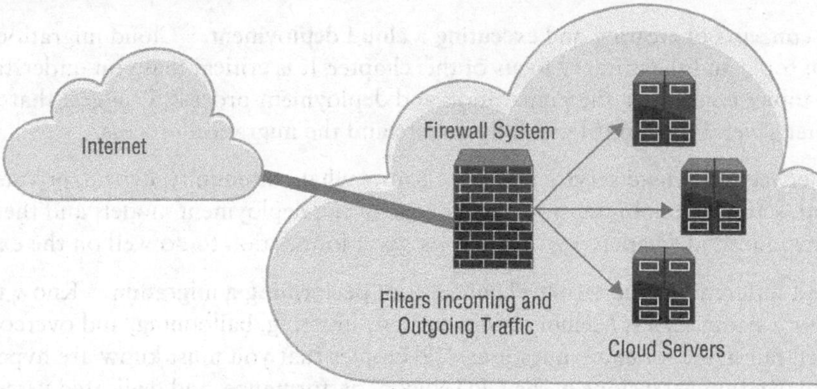

Summary

In this chapter, you learned about the concepts, practices, and technologies involved in deploying and migrating to the cloud. The chapter covered a lot of topics, including how to analyze and prepare for a migration and then how to execute the deployment plan.

To prepare for the migration, you should fully understand the basic cloud models of community, hybrid, private, and public. These are key concepts in cloud computing.

Other core migration topics include understanding the cloud networking infrastructure, including ports and protocols, VPNs, IDS/IPS, DMZs, and basic IP addressing using public and private IP addresses.

The chapter described how to size the virtualized resources such as CPU and memory for your VM servers with discussions of bursting, ballooning, and overcommitments. You learned about CPU designs and how hyperthreading is implemented in the virtualized cloud servers. High availability was discussed and will be explored in greater detail later in this book.

Storage is a key component in the cloud, and you learned about many storage different topics such as availability, replication, mirroring, and cloning. The chapter then discussed storage tiers and redundancy levels, including the RAID types. I detailed the primary storage types that include network-attached, direct-attached, and storage area networks. Then you learned that there are two types of storage provisioning used in the cloud: thick and thin.

To perform a migration, you must prepare your servers by doing any necessary migration conversions. Depending on your needs, a migration may be P2V, V2V, or V2P. Next, I talked about virtualization formats, application and data portability, and the potential issues of performing a migration either online or offline.

The different types of authentication and authorization included federations, single sign-on, multifactor, and directory services. Finally, we covered deploying networking services, which is important to understand not only for the exam but for your work in cloud computing.

Exam Essentials

Know the key concepts of creating and executing a cloud deployment. Cloud migrations are a key exam topic and the primary focus of this chapter. It is critical that you understand all the project topics concerning the preparation and deployment process. I suggest that you read this chapter several times until you fully understand the migration process.

Differentiate between the cloud service models. Know what community, hybrid, private, and public clouds are. By combining your knowledge of the deployment models and the service models introduced in Chapter 1, you'll have a good foundation to do well on the exam.

Understand and differentiate the technical concepts of performing a migration. Know the CPU and memory sizing topics. Memory topics such as bursting, ballooning, and overcommitments are all fair game for exam questions. CPU topics that you must know are hyperthreading, virtualization extensions in the CPU silicon, performance, and dedicated versus shared hardware resources.

Explain the storage technologies used in cloud computing. Storage plays an important role in running your operations in the cloud, and you learned about the various types of storage, redundancy, provisioning models, security, availability, and redundancy. Storage is a key exam topic.

Identify and be able to describe how to perform workload migrations. Know what V2V, P2V, and V2P migrations are and when you may need to perform each one. Understand the issues involved with storage migrations as well as how to determine whether an online or offline migration will be required.

Explain the different types of user and machine authentication and authorization techniques. Be able to identify and explain the different types of authentication. These include local, federated, directory servers, SSO, and MFA. Be able to select the best authentication method for a given set of requirements.

Explain the network services used in cloud computing. Core network services in the cloud include DNS, DHCP, TLS certificates, load balancers, firewalls, and IDS/IPS. These are all critical components for any cloud deployment model and application. Read this section over several times until you fully understand the basics of each technology and be able to identify when, where, and why each is used in the cloud network.

Written Lab

Fill in the blanks for the questions provided in the written lab. You can find the answers to the written labs in Appendix B.

1. A hypervisor function that allows the virtualization host to reclaim unused memory from a VM running on top of the hypervisor and to allocate that memory for other uses is referred to as ___________________.
2. A(n) ___________________ is very high-speed, highly redundant, and completely dedicated to interconnecting storage devices.
3. ___________________ refers to a system that will remain operational even after there has been a degradation of its systems. Such a system can maintain functionality because of its highly resilient design that takes into account the possibility of system failures and works to mitigate or work around any failures to maintain operations.
4. ___________________ copies the data to the primary storage system and simultaneously over the network to remote sites, and it ensures that all replicas are up-to-date and in sync with each other.
5. To move your VMs to the cloud, you may need to perform a(n) ___________________ migration.
6. ___________________ is the ability to move applications from one cloud provider to another without having to change the application code or architecture.
7. ___________________ allow multiple organizations to use the same credentials for authentication.
8. A(n) ___________________ offers performance enhancements, scalability, and encryption termination services for public web servers.
9. Taking sample performance metrics that need to be collected as part of the documentation process is referred to as creating a(n) ___________________.
10. The ___________________ monitors network traffic for malicious activity and actively attempts to prevent the attack.

Review Questions

The following questions are designed to test your understanding of this chapter's material. You can find the answers in Appendix A. For more information on how to obtain additional questions, please see this book's Introduction.

1. Carl is documenting his employer's cloud deployments and needs to label the cloud delivery model used by his single organization. As a Cloud+ consultant, what would you suggest he name his internal cloud?
   - A. Hybrid
   - B. Public
   - C. Private
   - D. Community
2. A national tax preparation firm is accessing industry-specific productivity applications in the cloud; many other tax preparation companies are also subscribing to the same service. What model of cloud are they accessing?
   - A. Hybrid
   - B. Public
   - C. Private
   - D. Community
3. Mary is a Cloud+ certified security consultant for her company. She is researching enhanced security access systems. What could she suggest that requires something you have and something you know?
   - A. Single sign-on
   - B. Confederations
   - C. Active Directory/LDAP
   - D. Multifactor
4. Pete is concerned about stored data that is replicated to a standby zone but not immediately. The delay means that there is going to be a short period of time where the data is not consistent. What storage replication service ensures eventual consistency?
   - A. Synchronous
   - B. Asynchronous
   - C. Block
   - D. Tier 1
   - E. File-based
   - F. RAID 6

5. Scott is planning his company's upload of stored data to the cloud. What are two common storage migration types? (Choose two.)

   A. Physical to virtual

   B. Block to object

   C. Online

   D. Offline

   E. Synchronous

   F. Asynchronous

6. Judy is migrating a Linux OS from running on a dual-slot, eight-core server in a private cloud to a VM in the public cloud. What type of migration would she perform?

   A. vMotion

   B. P2V

   C. Private to public

   D. V2V

   E. Synchronous replication

7. Christina has been asked by the firewall administration group to identify secure network protocols that can be used to prevent network analyzers from being able to read data in flight. Which of the following are considered secure network protocols that she recommends using? (Choose three.)

   A. SHHTP

   B. DHCP

   C. HTTPS

   D. DNS

   E. SSH

   F. SMTP

   G. FTPS

8. What technique makes it difficult for malicious hackers or hijackers to use or understand stolen data?

   A. PKI

   B. Obfuscation

   C. Cipher

   D. Symmetrical

9. Jerri is learning about cloud storage systems. She is interested in learning about high-speed network storage solutions. What would you recommend she focus her research on?

   A. Block access

   B. Zoning

   C. VMFS

   D. SAN

10. What is the process of determining the identity of a client usually by a login process?
   A. Authorization
   B. Accounting
   C. Authentication
   D. Federation
   E. Identity access

11. What are common management interfaces that are used to migrate and manage cloud-based resources? (Choose three.)
   A. Web console
   B. SNMP
   C. API
   D. PaaS
   E. CLI

12. VMs running on a hypervisor consume which of the following resources? (Choose three.)
   A. Bare-metal cores
   B. Virtual RAM
   C. SaaS
   D. Virtual CPUs
   E. RAID
   F. Memory pools

13. What system was developed to address the different types of storage needs a cloud consumer may require for availability, response times, backups, and economics?
   A. RAID
   B. Multipathing
   C. Tiering
   D. Policies

14. Terri is planning on implementing physical disk redundancy on her SQL database in the public cloud. She is creating specifications for her virtual machine image that will become the template for the database servers. What type of disk redundancy options could she implement to meet the needs of a SQL deployment?
   A. Multipathing
   B. RAID
   C. Masking
   D. Tiering

15. Which storage type stripes file data and performs a parity check of data over multiple disks that can recover from a hard disk failure?
    A. RAID 0
    B. RAID 1
    C. RAID 1+0
    D. RAID 5

16. Jill is reviewing a document from her secondary community cloud provider. What is the document that outlines specific metrics and the minimum performance that is offered by the cloud provider?
    A. SSL
    B. SLA
    C. Benchmark
    D. Baseline

17. Storage area networks support which type of storage? (Choose the best answer.)
    A. Meta
    B. Object
    C. Block
    D. File

18. What identity system gives multiple discrete organizations access to your NoSQL community cloud database via your cloud-based application server?
    A. Single sign-on
    B. Federations
    C. LDAP
    D. Authorization manager

19. When performing a migration from your on-site private cloud to a new community cloud data center, which of the following are project management pre-migrations action items? (Choose two.)
    A. RAID array durability rating
    B. VM file format
    C. Benchmark compatibility
    D. Online migration bandwidth

20. What systems monitor the network and report security issues?
    A. CloudShield
    B. Intrusion prevention system
    C. Firewall
    D. Intrusion detection system

Chapter

3

Security in the Cloud

THE FOLLOWING COMPTIA CLOUD+ EXAM OBJECTIVES ARE COVERED IN THIS CHAPTER:

✓ **2.1 Given a scenario, configure identity and access management.**

- Identification and authorization
  - Privileged access management
  - Logical access management
  - Account life-cycle management
    - Provision and deprovision accounts
  - Access controls
    - Role-based
    - Discretionary
    - Non-discretionary
    - Mandatory
- Certificate management
- Multifactor authentication (MFA)
- Single sign-on (SSO)
- Public key infrastructure (PKI)
- Secret management
- Key management

✓ **2.2 Given a scenario, secure a network in a cloud environment.**

- Protocols
- Encryption
  - IPsec
  - Transport Layer Security (TLS)
  - Hypertext Transfer Protocol Secure (HTTPS)

- Tunneling
    - Secure Shell (SSH)
    - Layer 2 tunneling protocol (L2TP)/Point-to-point tunneling protocol (PPTP)
    - Generic routing encapsulation (GRE)
- Log and event monitoring
- Network flows
- Hardening and configuration changes
    - Disabling unnecessary ports and services
    - Disabling weak protocols and ciphers
    - Firmware upgrades
    - Control ingress and egress traffic
        - Whitelisting or blacklisting
        - Proxy servers
    - Distributed denial-of-service (DDoS) protection

✓ **2.3 Given a scenario, apply the appropriate OS and application security controls.**

- Hardened baselines
    - Single function
- File integrity
- Log and event monitoring
- Mandatory access control
- Software firewall

✓ **2.4 Given a scenario, apply data security and compliance controls in cloud environments.**

- Access control
- Impact of laws and regulations
    - Legal hold

✓ **2.5 Given a scenario, implement measures to meet security requirements.**

- Tools

- Vulnerability scanners
- Port scanners

- Vulnerability assessment
  - Default and common credential scans
  - Credentialed scans
  - Network-based scans
  - Agent-based scans
  - Service availabilities
- Security patches
  - Hot fixes
  - Scheduled updates
  - Virtual patches
  - Signature updates
  - Rollups
- Risk register
- Prioritization of patch application
- Deactivate default accounts
- Impacts of security tools on systems and services
- Effects of cloud service models on security implementation

Although it's easy to pay lip service to making your systems as secure as possible, the fact is that security comes at a price. Convenience, speed, and money are the cost of security, and the better the security, the more you can expect to spend on all three. As such, the organization has to balance security against its other needs. You must be keenly aware of where these exchange points exist and how a particular security measure may affect other systems and operations. That's what this chapter is all about.

In this chapter, you will learn about cloud providers' security efforts in obtaining and maintaining compliance with many government and industry compliance initiatives. Also, you will learn about many of the security components, concepts, and configurations that are implemented by the cloud provider and the customer.

Security topics such as compliance, encryption technologies, and security configuration systems and methods will be covered. This chapter will also discuss protecting resources and access.

Cloud Security Compliance and Configurations

Cloud providers implement particular security controls and services to facilitate compliance with various industry and government regulatory guidelines. Proving compliance allows a cloud service provider to offer solutions specific to regulated industries such as finance, government, and healthcare, as well as to allow its customers to achieve compliance. Regardless of the jurisdiction under which your organization falls, there's a good chance that it will be able to operate in the cloud while remaining in compliance with its regulatory obligations.

To be able to contract and do business with a number of regulated entities, the cloud provider must be able to obtain and maintain many different regulatory compliance accreditations. Without meeting these regulatory requirements, the cloud provider would not be able to provide services for regulated companies that must follow strict requirements regarding their information technology resources. For example, an organization that deals with protected health information may have to prove that it's securely storing and controlling access to medical records. If the organization wants to migrate this information to the cloud, the requirement thus extends to the cloud provider as well. It's therefore in the cloud provider's financial interest to meet or exceed those requirements.

The cloud service providers may elect to obtain certifications to win additional business. For example, if they want to host processing of medical records in the United States, they will need to show that they are compliant with the *Health Insurance Portability and Accountability Act (HIPAA)*. The cloud provider must meet HIPAA compliance to be able to host applications and store records that fall under the HIPAA regulations.

As another example, if your company plans to offer payment card processing, it may need to meet the *Payment Card Industry Data Security Standard (PCI DSS)* to provide for data security and integrity. If the cloud infrastructure does not meet PCI DSS standards, it will not be able to participate in that marketplace.

To meet governance and regulatory compliance in the public cloud, the provider must go through audits to prove compliance, and extensive records must be created and retained. *Logging* is the generation of transaction records detailing the events that occur with or against resources. For example, any time a user reads a file, a log can be generated recording the time of access, username, source IP address, and so on. Logs are usually stored in case there's a need for later evaluation. In addition, changes made to the system must be recorded, and all of the required steps to maintain compliance must be retained. It is important to protect your log data by placing the log files in secure, encrypted storage that's backed up. Each regulatory requirement will specify a detailed listing of what logs are required to be collected to meet compliance standards. Often there is a compliance audit process to determine whether your deployment meets all requirements. Depending on the industry and the applicable laws, you may be able to go live with a deployment even if you're out of compliance, as long as you have a plan to address the shortcomings.

Cloud companies offer many utilities and tools to aid in meeting these compliance requirements. Cloud-based monitoring can make it easy to collect performance metrics and logs and track configuration changes. For example, a cloud provider can store application access log files and deliver those logs to analytic applications that search the logs for concerning activity. There are many third-party tools and offerings on the market to enhance and outsource your security and regulatory compliance requirements.

As another example, log data can be visualized in a dashboard for a constantly updated real-time visual display of your operations. This information can also be stored in a database, and specialized applications can monitor and report compliance metrics.

Cloud providers make it possible to log configuration changes made on your systems with user and date timestamps that record specifically what configuration changes were made to each resource. These logging facilities record what was changed and how it was changed. For example, if a user deleted an elastic storage volume, the log entry would record the resource affected, the action, the identity that performed it, and a timestamp. You can usually configure the particulars of what is logged so that you get only those events in which you're interested. Logging facilities can usually be configured, which means you can choose whether to log successful or failed attempts to perform some action.

Establishing Your Company's Security Policies

Even though your cloud provider will have extensive security policies and procedures in place, ultimately you are responsible for your data and cloud operations. A *security policy* is a document that defines your company's cloud controls, organizational policies, responsibilities, and underlying technologies to secure your cloud deployment. A related document called a *risk register* tracks the probability and impact of various security risks. What the risk register looks like depends on the particular risks you're concerned about. In the context of information security, some of the more significant risks are regarding unauthorized access, loss of availability, and financial impacts. By ranking risks on a grid according to likelihood and impact, you can visually identify the most significant risks and prioritize accordingly. It goes without saying that the risk register should inform your security policy.

Security policies can touch on topics such as account credentials, authentication, authorization, and logging. A security policy might outline the need to encrypt the data in flight and at rest, and it defines minimum requirements regarding the type of encryption. But a comprehensive information security policy should include input from all parts of the organization, not just the IT department. The policy should be developed with a view toward preventing breaches, but it should also detail the steps to mitigate and respond to breaches should they occur.

Selecting and Applying the Security Policies to Your Cloud Operations

After the security policy has been approved by your company, it's time to adopt the requirements outlined in the policy. All policies must be converted to actual configurations and applied to the devices and services running on your cloud fleet. For example, when addressing identity requirements, it is possible that the corporate security policy may require strong passwords over a certain length, use of special characters, and forced password changes. The usual change request process will be followed to implement and test these types of changes. Staying consistent with the security policy is an ongoing effort that will encompass a large number of devices, including workstations, networking equipment, storage systems, operating systems, and software configurations. The complete list will depend on each organization's needs and requirements. It's important to keep your security policies up-to-date to address to the ever-changing security threat landscape.

Some Common Regulatory Requirements

Cloud providers go to great efforts to become compliant with a large number of industry and governmental compliance requirements in order to attain certifications or recommendations to help them solicit business from companies and government agencies that must meet one or more of these requirements. Although they are extensive and vary by jurisdiction around the world, here you will see an overview of some of the most common regulatory requirements in the U.S. marketplace. If you are in a different market, you can check with your local regulatory requirements, which may be similar. The following list is an example of some of the many governmental and industry regulatory requirements:

- A *Service Organization Controls 1 (SOC 1)* report, also known as ISAE 3402 and formerly known as SSAE 16, outlines the internal controls of financial reporting operations. For example, a cloud provider would meet the requirements if it has outlined in detail its operational financial reporting procedures in compliance with the steps in SOC 1. Customers such as medical claims processing, payroll processing, or loan servicing companies may require SOC 1 compliance from their service providers.
- A *Service Organization Controls 2 (SOC 2)* report concerns a business's nonfinancial reporting controls for the availability, confidentiality, privacy, processing integrity, and security of a system. Given the history of IT security breaches, SOC 2 fills the need for information on the security controls behind financial transactions.
- A *Service Organization Controls 3 (SOC 3)* report is for the public disclosure of financial controls and security reporting. Because the SOC 2 report can contain sensitive and technical information, the SOC 3 report was created to offer a diluted, marketing-oriented, or nontechnical summary of the SOC 2 report.
- The *Federal Information Security Management Act (FISMA)* is a U.S. federal law that outlines the framework to protect federal government information, operations, and facilities. FISMA is a comprehensive outline for data security and is offered by cloud companies hosting U.S. government processing in their data centers.
- The *Federal Risk and Authorization Management Program (FedRAMP)* is a U.S. federal program that outlines the standards for security assessments, authorization, and continuous monitoring for cloud products and services. For a cloud provider to host federal government systems, they will need to be FedRAMP compliant.
- The *Department of Defense Information Assurance Certification and Accreditation Process (DIACAP)* is the process for computer systems' IT compliance. DIACAP compliance is required to be certified to meet the U.S. Department of Defense security requirements for contractors. DoD outsources commercial interconnections to the DoD and other systems. Cloud providers doing business with or connecting to the U.S. Department of Defense need to comply with the DIACAP requirements.
- The *Payment Card Industry Data Security Standard (PCI DSS)* sets the requirements to guarantee that companies that process, store, or transmit credit card information offer secure processing and handling of credit card data. PCI requirements are important for companies that store, process, and transmit credit card information or connect to third-party credit-processing companies. Cloud companies may be PCI DSS compliant, but as the cloud customer you must also meet the requirements, and you will have to undergo a PCI audit for compliance.
- *ISO 27001* ensures that the cloud provider meets all regulatory and statutory requirements for its product and service offerings. ISO refers to the International Organization for Standardization. ISO 27001 includes the seven quality management principles upon which the ISO 9001 certification is based. This standard is an extension of a cloud

provider's existing quality management certifications from the ISO and demonstrates confidence, credibility, satisfaction, and trust between the cloud company and its customers, providers, stakeholders, and the general community.

- The *International Traffic in Arms Regulations (ITAR)* are U.S. government regulations that affect the technology industry. ITAR restricts the dissemination of information to certain foreign entities that could assist in the import or export of arms. ITAR has a list of data security requirements that cloud companies can certify as being compliant with to meet these regulations.
- *FIPS 140-2* is a National Institute of Standards and Technology (NIST) publication that coordinates the requirements and standards for cryptographic systems that can be implemented in hardware or software. Systems that meet FIPS-140-2 can be approved for U.S. government use.
- The *Motion Picture Society of America (MPAA)* has published a set of best practices for storing, processing, and delivering protected media and content securely over the Internet. MPAA is not a certification, but it provides guidance and recommendations on best practices to assess risk and the security of protected content. Cloud providers can align their offerings to the MPAA guidance for the processing of MPAA-protected media.
- The *Health Insurance Portability and Accountability Act (HIPAA)* defines standards for protecting personal health information including medical records. Companies that work with protected health information must ensure that all of the required physical, network, and process security measures are in place and followed to meet HIPAA compliance requirements.

Protecting Your Data

Your data is your responsibility, meaning that your company must take the steps necessary to protect it in your private data center as well as in the cloud. Cloud companies offer an extensive array of facilities to protect your data, including off-site replication and resilient storage technologies that provide impressive durability and availability. Data in the cloud can be stored in different tiers that offer different levels of protection at different cost levels.

Most cloud providers offer the option of encrypting your data both in flight and at rest. You may have the option of using their encryption key management offerings, or you can use your own if desired or required for compliance purposes.

Most cloud providers give you the option to replicate your data to different regions, so you always have a backup that's geographically distant from the source. Also, you can choose to restrict data to particular regions to satisfy regulations that may prohibit data from crossing a particular geopolitical boundary.

Performing Compliance Audits

I cannot stress this enough: you own your data and your operations. You are renting infrastructure, storage, and compute services from the cloud provider. However, ultimately, they are not responsible for what happens to your data—you are. They can offer the most secure platform in the world, but if you spin up public-facing servers with connections to sensitive data stores and do not implement any, or implement incorrect, security configurations, you will probably get hacked. You must secure your cloud operations on top of what the cloud provider is already doing for you. They will let you know what they have secured and where your responsibility lies. Many providers even offer security audits of your configurations and will make suggestions for remediating common issues.

If your organization requires a particular regulatory certification to operate, it may be the case that for you to operate in a public cloud, the provider must have the same certification. For example, a company that processes medical records must certify that its operations are HIPAA-compliant. If the company decides to move its operations to the public cloud, it should make sure that the cloud provider it chooses attests that it is also HIPAA-compliant. In addition, when you migrate to the cloud, it's your responsibility to ensure that your systems in the cloud don't run afoul of any regulations your organization falls under. Remember, it is your operations and data.

This example applies to many other industries and government edicts from around the world. It is important that you understand and comply with all regulatory needs for your business, which may require complying with audits or proving that you meet the law.

Another area of concern that may arise when dealing with regulatory and compliance issues is called legal hold or litigation hold. A *legal hold* requires an organization to preserve data that may be relevant to active or anticipated legal disputes or investigations. One purpose of legal hold is to protect potential evidence from destruction. If there are processes that automatically delete or modify data past a certain age, the legal hold process may require quickly making copies of the relevant data and safeguarding it indefinitely. Organizations that are likely to face a legal hold often include in their employee training details on the legal hold process.

Vulnerability Assessments

Some regulations may require periodic vulnerability assessments to determine whether systems are open to known exploits. Vulnerability scans can significantly impact system performance, so they're often scheduled during off-hours to avoid negatively affecting users.

What you should scan depends on the cloud service model as well as the regulatory requirements. For example, if you're running web services on VMs that are open to the Internet, you may need to scan for operating system and application vulnerabilities. If you find any, your remediation options may include patching them if possible, disabling unneeded services, or implementing additional firewall rules to mitigate them. In the infrastructure-as-a-service (IaaS) model, you have control over particular services and can fix the issues that you find.

On the other hand, if you're using the software-as-a-service (SaaS) service model, performing vulnerability scans may not be an option because the cloud provider is responsible for the application. Most cloud providers require you to get permission prior to performing vulnerability scans so that the provider doesn't mistake your scan for malicious activity. Chances are that you won't get permission to scan SaaS applications. However, you can still assess the particular software versions that the provider is using to see if there are any known vulnerabilities.

Encrypting Your Data

The purpose of *encryption* is to protect the confidentiality, integrity, and availability of data. (This is popularly called the *CIA Triad*). *Confidentiality* means that those who aren't authorized to access data can't do so, *availability* means that those who are authorized to access data can do so in a timely manner, and *integrity* refers to assurance that the data has not been corrupted maliciously or accidentally modified.

IP Security

IP Security (IPsec) is a protocol suite that provides integrity, confidentiality, and authentication of Internet Protocol (IP) packets. IPsec is most commonly used to create virtual private networks (VPNs) over insecure networks like the Internet. There are two primary modes of operation with IPsec: transport mode and tunnel mode. The main difference lies in where the IPsec functions take place.

In *transport mode*, only the payload of the IP packet is encrypted. The IP header that contains the source and destination IP addresses is not encrypted. Anyone sniffing the packet along the way can see the IP header in plaintext, but the payload is in *ciphertext*. Transport mode offers end-to-end encryption since the payload never traverses any network unencrypted.

In *tunnel mode*, the entire IP packet, including the header, is encrypted. The encrypted packet is encapsulated inside an IPsec packet, thus hiding the original source and destination addresses. Most IPsec VPNs use tunnel mode because it allows encryption of IP packets between any two hosts. In a site-to-site VPN, a router or firewall at the edge of each site encrypts and decrypts IP packets using IPsec in tunnel mode, as shown in Figure 3.1. This arrangement offloads security and processing from the host machines and enables a central point of control. The trade-off is that complete end-to-end security is not provided since the unencrypted packets between the router or firewall terminating the encrypted tunnel and the local endpoint will not be secured with IPsec.

FIGURE 3.1 IPsec tunnel from remote site to cloud data center

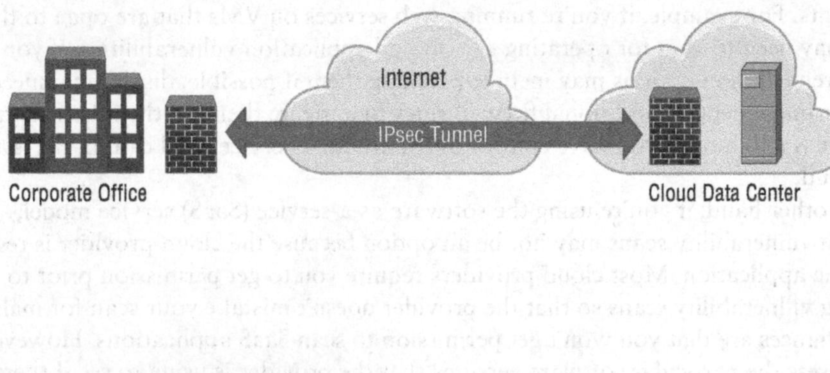

IPsec uses two protocols. The first is the security *authentication header (AH)* and the second is the *encapsulating security payload (ESP)*. Both the AH and the ESP provide slightly different functions:

- The AH provides authentication and data integrity. Authentication is provided by keyed hash functions that are called *message authentication codes (MACs)*. The AH also offers data integrity, provides the ability to determine whether the packet has been modified in transit, and has anti-replay services for additional security. The AH does not provide encryption.
- In tunnel mode, the ESP provides authentication, data integrity, and encryption for the entire IP packet. In transport mode, however, it only provides encryption of the IP payload.

Transport Layer Security

Transport Layer Security (TLS) and its predecessor, *Secure Sockets Layer (SSL)*, provide authentication and encryption for traffic sent over a network. SSL is no longer used; it was replaced with TLS. Despite this, many people still refer to TLS as SSL, so you'll sometimes see it referred to as SSL/TLS.

Its most common use implementation is the Hypertext Transfer Protocol Secure (HTTPS) protocol, which is used to encrypt HTTP payloads. In addition to encryption, HTTPS allows a web browser to authenticate the identity of a website. When a browser connects to a secure website and a TCP connection is made, the SSL handshake takes place and is initiated by the client's web browser. The browser then transmits to the server the SSL/TLS version, the encryption method it prefers to use, and, if using compression, what type to use. The server will select the highest version of SSL/TLS that it supports and agree to an encryption method offered by the client. If compression is to be used, it will also select a compression algorithm to use. When the basic handshake is completed, the server will send a certificate using *public key infrastructure (PKI)* services to the client. The certificate must be trusted by either the client or a certificate authority that the client trusts; a list of trusted authorities is usually stored in the browser or the operating system.

After the client performs the certificate verification function to determine that the web server is really who it claims to be, the client will generate a symmetrical key, called the *session key*, and then use the session keys exchanged for secure transmission of data. The TLS session is now established.

Now that you have a connection, every packet will be signed with a MAC. You can now ensure that the sender and receiver are in fact the originators of the data and not someone in the middle claiming to be the website or the client. The data cannot be modified by an attacker, and the attacker will not be able to read the data since it is encrypted.

Other Common Ciphers

A *cipher* encrypts data by taking readable plaintext and applying to it a set of transformations to turn it into unintelligible gibberish. Reversing a cipher—deciphering—requires some knowledge about the transformations used to encrypt the plaintext data. Ciphers can range from the very basic to the highly complex. A simple cipher can realign data in the stream to hide its meaning—for example, replacing any character B with a number such as 7. Knowing the cipher at the remote end, you can reverse the process to recover the original data. Doing this for all letters in the alphabet would create a basic cipher.

In modern computing, more complex methods are employed that use a secret or private key and an algorithm that combines the key with the plaintext. There are two basic types of ciphers: a block cipher and a stream cypher. They differ as to how the encryption is applied. With a *block cipher*, the data is broken up into blocks, and then the encryption process is run on each block. A *stream cipher* applies the encryption to each byte.

When the same key is used for both encryption and decryption, it's called *symmetric encryption*. Symmetric encryption is fast, but its weakness is that anyone who knows the key can decrypt the message. Stream ciphers commonly use symmetric encryption.

Asymmetric encryption makes use of two different keys. The receiver creates a public key and a private key that are mathematically related. This is also called *public key cryptography*. The receiver shares only its public key with the sender. The sender encrypts a message using the receiver's public key, and the receiver decrypts the message using its own private key. Even though the message is encrypted with the public key, it can be decrypted only with the private key and not the public key. This way, asymmetric encryption ensures that only the intended recipient can decode the message. The downside is that it's more computationally intensive.

HTTPS uses both asymmetric and symmetric encryption. The sender and receiver use asymmetric encryption initially to exchange a symmetric key, and from then on, they use the symmetric key to encrypt and decrypt data. This approach overcomes the shortcomings of both encryption schemes.

So, with that introduction to ciphers in mind, let's investigate some of the most common ciphers found in the security world.

- *Advanced Encryption Standard (AES)* is a symmetrical block cipher that has options to use three key lengths, including 128, 192, and 256 bits. With encryption, the longer the key length, the harder and longer it will be to break the encryption. AES with a 256-bit key length (AES-256) is a very secure standard, and it would take an extremely long time and a lot of processing power even to come close to brute-forcing the key by trying every possible combination. The 256-bit key is used to encrypt and decrypt traffic, and the same key is used in both directions. AES has been approved and adopted by many governments, including the United States and Canada, to encrypt sensitive data. AES has also been adopted as a standard by the National Institute of Standards and Technology (NIST).
- The *Triple Data Encryption Standard (3DES)* was developed in 1977 and has largely been replaced by AES. 3DES is a symmetrical cipher, and it is based on the DES cipher, which is weak and easily compromised. 3DES runs data through the original DES cipher three times, hence the name. Although more secure and DES, 3DES is considered insecure and NIST no longer recommends it. 3DES uses key lengths of 56, 112, or 168 bits.

- *RSA* is named after the developers of the protocol, Ron Rivest, Adi Shamir, and Leonard Adleman. RSA is an asymmetrical encryption implementation that uses a private key and a public key.
- The *Digital Signature Algorithm (DSA)* operates much the same way as RSA does, but it is slower than RSA for encryption but faster for decryption. Although DSA and RSA serve the same function and operate in much the same way, RSA is more commonly found in cloud implementations.
- *RC4 (Rivest Cipher 4)* is a symmetric stream cipher named after its developer, Ron Rivest. RC4 was commonly used to secure wireless connections and web transactions as an encryption protocol used in SSL. It's susceptible to compromise by hackers and is no longer in use. Most browsers and security implementations no longer support RC4.
- *RC5 (Rivest Cipher 5)* is the replacement for RC4. It is also a symmetrical block cipher algorithm that uses a variable-length key.

File Integrity

It can be easy to modify files, and in the context of security, that can be a big problem. Malicious hackers have long modified log files to cover their tracks. Criminals modify database entries to commit fraud. Malware modifies executable files to create backdoors and propagate itself through networks.

The goal of file integrity is to detect when a file has been changed. File integrity works using hashes. A *hash* is a unique value derived from the contents of the file. A *hashing algorithm* is a one-way function that runs through each byte of the file and yields a fixed-size string called a hash. No matter how many times you calculate the hash of a file, the hash will be the same, provided the file hasn't changed. But if even only one byte of the file changes, the entire hash changes. By calculating a cryptographic hash of a file and storing that hash separately from it, detecting whether a file has changed involves simply taking a hash of the file in question and comparing it to the original hash. If the hashes are different, you know the file has changed.

File integrity requires storing the hashes separately from the file itself, preferably in a write-only system where it can't be deleted or overwritten. File integrity does no good if a hacker can modify a log file *and* the recorded hash. In the cloud, logging facilities sometimes offer the option of enabling file integrity for log files.

Understanding Public Key Infrastructure

A *public key infrastructure (PKI)* is a standardized set of roles, policies, and procedures used to create, manage, distribute, use, store, and revoke digital certificates and manage public/private key encryption. As the name implies, it is a framework and not a specific protocol. Here you will get an overview of what it is and why you use it in the cloud.

PKI provides for identity, authorization, and encryption services that are central to implementing security in the cloud. PKI is an industry-standard framework that provides authorization and enforces security policies. One foundational element of PKI is digital certificates. Certificates are used in authentication, whether it's authenticating a website or a user. HTTPS makes heavy use of certificates, so we'll use it as a familiar example to illustrate the principles of PKI.

A *certificate authority (CA)* is a trusted entity that issues digital certificates. A website owner sends a certificate request to a CA requesting a certificate for a particular domain name. In certificate parlance, the domain name is called the *common name*, or if the certificate is for multiple domain names, they're called *subject alternative names (SANs)*. The CA creates a certificate that it signs using its private key. This creates a digital signature that becomes part of the certificate. Certificates have an expiration date and are valid only for that period of time. The website owner installs the certificate on their site.

When a user visits the site using HTTPS, the web server sends its certificate to the browser. The browser checks that the certificate is valid by checking whether the certificate was signed by a trusted CA. Web browsers and operating systems have copies of CA root certificates that contain the CA's public key. (One of the other goals of PKI is the distribution of public keys for asymmetric cryptography.) If the certificate is signed by a trusted CA and hasn't expired, the browser considers the website to have been authenticated. At that point, it establishes an encrypted connection to the site. This is a simplified explanation of the process, since the details are beyond the scope of the exam. Table 3.1 shows the five major parts of the PKI framework.

TABLE 3.1 Major components of a PKI framework

PKI service	Description
Certificate authority (CA)	Central authority of trust; authenticates the identity of individuals, computers, and other entities in the network; issues root certificates
Registration authority (RA)	Issues certificates for use as permitted by the CA
Certificate database	Stores certificate requests and issued and revoked certificates from the CA or RA
Certificate store	Stores issued certificates and pending or rejected certificate requests from the local computer
Key archival server	Stores the encrypted private keys in a highly secure certificate database in case the certificate database is lost and for disaster recovery

PKI is also used in file encryption and in two-factor authentication with smartcards and token-based systems. Cloud applications may also use the PKI certificates such as email, databases, document signing, mobile device security, and many other applications. In corporate cloud environments, PKI is commonly used to authenticate users trying to access data and to validate transactions.

Major cloud providers offer companies PKI as a service (PKIaaS) to allow you to use PKI managed services without the need to build and manage your own PKI implementation. There are also cryptography as a service (CaaS) cloud providers who provide PKI services such as hardware and software tokens, authentication services, and encryption offerings.

NOTE For a deeper understanding of security, check out CompTIA's Security+ certification.

Remote Access Protocols

Since your cloud data centers are by definition distant from the location from which you will be accessing them, you will need to access the operations, consoles, configuration consoles, dashboard, and a host of other cloud services remotely.

In this section, we will primarily address the security of remote access as it pertains to managing your cloud operations. You will most likely use some sort of encrypted remote access VPN technology that you will learn about in this section. We will also discuss how to lock down your access locations and how to strengthen your remote access security posture.

Generic Routing Encapsulation

Generic Routing Encapsulation (GRE) is a standardized network tunneling protocol that can encapsulate any network layer protocol inside an IP packet. GRE has many uses, including tunneling IPv6 traffic over an IPv4 network, and vice versa. GRE is most commonly combined with IPsec to create encrypted VPN tunnels across a public network like the Internet. GRE was developed by Cisco Systems.

Layer 2 Tunneling Protocol

The *Layer 2 Tunneling Protocol (L2TP)* is a protocol that can transport a variety of packets (including Ethernet frames) over IP networks. It used to be a popular choice for VPNs, and some VPN servers still support L2TP even though it is an older protocol and not as widely used as it was in the past because it does not natively provide encryption (although you can use IPsec for this). L2TP was developed by Cisco Systems and Microsoft and ratified as a standard in 1999.

Point-to-Point Tunneling Protocol

The *Point-to-Point Tunneling Protocol (PPTP)* is a deprecated protocol that is similar to L2TP in that it can encapsulate layer 2 point-to-point protocol (PPP) frames in GRE packets, allowing for transport over IP networks. PPTP doesn't natively provide encryption and is considered to be obsolete.

Automating Cloud Security

Cloud security can be automated by combining many of the service offerings to architect complete systems for monitoring, reporting, and responding to security events. For example, logging data can be collected and placed in a cloud storage system; then the files are read by a log file analytics applications such as Splunk, which may be offered as a cloud application service. Third-party and homegrown security operations can also obtain this monitoring data and run scripts that monitor for security threats.

When events occur that require action, systems can be triggered and automation scripts run to take action without human intervention. The scripts can be run on network management systems, intrusion prevention appliances or VMs, or microservices, as well as other sources such as custom applications.

Automation allows for rapid response to security events and can stop an attempted breach in progress as well as record all events to forensic analysis of the event. How to implement cloud security will be covered in more depth in Chapter 4, "Implementing Cloud Security."

Log and Event Monitoring

Logging is one of the foundational elements of good security. Knowing who did what, where, and when is invaluable information when troubleshooting or investigating incidents. Event log entries generally consist of a timestamp, the action performed, and the entity that performed the action (such as a username). Entries may also include the resource affected and outcomes, such as whether the action was successful.

All major cloud providers offer the ability to log events that occur against resources in your cloud account—for example, logging into the web management console, creating or deleting a VM, taking a snapshot of a block storage volume, or even uploading a file to object storage. These sort of events that occur at the cloud management level are called *application programming interface (API)* events. The level of logging can be extremely granular, giving you a wide range of options for what you log. You can selectively log only actions of interest, or you can log everything. For instance, if you want to log every time someone downloads a file from an object storage bucket, you can do that. Some other things that can be logged are network flow information and DNS queries.

It's important to understand that the cloud provider can log only events that it knows about. Obviously, the provider is aware of discrete cloud resources that you create using its services. What you can log generally depends on the cloud service model. In the IaaS model, most logging is going to be your responsibility, whereas in the SaaS model the cloud provider will likely log everything. In the IaaS model, if you deploy a VM, the provider knows the details of it, such as its network configuration, what volumes are attached to it, and whether it's running. The cloud provider does not, however, necessarily know what software is running on the VM. That's because in the IaaS model, you're responsible for what you put on it. If you're running an Apache web server, the cloud provider won't automatically grab the web server logs and keep them for you. That doesn't mean, however, that you have to manage logs on your own. Most cloud providers offer the ability to export or stream application logs to their logging service. But it's something you have to configure explicitly (and usually pay extra for).

In addition to logging, you can likely have your cloud provider alert you to certain events via email, SMS, or other mechanisms. In addition to logging it, you might also want to get an email every time there's an autoscaling event. You can use such notifications to trigger other workflows.

Distributed Denial-of-Service Protection

A *distributed denial-of-service (DDoS) attack* is one in which attackers remotely trigger a large number of devices to send mass traffic to a victim server simultaneously in order to overwhelm its resources. Attackers gain control of these devices via malware that silently gives the attacker remote control over them. This is called a command-and-control or botnet setup. Different methods can be used to carry out a DDoS attack, but they all have one goal in common: to render the victim server unusable and thus deny service to those trying to reach it.

Cloud providers employ defenses against DDoS attacks to protect their own infrastructure. Common attacks include UDP reflection and TCP SYN flood attacks. There are also application-specific attacks, such as HTTP flood attacks that attempt to overwhelm a web server with HTTP `GET` or `POST` requests. Guarding against application-specific attacks requires a firewall that understands the application protocol. A web application firewall (WAF) is a good example of one such firewall that can protect against these HTTP attacks.

Security Best Practices

In this section, you will learn about security best practices that you should consider for your computing environment, be it in the cloud or in a data center. There is no one-size-fits-all approach to security, and your organization's requirements may call for more or less stringent measures than the ones that follow. Use this section as a guide and a starting point, and tailor your security policies accordingly.

Securing Accounts

Default accounts should be disabled or have their credentials changed. A quick search can easily find default usernames and passwords for a variety of off-the-shelf applications and systems. Attackers routinely try these credentials first, so leaving them unchanged creates a large security hole that may allow hackers to penetrate your system. If you can't disable or change the credentials of a default account, remove as many permissions from the account as possible to reduce the attack surface area.

At a minimum, implement password policies to enforce long, hard-to-guess passwords. This is especially important for administrator and service accounts. Prohibiting or limiting password reuse, expiring passwords, and requiring a mix of letters, numbers, and symbols are other common techniques to coax users into creating strong passwords.

Disabling Unused Accounts

One oft-neglected area is disabling unused user accounts. When a user leaves the organization, disabling their account should generally be part of the offboarding process. It's especially common for organizations not to disable accounts belonging to former managers or system administrators for fear that doing so will break some unknown service or process that depends on that particular account. Leaving the account enabled might be convenient, but it leaves the door open for an unauthorized person to use the account, particularly if they know the password. Hence, it's best to disable unused accounts as soon as possible, and perhaps even delete them after a period of time.

Disabling Unused Services

One of the basic tenets of securing a network is that if you do not need it, turn it off. When you install a new operating system, by default many services are enabled that may expose your system to a malicious attack.

The practice of *hardening a system* essentially means to remove or disable any unused applications or services. To harden the system, you must determine which ports and services are running on the machine and investigate whether they are required for the server's purpose. If the service isn't needed, remove it or shut it down to reduce the attack surface area. Both Windows and Linux may have services running that are enabled by default and may be of no use to you. By design, a freshly installed server OS will be ready to perform most any task with just a few commands. In practice, however, each server generally needs to perform only a handful of well-defined functions. A database server, for example, should have its inbound network access locked down to the IP ranges that need to access it. Likewise, it probably shouldn't be running file, print, or web services. Each server roles should inform how you harden it—its *hardening baseline*.

Hackers will often perform network port scans to determine which TCP or UDP ports are open and tailor their attacks accordingly. An application, even if it's rejecting incoming requests, may still respond to port scans, alerting the would-be attacker to its presence. Disabling or uninstalling unneeded applications can help thwart this sort of reconnaissance. Firewalls still play a role in blocking network reconnaissance and attacks from the outside, but if a hacker can gain access to your internal network—perhaps by taking over a user's workstation or other server—it can evade detection by your firewalls. The approach of hardening all of your systems, not just those at the perimeter, is called *defense-in-depth*.

Operating system vendors will often publish white papers and checklists that can be followed to harden their systems. They may also offer specific releases that have already been hardened for specific use cases. For example, an operating system may offer unneeded services such as printing, universal plug-and-play, file sharing, or even remote access tools. Even seemingly innocuous services can fall to new and unknown *zero-day exploits*. The bottom line: if you don't need a service, disable it. You can always enable it if it turns out that you need it later.

Disable/Rename Default Accounts

Applications and operating systems often have default accounts that are required for initial configuration and ongoing interprocess communications. The user documentation will often publish what username and password is to be used to access these systems and how to make configuration changes. This may be an initial requirement, but it is also a massive security hole. You must disable all applications and operating system default accounts or—if the accounts are needed—change the username and password to prevent a breach.

Networking appliances such as switches, routers, load balancers, and firewalls should also be checked. Network management using the *Simple Network Management Protocol (SNMP)* may come activated with well-known community strings that are wide open for exploitation.

Host-Based Firewall Security

Hardware-based perimeter firewalls are a mainstay of any security implementation, and they provide a first line of defense as well as segmentation in the cloud. In addition to this, a host-based firewall software can then be configured with rules or policies that allow connections only to the applications it is hosting and from known source networks. In fact, many operating systems have firewalls preinstalled as part of the release. A host-based firewall performs the same functions as a perimeter firewall, allowing filtering based on network addresses, ports, and protocols. A combination of a certain protocol, source or destination IP address, and source or destination port is called a *network flow*. Modern firewalls, including host-based firewalls, use flow information to differentiate one application's traffic from another. Host-based firewalls are important for stopping attacks from the inside, such as a worm spreading through the network or a hacker using a compromised server as a "jump box" or bastion host to reach other machines on the internal network.

Antivirus Protection

Antivirus software can identify, prevent, or remove viruses or malicious software from a system. Some operating systems ship with antivirus software, although there are many third-party alternatives that you can choose from that might better meet your needs. Much like IDSs/IPSs, antivirus software uses signatures to identify malware. As such, you have to keep the virus and malware signature definitions up-to-date to be protected against the latest threats.

Antivirus software is generally only installed on workstations and servers. Most virus infections occur when an unsuspecting user inadvertently downloads and executes malware, perhaps from a website. Purpose-built appliances such as firewalls aren't used in this way, are hardened by default, and generally don't allow you to install arbitrary applications, so the risk of infection is extremely low.

Keeping Your Servers Up-to-Date by Applying the Latest Patches

There seems to be a constant release of patches and fixes for operating systems, applications, and system firmware to address bugs and vulnerabilities. When a vulnerability is found, malicious hackers can be quick to exploit the system before it has had patches applied to it.

Vendor support sites, automation software, operating systems utilities, and email subscriptions can be tracked to keep up with updates that are required.

Many systems can be configured to detect and install patches automatically, which can be both a blessing and a curse. You may need to install critical security patches in a timely manner to prevent a breach. But patches for critical security issues may be rushed out before being sufficiently tested, so installing them might result in a crash or even data loss. Ironically, a rushed patch might even open other security holes. It is generally preferable to investigate patches and test for stability and install them during a maintenance window. If you're following a defense-in-depth approach, delaying patches for a short time is not likely to increase your risk significantly. However, if you're experiencing an attack that would be mitigated by a patch, it may be necessary to install the patch without testing it.

Proxies

A *proxy server*, as the name suggests, is an intermediate server that sits between two network endpoints, allowing it to intercept, analyze, and even block traffic. Web proxies often sit at the edge of organizational networks and perform content filtering. They may also aid in data loss prevention by blocking sensitive information from leaving the network.

Organizations that offer Internet-facing web services may use something called a *reverse proxy* to protect the back-end servers. A reverse proxy sits at the edge of a network and intercepts incoming HTTP(S) requests. It then opens up a separate connection between itself and a back-end web server and passes or proxies the request to the server. A reverse proxy is in a position to intercept and block application level (layer 7) attacks as well as perform load balancing.

Access Control

In this section, you will learn about access and authorization of your cloud-based operations. Access control includes many different areas of security. You will learn about object access, which includes not just users and groups of users but also machine-to-machine authorization and security at the network and storage levels as well as the services in the cloud. You will then learn about security as it applies to service models and learn more about the authentication process.

Accessing Cloud-Based Objects

A cloud *object* is any resource that you create in the cloud. Objects can include VMs, elastic load balancers, managed database servers, block storage volumes, and elastic filesystems. Controlling who can access objects and what actions they are allowed to take is a critical component of maintaining proper security in the cloud. In this section, you will learn about the authorization and access to cloud-based objects.

The Authentication and Authorization Processes

Before a user can manage objects in the cloud, they must go through the *authentication process,* which entails identifying themselves using a set of credentials. Most of the time these credentials consist of a username and a password. But they can also be security tokens or API keys.

Once the user has been *authenticated,* what they're allowed to do depends on their authorizations, which define what actions they're allowed to perform and against what objects. Authorizations can be extremely granular, even permitting or denying access during certain times of the day or from certain IP addresses. By defining granular rules in the authorization process, you can meet even the most stringent security requirements.

Many cloud providers offer an automated assessment of your cloud security posture, looking for overly permissive authorizations, old credentials, or lax password rules.

User Accounts

User accounts are created for each and every user who needs to gain access to the cloud objects and resources. A user account is usually associated with an individual person but could be expanded to include other entities such as servers or applications that need to access cloud objects. (In data center parlance, these accounts are called *service accounts.*)

More generally, user and service accounts are called *identities.* Once you create an identity, you can define the authorizations granted to it. Authorizations can be assigned directly to each identity in most cloud management systems. However, the preferred practice used to authorize users is to place them into groups, as we will discuss in the next section.

User Groups

User groups can simplify assignment of permissions to users. Rather than assigning permissions directly to users, you can create a user group and assign permissions to that. You then add users to the group, and they inherit the permissions assigned to the group. Groups make management more effective and streamlined than managing a large number of individual user accounts. If a large number of users need the same permissions—perhaps users who share the same job role or function—it may be worth creating a group for them. For example, the help desk will likely require different permissions than server administrators, so you'd create separate groups for each.

Network-Based Access Control

Network-based access control permits or denies packets based on information in the packets themselves. The most familiar example is access control lists (ACLs), which work based on things like IP addresses, protocols, and port numbers. But network-based access control can use additional rules, such as whether the user or device sending the packets is authorized. For example, an administrative user may be allowed to connect to a server using Secure Shell (SSH), whereas a regular user would not.

When it comes to network-based access control, there are two approaches, and which one you choose depends on how strict you want to be. When you have an ACL that permits traffic by default but makes exceptions to block only particular types of packets, it's called a *blacklist*. Because blacklists are permissive and don't block any application traffic by default, they can make troubleshooting easier.

A *whitelist* is the inverse. It denies traffic by default but makes exceptions to permit only needed ports and protocols. This is substantially more secure, but it can create endless headaches when you're troubleshooting network connectivity problems. If you install a new application that needs to communicate using a certain protocol and port but you fail to explicitly permit that traffic, the application won't work properly.

Again, there's no one-size-fits-all approach to security. Some organizations try to strike a balance by using whitelists that allow wide ranges of ports and protocols. It is a common cloud security practice to use a layered security approach that implements security at all levels, including the network, for a broad definition of access and then define authorization policies at the server, storage, and application layers in a more granular fashion for a complete security implementation.

Cloud Service Models and Security

As you will recall from Chapter 1, "Introducing Cloud Computing Configurations and Deployments," there are three primary cloud service models: IaaS, PaaS, and SaaS. The most basic offering is infrastructure as a service. In this service model, the service provider is responsible for all cloud infrastructure up to the hypervisor level. The customer is responsible for the VM, as shown in Figure 3.2.

FIGURE 3.2 IaaS security model

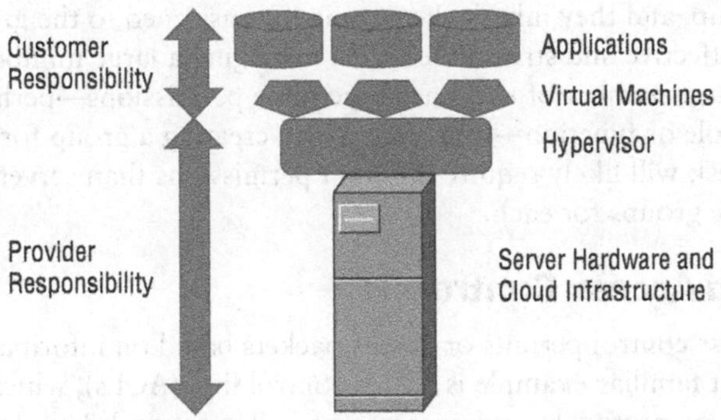

Platform as a service offers the compute and operating systems as a service and allows customers to install their applications on the cloud platform. The security demarcation for PaaS is that the cloud provider assumes responsibility for security up to the operating system, and the customer manages the application and operating system configuration, as shown in Figure 3.3.

FIGURE 3.3 PaaS security model

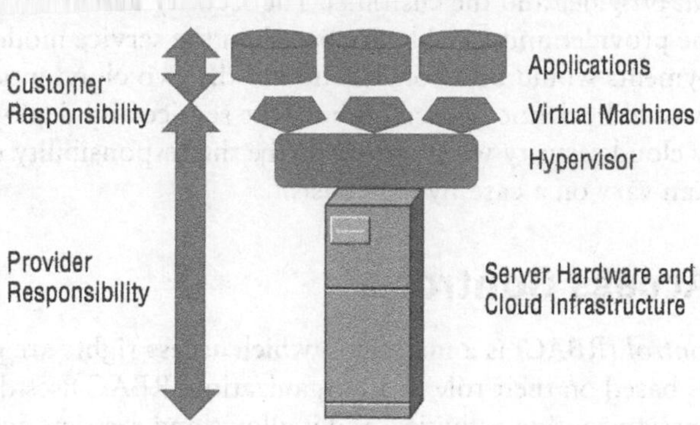

The software as a service model is where the customer of the service accesses application software that is owned and controlled by the cloud company, which has complete responsibility for the management and support of the application, as shown in Figure 3.4.

FIGURE 3.4 SaaS security model

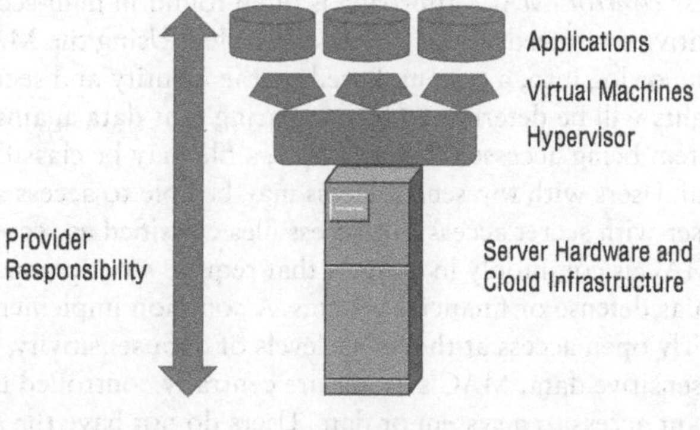

Cloud Deployment Models and Security

Chapter 2, "Cloud Deployments," introduced cloud deployment models and mentioned that a good understanding of the models is critical because they provide an overall structure to cloud computing. You also learned that deployment models are important to know, not only for the Cloud+ exam, but also for your day-to-day work as a cloud professional.

The primary deployment models are private, public, hybrid, and community. Security policies and responsibilities will vary based on the deployment model and each organization's specific definitions of who accepts security responsibility. However, you can assume that in a private cloud there is most likely one private organization that owns and operates the private cloud and that would assume the responsibility for the operation.

With a public cloud deployment model, the security responsibility would be shared between the public cloud provider and the customer. The security demarcation would be defined in agreement with the provider and would vary based on the service model.

The hybrid deployments would be a combination of the two cloud models that are interconnected and would be defined based on both the service and deployment security policies. Community cloud security would generally be the responsibility of the community cloud operator but can vary on a case-by-case basis.

Role-Based Access Control

Role-based access control (RBAC) is a method in which access rights are granted to, or restricted from, users based on their role in an organization. RBAC uses different defined permission levels to assign routine activities, and it allows and restricts access to cloud resources based on these roles. The roles are defined based on the task, and users are then assigned to the roles. Based on the permissions allowed in the roles, the users will inherit those rights. RBAC is also called *nondiscretionary access control*.

Mandatory Access Control

The *mandatory access control (MAC)* approach is often found in high-security environments where access to sensitive data needs to be tightly controlled. Using the MAC approach, a user will authenticate, or log into, a system. Based on the identity and security levels of the individual, access rights will be determined by comparing that data against the security properties of the system being accessed. For example, a file may be classified as top secret, secret, or confidential. Users with top secret access may be able to access all files on the system, whereas a user with secret access can access files classified as secret or confidential, but not top secret. MAC is commonly in systems that require strict compartmentalization of information, such as defense or financial systems. A common implementation of a MAC system will allow fairly open access at the lower levels of data sensitivity, with tighter controls over the more sensitive data. MAC systems are centrally controlled using a defined security policy to grant access to a system or data. Users do not have the ability to change or overwrite this policy and grant access to other users.

Discretionary Access Control

Discretionary access controls differ from mandatory access controls by giving users the ability to grant or assign rights to objects that they own, as compared to the centrally controlled method used by mandatory access controls. Users with control over a system or data directory, for example, can use their discretionary access control rights to give other users or systems rights to those systems and directories. The discretionary approach allows users with the correct permissions to manage rights. These users own the objects and are allowed to make decisions on rights such as security, read-only, read-write, and execute on those objects.

Multifactor Authentication

Multifactor authentication (MFA) is an access control technique that requires several pieces of information to be granted access. Multifactor implementations usually require you to present something you know, such as a username/password combination, and something you have, such as a smartcard, a fingerprint, or a constantly changing token number from an ID card.

An example of multifactor authentication is when you withdraw money from an ATM. The two-factor authentication includes something you have, which is your ATM card, and something you know, which is your PIN.

Since you have more than one requirement for authentication to access a system, multifactor systems are inherently more secure than single-factor systems such as a username/password combination.

Cloud vendors offer the option for two-factor authentication to access and administer your cloud deployment. This adds a second layer of access security and is a good security measure to adopt a multifactor framework. A number of companies offer token-generation hardware that is small enough to fit on your keychain and applications that can be installed on a smartphone.

When you log into your cloud management console or other services, you will be prompted for a token ID, which you will read from your token generator. You type in the five- or six-digit number along with your username and password to gain admission. Multifactor authentication is widely used in the cloud and corporate environments.

Single Sign-On

Single sign-on (SSO) is an approach that reduces the number of times a user has to authenticate. SSO allows a user to log in just one time and be granted access rights to multiple systems. For example, a user may log into their workstation and then connect to an application running in the cloud. Using SSO, the user won't need to log into the application separately. Instead, their authentication from logging into their workstation will carry over to the application, and they'll be granted appropriate access. Using SSO, you can centralize the authentication of multiple systems into just one area, easing user administration significantly.

Single sign-on eliminates the need to remember multiple username and password combinations and saves the time of having to enter your authentication information repeatedly across a network. SSO is also effective when terminating a session. When a user logs off their workstation, any other active sessions they may have with other systems will also be logged out.

Summary

Information security is about protecting the confidentiality, integrity, and availability of data. It's easy to pay lip service to making your systems as secure as possible, but security comes at a price. The better your security, the more convenience, speed, and money you should be prepared to sacrifice. Every organization must decide how to balance security against its other needs. You need to know where these trade-offs exist and how implementing a particular security measure may impact the organization.

The topic of security is prominent in the cloud community, and CompTIA has a strong emphasis on security on the exam. It is important to understand security, encryption, authentication, and authorization.

This chapter started out with a macro view of the topic of cloud security. You then learned about the need for compliance and what compliance really is by exploring many regulations that apply to private industry and government organizations. Then you learned about developing security policies, meeting these requirements, and performing audits to ensure compliance.

Encryption of your data was the next topic. Encryption goes beyond just making data indecipherable to unauthorized parties. It entails integrity and assurance that the data hasn't been surreptitiously or inadvertently modified. Understand the difference between ciphers and hashes. A cipher is what performs encryption, whereas a hash is a one-way function that converts data into a unique string, usually of fixed size. By taking the hash of a file, and subsequently taking a hash of the same file later, you can determine with certainty whether the file has changed. If the hashes match, the file hasn't changed. If the hashes don't match, the file was modified.

You learned some steps required to harden your cloud resources against attack. Disabling default and unused accounts, disabling unused servers, implementing firewalls, installing antivirus applications, and keeping your patches up-to-date are basic habits that are appropriate for most organizations.

The chapter concluded by discussing user access, specifically the authentication and authorization of users and systems. Many different types of access technologies were explained such as role-based, single sign-on, and groups. You then learned how to secure various objects in the cloud such as VMs, storage assets, and networks.

Exam Essentials

Know about cloud security compliance. Know that a company's security policy is an internal document that outlines its security posture and lists all topics related to security.

Understand that companies must meet certain regulatory compliance statutes. Know that HIPAA compliance is required for the processing and storing of medical data, that PCI DSS compliance is required for credit card processing, and that there are a range of U.S. federal cloud requirements such as DIACAP, FedRAMP, and FIPS 140-2.

Understand compliance. Know that even if a cloud provider is compliant with a regulation, that compliance doesn't automatically extend to your organization. You must architect and implement your systems to the relevant compliance standards. For example, if a cloud provider is PCI DSS compliant but you leave credit card numbers sitting out in a publicly accessible object storage bucket, you won't pass a compliance audit.

Be able to identify data encryption types and techniques. Know what IPsec is and the difference between transport and tunnel modes. Understand ciphers, the public key infrastructure, encryption types, and common implementations of encryption technologies such as TLS and VPNs.

Know the various remote access technologies. Common remote access protocols include L2TP, PPTP, and GRE.

Understand the devices that need to be hardened in your cloud fleet. Disable all unused services, deploy a firewall, implement antivirus protection, keep your servers patched and up-to-date, and shut down default user accounts.

Be able to explain authentication and authorization. Understand the concepts of user and service accounts and groups. Know the difference between authentication and authorization. Authentication is concerned with identifying a user, whereas authorization deals with what that user is allowed to do.

Know who has security responsibility for the various cloud services' models. For IaaS, you have full responsibility from the operating system up to the application level, and the cloud service provider maintains responsibility from the hypervisor down to the cloud data center infrastructure. PaaS allows the cloud service provider to take responsibility for everything except the application. In the SaaS model, the cloud service provider takes security responsibility up to the application level. However, it is important to understand that ultimately you are responsible for your data and for meeting compliance requirements.

Know the different types of access controls. Be able to identify and understand the many types of access control, including mandatory, discretionary, nondiscretionary, multifactor, and single sign-on.

Written Lab

Fill in the blanks for the questions provided in the written lab. You can find the answers to the written labs in Appendix B.

1. Multifactor authentication must include something you ________________ and something you ________________.
2. A(n) ________________ is the document that defines your company's cloud controls, organizational policies, responsibilities, and underlying technologies to secure your cloud deployment.
3. ________________ controls give users the ability to grant or assign rights to objects and make decisions for themselves as compared to the centrally controlled method.
4. ________________ is an approach that reduces the need to sign into multiple systems for access.

5. A(n) ________________ is defined as any method of encrypting data by concealing its readability and meaning.
6. ________________ allows for software scripted responses to security events and can stop an attempted breach in progress. These systems can provide hands-off recording of all events to forensic analysis of the event.
7. A cloud ________________ can be a file stored in a storage system, a virtual machine, a load balancer, or any other system running in the cloud, and it is an item that can be accessed and manipulated in the cloud.
8. Public clouds implement a(n) ________________ security model.
9. A(n) ________________ is a standardized set of roles, policies, and procedures used to create, manage, distribute, use, store, and revoke digital certificates and manage public/private key encryption.
10. In the ________________ service model, the cloud service provider assumes security responsibility up to and including that application level.

Review Questions

The following questions are designed to test your understanding of this chapter's material. For more information on how to obtain additional questions, please see this book's Introduction. You can find the answers in Appendix A.

1. Harry is investigating cloud service models and wants to outsource the security responsibility to the cloud company and not have to take responsibility for maintaining and patching the operating systems. Which service model will meet his requirements?

   A. IaaS

   B. PaaS

   C. SaaS

   D. CaaS

2. What is the name of the process when a cloud administrator uses their token, username, and password to log into the cloud console? (Choose two.)

   A. Authorization

   B. Two-factor

   C. Authentication

   D. Role-based access

3. Robert has been tasked with creating an access control solution for his company's fleet of servers in a hybrid cloud configuration. He has been asked to define the required tasks and then to put users, groups, and servers into this task-based implementation. What type of access control should Robert deploy?

   A. Mandatory access control

   B. Nondiscretionary

   C. Role-based

   D. Multifactor

4. What is a report for the public disclosure of financial controls and security reporting that does not contain sensitive and technical information called?

   A. SOC 1

   B. SOC 2

   C. SOC 3

   D. ISO 27001

   E. FIPS 140-2

5. What is the National Institute of Standards and Technology publication that coordinates the requirements and standards for cryptography modules?

   A. PCI DSS

   B. FIPS 140-2

C. ISO 27001
D. FedRAMP

6. What is a compliance requirement to be certified to meet the U.S. Department of Defense (DoD) security requirements for contractors working with the DoD?
   A. FedRAMP
   B. DIACAP
   C. FISMA
   D. 123

7. Mary's boss has asked her to investigate moving the company's medical records to the cloud. What compliance mandate must the cloud provider meet for Mary to recommend deploying her company's operations to the cloud?
   A. SOC 3
   B. HIPAA
   C. MPAA
   D. ISA 2701

8. Sue is preparing a change management process to harden various resources. What resources are her responsibility to harden? (Choose three.)
   A. Web servers running on a fleet of VMs
   B. Self-hosted MySQL server
   C. Managed elastic filesystem
   D. Linux virtual snapshot image
   E. On-premises DHCP server

9. Harry is the cloud administrator for a company that stores object-based data in a public cloud. Because of regulatory restrictions on user access to sensitive security data, what type of access control would you suggest he implement to meet his company's security policies?
   A. Mandatory access control
   B. Nondiscretionary
   C. Roles
   D. Multifactor

10. Christina is investigating obtaining compliance for her employer, which is a large public cloud company. She has been asked to provide a report on the process to enable her company to host a large U.S. federal government database. Which compliance certification is she investigating?
    A. HIPAA
    B. FedRAMP
    C. DIACAP
    D. FISMA

11. What is the process document that outlines your company's responsibilities for safely deploying your fleet of servers in the public cloud?

    A. DIACAP

    B. Security policy

    C. Service level agreement

    D. SOC 2

12. Hank goes to his local bank and inserts his card into the ATM and then enters his PIN on the keypad. What type of authentication is he participating in?

    A. SSO

    B. Two-factor

    C. LDAP

    D. User-based

13. You work in the financial services industry and are required to encrypt your data at rest in the public cloud to comply with securities regulations. You want to implement a strong encryption protocol that is widely approved by industry best practices. Which one of the following meets your requirements?

    A. 3DES

    B. RSA

    C. AES-256

    D. Rivest Cipher 5

14. Single sign-on services allow a user to log into the system one time and be granted device access without having to perform multiple system authentications. What two technologies enable SSO systems? (Choose two.)

    A. PKI

    B. LDAP

    C. Active Directory

    D. Roles

15. Which of the following functions might a reverse proxy perform?

    A. Content filtering

    B. Load balancing

    C. Data loss prevention

    D. Issuing digital certificates

16. Sarah has been tasked to implement a strong user authentication strategy to secure dashboard access to her SaaS cloud services. She wants to use temporarily issued tokens to prevent unauthorized users from accessing her cloud administrator's account. What type of authentication would you recommend that Sarah implement?

    A. Multifactor

    B. Mandatory access control

C. Roles

D. Nondiscretionary

17. Brad has been tasked with encrypting traffic to and from his e-commerce application running in a community cloud. He is investigating a standards-based secure solution that web customers can easily implement to ensure secure transactions. What is a good solution that you would recommend to Brad?

A. AH/ESP

B. AES 256

C. TLS

D. IPsec

18. You have been asked to investigate cloud-based VPN access from your corporate data center that offers data integrity and confidentiality. Your manager does not want to incur the costs of a dedicated circuit to the cloud provider. What connection protocol should you suggest?

A. AES

B. SOC-3

C. IPsec

D. RC5

19. Bob is compiling a list of security tasks to implement to harden his public cloud posture. What are four recommendations that you would suggest? (Choose four.)

A. Install antivirus protection software on public-facing servers.

B. Shut down unused services.

C. Implement whitelisting for public-facing web servers.

D. Implement a host-based firewall or security groups.

E. Allow all storage volumes' authenticated users full access.

F. Disable all default accounts.

G. Grant ephemeral ports access to the DMZ.

20. Jill plans to optimize and control user access by implementing a technology that will allow access to all allowed systems at the time of user authentication. She is implementing the LDAP protocol to enable this service. What does she plan to deploy?

A. Token-based 2FA

B. SSO

C. RSA

D. Nondiscretionary

Chapter 4

Implementing Cloud Security

THE FOLLOWING COMPTIA CLOUD+ EXAM OBJECTIVES ARE COVERED IN THIS CHAPTER:

✓ **2.0 Security**

- 2.1 Given a scenario, configure identity and access management.
    - Multifactor authentication (MFA)
- 2.3 Given a scenario, apply the appropriate OS and application security controls.
    - Antivirus/anti-malware/endpoint detection and response (EDR)
    - Host-based IDS (HIDS)/Host-based IPS (HIPS)
    - Encryption
    - Application programming interface (API) endpoint
    - Application
    - OS
    - Storage
    - Filesystem
- 2.4 Given a scenario, apply data security and compliance controls in cloud environments.
    - Encryption
    - Integrity
    - Hashing algorithms
    - Digital signatures
    - File integrity monitoring (FIM)
    - Classification

- Segmentation
- Cloud access security broker (CASB)

✓ **4.0 Operations and Support**

- 4.2 Given a scenario, maintain efficient operation of a cloud environment.
  - Dashboard and reporting
- 4.4 Given a scenario, apply proper automation and orchestration techniques.
  - Secure scripting
    - No hardcoded passwords
    - Use of individual service accounts
    - Password vaults
    - Key-based authentication
  - Orchestration sequencing

In this chapter, you'll learn about implementing and automating security in the cloud.

Implementing Security in the Cloud

This section focuses on data classification, the segmentation of storage and compute resources, encryption, and multifactor authentication. Then you will learn about meeting regulatory and compliance requirements.

Data Classification

Data classification organizes data into different tiers or categories for various purposes. The most common purpose is to restrict access to certain people, particularly in environments where compartmentalization of knowledge is critical, such as the military. Classification can be used to identify sensitive data and to mark something as requiring encryption. Other reasons include the need to retain or delete data based on its age or purpose. There may be regulatory requirements to hold onto certain types of data for a period of time. Likewise, an organization may want to dispose of other types of data as soon as possible.

Data can be organized into any defined category and managed according to that classification's needs. *Metadata* is data that is attached to a file and that can be thought of as a tag that explains, categorizes, or classifies the data. Metadata might include the creator of a file, the program that created it, or a timestamp indicating when the file was last accessed. Metadata can aid in searching and organizing data. Many metadata tags can be applied to data, and they are usually in a type-value format, where a tag type is defined and then a value is given for the type. For example, a type could be *public*, and the value could be a country such as *Germany*, so the pair would be *public: Germany*. Public cloud vendors offer classifications for accessing data and allow you to assign metadata based on your needs.

A common classification need is based on the sensitivity of the data, such as levels of confidentiality or importance. If your organization were to classify its data into three security categories such as Restricted, Private, and Public, then the appropriate level of security policy could be applied to each classification. Public would require the least amount of security, followed by Private, to which your organization would need to apply additional security policies. With the Restricted category, your company's security policies may require highly restricted access to encryption in transit and at rest to meet any compliance requirements such as Health Insurance Portability and Accountability Act (HIPAA), the Sarbanes–Oxley

Act (SOX), or the Payment Card Industry Data Security Standard (PCI DSS). For example, consider a healthcare provider that collects patient health and payment information. Any files that contain a patient's Social Security number may need to be classified as private to comply with HIPAA regulations. Likewise, if the healthcare provider keeps the patient's credit card on file, they would need to classify and encrypt it appropriately to comply with PCI DSS requirements.

Classification is often done automatically based on the metadata or contents of a file. But it can also be an involved, manual process. Each organization must define the criteria to classify its data and then determine how to apply policies based on each classification. Employees may need to be trained on how to identify and classify data and implement the required security standards necessary for each classification level.

Classification policies need to be clearly outlined in your company's data policy documents and any other documents that are required for regulatory compliance. Policies should explain the types of classifications, how they are determined, and what data belongs in each category. Policies should also include how each class of data should be treated, including the security operations required for the data; how the data can be transmitted, received, backed up, and stored; and what the risks and penalties are for failing to classify data properly or treat it properly according to its classification.

Data classification also helps organizations manage large amounts of data by enabling greater and more precise visibility of what the data is and how it is stored, accessed, and protected. It's important for an organization to revisit its classification policies and implementations routinely in order to determine whether there is a need to reclassify that data, since its status may have changed over time.

Segmenting Your Deployment

Cloud segmentation is the process of dividing your cloud deployment into sections to allow granular security policies to be applied. By applying segmentation to your cloud deployment, you can implement a multilayered security approach that aligns with a defense-in-depth security model.

Cloud networks can be segmented by function, and then security policies can be applied to each segment. Segments can include the public-facing web servers and then an additional segment for the application layer and a third for the database. By creating multiple segments, greater security and controls can be applied to the flow of data into and out of each segment. A strong security posture on the cloud network periphery is critical to defining who you allow into and out of your network. Security policies can be applied using network access control lists, security groups, user access permissions, user groups, roles, and application firewall configurations that are designed to meet your company's security requirements. These security policies protect, for example, data in storage systems, databases, and application servers from unauthorized access or attacks.

Networks can also be segmented by creating more than one virtual private cloud and interconnecting the virtual private clouds (VPCs) with security policies in place to define the permit/deny rules of the traffic flow between the VPCs. In this approach, each VPC can be dedicated to a specific function such as production workload or development and can be isolated from the other processes running in your cloud deployment.

Cloud networks can also be further segmented using subnets. You can place like functions into a subnet and apply a policy to control traffic flow into and out of a subnet. This approach becomes especially useful if you want to restrict or allow access to or from the public Internet. A subnet that is reachable from the Internet is a public subnet, whereas a subnet that isn't reachable from the Internet is a private or protected subnet.

A subnet may be tied to an availability zone, which usually corresponds to a particular data center. If you spread like resources among multiple subnets, you should ensure that the subnets are in different availability zones for reliability and resiliency. For example, if you have a fleet of web servers, you may have half the servers in a public subnet in one availability zone and the other half in a different subnet that's in a different zone. If one zone fails, taking half of the web servers with it, the other zone continues to provide service. This type of deployment is often referred to as a *multi-availability zone architecture*.

Storage Segmentation

Storage segmentation is used to separate cloud data stores and storage offerings to meet a customer's requirements. Using the cloud provider's provisioning tools, you can provision different storage types according to your performance and security needs. As you recall, the three primary storage types are filesystem-, block-, and object-based storage. Each meets different storage use cases and needs.

For example, a database that requires very high read-write I/O operations will best be served using a block storage media that utilizes multiple solid-state drives and is optimized for a high rate of I/O operations, whereas another database may have a low read-write requirement and could make use of standard magnetic drives at a substantially lower cost.

Data that needs to be archived for long-term storage to meet regulatory requirements can be kept in less expensive object storage for the long term. For example, the same database that normally lives on block storage can be snapshotted and backed up to object storage. This can yield significant cost savings while keeping the data accessible within a reasonable time frame if needed.

When you're using block storage to back up a virtual machine, the storage volume can be configured as *durable storage* or *nondurable storage*. With nondurable storage volumes—also known as *ephemeral volumes*—if the virtual machine is deleted or stopped, data will be lost. Nondurable storage is appropriate for temporary files that benefit from low latency, such as high-speed caches. Generally, losing data on a nondurable storage volume is inconsequential, so they're not backed up. Data on durable storage volumes, on the other hand, will not be deleted and as such retain data even if the virtual machine is stopped or terminated. When a VM is snapshotted, it's usually only the durable storage volume(s) that are backed up.

Computing Segmentation

Computing segmentation is a best practice that refers to the isolation of compute resources to reduce the attack surface. One of the most common examples is the *three-tier architecture* often found in web hosting designs. Internet-facing web servers are placed in a public-facing segment or tier that allows users to access the servers using common web access protocols, such as HTTP and HTTPS. The web servers communicate with a fleet of application servers that are placed in a second tier that allows only connections from the upstream web servers and not the public Internet. Finally, there's a third tier containing database servers. Only the application servers are allowed to connect to the database servers. This layered approach provides containment if, for instance, a server in the web tier is hacked. Even if a hacker compromises a web server, the isolation of the application and database servers can protect those components from further attacks.

Other applications that make use of segmenting compute resources is big data hosting in the cloud. A big data configuration will often implement a very large fleet of virtual machines, which can number into the hundreds and sometimes the thousands of servers. There is heavy and delay-sensitive traffic loads between the big data servers. By placing all big data servers into their own compute segments that are physically close together, the high network I/O needs can be addressed and the security needs defined for the segment.

Implementing Encryption

Many regulations and corporate policies require that data be encrypted not only when it is in transit or *in flight*, but also when it's in a storage system, often called *data at rest*. For example, financial or healthcare data may need to be encrypted at rest.

Encryption and decryption introduce delays that are negligible for small amounts of data. But these small delays can compound for highly transactional data—that is, data that is constantly read and written. Be sure to take this overhead into account when scoping your storage requirements.

Encryption can occur at different levels of the storage process. Operating systems such as Linux or Windows can encrypt filesystems. Cloud providers offer encryption options for object and block storage. Modern hardware contains silicon chips called application-specific integrated circuits (ASICs) to offload the compute-intensive encryption from the core CPUs for greater efficiency.

The actual implementation and configuration of encryption can be simple. For example, when creating a block storage volume or object storage bucket, you can enable encryption by just selecting a check box. Many cloud providers have extensive automation systems in place that abstract the complexity and hide the sometimes highly complex configurations from their customers. The cloud provider may allow you to enable encryption after the fact, or they may only allow you to choose encryption at the time of creation of the storage system or database. The only way to add encryption after you have brought up your services may be to create a new encrypted deployment and then migrate the data over from your original nonencrypted deployment. Most regulatory structures, such as PCI and HIPAA, require that the storage data also be encrypted when making backup and archived copies and that each storage drive be tracked and its location known at all times.

Applying Multifactor Authentication

In Chapter 3, "Security in the Cloud," you learned that *multifactor authentication* (MFA) includes something that you have, such as a one-time token generator or smartcard, and something that you know, like a PIN or password. Figure 4.1 shows an example of an MFA login screen.

FIGURE 4.1 Multifactor authentication login screen

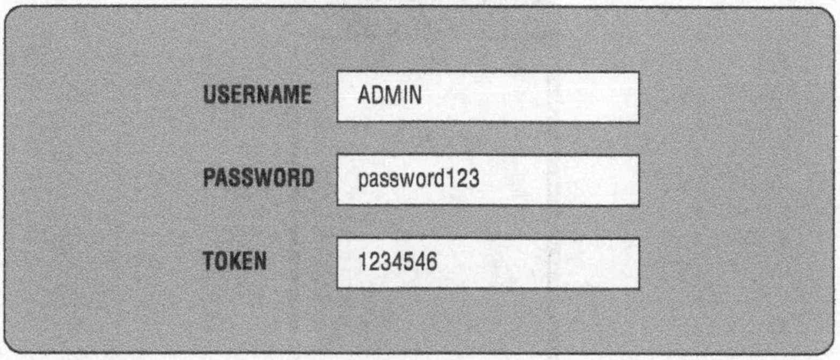

Cloud providers offer a web-based identity management console that you can use to configure user accounts to which you can then assign permissions to access cloud resources. When setting up a user, you can enable MFA for the user. There are also options to use application programming interfaces (APIs) and command-line interfaces to script the MFA configurations.

You can select from several different MFA systems. Hardware tokens are small devices that display a changing authentication code. This code is usually valid for only a few minutes at most and needs to be typed into the authentication dialog box along with the user's username and password. Hardware-based token systems are available from several different global suppliers such as Gemalto and RSA. An example hardware token is shown in Figure 4.2.

FIGURE 4.2 Hardware-based multifactor authentication token

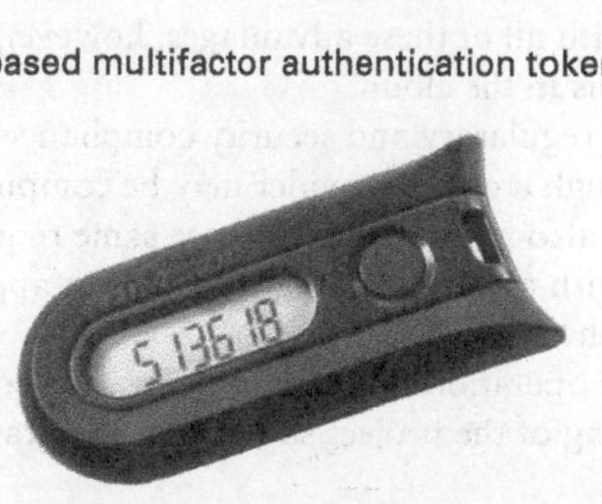

Software-based versions of the hardware MFA tokens are also available. These virtual devices can be installed on laptops, tablets, or smartphones, and they perform the same function as the hardware keychain versions. But instead of having to carry around another device, you can just pull out your mobile phone and access your token. Figure 4.3 shows an example of a software-based token.

FIGURE 4.3 Smartphone-based multifactor authentication token

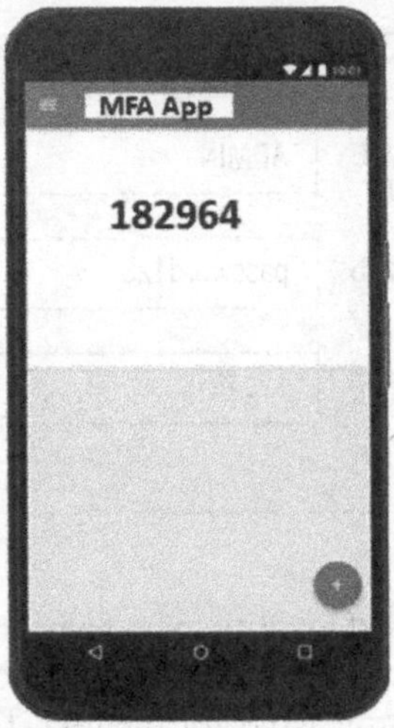

Regulatory and Compliance Issues During Implementation

The cloud offers many advantages over the traditional compute model, including rapid provisioning, the ability to add capacity dynamically, minimal capital expenditures, and access to cutting-edge technology that has traditionally been available only to organizations with large technology budgets. With all of these advantages, however, come a few challenges when implementing your operations in the cloud.

You're responsible for all regulatory and security compliance requirements for your cloud deployment. Even though a cloud provider may be compliant for a specific regulation, this does not absolve you of also having to meet those same requirements on the cloud's platform. Being compliant with all laws and regulations that apply to your deployment is your responsibility and not the cloud provider's.

When implementing your operations in the cloud, it is best to plan to meet all compliance issues from the beginning of the project so that your migration is not delayed with unforeseen compliance requirements. Planning for compliance should start when defining your original requirements and proceed through the design, implementation, and validation phases. After the deployment, extensive testing and validation must be performed to ensure that your migration is working as expected and all compliance configurations are operational. Often, there are reference designs available to guide you on creating the proper architecture to meet specific regulatory requirements. Many third-party agencies and service providers are also available to assist in the process of meeting your specific regulatory requirements when migrating to the cloud. Only after all of the planning, implementing, and validations have been completed is it advisable to proceed to compliance testing with the regulatory authorities.

Cloud Access Security Broker

One challenge that organizations face is consistently applying security policies across cloud-based and on-premises resources. Suppose a company has their security policy configurations down to a science for their IaaS resources—VMs, network and user access control, and so on. But this same company also uses a line-of-business SaaS application, and the security configurations for it are way out of compliance with certain regulations under which the company falls. Such blind spots can occur for a variety of reasons, but often they occur when a department or business unit procures a third-party SaaS application and begins using it without involving the IT organization.

A *cloud access security broker (CASB)* is software that monitors and enforces security policies regarding the user of cloud-based applications. A CASB monitors what cloud-based applications users are accessing and may restrict their access or permit it only under certain circumstances. An agent-based CASB is installed on the device to be monitored, and therefore it isn't very useful for devices that are outside of the organization's control (such as mobile phones). An agentless CASB is typically a hardware or virtual appliance that sits in line between the organization's network and the cloud. It can thus intercept cloud-bound traffic even from user-owned devices and ensure that the user's device and what the user is doing are compliant with the organization's policies.

Automating Cloud Security

Security automation can allow code to replace many of the processes that had to be performed manually in the past, such as creating, configuring, monitoring, and deleting resources. Scripts can be implemented to apply security policy and configurations to new devices such as virtual machines when they are created. This allows for a uniform and consistent security policy for your organization. Event triggers can be defined for security events that can, in turn, call software automation processes to address the alarm.

Applications can be designed with security in mind, operating systems have the ability to automate updates with patch management software, and network security and monitoring systems generate log files and alerts that can be used to instigate an automated security operation.

Automation Tools

In this section, you'll learn about the components and technologies available to create automation tools. You may often hear the cloud described as one big programmable interface by those who have worked with it for many years. The ability to interact with the cloud programmatically is what makes all the cloud economics and operations possible. Implementing a well-defined and agreed-upon set of software interfaces that allow devices to intercommunicate with each other ensures that the magic of cloud computing can happen.

Application Programming Interfaces

An *application programming interface (API)* is a means to access, control, and configure an application or service programmatically. In most cases, any time you make a configuration change on any cloud-based object, whether it is using a web GUI or a command-line interface, you are actually communicating with the device via an API.

The API defines how software components interact with one another. APIs provide the means to enable automation of the complete stack, from the physical devices to the applications and everything in between. Systems that offer an API will publish the documentation for it, allowing software developers and system administrators to write scripts or tools to interact with those systems.

In the cloud, you interact with an API using its network endpoint. For example, a cloud object storage service will likely have a public API endpoint that you can use to create buckets, upload or delete files, and set permissions. Commands that you send to an API are called *requests*, and they must contain enough information to complete the request. At a minimum, you'll need to specify the action to perform, which will involve creating, deleting, or modifying a resource. Using the preceding object storage example, to delete a bucket you'd have to specify the action (delete) and the resource (the identifier of the bucket).

To make interacting with the endpoint easier, many of them use the *Representational State Transfer (REST)* standard that makes use of HTTP operations, particularly `GET`, `POST`, `PUT`, and `DELETE`. These operations usually translate to the following API actions:

`GET`: Get or read the configuration of a resource, such as listing the contents of a bucket.

`POST`: Create a resource, such as a new VM.

`PUT`: Modify a resource, such as setting permissions on a file to make it read-only.

`DELETE`: Delete a resource.

In addition to the operation, an API request may need to reference the resource being acted on. Importantly, the request probably also needs to include some credentials for authentication. All this information is packaged into a tidy data format and sent to the endpoint. The two most common formats that you'll encounter are *JavaScript Object Notation (JSON)* and *Extensible Markup Language (XML)*.

Once you send an API request, the endpoint almost always replies with a response indicating whether the request was successful. There are numerous ways to craft and send API requests and process responses. A common coding language for automation is *Python*. Many Python libraries are available that make interacting with RESTful APIs easier. Of course, you're not limited to Python. Common scripting languages such as Bash and PowerShell also support interacting with APIs. Cloud providers sometimes provide free, tested automation scripts in various languages. You can also find a wide variety of scripts on GitHub.

Command Line

A *command-line interface (CLI)* is a text-based tool used to configure, manage, and troubleshoot devices and services. You're undoubtedly familiar with using the shell or command prompt of your favorite OS. Major cloud providers support their own CLI that's geared toward interacting with their service. Although it's not as user friendly as using a *graphical user interface (GUI)*, such as a web management console, the CLI's complexity and power enables automation through configuration scripts. With some practice, using a CLI can prove faster than using a GUI. In short, almost anything that you can do with the web interface, you can do with the CLI—and then some.

Portals and Dashboards

Cloud providers allow you to create dashboards to monitor your cloud resources. Figure 4.4 shows a sample dashboard featuring some key metrics for a VM running in the cloud. You can configure monitoring to generate an alert or take some action when a particular metric crosses a certain threshold. For example, if the average CPU utilization of a VM remains too high, you might want to receive an email to that effect.

Alerting is a key enabler of automation. You can configure automated responses to various alerts. Using the preceding example, if you have a fleet of web servers, and on an especially busy day their overall average CPU utilization remains too high, you might use the cloud provider's web interface to configure an alarm that will trigger an autoscaling process to provision additional servers to lighten the load.

The same approach can be taken with troubleshooting. If an application running on a VM begins experiencing a large number of errors, the best course of action may just be to delete and re-create the VM from a known, good template. This can be automated as well. For example, you can send application logs to the cloud provider's monitoring service and configure it to look for entries that indicate application errors. When such errors are detected, the service fires off an alarm that terminates the offending VM and launches a new one in its place.

FIGURE 4.4 Dashboard applications show cloud health reports using a browser.

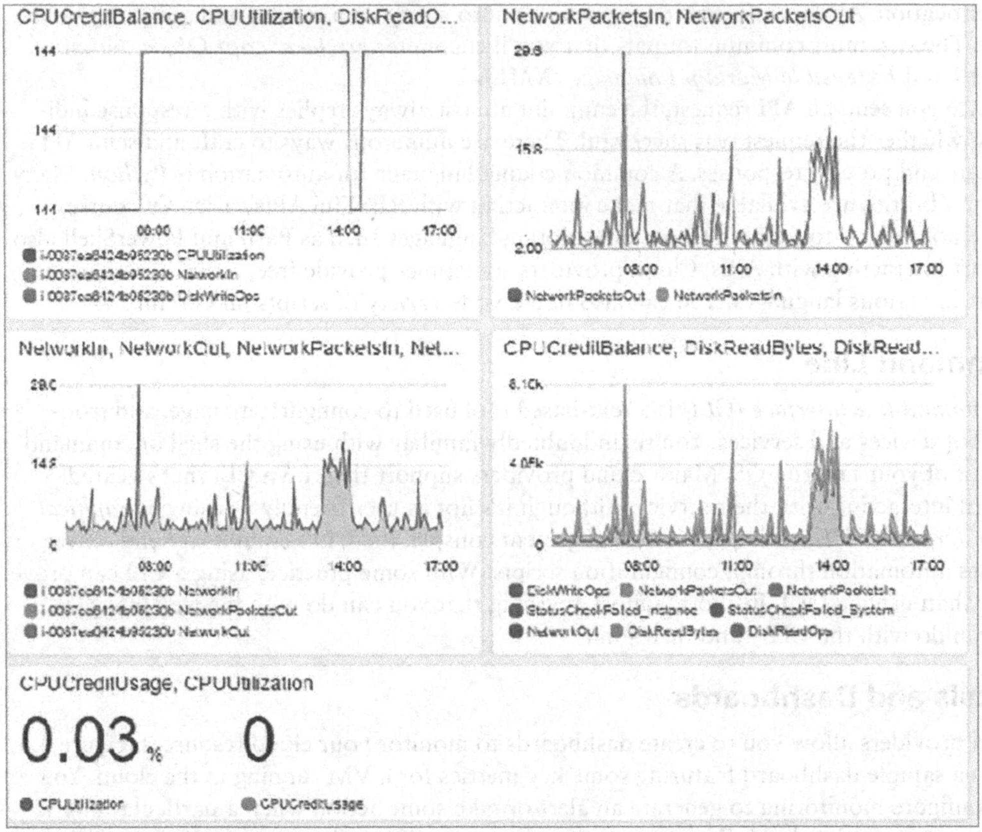

Techniques for Implementing Cloud Security

As you have learned, the shared responsibility model defines the areas you will secure and for what sections the cloud provider assumes responsibility. There are several well-defined approaches you should follow when implementing cloud security. The first is the use of orchestration systems that offer automation for the security overlay of your cloud as a core component. Another common method of implementing security is to run preconfigured scripts that apply policy and security configurations. The final implementation technique discussed in this section is using a customized approach with specific tools designed for cloud security.

Orchestration Systems

Orchestration systems can discover your cloud resources and conduct vulnerability assessments against them. Additional services include compliance management for the many different regulatory compliance requirements that you have to meet. Some orchestration systems may also be able to configure security features automatically, such as logging and intrusion detection and prevention.

Orchestration systems are part of a cloud provider's basic offerings and are most often included at no charge, since they are often a requirement to launch your cloud services. Orchestration systems may be middleware that has a web front end visible to the cloud customer and the APIs to interface with the virtual services in the cloud on the back end.

Most large network management software companies offer commercial orchestration systems. There is a robust open source community offering popular packages such as Chef, Docker, Kubernetes, Puppet, and OpenStack. If you don't want to go it alone, you can contract with a *managed security as a service (MSaaS)* company to handle everything for you.

Script-Based Services

Scripting is a method of automatically running configuration commands, such as commands to deploy cloud resources and configure security policies. Scripts can be run on a virtual machine at startup to apply updates, install applications, and automate the cloud security deployment. Scripts can be run based on time of day using the `CRON` utility or based on an event trigger from network management systems. It is a common practice to deploy a management, or *jump server*, in your fleet of compute instances in the cloud. The jump server can be left up and running at all times and used for management tasks such as running automation scripts.

When writing scripts, it's important to understand and follow the principles of secure scripting. If you can avoid it, don't run a script under your own credentials. Instead, use a dedicated identity or service account for this purpose. Don't hard-code any passwords or secret keys in your script. Hard-coding credentials makes it easier for others to get at those credentials, and whenever the password changes, you have to update the script. Instead of hard-coding credentials, you have a couple of better options.

The first option is to use the cloud provider's authentication system to obtain a temporary authentication key. You can obtain such a key by providing your authentication credentials at runtime and passing the temporary key into the script.

The second option is to use a *secrets manager* or *password vault* to store credentials. Most cloud providers provide a secrets manager service to store credentials securely in an encrypted vault. You craft the script in such a way that when it needs a set of credentials, it calls out to the secrets manager, which in turn returns the needed information. The script doesn't save the credentials but uses them only at runtime and then forgets them. If the credentials ever change, you just update the entry in the secrets manager.

Customized Security Implementation Approaches

Many cloud vendors and equipment suppliers offer applications to implement security configurations in your cloud deployment. For example, a firewall company may offer a configuration and management application based on a technology such as Java or a web front end to an API on the firewall. These specialized interfaces are useful in implementing cloud security since they are tightly integrated with the vendor's product set. A firewall vendor may deploy a virtual firewall in the cloud as a service and integrate custom configuration applications into the cloud provider's management platforms.

Security Services

In the cloud, applications or devices that perform specific functions are often available as a service. Cloud-based security services include devices such as firewalls, intrusion detection and prevention systems, authentication, authorization, and accounting services; security key management; inspection services that scan and report on security configurations; denial-of-service prevention; and data classification services. In addition to this long list of security services, the fast pace of the cloud marketplace means that new offerings are constantly being introduced and existing services are being enhanced and expanded.

Firewalls

A *firewall* sits in line in a network so that all traffic must pass through it. Firewalls will have rule sets, or policies, configured to permit or deny traffic. In addition to performing basic packet filtering, they can monitor TCP, UDP, and ICMP flows for attacks against particular network protocols. Some firewalls, such as web application firewalls, can even monitor application protocol traffic to guard against application-specific attacks.

The firewall rules that you apply to a VM in the cloud apply either at the VM interface level or at the subnet level. Inside your cloud infrastructure, firewalls are used to segment the network and to isolate critical systems from the rest of the network.

In addition to this, you may decide to place a virtual firewall appliance—deployed on a VM—at the border or *perimeter* of your cloud network—between your cloud site and the Internet, for example. Figure 4.5 shows the placement of a perimeter firewall.

FIGURE 4.5 Firewalls define what traffic is allowed in and out of the network.

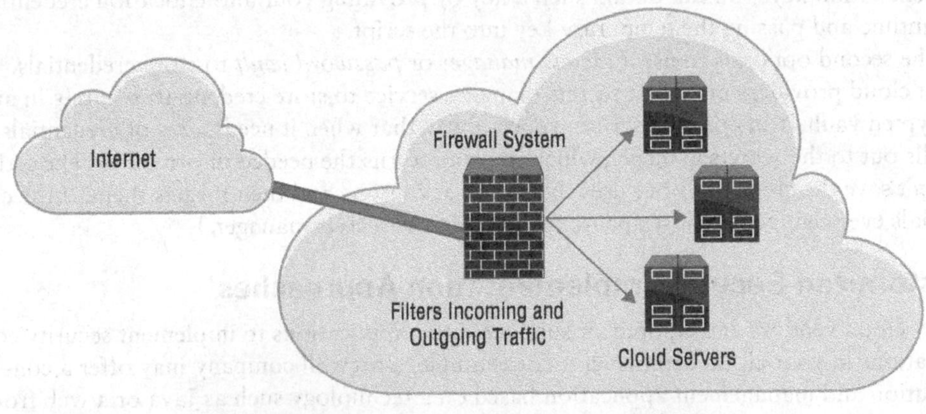

Antivirus and Malware Prevention

Antivirus and antimalware software plays a critical role in the virtualized world of the cloud just as it does in the corporate data center or at home. You can purchase protection software in the marketplace from the same antivirus companies and in the same manner as you are currently doing. Some cloud providers offer antivirus and malware protection services, and if you hire a third-party managed security provider, it will most likely offer the service as part of its standard product portfolio.

Endpoint Detection and Response

End users may access your cloud resources from a variety of devices—laptops, workstations, or smartphones. It's become increasingly popular for employees to use their own devices. Allowing these potentially insecure devices to access cloud resources can pose a significant risk, especially if they're downloading sensitive data onto those devices. A user-owned device is likely to use unencrypted storage, and if the device is stolen, getting that sensitive data might be a trivial process. A device may be infected with malware or be behind on security patches, making it vulnerable to attack. A compromised user device can allow a hacker to access cloud resources surreptitiously without the user even knowing it.

Endpoint detection and response (EDR) requires a user's device to pass certain security checks before they can access IT resources. Such checks include making sure that antivirus software is functioning, definitions are up-to-date, and certain potentially suspicious programs (like spyware or hacking tools) aren't running or installed. EDR may also check that the user is not connecting from an insecure location like a public hotspot or a foreign country.

EDR doesn't just do a one-and-done check. It continually monitors for suspicious activity. For example, if a user connects to a corporate database and begins downloading large volumes of data, EDR can record and even alert on that activity. Continuous monitoring can also head off an attack in progress. If a worm has penetrated a user's home network and begins sending suspicious traffic, EDR can allow IT staff to see and respond to the threat before the worm has a chance to spread further.

Intrusion Detection and Prevention

Intrusion detection systems (IDSs) and *intrusion prevention systems (IPSs)* play as important of a role in the cloud as they do in the private cloud or corporate data center. As you learned in Chapter 2, "Cloud Deployments," IDSs and IPSs are similar in that they are used to monitor network traffic, looking for suspicious activity. Both solutions can detect, in real time, suspicious activity on the network.

Intrusion systems monitor traffic, looking for signatures of network activity that indicate an intrusion based on predefined rule sets that are kept up-to-date by the IDS/IPS vendors. The IDS will alert a management system, or it can be configured to send out emails or text notifications if an attack is discovered. However, the IDS will not take action to remedy the situation—it only monitors and reports.

The IPS is more advanced than the IDS, and it can actively take measures to mitigate the attack with configuration scripts and methods to stop an attack that is under way. The IPS communicates with network devices such as routers and firewalls to apply rules to block the attack.

Most cloud providers will manage their own internal IDS/IPS systems as part of their security posture in the shared security model. MSaaS vendors offer intrusion systems, either as part of their base offerings or as an add-on service. IDS/IPS software companies offer cloud-based versions of their commercial products, with the advantage of templates that can be used to ease the installation, configuration, and management of IDS/IPSs.

When implementing IDS/IPS security in the cloud, investigate your options early in the planning process because offerings can vary widely. Sensors are offered as a native option, or customers can install their own implementations. Many preconfigured virtual machine images of popular commercial and open source IDS/IPS offerings are available in cloud provider marketplaces. These can be especially useful; many intrusion detection and prevention vendors offer a try-before-you-buy option.

Malware detection systems follow the same model as intrusion systems and should be installed on susceptible servers and systems in the cloud, just as they would be in a commercial data center. Companies such as Metaflow offer malware prevention and detection services that are designed for cloud-based operations and can even be deployed at the hypervisor level. Be aware that the cloud service provider most likely is also monitoring for malware and may take steps to stop it.

Host-Based Intrusion Detection Systems

Host-based intrusion detection systems (HIDSs) are applications that run on a server or workstation and perform the same security functions as a network-based IDS. A HIDS may function as a standalone application, or it may report back to a central controller for management and reporting. With IaaS deployments, you will have full control over the operating systems and their configurations in your deployment. This gives you the ability to install your preferred HIDS. For PaaS and SaaS, whether the underlying hosts use HIDS is up to the cloud service provider.

When an attack occurs, a HIDS can record the state of the host at the time of the attack, which programs were affected, and what systems or services were started or modified. It can also capture log files for subsequent analysis. HIDSs are a valuable aid in managing compliance and gathering forensic data in the event of a security breach.

TIP Running antivirus, antimalware, or a HIDS on a VM will likely increase its CPU load. Keep this in mind when sizing your VMs.

Physical Security of Cloud Systems

Security has a critical role to play in any IT deployment, and the cloud is no different. The critical need to protect and secure systems remains the same regardless of where the compute systems reside.

The cloud provider will ensure that it has secured its infrastructure and facilities. Data center personnel will be screened and only allowed in data center areas where they have a need to be. Most cloud data centers are inside of nondescript buildings with no company markings, and the cloud provider takes measures to keep their operations confidential. Since insider attacks are common in IT, the providers take all the steps necessary to mitigate the risk, including doing personnel background checks and monitoring for suspicious activity.

Automation's Impact on Critical Systems

Automation can relieve you of repetitive tasks, facilitate unified deployments, and allow for rapid response to events. Monitoring systems can look for events that indicate an anomaly in the operation of the cloud infrastructure. These events can trigger automated scripts that correct the issue without human intervention, or they can alert the operations staff of the issue. Automation systems are always running in the background of the cloud data center to maintain the uptime of all physical and virtual devices.

Summary

The Cloud+ exam has a strong security focus, which makes the topics in this chapter critical to understand before you take the exam. This chapter focused on the implementation of security in the cloud.

Data classification serves many purposes, including compliance, security, cost control, and data life cycle management. Data can be classified according to its contents as well as its metadata. Cloud providers offer automated, AI-based data classification tools that can help you organize large amounts of data and how it's being used.

You learned that by segmenting your cloud deployment, you can apply granular security policies to each segment, thus reducing the attack surface and "blast radius" of an attack. By carefully segmenting your cloud resources, you can contain or at least limit the scope of an attack if it occurs. You learned how to segment the network, storage, and compute resources, and you were then given an overview of how security can be applied to these segments.

Encryption plays a central role in security. This chapter covered the different ciphers and implementations of encryption that are common in the cloud. Data can be encrypted at rest on storage or in transit as it moves across a network. Encryption is almost universally a must for compliance.

Multifactor authentication adds an extra layer of protection to the authentication process. In addition to providing credentials such as a username and password, MFA requires you to present proof of something that you have, such as a rotating number that is present on a hardware device, on your keychain, or as an application on your phone or laptop. This prevents someone from signing in as you if they discover your credentials. Keep in mind that this added security is a two-edged sword; if you do not have access to your MFA device, you will not be able to log in.

Cloud providers implement APIs to allow programmatic access to their services. When you're managing your cloud infrastructure, whether you're using a web management interface or a command-line interface, behind the scenes you're actually interacting with the cloud provider's API. It is important to understand APIs, what they are, and how they are used, because they are the central programmability interface for cloud services and objects. You don't need to be a programmer, but you should grasp the concepts of API endpoints, requests, and responses. Many APIs use the REST model and represent data in JSON or XML format.

In addition to APIs, there are many overlay applications that abstract the coding needed to communicate with a device using an API. Web-based front ends and vendor applications are available for ease of use in automating and configuring cloud resources. Portals and dashboards are often made available by cloud vendors; they offer a graphical view of your deployment and can be customized with a focus on security monitoring.

Good security requires a defense-in-depth approach. Cloud providers therefore offer security services geared toward many of the different types of resources that you might deploy. Firewalls, intrusion detection and prevention systems, and antivirus and antimalware applications are just a few examples of standard services.

Exam Essentials

Know what data classification is. Data classification is the organization of data into different tiers or categories for the purpose of making data available as required and to meet regulatory requirements, mitigate and manage risk, and secure data. Data can be organized into any defined category and managed according to that category's needs. Metadata is data that is attached to a file and can be thought of as a tag that explains, categorizes, or classifies that data. Metadata allows the data to be tracked as a group and be searched, and it can reduce duplication of like data that can help reduce or even eliminate storage requirements.

Understand segmentation of cloud resources. *Cloud segmentation* is the process of dividing your cloud deployment into sections to allow for granular security policies to be applied. By applying segmentation to your cloud deployment, you can implement a multilayered security approach that aligns with a defense-at-depth security model.

Know how to implement encryption in the cloud. There are regulations and corporate policies that require data to be encrypted not only as it is transmitted across the network but also when it is in a storage system. Be able to read scenario-based questions and determine the type of encryption application that is applicable.

Understand multifactor authentication. Multifactor authentication includes something you know (username and password) and something you have (an MFA device that displays a changing numerical token). When authenticating to systems, you will be prompted for a username and password and also be asked to type in the number given on the rotating token generator. Multifactor authentication offers a higher level of security than using a simple username/password combination.

Understand and differentiate regulatory compliance issues as they relate to the implementation of cloud security. Be able to answer questions related to the implementation of regulatory and compliance requirements. Compliance starts early in the planning process of a cloud deployment and continues through the design, implementation, and validation phases.

When implementing your operations in the cloud, it is best to meet all compliance issues from the beginning of the project so that your migration is not delayed with unforeseen compliance requirements. The exam may include scenario-based questions about specific industries or laws, and you should be able to answer that they are related to compliance.

Know the basics of automation and programmable interfaces. It's possible to automate many of your ongoing cloud security operations. Security automation can allow code to replace many of the processes that had to be performed manually in the past. Questions that reference APIs, REST, JSON, or CLI are likely related to programmability and automation. You do not need to know how to program, but you do need to understand the concepts behind how APIs work.

Identify the different ways that security is implemented. You may be required to identify different methods of implementing security. Examples include using orchestration systems, scripting techniques, and customized automation systems.

Know security services. For the exam, you should understand the basic operations of firewalls, intrusion detection and prevention services, host-based intrusion, and common antivirus and antimalware software implementations. Be able to differentiate between IPS and IDS.

Written Lab

Fill in the blanks for the questions provided in the written lab. You can find the answers to the written labs in Appendix B.

1. The process of organizing information into different tiers or categories is referred to as ________________ ________________.
2. Dividing your cloud fleet of servers into smaller discrete areas for the purpose of applying a granular security policy is known as ________________.
3. Data that is obfuscated on a RAID 5 storage array is ________________ ________________ encryption.
4. Multifactor authentication includes something you ________________ and something you________________.
5. Programmatic configuration of cloud resources is commonly referred to as ________________.
6. A(n) ________________ allows for programmatic interaction with cloud resources.

7. A(n) ______ ______ ______ is a user-friendly interface to a service's APIs.
8. Network-based ______ ______ ______ take active security breach countermeasures.
9. The processes of encryption and decryption may place an additional load on a machine's ______.
10. Security ______ can allow code to replace many processes that had to be performed manually in the past.

Review Questions

The following questions are designed to test your understanding of this chapter's material. For more information on how to obtain additional questions, please see this book's Introduction. You can find the answers in Appendix A.

1. Robert has been tasked with creating a security implementation that segments his employer's e-commerce design to allow for policy enforcement. What are some of the areas that he is investigating? (Choose three.)
   - **A.** Network
   - **B.** Automation
   - **C.** Storage
   - **D.** Compute
   - **E.** APIs
   - **F.** JSON/XML
2. Where can MFA tokens be obtained? (Choose two.)
   - **A.** Python app
   - **B.** Smartphone app
   - **C.** Automation systems
   - **D.** Keyfob
   - **E.** Cloud vendor management dashboard
3. Hank just completed running some security automation scripts on his new fleet of application virtual machines. After applying intrusion detection, virus, and malware protection on the Linux images, he notices an increase in which VM metric on his management dashboard?
   - **A.** DMA
   - **B.** BIOS
   - **C.** CPU
   - **D.** IPSec
   - **E.** I/O
4. What technology was instrumental in the growth of cloud services?
   - **A.** XML
   - **B.** Python
   - **C.** Automation
   - **D.** Authentication
   - **E.** Scripting
   - **F.** Workflow services
   - **G.** Encryption

5. Carl is planning his cloud migration and must meet HIPAA requirements for confidential storage of data at rest in the cloud. What services must be addressed by Carl? (Choose two.)
   A. Virtual private network
   B. Storage
   C. Client-side
   D. Database
6. What is a common cloud-based GUI used to get an overview of your security operations?
   A. Puppet automation
   B. Gemalto system
   C. Dashboard
   D. Vendor-based security appliance
7. Who is responsible for the security of customer data stored in the cloud?
   A. Cloud provider
   B. Compliance agency
   C. Cloud customer
   D. Shared responsibility
8. What are systems that automate cloud operations called?
   A. Authentication
   B. Federations
   C. Orchestration
   D. Ephemeral
   E. API
9. RESTful APIs using XML and JSON can be used to provision what cloud-based services? (Choose all that apply.)
   A. Firewalls
   B. Load balancers
   C. Virtual machines
   D. DNS servers
   E. Durable storage volumes
10. Jim has a critical server in the application tier of his cloud-based deployment. He is looking at a device-specific security solution to add defense-in-depth capabilities to his currently deployed network-based security defenses. He has been researching ways to mitigate potential hacking attempts. What is a good solution for him?
   A. DMZ
   B. IDS

C. IPS
D. Classifications automation
E. HIDS

11. A constantly changing six-digit numerical token is used in what type of cloud service?
    A. XML
    B. TLS
    C. SSL
    D. MFA
    E. JSON

12. You're developing a web-based dashboard that must pull data from many different cloud locations and devices. Which of the following will you need to use?
    A. Python
    B. XML
    C. API
    D. SNMP
    E. TLS

13. Samantha has been tasked to meet FedRAMP compliance for her customer's new contract. Where should she integrate compliance in her project? (Choose four.)
    A. Handoff
    B. Design
    C. Implementation
    D. Automation rollout
    E. Planning
    F. Validation
    G. HIDS
    H. JSON/XML scripting

14. Sharon is investigating a standards-based construct to enable automation on her load balancers. What is a good lightweight data-interchange format standard that is easily readable and for computing systems to parse and generate? (Choose two.)
    A. XML
    B. JSON
    C. REST
    D. Python

15. Mike has been investigating multiple hacking attempts on his cloud e-commerce web servers. He wants to add a front end with a service that actively takes countermeasures to shut down the hacking attempts. What application would you suggest that Mike deploy?
   - **A.** DMZ
   - **B.** IDS
   - **C.** IPS
   - **D.** RAID
   - **E.** HIDS

16. Hank works in his e-commerce company's IT security group and has been tasked to investigate options that will allow customers to securely access over the web their personal records stored on the cloud deployment from their smartphones. What is the most common protocol for in-flight encryption?
   - **A.** MD5
   - **B.** TLS
   - **C.** IPsec
   - **D.** VPN

17. Storage that does not survive a virtual machine shutdown is referred to as what? (Choose two.)
   - **A.** Durable
   - **B.** RAID
   - **C.** Ephemeral
   - **D.** Nondurable
   - **E.** Tiered

18. Cloud segmentation enhances security for cloud-based applications. What services is it a best practice to segment?
   - **A.** Python
   - **B.** Compute
   - **C.** RAM
   - **D.** VPN

19. What is a long-standing text-based interface that is used to configure network services both locally and remotely?
   - **A.** GUI
   - **B.** CLI
   - **C.** REST
   - **D.** SNMP
   - **E.** API

20. Your company has purchased an IPS. When reading the documentation, you notice a link to download a Java application to monitor and configure the IPS. What kind of management application is this?

A. CLI

B. HTTP

C. GUI

D. API

E. REST

Chapter 5

Maintaining Cloud Operations

THE FOLLOWING COMPTIA CLOUD+ EXAM OBJECTIVES ARE COVERED IN THIS CHAPTER:

✓ **1.3 Explain the importance of high availability and scaling in cloud environments.**

- Clusters

✓ **1.4 Given a scenario, analyze the solution design in support of the business requirements.**

- Environments
  - Deployment
  - Quality assurance (QA)
  - Staging
  - Blue-green
  - Production
  - Disaster recovery (DR)

✓ **2.3 Given a scenario, apply the appropriate OS and application security controls.**

- Builds
  - Stable
  - Long-term support (LTS)
  - Beta
  - Canary
- Operating system (OS) upgrades

✓ **2.4 Given a scenario, apply data security and compliance controls in cloud environments.**

- Records management
  - Versioning
  - Retention
  - Destruction
  - Write once read many

✓ **4.2 Given a scenario, maintain efficient operation of a cloud environment.**

- Confirm completion of backups
- Patching
  - Features or enhancements
  - Fixes for broken or critical infrastructure or applications
  - Scope of cloud elements to be patched
    - Hypervisors
    - VMs
    - Virtual appliances
    - Networking components
    - Applications
    - Storage components
    - Firmware
    - Software
    - OS
  - Policies
    - n-1
  - Rollbacks
- Upgrade methods
  - Rolling upgrades
  - Blue-green

        - Canary
        - Active-passive
        - Development/QA/production/DR

✓ **4.4 Given a scenario, apply proper automation and orchestration techniques.**

    - Infrastructure as code
        - Infrastructure components and their integration
    - Continuous integration/continuous deployment (CI/CD)
    - Version control
    - Automation activities
        - Routine operations
        - Updates
        - Scaling
        - Shutdowns
        - Restarts
        - Create internal APIs
    - Orchestration sequencing

✓ **4.5 Given a scenario, perform appropriate backup and restore operations.**

    - Backup types
        - Incremental
        - Differential
        - Full
        - Synthetic full
        - Snapshot
    - Backup objects
        - Application-level backup
        - Filesystem backup
        - Database dumps
        - Configuration files

- Backup targets
  - Tape
  - Disk
  - Object
- Backup and restore policies
  - Retention
  - Schedules
  - Location
  - SLAs
  - Recovery time objective (RTO)
  - Recovery point objective (RPO)
  - Mean time to recovery (MTTR)
  - 3-2-1 rule
    - Three copies of data
    - Two different media
    - One copy off-site
- Restoration methods
  - In place
  - Alternate location
  - Restore files
  - Snapshot

In this chapter, you'll learn about the maintenance and ongoing operations of your cloud deployment. You'll learn about the various methods and operational approaches of performing software patches and updates. This chapter will also cover backup and disaster recovery operations. We'll explore the operational aspects of backing up your cloud resources and recovering from failures. The primary enabling technology of cloud computing is automation, so we'll discuss how automation can help simplify and streamline these maintenance tasks.

Applying Security Patches

Almost all software has bugs that must be patched to prevent undesirable and sometimes catastrophic consequences. Some bugs are benign, perhaps annoying, whereas other bugs can create gaping security holes that can put your data at risk. When a vulnerability is discovered, the details are often published or leaked to the media. People with less than wholesome intentions can use this information to craft exploits by taking advantage of these bugs with the knowledge that most systems are out-of-date and not protected.

With this in mind, it's important to keep on top of the security landscape and have a planned approach to patch management. This section will focus on the subject of securing your cloud resources by keeping your systems up-to-date.

As part of a shared responsibility model, the cloud provider will secure some of the infrastructure, and the cloud customer will be required to address security concerns based on the service model under which they are operating. A complete patch management approach must be developed, implemented, and adhered to in order to prevent a security breach.

Patching Cloud Resources

When discussing security in this chapter, I will break it down based on elements in the cloud that may require patches to be installed to mitigate security concerns. Although this is not anywhere close to a complete list of devices or services, I will discuss patching hypervisors, VMs, appliances, networking components, applications, storage systems, and clustered devices, which cover a large swath of cloud systems.

Hypervisors

As you now know, a hypervisor is the software that virtualizes server hardware, enabling it to be shared among virtual machines (VMs). This is of course critical software that is often hidden from sight but at the core of a virtualized data center.

Since there are many VMs running on each hypervisor and given that the hypervisor is a core component of the server, most, if not all, operations on the hypervisor will require that it be taken offline when patching or upgrading takes place. To prevent the disruption of the operations of every VM running on top of the hypervisors, each VM will need to be migrated to another server before any patches are performed on the hypervisor.

Once all active services have been migrated off the server, then patching can be performed on the hypervisor while it's offline. Hypervisor code will require periodic maintenance to address security vulnerabilities, fix feature deficiencies, and add functionality.

The cloud provider usually manages the hypervisor and is thus responsible for patching it. Under some offerings, however, the cloud provider may give you control over the hypervisor, in which case patching may be your responsibility. This is likely the case if you're using bare-metal servers on which you've installed a hypervisor.

Virtual Machines

The operating system and software on a VM will require patch management as well. There are third-party patch management applications that track patches and download, implement, and validate the installation of the patched software automatically. Some cloud providers provide their own patch management systems that integrate with their native cloud management interface, allowing you to incorporate patch management into your existing workflows easily.

One approach to patching VMs is to patch the existing VMs online. For example, if you need to patch the web server running on a VM, you remove that VM from load balancing and install the patches. Then you add the VM back into the load balancing target group. You can patch all VMs at once or do rolling updates where you patch one or a few at a time.

Another approach to patching involves patching offline VM images and then deploying them. In this approach, you leave the existing VMs alone, but install and test patches on a template image that you then deploy to replace the existing VMs. This approach allows for testing of new patches prior to deployment to production. But regardless of the approach you use, it's best to set aside a maintenance window for applying patches.

Virtual Appliances

Just as VMs require a patch management process to ensure that they are kept up-to-date and secure from exploits, so too virtual appliances need to be patched. A *virtual appliance* is a specialized application or suite of applications running on Linux, so it has its own set of deficiencies and vulnerabilities that require ongoing patch management.

Virtual appliances include firewalls, load balancers, and IDSs/IPSs, for example. Vendors license these products to you, and although they may offer patches and upgrades, it's usually your responsibility to perform the ongoing maintenance of these applications. Most offer support agreements that allow access to vendor support forums, technical support teams, and software updates.

There are many different virtual appliance offerings from many different companies. Each vendor offering virtual appliances will have its own security and patch management offerings based on its own product offerings.

Applications

The application or development teams will generally be responsible for patching and maintaining systems at the application level. If the application was developed internally, or you are running an IaaS or PaaS service, then you'll be responsible for application maintenance.

However, if you are purchasing a software-as-a-service (SaaS) solution from your cloud provider, then the provider will assume responsibility for maintaining and ensuring that the applications are current and secure.

Many applications will check automatically with a central repository to make sure that they are current, and if they are not, they can download and either install the update or prompt you that there is an update available and allow you to manage the process.

Automation software, such as Puppet or Chef, can also patch applications if configured to do so. Automated scripts can also be run on the servers that check for and install application updates.

Storage Systems

SAN Fibre Channel switches, storage controller heads, host bus adapters, and RAID controller software all go through the revision cycle just like any other system that runs on software. Because of their critical nature and need for constant uptime, storage systems are highly redundant. This allows for some flexibility in performing updates as one part of the storage systems that can be temporarily taken offline for maintenance while the backup system assumes full operational responsibility. The cloud provider will generally be responsible for keeping these systems updated.

Clusters

Clusters are groups of computers interconnected by a local area network. Clusters can be configured in many different topologies depending on the use case and the different solutions for which they are designed. However, all clusters are designed for high availability, which can allow you to install patches with zero downtime. Depending on the capabilities of the cluster software, most individual components in a cluster can be taken offline without the need to take the whole cluster down. This flexibility allows individual systems to be upgraded while the cluster is live. Another common approach is to upload the patch to a master or controller node in a cluster and have the cluster management software perform the upgrades internally.

Patching Methodologies

By making sure that all of your systems have current patches installed, you can reduce your attack footprint and protect yourself by addressing known bugs that may affect your operations. You can take different approaches when patching your systems, and there are different types of patches for different requirements that you'll explore in this section.

It's best to make sure that your applications have the same patches installed—that is, keep them at the same version, revision, or patch level. Doing so will allow you to have a known baseline for you to operate on and to troubleshoot. Patch management applications keep track of patch levels, which is a necessity in larger deployments. For small deployments that don't warrant investment in patch management, some administrators use a basic spreadsheet and manually track software version levels that are installed on platforms either on-premises or in the cloud.

Given that there are often a large number of patches released every week or month, it can become a chore to track them and decide which ones demand immediate attention to solve a critical issue and which ones are minor or cosmetic and can be safely ignored. You must also know the proper order in which to install these patches.

It's helpful to classify the risk that each patch mitigates. For example, an unpatched vulnerability that leaves a web application open to attack might be mitigated if the application is behind a web application firewall. The likelihood of an attack should be assessed, including how critical the system is. Is there a bigger operational risk installing the patch than leaving the system as it currently is configured? It usually comes down to how severe the threat is, the potential impact it may have on your operations, the probability that you could get exploited by your unpatched systems, and the cost of time and the monetary impact to recover if you were to be attacked by choosing not to install the patch.

Production Systems

Applying patches in the production environment is inherently risky. Production updates will need to follow the change management process, and a plan should be developed that outlines the upgrade steps, the validation and testing process, and the rollback process should the patch cause undesirable results.

All patches should be tested prior to a production rollout. If you have a large fleet of servers, automating the process can help to ensure consistency. Many automation systems, such as Puppet, Chef, or Ansible, allow you to automate updates. After the rollout, you should validate that the patches were installed successfully. Test to make sure that the system is operating as expected, and if you uncover any issues, have a rollback plan in place to restore the system to its original state.

There is a risk to patching production servers, but you may not have a choice depending on the severity of the bug that needs to be corrected. If time allows, you may consider rolling out patches gradually to a few systems at a time, leaving the rest available to handle regular workloads.

Development Systems

Patching systems in the development stage allows for full integration of system patches prior to QA testing and rollout of your applications. The DevOps team should evaluate the patches and integrate them into their product as soon as practical. If this isn't feasible, then patches can be deployed in the staging environment. This approach avoids the need to patch systems after they've been deployed into production.

Quality Assurance

Updates should be validated by the software vendor, the cloud company, and your operations staff in order to determine how the patch will perform in production. It's important that you establish a quality assurance test bed that allows you to test the patch in your specific environment in order to identify dependencies, interoperability issues, unknowns, and, most of all, whether the update fixes the problem you are experiencing!

For the software vendor that has developed the patch, it's absolutely critical that the vendor performs a full suite of QA tests of the package. This testing is done to verify that the fix does in fact fix the issue that it was intended to fix. Also, QA tests are done to make sure that the fix does not interfere with other processes and that there are no memory or buffer issues experienced with the patched version of software.

Rolling Updates

Rolling updates is the constant delivery of software updates or patches to operating systems or applications. Other terms that are synonymous with rolling updates are *rolling releases* and *continuous delivery*. Rolling updates are generally related to small but frequent updates. Rolling updates are common in the Linux world and are often delivered as a package accessed remotely over the Internet. A rolling update is performed sequentially, with one system being patched at a time; when the first system's patch is complete, the next system is patched, as shown in Figure 5.1.

FIGURE 5.1 Rolling updates are performed sequentially.

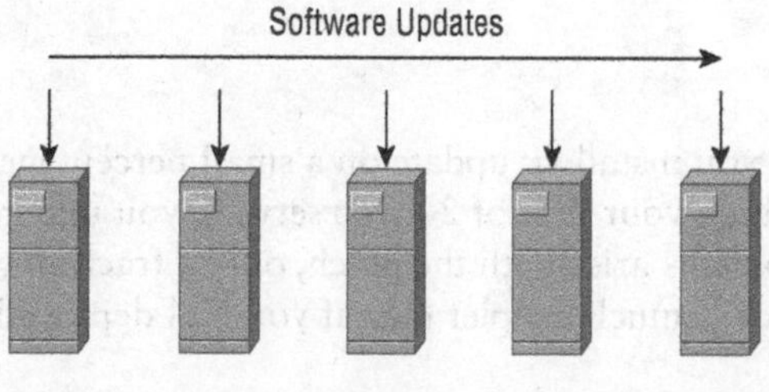

Blue-Green

Blue-green is a deployment method used to update a production environment with minimal interruption. As such, it can be used not just for patching but for any changes. In a blue-green deployment, the existing environment is left untouched. You create a new, identical environment that you then patch or otherwise update as needed. When ready, you move all production workloads to the newly updated environment.

Each environment can function independently and handle the complete workload without assistance from the other. One of the two identical environments is referred to as *blue*, and the other is called *green*. This model allows you to implement, test, and validate software updates in the inactive environment without affecting production. Once this operation has been performed and you feel comfortable with the updates, you can activate the inactive environment and deactivate the other. Blue and green are arbitrary names that are merely used to differentiate between two sides.

The blue-green model avoids downtime by supplying two identical deployments that allow you to operate while one is active and have the other on standby. Updating the inactive one does not affect the active one, and it allows for thorough testing before going live. The blue-green approach also works well for new application deployments in critical implementations with high uptime requirements or for critical customer-facing applications. Rollbacks are as fast as redirecting traffic to the standby. The downside is that this approach requires a massive fleet of servers since you must allocate as many resources in standby mode as you do for your production fleet of servers. Figure 5.2 illustrates a blue-green deployment.

FIGURE 5.2 Blue-green deployment

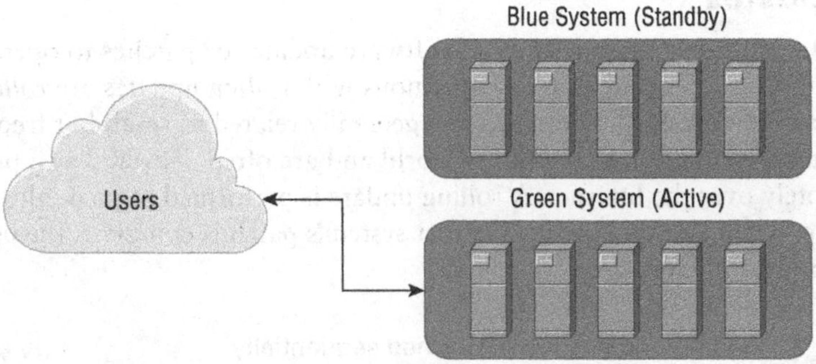

Canary

In a *canary* deployment, you install an update on a small percentage of systems. For example, if you are patching your fleet of 20 web servers, you may patch only two of them, or 10 percent. If any problems arise with the patch, only a fraction of users will be affected, and performing a rollback is much simpler than if you had deployed the patch to all servers.

Clustering and Failover

A *cluster* is a group of servers operating in tandem to process a shared workload. A cluster typically consists of a master node that coordinates processing among cluster members. You can manage a cluster as a single system and not be concerned with all the individual systems that make up the cluster. Patches can be downloaded to the master node, which will push out and install the updates to the other systems in the cluster. Depending on the system and its capabilities, a cluster can be upgraded while maintaining full operational capabilities, less the reduced capacity of individual nodes being taken offline for upgrades. The devices in the cluster work together to support a high-availability platform for applications and services, as shown in Figure 5.3. If any node in a cluster were to fail, other nodes would pick up the operations and continue without any downtime.

FIGURE 5.3 Cluster updates on each server with no downtime

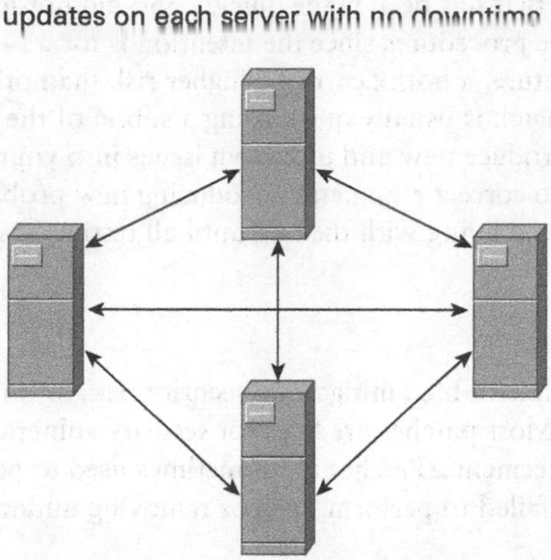

Patching Order of Operations and Dependencies

When applying patches, it's sometimes necessary to apply patches in a certain order because of dependencies. A server may need to be rebooted after installing certain patches and before subsequent patches can be installed. Take into account the additional time required for such patches. System documentation or release notes will explain the steps and in what specific order they should be performed. Any packages, especially on Linux systems, ship with package managers that abstract the dependencies and are applied without any user intervention.

Updating Cloud Elements

Software updates are a necessary part of the computing landscape. Bugs, regulatory requirements, security concerns, and the market demand for new features or capabilities all drive the continual stream of updates.

In this section, you'll learn about the various types of updates that are available and the problems they are intended to solve. During your career in cloud computing, you'll find that these terms are often used interchangeably. This section will allow you to understand what the terms really are and how they should be used. Out in the field, your mileage will vary widely!

Hotfix

A *hotfix* is a software update type that is intended to fix a specific problem quickly. A hotfix may be custome-specific and not released to the public or available to everyone. Patches are often developed and deployed rapidly without undergoing thorough testing. Many times, a hotfix is a bug fix that has been made quickly and did not follow the normal quality assurance or formal release procedures since the intention is for a rapid deployment.

Because of its urgent nature, a hotfix carries a higher risk than other approaches to patching software. Testing the patch is usually quick using a subset of the full QA test suites. Installing a hotfix may introduce new and unknown issues into your environment. The risk of installing a hotfix to correct a bug and introducing new problems must be weighed against not taking action and living with the bug until all testing has been completed.

Patch

A *patch* is an update that fixes a bug, mitigates a security risk, or improves the reliability or performance of a system. Most patches are fixes for security vulnerabilities. Patches typically do not offer feature enhancements. Patches are sometimes used to perform housekeeping that developers may have failed to perform, such as removing undocumented features.

Version Update

A *version update* is the process of replacing a software product with a newer version of the same product. Version updates can add new features, bring the system up-to-date, and provide a rollup of all previous patches to improve the product. Upgrading entails replacing the current, older version of the same product with a newer version. Often, a version update includes major feature enhancements and capabilities. As such, there may be a charge associated with the upgrade. Think of upgrading to the hottest new release of Microsoft Windows Server.

The most current release of an application is called *n*, so if you are one release behind the latest, you're said to be at n-1. Many organizations adopt an n-1 policy to avoid potential problems caused by the latest release. But not all version updates are created equal. Here are a few different types you should know:

Stable This is the type of version update most individuals and organizations want. *Stable* releases have been thoroughly tested and are expected just to work. The developer tends to stand behind stable releases, and you can typically acquire a support contract for them. Stable versions are usually released on a frequent and recurring basis, allowing you to stay up-to-date while minimizing the risks inherent in upgrades.

Long-Term Support (LTS) *LTS* versions are released on a scheduled cadence and have a defined support lifetime. LTS builds are meant for organizations that aren't comfortable with frequent updates or that require a high level of reliability and quality that may not be present in stable releases. LTS releases may lack the latest and greatest features.

Beta *Beta* versions offer new features or fixes, but they tend to be buggy and thus inappropriate for production use. Software developers offer beta versions as a way of testing new features or fixes in the real world, not just in controlled test environments. Organizations may use beta versions for proofs of concept or to test a new feature or bug fix.

Rollback

A *rollback* is the process of uninstalling updates with the intention of returning the software to its previous state. If a software update failed, did not correct the issue as expected, or introduced new issues, then a rollback may need to be performed.

The process of performing a rollback is dependent on each system. If it's a VM, then you can take a snapshot of the VM before installing the patch. If you need to perform a rollback, just revert to the snapshot. Some applications and operating systems have scripts or utilities that automate the rollback procedure. In other cases, it may be necessary to reinstall the original software package to overwrite the patch.

The term *rollback* is also common when working with databases, and it refers to an operation that can return the database to a known previous state to maintain database integrity. If there is a severe database issue, you can roll back to the last good backup.

Workflow Automation

A *workflow* is a defined sequence of stages in which one or more actions can occur. These actions may yield outputs that can then be passed along to the next stage. For example, ordering an item online triggers a workflow that consists of actions such as payment processing, shipping, and tracking. Each stage of the workflow depends on the success of the previous stage, as well as some outputs or artifacts from the stage. For instance, you can't track a package until you obtain a tracking number, which is an artifact of the shipping process. Think of a workflow as a flowchart that uses automation tools to carry out the process steps of the flowchart.

Workflow automation tracks and monitors the workflow sequence to see it through to completion. Workflow automation reduces errors since it follows a defined sequence of events, which ensures that all previous steps are completed before passing to the next step. This allows for consistency and eliminates human error.

Workflows can be created and used as templates for large system upgrades that automate the process of updating cloud-based systems in a systematic and predictable manner. If there are software dependencies that require one patch to be installed before another patch, for example, then a workflow can be created that tracks and verifies that the order of operations have been completed before passing to the next workflow step.

Runbooks

Automation platforms use *runbooks* to define the tasks that the automation software should carry out—essentially, a script. Runbooks can be created to automate the installation of software updates. Runbooks can be used to automate tasks for other operations such as responding to events or alarms or performing routine system maintenance.

Multiple runbooks can be created, with each one dedicated to performing a specific automated task. When an event occurs, the automation and orchestration applications can execute a specific runbook to perform an action based on the event. For example, if a VM should fail, the management software could call a runbook that runs a series of diagnostics, attempts to restart the VM, tests for completion, and installs a new VM using a predefined image if the restart fails. If a new VM is created, a runbook could be used to install all updates and applications that are required.

Orchestration

Orchestration systems automate workflows in a way that minimizes the need for human intervention. They are often couched in terms such as service-orientated architecture, automated provisioning, converged infrastructure, or dynamic data center. Orchestration systems play a key role in deploying new services and systems as well as responding to operational events such as a loss of network services that may necessitate switching to a backup system or calling programs to restart a failed system. Orchestration systems carry out the automated operations in the modern cloud that used to be done manually in the data center.

The main function of orchestration systems is to automate a series of tasks that must be completed to accomplish an operation. These tasks are combined into a workflow that defines the order of events and steps needed to complete the operation. The orchestration system uses software systems and processes to carry out the workflow. Orchestration abstracts and hides much of the complexity of modern cloud systems, and it also reduces operational errors by executing tested cloud systems, scripts, workflows, or runbooks to make sure that the systems are configured correctly.

Cloud providers usually offer a web management console or command-line interface (CLI) as a front end to their automation systems. End users will not be able to access these systems directly, but they can input order or configuration requests that trigger the orchestration systems running in the background. The web front ends also act as a dashboard that allows you to monitor the activities in real time as the orchestration system carries out its operations. There are also APIs, typically published for software developers, to access these systems programmatically.

Some orchestration systems allow for an approach called *infrastructure-as-code (IaC)*. IaC lets you use code to define the end state of your systems. For example, if you want to install a particular version of an application on a fleet of VMs, you simply set the desired version number, and the orchestration system figures out how to make it happen. Contrast this with a more imperative approach such as scripting, where you would have to spell out the exact steps to download and install the version of the application you want.

Continuous Integration and Continuous Deployment

Continuous integration (CI) and *continuous deployment* or *delivery (CD)* are methods that software developers use to deliver new versions of applications rapidly. In CI, developers use a version control system like Git to make changes to source code in a shared repository. During what is called the *build stage*, an automated system might compile the code into an installable package. A key purpose of CI is to make sure that new code works as expected, so the build stage can also include automated tests to verify that new features work and that changes didn't break functions that were already working.

CD enables regular, automatic updates. There's a lot of overlap between CI and CD, but CD adds the final step of deploying the application to production. A CD workflow or pipeline might include a testing stage, but it always includes a deployment stage. Given that CI and CD functions overlap, someone combined them and coined the term CI/CD pipeline.

Virtualization Automation Tools and Activities

This section will address the various issues of patching VMs. You'll learn about creating snapshots and clones of VMs. We'll also discuss common practices about which you should be aware when performing maintenance such as temporarily disabling monitoring so as not to generate unnecessary alarms on systems undergoing routine maintenance.

Snapshots

A *snapshot* is a point-in-time image of a VM's disk(s). It includes the complete set of operating systems and all the applications that are stored on it. The snapshot will record the data on the disk, its current state, and the VM's configuration at that instant in time, as illustrated in Figure 5.4.

FIGURE 5.4 Virtual machine snapshot

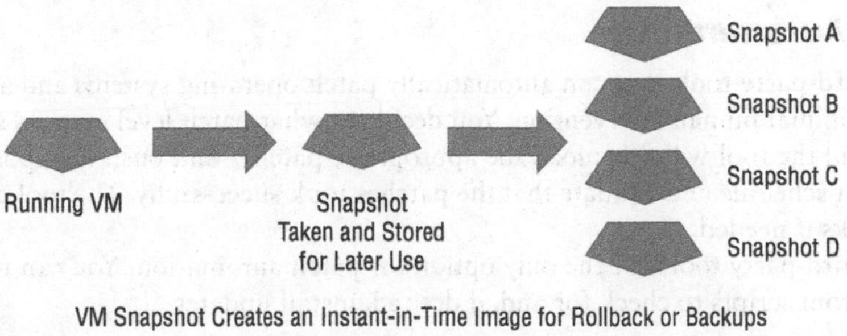

Taking a snapshot is a quick way of backing up the VM's state without having to copy it. The snapshotted state of the VM is preserved, and subsequent changes are stored separately. This makes it easy to revert the VM to its snapshotted state. If the snapshot is no longer needed, it can be deleted.

The process of taking a snapshot is usually performed with the management tools that are used to administer the virtual environment. When a snapshot is created while the VM is running, it's called a *crash-consistent snapshot*. If the snapshot is created while the VM is shut down, it's called an *application-consistent snapshot*.

Cloning Virtual Devices

There is a second type of VM replication called *cloning*, as shown in Figure 5.5. Cloning involves making a copy of the VM, unlike a snapshot, which simply preserves a VM's state at a point in time. Cloning is usually done to create a fleet of near-identical servers from a single golden master VM. After cloning, each VM usually goes through a cleaning process to change unique elements such as the server name, universal unique identifier (UUID), and MAC and IP addresses of the cloned server.

FIGURE 5.5 Virtual machine cloning

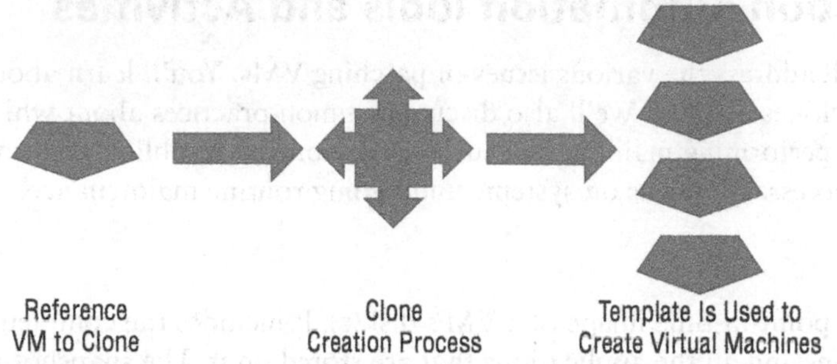

NOTE

Use snapshots when you need to preserve a VM's state prior to making changes to it. Clone a VM if you need create a new VM from it.

Patching Automation

There are third-party tools that can automatically patch operating systems and applications with minimal human intervention. You decide at what patch level systems should be operating, and the tool will download the appropriate patches and push the updates out to the VMs on a schedule and validate that the patches took successfully. The tool can also perform rollbacks if needed.

Using a third-party tool isn't the only option for patch automation. You can write and schedule custom scripts to check for and, if desired, install updates.

Restarting Systems

Software updates may require rebooting a VM, possibly multiple times. The restart process can be monitored through the management systems and dashboards that are offered by the cloud provider. Depending on the application and operation being performed, the dashboard may not be notified of a restart at the application level. The ability to notify the monitoring systems may depend on the management and reporting capabilities of the system that is being restarted.

Shutting Down Systems

A shutdown may be desired if you choose to retain the VM and its applications but do not need it to be active. You may also want to shut down VMs momentarily in order to create an application-consistent snapshot or clone. Most cloud providers will not charge your compute cycles for a VM that is not running. However, if the VM is using a block storage volume, you may continue to be charged for the space that volume consumes. So, having VMs that are shut down makes sense as a cost-saving measure that allows you to bring fully configured computing capacity online quickly later as needed.

Enabling Maintenance Mode

When performing maintenance on a server in the cloud, it's a best practice to put it into *maintenance mode*. When a server is undergoing maintenance, it may be in a state that it will not respond to health checks, API calls, Simple Network Management Protocol (SNMP), or any other means used to monitor its health by network management systems. This failure to respond to various monitoring methods may cause false alarms and trigger automated troubleshooting systems. When a server is in maintenance mode, the management systems will not respond to alarms from the server being down for maintenance.

Enabling/Disabling System Alerts

Alerting allows a virtual server to send management data to monitoring systems informing them of either predefined or custom events. Alerts can be in the form of traps, logging information, or data generated by management software running on the server. In the cloud dashboard or management console, many cloud providers allow you to enable or disable the alerting system. When you initially create a virtual server, you may set alerting to be enabled for that VM, and the automation systems will create a managed object for that server in the monitoring systems. As discussed earlier, it's a best practice to disable alerts prior to taking a server offline for maintenance.

Storage Operations

In this section, you'll learn about *storage operations* related to backing up and restoring your data. You will become familiar with the different types of backups and the best use cases for each one. Backups are a critical piece of your overall IT strategy and will usually be required for regulatory compliance and corporate policy.

Backups may be performed by the cloud provider as part of its service offerings and as a managed service. Cloud customers may also want to implement their own backup strategy to meet their specific needs.

Types of Backups

Many different types of backups are available to meet use cases and objectives. I will cover the most common backups that are objectives for the Cloud+ exam.

When thinking about backups, you should know two metrics. Your *recovery time objective (RTO)* is the maximum time you're willing to wait to recover data and get back up and running after a failure. Your *recovery point objective (RPO)* is the maximum amount of data that you're willing to lose.

If you have a low RTO, you'll need to consider how quickly you can recover using your chosen backup methods. For example, recovering data from tapes is probably going to take longer than recovering from hard drives. If you have a low RPO, then you'll need to back up more frequently. As you read through the rest of this chapter, think about how your backup choices will affect your ability to meet your RTO and RPO.

Image Backups

Image backups are byte-by-byte copies of complete block storage volumes. This technology is often called *disaster backup*, *cloning*, *ghosting*, *image backups*, or *block-level backups*. You use image backups to prepare for disasters resulting from losing VMs, or to roll back an image after an update has failed or from a server that will not boot or is corrupted. Image backups are also used to provision workstations rapidly for end users. The process works by copying or imaging a source hard drive with all the desired applications and configurations and then copying that image to other computers. Figure 5.6 shows the process of creating an image backup.

FIGURE 5.6 Image backup

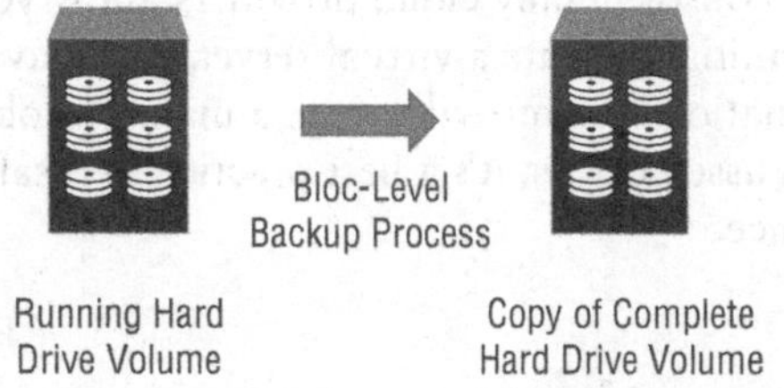

LUN Cloning

LUN cloning is the process of creating an identical copy of a unit of block storage. Just as cloning a VM involves using an existing VM to create *another* one, when cloning a storage area network (SAN) LUN, you're creating another LUN. One advantage of a LUN clone is that it can double as a backup because that's what it is. A disadvantage, however, is that a clone takes up as much storage space as the original source since all the data is copied in the clone operation. There is also a performance hit with cloning in that overhead is involved when writing data to the cloned copy from the source while the source is actively serving production storage operations.

File Backups

File backups, sometimes called filesystem backups, are what people normally think of when backing up a server or personal system. File backups, as shown in Figure 5.7, are the storage of folders and files that you select with your backup software to copy to another storage location for later access if needed. File backups are generally smaller in space requirements, are more efficient, and have more options during restorations than complete image backups.

FIGURE 5.7 File backup

Snapshots

Storage *snapshots* are a point-in-time copy of a storage volume or image that can be used as a backup to shorten RTO and RPO. There are several variations of snapshots. The two most prominent are the copy-on-write and redirect-on-write snapshots.

The *copy-on-write snapshot* is based on reserved storage capacity that is required to store the snapshot of your data. After the snapshot is performed, the original data remains untouched. Any changes, such as adds or deletes, are stored separately from the original data. When there's a change to the snapshotted data, the storage system moves the original blocks to a reserved snapshot storage area. The original block is then changed.

A copy-on-write snapshot requires an original copy of the data and stores changes to the reserved storage. The primary advantages of copy-on-write snapshots are that they're immediate and use minimal backup storage space. However, there will be a negative effect on storage write performance because the original volume must store the backup data to the copy-on-write backup storage space before accepting the write request. Note that the snapshot data is in sync with the time that the snapshot was taken.

The *redirect-on-write snapshot* process has a different approach. When a storage write operation takes place, the redirect-on-write snapshot will not store the new data over the existing block. Instead, it will create a pointer that tells the snapshot image where the original block is located on the original storage volume. These pointers allow a system accessing the snapshot to reference the data at the point in time the snapshot was taken and uses less storage I/O operations than a copy-on-write snapshot. This process allows for a more efficient storage system with less overhead and a faster response.

Database Backups

There are a couple of ways to back up a database. One method is to back up the volume on which the database is stored. This approach allows remounting the volume, and thus the database itself, on another VM. In between snapshots, it's also important to back up the database transaction logs frequently, around every 5 to 15 minutes. Another method is to perform a full database backup—colloquially called taking a database dump—which saves the database as a file or collection of files.

Application-Level Backups

Some applications offer the ability to back up and restore their own configuration files and data files. *Application-level backups* can come in handy when you want to install a fresh copy of an application but restore the application to a previous state. A database dump is an example of an application-level backup. You can install a fresh copy of your database software and then restore an existing database to it. This process can be cleaner and less time-consuming than restoring from a block-level image backup.

Full Backups

A *full backup* is a complete copy of data. Although this sounds a lot like a clone, one difference is that full backups are typically compressed and may even be encrypted. For example, whereas a clone of a volume creates an exact block copy of the original, a full backup operates at the file level and may make changes to the metadata of backed-up files.

Full backups are generally performed on an infrequent backup schedule with smaller, incremental backups occurring more frequently. Full backups offer the advantage of a complete and up-to-date copy of your data in one operation. They have the disadvantage of taking a long time to perform because all the data in a storage system must be copied instead of just the modified data from the last backup. Full backups also require a significant amount of storage capacity since the complete dataset is copied in the operation.

Differential Backups

A *differential backup* uses the latest full backup as a source dataset, and with each additional sequential backup operation the differential backup will identify and back up only the data that has been modified since the last full backup was performed. This approach allows for an efficient and significantly smaller backup operation. Restoring a differential backup takes only two steps: restoring the full backup and then restoring the most recent differential backup.

A differential backup contains all the changed data since the last full backup. For example, suppose that you perform a full backup on Sunday and then do daily differential backups for the rest of the week. The first differential backup that runs on Monday will include the file changes made since the time of the full backup that was performed on Sunday. The next differential backup that runs on Tuesday will contain the changed data from both Monday and Tuesday, and so forth.

Incremental Backups

Incremental backups capture all changes since the last incremental backup, if available. Otherwise, it captures all changes since the last full backup. Incremental backups can be run, for example, on a nightly basis and capture the changes that were made since the previous backup was run the night before. This approach allows for an efficient backup operation since only the changes from the past 24 hours are stored on the backup media. Incremental backups are quicker and less resource-intensive than a full backup.

One downside of using incremental backups is that the recovery time objective can be longer since the last full backup must be restored; then all the incremental backup images taken since the last full restore would have to be retrieved and copied over the full restore to bring it up to the current point of the last differential update.

Synthetic Full Backup

A *synthetic full backup* is an outdated full backup that's brought up-to-date with a complete series of later incremental backups. An advantage of this approach is that a full backup can be constructed offline without having the time and performance penalty of taking another full backup.

When a block of data on a storage device is modified, it will be flagged as having been changed since the last backup. When a backup operation is performed, if it's a full, incremental, or differential backup, the flag can be reset to indicate that the data has been backed up. The tags indicate to the backup software if an operation needs to be performed or skipped because there were no changes. When the block is later modified, the flag will be set again to indicate that there were changes made to it since the last backup.

Backup Targets

The *backup target* is the endpoint or storage system where the backup data is to be stored. In a data center, backup targets include disks, tape drives, or optical media. In the cloud, backup targets are file/object stores, block storage volumes, managed filesystems, and virtual tape libraries. The way that the source data is stored generally dictates the type of backup target you'll choose. For instance, you can back up a block storage volume by taking a snapshot of it and storing the snapshot in object storage. As another example, backing up a database may involve copying the database to another database server while also taking a database dump.

Regardless of how your source data is stored, a best practice is to use the 3-2-1 rule. This rule states that you should have three copies of data stored on two different media types, with one backup being kept off-site. Many organizations maintain a disaster recovery (DR) site or region to use if the main data center or region fails. In this case, backing data up to the DR site would suffice as an off-site backup.

Replicas

Replicas serve as a live, secondary data store. For example, with many popular databases, you can create one or more read replicas that can be stored in local or remote data centers. These replicas are updated in real time from the master, and the database can access them instead of the master replica. This approach allows the database to scale and handle very high read rates.

Another example of replicas is *content delivery networks (CDNs)*. A CDN consists of geographically distributed edge locations that each store a copy of the same data—typically video, audio, or web assets. By having copies of the data close to the users that need it, a CDN can offer enhanced performance and resiliency if the primary data source becomes unavailable.

Operating systems, storage management software, applications, and virtualization management systems offer storage replication, where data that is stored in a volume is automatically replicated to another system for availability and redundancy purposes. When a file—such as a video—is stored in the primary storage system, the replication software will automatically copy the same file to another location. This location is also known as a replica.

Local Backups

Local backups are stored in proximity to the original data. For example, cloning a VM's disk volume and storing it on the same storage system as the VM would be a local backup. The advantage of local backups is speed. The disadvantage is that if something happens to the storage system, both the original and backup data would be lost, as shown in Figure 5.8.

FIGURE 5.8 Local backup

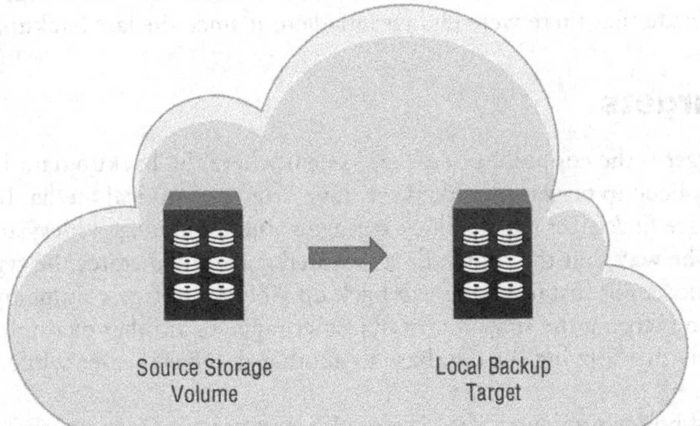

Remote Backups

Remote backups are stored separately from the original data and usually at a significant geographic distance. Remote backups have the advantage of surviving catastrophic incidents that affect the original storage system, such as fires or natural disasters. Many corporate and most regulatory requirements will specify that the backup data be located at a separate data center from the origin data center and that the two locations be geographically some distance apart from each other, as illustrated in Figure 5.9. Many cloud providers interconnect their data centers into regions and availability zones using high-speed, directly connected, fiber networks that allow large backup sets to traverse the data network between the data centers and makes remote backups feasible.

FIGURE 5.9 Remote backup

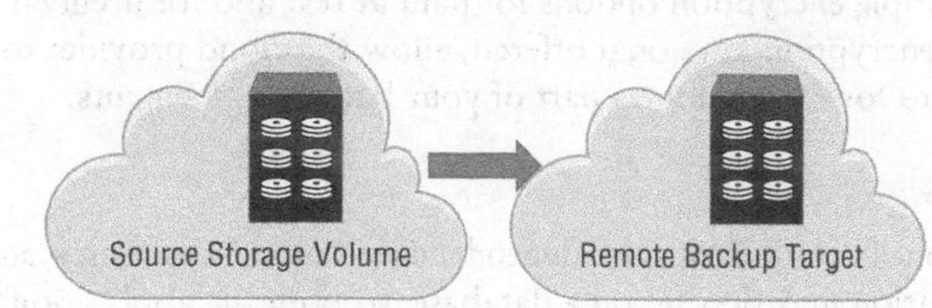

Backup and Restore Operations

So far, we've covered what to back up and where. In this section, you'll learn some operational considerations for the "when" and "how" of backing up and restoring data.

Backup Service Level Agreements

Cloud service providers that offer backups as a managed service will publish *service level agreements (SLAs)* that outline their offered service levels for backup operations to the cloud consumer. Examples of the items that may appear in the SLA include guaranteed availability for a percentage of the month, as well as maintenance windows when the service may not be available. The SLA will also include details on the service and a statement of what is and what is not covered under the SLA. The SLA defines the boundaries of what the service provider is responsible for and how the service provider will compensate you if they fail to meet the SLA—usually by providing monetary credits.

Scheduling

The *backup window* is the time during which the backup operation may run. The backup applications allow you to define when the backup operation takes place and what type of backup is to be performed. For example, a full backup can be scheduled for 1:00 a.m. to 5:30 a.m. every Sunday, and then incremental backups on every other day of the week can take place from 1:00 a.m. to 2:00 a.m. The schedule and backup window must allow for enough time for the backup operation to complete and take into account the volume of data and the time to transport the data across a network and to write the data to storage media.

Backup Configurations

The configuration and management of backups will depend on the level of service that you have purchased from the cloud service provider. Most cloud providers will offer storage as a managed service that allows you to define your backup and data life cycle operations using a web interface, command-line interface, or API. Once you've defined your backup configurations, the cloud provider will use automation and orchestration systems to carry out your backup requests.

The service provider backup options can be quite extensive. For example, you can define which storage tier to use to store your data. For rarely used data that must be archived, you may choose an inexpensive storage tier with an SLA that allows for a longer restore time. You can define the region(s) to store the data to meet regulatory or corporate requirements for the location of the data and geographical separation of the online and backup data. Most providers offer multiple encryption options for data at rest and for archival needs. You can manage your own encryption keys or, if offered, allow the cloud provider to provide key management services for encryption as part of your backup agreements.

Dependencies

When thinking about backups, consider dependencies that exist among systems. For example, an application may depend on a database, so both the application files and database need to be backed up—and just backing them up might not be enough. The restore process must ensure that both the application and database interoperate properly. A backup is only as good as your ability to restore from it, so testing restore operations is crucial to making sure that your backup strategy is sound.

Online vs. Offline

Offline storage allows the storage medium to be removed from the storage system and reattached or mounted at a later time. Mounting offline storage requires physically moving the medium to the storage system. For example, an administrator or robot may have to retrieve a tape and insert it into a tape drive. Some other examples of offline storage are DVD, CD, or removable portable devices such as USB drives. Offline storage media can be transported to remote storage facilities or stored in vaults for protection. The offline architecture allows the backed-up data to be stored safely in a secure location and is generally a cost-effective method to store long-term data that is infrequently accessed. In contrast, *online storage* media remains attached to the rest of the storage system and can be accessed at any time. Online is the most common storage design, and with backups, this design offers an always available method to store and retrieve data.

Retention

Regulatory requirements may dictate how and how long you must retain backups. Just as with any other data, be aware of these requirements so that you know when you may and may not destroy old backups.

If keeping backups in object storage, you can use versioning to ensure that backups aren't accidentally deleted. Write-once, read-many media (WORM) can be written to only once, ensuring that once backed up, the data can't be changed (although the media can always be destroyed). Some media types that offer WORM capability are tape drives, hard drives, and SD cards.

Summary

The ongoing maintenance and support of cloud deployments is a primary focus for many Cloud+ certified professionals. The world job market has a strong requirement for knowledgeable cloud support personnel as the transfer from private to cloud computing grows year after year. This chapter's focus was on many of the core topics of cloud maintenance.

The chapter started with a discussion of applying software patches to the most common cloud elements, such as the hypervisor, VMs, network systems, applications, storage, and compute clusters. You learned about patching software and the different issues that you must take into account when patching production, development, and QA deployments. Patching methodologies were introduced, including rolling updates, blue-green, and clusters. Even with the cloud provider responsible for the maintenance of the cloud infrastructure, you must be aware of its operations and know what your maintenance responsibilities are and what systems fall under your management domain.

There are different types of software updates with which cloud professionals will need to be familiar, including hotfix, patch, and version updates. You also learned about removing these updates by performing rollback operations.

The cloud is like one big software platform with APIs to configure and control its operations. With hyperscale cloud computing, the massive numbers of ongoing changes taking place at any point in time is staggering. The only way that a modern cloud system can function is with the use of automation systems. This chapter reviewed workflow automation, runbooks, and orchestration systems as they relate to ongoing maintenance. You learned about the details of automated patches that must be addressed such as shutting down and restarting systems, understanding why it's a good practice to put systems into maintenance mode, and disabling system alerts to prevent false alarms.

A critical part of ongoing operations is the protection and care of your user data. The different types of backups were discussed such as snapshots, copy/redirect-on-write, cloning, full, differential, and incremental.

Next you learned about backup targets, replicas, and the advantages and disadvantages of local and remote backups. You then explored service level agreements, the issues with scheduling backups, different backup configurations, and the differences between online and offline backup operations.

Exam Essentials

Know the common systems that need ongoing patch management. The most common systems that are operating in the cloud are hypervisors, virtual machines, virtual appliances, software applications, and clustered systems. Also, networking components, such as switches, routers, load balancers, firewalls, NAT systems, and many others, will need to be patched to remain current and secure. Storage systems are also included here.

Differentiate between the different types of updates. You can expect the exam to ask you questions about the different types of updates. An update procedure will be described in the question, and you'll need to identify what type of update it is. It's important that you be able to distinguish the differences between these types such as blue-green, rolling updates, production, development, and QA.

Understand automation and the basic support operations that can be performed. Automation systems play an important role in cloud computing. You need to know what runbooks, workflow, and orchestration systems are.

Know virtualization operations that are common in the ongoing support and maintenance of cloud operations. Be able to answer exam questions concerning what a snapshot is and its purpose. Know the differences between snapshots (which are backups) and cloning (which is a master copy of an image that is used for repetitive deployments).

Explain the storage operations in ongoing cloud maintenance. You can expect that the exam will test you on your storage knowledge since it's a critical component of all cloud operations. Know the types of backups and be able to identify questions that differentiate between full, differential, and incremental backups.

Differentiate between the different types of backup targets. Prepare for scenario questions that may describe a particular backup target solution and be able to select the correct type. Replicates, local, and remote are all common target types.

Understand backup and restore topics. Know that there are service level agreements that address backup operations, that backups can be scheduled for automated operations, and that service providers offer many different configuration options.

Written Lab

Fill in the blanks for the questions provided in the written lab. You can find the answers to the written labs in Appendix B.

1. The ________________ ________________ model is a software deployment methodology that uses two configurations for production that are identical to each other.
2. A constant delivery of software updates or patches to operating systems or applications is referred to as a(n) ________________ ________________.
3. If you experience undesirable results after deploying a patch to a fleet of VMs, you may be required to perform a(n) ________________ to withdraw the patch from operations.
4. ________________ are used to restore an existing virtual server, and ________________ is when you take a VM and use it to create a new and separate VM.
5. The endpoint or storage system where the backup data is to be stored is commonly referred to as the ________________ ________________.
6. ________________ are backup copies of data that can be stored either locally or remotely and act as an alternative data store from your main production operations.
7. A(n) ________________ is a software update type that is intended to fix an immediate and specific problem with a quick release procedure.
8. A (n) ________________ ________________ uses the latest full backup as a source dataset, and with each additional sequential backup operation, this type of backup will identify only the data that has been modified since the last backup was performed and not the complete backup set. This allows for an efficient and significantly smaller backup operation.
9. When installing patches on a server and knowing that the server will be down and unresponsive for a period of time, it's important to disable ________________ when performing maintenance.
10. A(n) ________________ ________________ is the time available for the backup operation to run while the target storage system is either offline or lightly used.

Review Questions

The following questions are designed to test your understanding of this chapter's material. For more information on how to obtain additional questions, please see this book's Introduction. You can find the answers in Appendix A.

1. What backup type offers the advantage of a complete and up-to-date copy of your data in one operation?
   A. Full
   B. Differential
   C. Incremental
   D. Online
2. When applying a series of patches to your fleet of middleware servers in the cloud, you are concerned about the monitoring systems generating invalid alerts. What part of the server maintenance process would cause this? (Choose two.)
   A. API polling
   B. Rolling upgrades
   C. Shutdown
   D. Restart
3. What are common automation systems that are used for patch management? (Choose three.)
   A. Chef
   B. Cloudpatch
   C. Ansible
   D. DevOps
   E. Puppet
   F. Cloud Deploy
4. What type of software change is designed to address a known bug or issue and to bring a system up-to-date with previous bug fixes?
   A. Hotfix
   B. Patch
   C. Version update
   D. Rollout
5. What backup method creates a master copy of a system image and uses it as a template to create additional systems?
   A. Full backup
   B. Snapshot
   C. Clone
   D. Replicate

6. What backup method creates a file-based image of the current state of a VM, including the complete operating system and all applications that are stored on it?
   - **A.** Full backup
   - **B.** Snapshot
   - **C.** Clone
   - **D.** Replicate
7. To meet regulatory requirements, your company must provide geographical separation between active and backup data of certain medical records that your company collects and processes. The requirements stipulate that the data cannot leave the country and must be in two or more data centers. As the cloud professional for your company, what recommendations would you offer to meet these requirements?
   - **A.** Remote
   - **B.** Offline
   - **C.** Target
   - **D.** Incremental
8. What type of software update may offer new features and benefits in addition to bug fixes?
   - **A.** Hotfix
   - **B.** Patch
   - **C.** Version update
   - **D.** Rollout
9. Which of the following offers a structured process for a series of actions that should be taken in order to complete a process?
   - **A.** Automation
   - **B.** Workflow
   - **C.** Orchestration
   - **D.** Application programming interface (API)
10. These cloud-based systems abstract and hide much of the complexity of modern cloud systems and also reduce operational errors by executing tested cloud systems, scripts, workflows, or runbooks to make sure that the systems are configured correctly.
    - **A.** XML
    - **B.** SDN
    - **C.** Orchestration
    - **D.** REST/API

11. When a server is undergoing updates, it may be in a state that it will not respond to health checks, API calls, SNMP, or any other means used to monitor its health by network management systems. This may cause false alarms and trigger automated troubleshooting systems. What can be done to prevent false alarms? (Choose two.)

   A. Put the system into maintenance mode.

   B. Edit workflow scripts.

   C. Assign a workflow to the orchestration rollout.

   D. Disable system alerts.

12. What type of software change is designed for rapid deployment and to correct a specific and critical issue?

   A. Hotfix

   B. Patch

   C. Version update

   D. Rollout

13. What type of backup system is intended to provide quick restore access if needed?

   A. Virtual Storage Area Network (SAN)

   B. Fibre Channel over Ethernet (FCOE)

   C. Online

   D. Replica

14. Which of the following is a tightly coupled computer system that allows for software patching without incurring downtime?

   A. Blue-green

   B. RAID

   C. Cluster

   D. Availability zone

15. Your IaaS cloud company has announced that there will be a brief outage for regularly scheduled maintenance over the weekend to apply a critical hotfix to vital infrastructure. What are the systems they may be applying patches to? (Choose three.)

   A. VM

   B. Load balancer

   C. Hypervisor

   D. NoSQL database

   E. Router

   F. Email server

16. You have been asked to update your entire fleet of Internet-facing web servers to remediate a critical bug. Your supervisor has agreed to operate under reduced computing capacity during the process but stipulates that there can be no downtime. What upgrade approach should you recommend that your company follow to meet these requirements?
    A. Orchestration
    B. Rolling
    C. Hotfix
    D. Blue-green
17. Before a new patch is released to the public, the release manager at a large software development house has requested a report that shows the pass/fail data to verify that the fix does, in fact, work. He is requesting data about the issue it was intended to fix and the results of the tests performed to make sure that the fix does not interfere with other processes and that there are no memory or buffer issues experienced with the patched version of software. What process is he verifying?
    A. Rollout
    B. Orchestration
    C. Automation
    D. QA
18. You company's primary application is critical to the power generation industry and must be highly available. When critical patches need to be installed, downtime is not an option that your customers can tolerate. You have designed a web architecture to take this into account and that allows you to have an exact copy of your production fleet that can be brought online to replace your existing deployment for patching and maintenance. What type of model did you implement?
    A. Cluster
    B. DevOps
    C. Blue-green
    D. Rolling
19. What type of backup operation is based on the change of the source data since the last backup was performed?
    A. Full
    B. Differential
    C. Incremental
    D. Online
20. What backup solution requires an administrator or tape jukebox to make it available by inserting a tape or other media into a storage system for retrieval?
    A. SAN A/B
    B. FCON
    C. Cluster
    D. Offline

Chapter 6

Disaster Recovery, Business Continuity, and Ongoing Maintenance

THE FOLLOWING COMPTIA CLOUD+ EXAM OBJECTIVES ARE COVERED IN THIS CHAPTER:

✓ 4.6 Given a scenario, perform disaster recovery tasks.

- Failovers
- Failback
- Restore backups
- Replication
- Network configurations
- On-premises and cloud sites
  - Hot
  - Warm
  - Cold
- Requirements
  - RPO
  - RTO
  - SLA
  - Corporate guidelines
- Documentation
  - DR kit
  - Playbook
  - Network diagram
- Geographical datacenter requirements

Implementing a Disaster Recovery and Business Continuity Plan

Cloud computing operations can be amazingly complex, as you have learned throughout this book. Failures can and will happen—often when least expected. It is important for you to plan for disruptions ahead of time so that you can be ready when they occur.

Some outages, such as a web server failure, are relatively easy to plan for by implementing multiple web servers behind a load balancer. Virtual machines can easily be replaced or moved quickly to new hardware platforms in the event of an outage.

This section will discuss disaster recovery and business continuity. You'll learn how to prepare for a disaster and the different architectures and reference designs you should consider when creating a disaster recovery plan.

The cloud service provider maintains hosting facilities that are designed and built to be highly resilient and offer protection from service disruptions. Redundant systems for power, cooling, networking, storage, and computing are implemented in the cloud to reduce the frequency and probability of outages and to recover critical systems quickly in the event of an outage.

As you move computing operations to the cloud, it remains your responsibility to plan for, and be able to recover from, any disruptions. Many types of natural disasters, such as weather-related events, may cause power or communication interruptions in the data center. Other events that may cause disruptions are software bugs; key infrastructure outages, such as power and cooling systems; cyberattacks; virus infections; critical service or equipment suppliers going out of business; or labor disruptions. This section will investigate the methods and concepts for recovering from a service disruption. You'll learn about the options available for proactive planning for an outage and investigate how to build resiliency into your cloud deployment.

You'll also learn about deploying cloud operations, with business continuity as a design requirement, which will allow your operations to recover quickly in the event of a service disruption.

Service Provider Responsibilities and Capabilities

In this section, we will go over the responsibilities of the cloud service provider for disaster recovery and ongoing maintenance. You'll learn about their capabilities, what is generally included in a service level agreement (SLA), and the process of recovering from a disaster. There are many terms associated with disaster recovery that will be discussed in this section, and it is important that you completely understand these terms because they are a focus of the Cloud+ exam.

Recovery Point Objective

The *recovery point objective (RPO)* is the restore point you recover to in the event of an outage. Basically, the RPO indicates the amount of data that may be lost when restarting the operations after a disaster.

An example to help you understand the RPO is that if you have a database storing sales from your online e-commerce site and it is set to create a backup every two hours, then the RPO would be a maximum of two hours. If you had a disaster strike and as part of the recovery process you switched over to a backup site, the RPO would define how fresh the data would be at the new site. If the site is used for financial or other critical transactions, such as healthcare, the RPO would need to be close to zero since losing any data could be catastrophic. However, if you had an outage on a noncritical system where losing recent data would have no impact, then the recovery point could be longer and not have any lasting negative effect on the business. When you are performing business continuity planning, the RPO plays a critical role in the design of the cloud computing architecture.

Recovery Time Objective

The *recovery time objective (RTO)* is the amount of time a system can be offline during a disaster. It is the amount of time it takes to get operations back up and operational after a failure. When planning for business continuity, the cost of the downtime must be taken into consideration. Ask yourself what the impact to business operations will be if the cloud operations or a section of them were to fail. If the site is an active e-commerce operation during the busy holiday selling season, the outage can cost the company a large amount of lost revenue each minute that the site cannot be reached by customers. In this case, the RTO would need to be a short amount of time. However, if the failure is a noncritical system that has no impact on operations, the RTO can be days or even weeks to bring the systems back online. As you can see, the RTO value will be a critical metric for your cloud business continuity design and operations.

Corporate Policies and Guidelines

The role that information technology plays in any modern corporation has become absolutely critical to the daily operations of any organization, so the organization needs to develop a business continuity and disaster recovery plan. This is much more than a technology document—it has a direct impact on a company's ongoing operations and possibly even its survival. The plan should include operational and governance considerations. The executive committee and even the company's board will need to decide the RPO and RTO objectives and build a plan around that. These metrics will drive the decisions on the various disaster recovery approaches that can be implemented.

There is an old saying that explains this well: "When you fail to prepare, you prepare to fail."

The business continuity plan should include not only the restoration of network operations but also topics such as moving into a new office space if there is a loss of access to facilities due to natural disasters such as storms, floods, or earthquakes. Another issue that may arise in a disaster is that many of the company's employees may not be able to work for a period of time, so the company must plan how to operate in such a situation.

The first step in implementing any *disaster recovery (DR)* offering is to evaluate your organization's needs. Based on the needs outline, you can choose a cloud provider that offers the specific services that you require to meet your stated needs. Once you have these steps completed, you can architect and implement an effective DR plan that meets your requirements and budget.

Once the DR plan has been implemented, it is absolutely critical to test the design and effectiveness against the documents. This step offers you a great opportunity to uncover any unforeseen process or technical issues that should be modified. Also, as time goes on, your DR needs will most likely change, and your plan will have to be modified. As such, it is important to revisit your company's DR requirements over time, test, and adjust accordingly.

Cloud Service Provider Policies and Guidelines

Cloud providers have extensive DR planning and operational designs. They must be prepared for any disaster to be able to offer their customers service level agreements that commit to defined recovery objectives. All of the major public cloud provider's networks have been designed for recoverability and survivability.

When a company is preparing and designing its disaster recovery plan, it should work closely with its cloud provider to understand their capabilities and limitations. These capabilities and limitations are outlined in policy, compliance, and guideline documents offered by the cloud provider to their customers. A cloud provider may also offer reference designs and case studies to assist their customers in planning for a disaster.

Disaster Recovery Network Capacity

During a disaster, network capacity plays an important role in the recovery and restorations of corporate operations. Wide area network (WAN) circuit bandwidth and connectivity are critical components of any DR plan.

When the recovery site comes online, it must be designed for peak network capacity and not get saturated with the new traffic of your recovered sites load. In addition to the site's regular peak load, the possibility of exceeding your normal peak traffic should be considered. During a disaster, your site may need additional bandwidth provisioned for data replication and backup. Customers checking order status and suppliers may have a higher interaction with your company, for example. You must address all possibilities for bandwidth starvation during a disaster event, such as the replication of storage traffic consuming so much network bandwidth that all other applications are starved for bandwidth. Do you want to consider adding bandwidth to address these issues? It is best to gain an understanding of any potential problems and deal with them well before you have a DR event and do not have the bandwidth in your network to handle the traffic!

Other network disaster recovery services that need to be addressed are Domain Name Services (DNS), Dynamic Host Configuration Protocol (DHCP), File Transfer Protocol (FTP), Active Directory (AD), Remote Authentication Dial-In User Service (RADIUS), and Terminal Access Controller Access-Control System (TACACS). These services are well suited for a multisite deployment that offers failover in case of an outage. Also, the cloud service provider will usually offer a variety of network services that include these services and others. Using the service provider's infrastructure may be a good DR option if you are already using its compute services, and it allows you to leverage the provider's extensive resources.

It is common for service providers to offer highly redundant network services that consist of data centers, sometimes called *availability zones*, which are interconnected with private high-speed and low-latency fiber connections.

Disaster Recovery ISP Limitations

A potentially critical issue in formulating and deploying an effective DR plan is to make sure that your Internet service provider (ISP) has the facilities that meet your requirements and that you have the correct services enabled so that the ISP does not present obstacles.

Issues to be addressed with the ISP include any charges that the ISP may place on you for bandwidth consumption and whether these charges are acceptable and in alignment with your expectations. Are there any monthly usage caps about which you need to be aware? These caps may cause the ISP to throttle or, worse yet, block the flow of traffic when exceeded. Is there enough ISP capacity to handle additional traffic load because of the DR event, such as data backup and replication processes taking place?

Disaster Recovery Models and Techniques

The cloud's resiliency, on-demand resources, and pay-as-you-go business model make it possible to implement a cost-effective DR plan. Public cloud regions and zones are designed for high availability and resiliency that can complement your company's disaster recovery requirements. The cost model and economics of this approach bring a complete and effective DR plan within the reach of even smaller companies that in the past may not have had the financial or technical resources available to implement a complete recovery. If your primary data center goes offline because of any number of events, such as a flood, earthquake, or any other type of disaster, the cloud can be used as your backup data center. Also, one cloud site can back up another, and this can often be automated.

Site Mirroring

Site mirroring can encompass multiple redundancy strategies that you'll explore in this section. *Site mirroring* refers to the process of keeping the backup site updated so that it's ready to assume the workload in the event of a primary site failure. Site mirroring provides an identical copy of the original site's data and applications at a remote site. By implementing a mirroring strategy, you can be better prepared to survive an outage event with little or no impact on your operations.

The cloud operations can be deployed in a *hot site* model where two fully redundant cloud data centers are in sync with each other, with the standby site backing up the primary in real time in the event of a failure, as shown in Figure 6.1. The hot site offers the most redundancy of any model. However, it is also the most expensive option, and it is used when having your cloud computing operations go offline is not an option.

FIGURE 6.1 Hot site mirroring

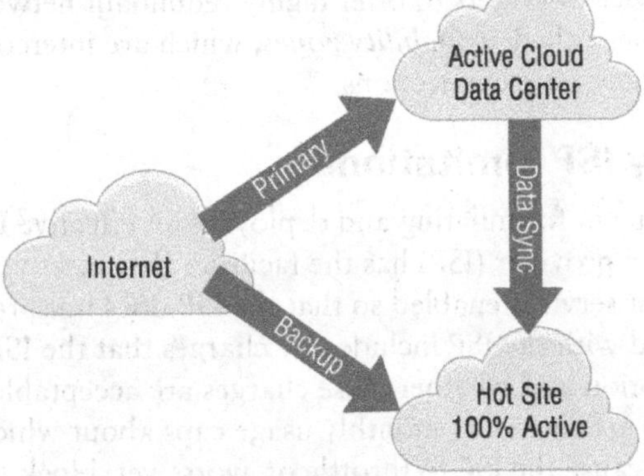

The *warm site* approach to recovering from a primary data center outage is when the remote backup site is offline except for critical data storage, which is usually a database. The warm site will host an operational database server that is in sync with the database server at the primary data center. This is sometimes referred to as the *candlelight design* or *pilot light design*. All other needed site infrastructure, such as servers, storage, load balancers, and networking, are either offline or not provisioned until the warm site is brought online after a failure at the primary data center, as shown in Figure 6.2. There will be a delay during the transition process, so you should consider that when thinking about your RTO.

FIGURE 6.2 Warm site

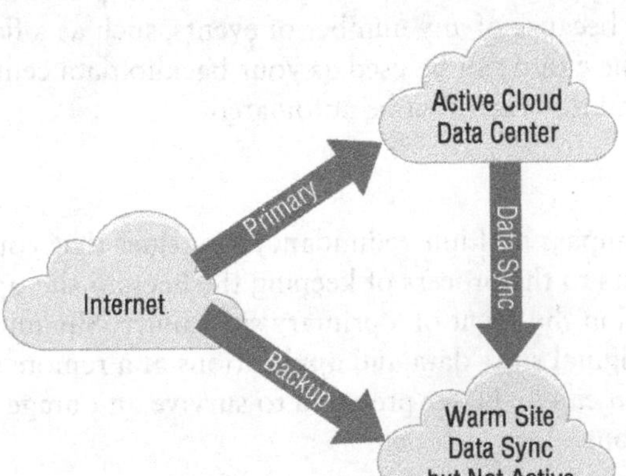

The warm site model is similar to the hot site, except there will be more work involved in the cutover process and usually much more time will be needed before it becomes operational and takes over processing from the failed primary site. Also, a lot of planning and testing must take place ahead of time in order to ensure that you can quickly bring the warm site online. The warm site approach is more cost-effective than the hot site solution since you are not being charged for services that are not active. The time to recover is much less than a cold site but, of course, higher than a hot site. However, the hot site approach will likely not lose data as compared to the warm site because the hot site is designed for a short RTO. With the warm site solution, transactions will not take place between the time that the primary data center goes offline and the time that the warm site comes up. For many cloud customers, the warm site is a good compromise between the expense of supporting a hot site and the extended downtime incurred with the cold site approach.

The *cold site* model is where a backup site is provisioned to take over operations in the event of a primary data center failure but the servers and infrastructure are not operational until needed. To recover from an outage, the cold site approach will need significant amounts of preparation before it is ready to be used. This effort means that it can take a long time for a cold site to come online. Figure 6.3 shows that the cold site does not have data replication or equipment installed. However, the cold site may be good for extended outages, and it is certainly more cost-effective than the hot or warm site approach. The servers at the cold site must be provisioned and configured in the event of an outage at the primary site. The cold site model of recovery means that all cloud operations will have to be brought online and configured at the cold site when the primary site has a failure. Automation tools may be used to accelerate the replication of the primary site's architecture, including servers, load balancers, storage, networking, and security, at the cold site location.

FIGURE 6.3 Cold site

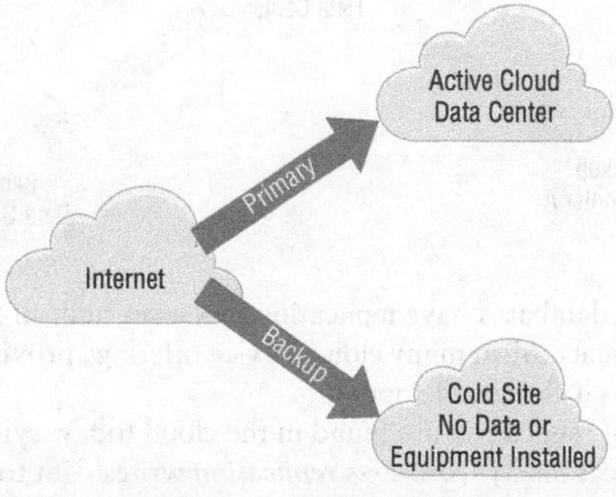

When deploying a cold site model for your business continuity planning, you must take into consideration that the time it takes to recover can be long, so a cold site solution may not be optimal for business-critical operations. For example, operational data such as databases will have to be transferred to the cold site and restored onto the database servers.

This transfer can take a long time, depending on the amount of data you have to send over a network and store in the storage arrays in the cold site data center. If the primary data center experiencing an outage is a mission-critical system, the monetary and goodwill costs can be very high and the time it takes to recover from a cold site may not be a cost-effective solution.

When operating a popular e-commerce site during a holiday shopping season, for instance, even a short outage can cost an organization a large amount of lost revenue, so a warm or hot site should be considered as a more optimal solution. If the site is mission-critical, a cold site will most likely not be the solution that best meets your requirements. However, if the cloud operations are not critical, or they can be down for the time it takes to bring the cold site online, the cost savings of the cold site approach may be the best disaster recovery solution. The advantage of using the cold site approach for recovery is that the charges for the cold site sitting idle will be minimal, which can be a significant cost savings to the business.

Replications

Replication is the transfer and synchronization of data between storage systems, and often between sites, as illustrated in Figure 6.4. For disaster recovery purposes and data security, your data must be replicated between sites. Remote copies of data have traditionally been achieved with storage backup applications. However, with the cloud, you can easily replicate VMs with all the applications, service packs, and data to a remote site.

FIGURE 6.4 Site-to-site replication of data

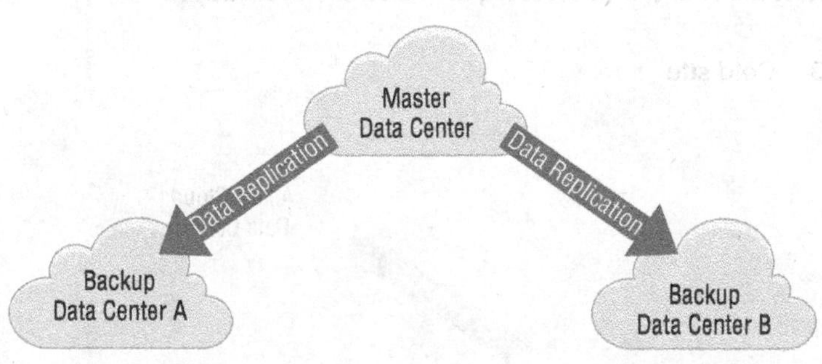

Applications such as databases have replication processes built-in that can be utilized based on your requirements. Also, many cloud service offerings provide data replication as an included feature or as a chargeable option.

Two primary types of replication are found in the cloud today: synchronous replication and asynchronous replication. *Synchronous replication* writes data to both the primary storage system and the replica simultaneously to ensure that the remote data is current, as shown in Figure 6.5. Synchronous replication allows you to store current data at a remote location from the primary data center that can be brought online with a short recovery time and limited loss of data.

FIGURE 6.5 Synchronous replication

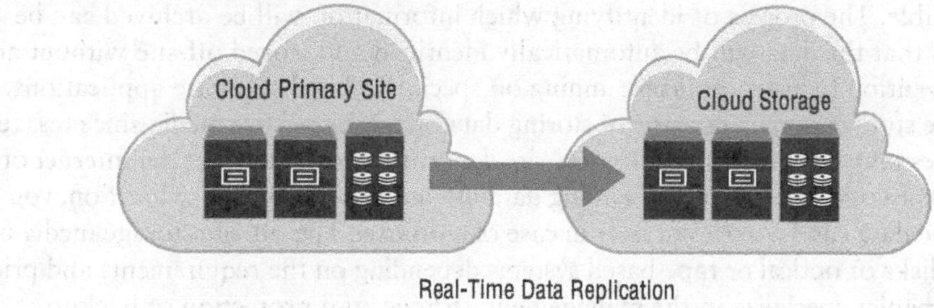

Synchronous replication offers high availability for mission-critical applications by storing data in a remote site that can assume processing responsibility with current data from the primary site. When implementing synchronous replication, disaster recovery hot and warm sites can be effectively implemented.

In *asynchronous replication*, the data is written to the primary first and then later a copy is written to the remote site on a schedule or after a set delay, as shown in Figure 6.6. Asynchronous replication works off a store-and-forward model and is a cost-effective protection and backup solution. With asynchronous replication, the data is first written to the primary storage system in the primary storage facility or cloud location. Because asynchronous replication is not in real time, it uses less bandwidth, making it more cost-effective than synchronous replication.

FIGURE 6.6 Asynchronous replication

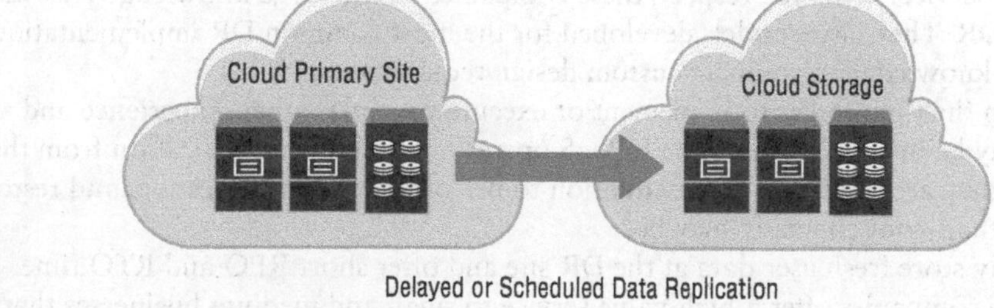

NOTE: Once configured, replication occurs continuously and automatically in the background.

Archiving Data

Data archiving moves inactive data, or data that is no longer being used, to a separate storage facility for long-term storage. It can be more cost-effective to store archived data in less expensive storage systems and still allow the cloud consumer access to that data for backup and retrieval as needed. Regulatory and company policies may require long-term retention of information. Archiving policies, often implemented in automated systems, allow these capabilities to be met and often at a low price since the data does not need to be immediately accessible. The process of identifying which information will be archived can be automated so that the data will be automatically identified and stored off-site without any manual intervention by using policies running on special archival software applications.

The off-site storage of data consists of storing data on less expensive media since fast read and write times may not be required. The off-site data can be accessed over the Internet or with a direct network connection. By sending data off-site from the primary location, you ensure that the data can be retrieved later in case of a disaster. The off-site storage media may be magnetic disks or optical or tape-based systems depending on the requirements and pricing.

Some companies specialize in the management, storage, and protection of backup information, which will relieve a company of the burden of managing off-site storage. Storing data off-site reduces the risk of data loss that could result from a natural disaster, a catastrophic failure of the storage system, human error, or any other calamity. Storing a copy off-site is a sound business practice, and it allows you to recover operations should the primary site fail.

Third-Party Offerings

Some companies offer consulting and management services aimed at assisting organizations with their DR requirements. Management consulting companies have business continuity practices that assist organizations with the process of developing and implementing a DR plan. This approach takes all legal, regulatory, industry, technology, and operational needs into consideration and develops a complete business continuity plan for your company.

With the hype of the cloud, and every technology company now being "cloud enabled," it should come as no surprise that there is such a thing as DRaaS—that's right, disaster recovery as a service! With due respect, these companies have a large knowledge base and specialize in DR. They have models developed for the most common DR implementations and have the knowledge to architect custom design requirements.

Also, when the time comes to implement or execute your plan, their experience and assistance may be invaluable. With the DRaaS operations at a different location from the disaster site, they are often in a better situation to perform the failover, testing, and restoration services than your company may be.

DRaaS may store fresh user data at the DR site and offer short RPO and RTO time frames. These companies offer a high-value service to small and medium businesses that may not have the resources internally to develop and manage their own DR plan. Using DRaaS providers saves an organization from investing capital and resources to maintain and operate off-site DR systems.

One downside, or potential for concern, is that you really are placing a lot of trust in the DRaaS company. Potentially, the survivability and validity of your company's ongoing operations after disaster strikes rests with the DRaaS provider's capabilities and ability to execute. Can the DRaaS company meet your RPO and RTO? Will the backup site function as planned? All of these issues require a high level of trust in your DRaaS and management consulting business partners.

Business Continuity

Business continuity is the ability to recover to an operational state quickly after a failure or outage. This section will focus on business continuity specifically as it pertains to cloud operations, and it will discuss some strategies to protect against outages. The best defense against an outage is a solid plan for recovery. A *business continuity plan* or playbook defines how to protect the company assets and to be able to survive a disaster.

Establishing a Business Continuity Plan

The first step in implementing any DR offering is to evaluate your organization's needs. Based on the needs outlined, you can architect and implement an effective DR plan that meets your requirements and budget. You then can choose a cloud provider that offers the specific services that you require to implement your plan.

Once the DR plan has been implemented, it is absolutely critical to test the design and effectiveness against the documents. This offers you a great opportunity to uncover any unforeseen process or technical issues that have to be modified. Also, as time goes on, your DR needs will most likely change and require modification. As such, it is important to revisit your company's DR requirements over time and adjust accordingly.

Determine Alternate Sites

The site placement for DR would include geographical separation from your primary location. You would not want the same hurricane or earthquake to take out your primary and DR sites at the same time, would you? Most corporate governance documents will stipulate that their operational data center has a certain degree of geographical separation from the DR site so that one event will not affect both of them. This can be true when using the public cloud as a DR facility. The cloud provider will outline a regional area where it has a presence and also a number of smaller data centers or availability zones in those regions.

Other factors that determine which alternate sites are desirable include regulations such as HIPAA or PCI DSS, or restrictions on data being stored in-country. The capabilities to meet these compliance requirements may also limit your options if the provider is not certified for compliance.

Define Continuity of Operations

What does it mean for your company when it contemplates business continuity? What are the operational requirements needed to function after a major event that disrupts operations? Your company must define these issues and many more as it prioritizes its operations and the steps that it must take to resume operations. These issues are well beyond a discussion of technology. The role of technology is to enable these requirements. As such, the organization's leadership must determine what is required for the business's continuity of operations and outline them in the document. Based on these requirements, business processes with the aid of technology can be used to carry out operational continuity.

Addressing Network Connectivity

Earlier in this chapter, we discussed the network connectivity from both the cloud service provider and the ISP or WAN provider. Network connectivity requirements should be investigated, and your current facilities may have to be upgraded to take into account your business continuity requirements.

The continuity plan should require that your network connectivity partners provide the needed capacity and an SLA that outlines specifically what they guarantee to offer you in the event of a DR operation. Care must be taken to ensure that you are prepared for peak data usage. Implementing your plan will likely produce additional network traffic, such as data replication, beyond your normal operations.

Deploying Edge Sites

It is common for large public cloud vendors to offer *points of presence* at locations around the world that allow them to have a presence but not a complete, fully operational data center in place. These are often called *edge facilities*, and they are placed at key locations worldwide or in the geographical areas covered by the service provider. Edge locations allow you and your customers the ability to connect locally to fast, low-latency connections at the DR location. They can also store, or cache, data at these locations for low-latency responses to local user requests. Provisioning resources at edge sites (also known as edge locations) is usually straightforward using the cloud provider's management dashboard or APIs.

Procuring Backup Equipment

If your backup site is in the cloud, there's no need to purchase additional equipment because the cloud provider handles that for you. However, if you are using a traditional data center, then you must incur all capital expenses for the IT equipment and software required for the backup site. This expense can be significant because a complete, or nearly complete, image of your production network would need to be procured and implemented. The equipment required would include all servers, storage, network, software, and any other hardware or software needed to restore services. This is usually not very economical or easy to keep up-to-date since it requires that the equipment sit idle and unused.

When procuring backup equipment, care must be taken to purchase and implement gear that can handle the anticipated workload. It may be temping, for example, to purchase a smaller server or router model since it is intended to be used only for disaster recovery. However, the risk is that when the servers go online, they may not have the capacity to handle the workload.

Recovery Site Availability

What would happen if there was a disaster and the disaster recovery site could not be accessed? Well, that would be a very bad situation! When devising and implementing a DR plan, you must consider all possible scenarios.

Also, if your DR plans require your IT staff to go on-site at the DR data center for implementation of your infrastructure, it is important that arrangements be made well ahead of personnel arriving on site. Data centers by their nature are secure facilities, and not just anyone can just pull into the parking lot and gain access to the data center floor. Not even close! Many cloud providers completely restrict anyone from entering their facilities. Others require a service ticket and employee clearance in advance to get access to the facility. You can also be expected to be escorted when in the facility and any equipment that you bring along to be inspected and approved before being installed.

Because of security concerns, data centers do not hang huge neon signs outside of their facilities flashing who they are! The cloud data centers are usually in nondescript facilities, often with no names on them, and seem to go out of their way to not be noticed. One give-away is the high fences, cameras, and floodlights. They look like secure fortresses. So, get a good set of directions before heading over to do your work.

Third-Party Disaster Recovery Vendors

There is, of course, a whole disaster recovery industry that has formed. Some data center companies offer specialized data centers and operations designed specifically for disaster recovery. Other companies offer services that manage the complete disaster recovery process from start to finish. Management consulting companies offer valuable consulting services for defining and implementing a company's business continuity and disaster recovery plan.

Establishing Service Level Agreements

An SLA outlines responsibilities and serves as a basic contract between you and the service provider. In this section, you'll learn about the disaster recovery topics that are often outlined in a typical SLA between you and the service provider.

A *disaster recovery SLA* will outline the fundamental issues of determining the business impact, performing a risk assessment, managing the risk, and planning for a disaster. Also, the SLA will include metrics such as the RPOs and RTOs for the services offered, and the SLA metrics are highly dependent on the type of offerings such as IaaS, PaaS, or SaaS. SLAs are used to determine the area of responsibility: what part of the recovery is the responsibility of the provider and what responsibilities the customer assumes.

As you learned earlier in this chapter, the RPO is the amount of data that can be lost because of an outage. The RTO is a measure of the amount of time a system can be offline during an outage. The SLA also outlines the levels of availability and response times when an emergency or critical event takes place.

The RTO and RPO metrics are used to create a measurable SLA that outlines for you when you can expect your systems to be back online after an outage. These SLAs are often dependent on the service offered and for what level of support you have contracted. For example, if the cloud provider is offering a managed database service, it would have a much greater responsibility and be accepting a higher complexity level of recovery if they were an IaaS provider and had responsibility for all your running servers, applications, and other cloud services.

I should point out that while you would like all systems to fail over instantly and come online with little or no impact on your operations, this is generally not possible. In the event of a large-scale outage, such as a data center losing power or a fiber cut isolating the data center, a lot of operations must take place to move the workloads to a backup location. The possibility of data loss or an extended outage taking place will always exist.

The failover will require that the virtual infrastructure be configured or activated at a remote location and that the data be current enough to meet the RPO. Several operations must take place, and there are often dependencies where one section must be activated before the next steps in the workflow are addressed. For example, the servers and networking must be active before the database can be brought up and connected, the database must have current replicas, and so forth. Steps must occur in a certain order.

The SLA's agreed-upon levels can have variable costs associated with them. If there are very short RPO or RTO requirements, then additional resources and potential infrastructure will have to be allocated, which means a higher-cost service to you for the solution.

Cloud Maintenance

Maintenance activities are a fact of life in any IT operation, including the cloud. We have covered this subject throughout this book as it pertains to the various aspects of ongoing operations. This section will go a little deeper and explore the issues of maintenance operations and not the detailed technology maintenance requirements discussed earlier.

With the shared responsibilities between the cloud provider and customer, it is important to understand who is performing what maintenance and when and what the impact is going to be. With highly redundant cloud data centers and an architecture designed for high availability, there are often maintenance activities that take place and have no impact on operations. If the cloud vendor is performing the maintenance, they will generally post the operation's notice on their maintenance dashboard or send out notification emails to subscribers that outline the work to be done, the time frames, and what the expected impact will be. It is common to see regular status updates when the operations are taking place and an "all clear" message when the maintenance event is completed.

If you are performing maintenance on your cloud deployments, it is advisable to follow the change management process that you learned about in Chapter 2, "Cloud Deployments." If you are undertaking planned maintenance, the formal change process reduces the risk of the undertaking. If it is an unplanned event, then the objective is to get the systems operational and back into production as soon as possible. This should be followed up with a review and postmortem analysis after the excitement is over!

Establishing Maintenance Windows

Your IT operations group must define when changes may take place. These are driven by business operational objectives. For example, it you are a retailer, you would limit any changes leading up to and during the holiday selling season. Many companies have heavy compute operations during end-of-month or fiscal-quarter processing. In most cases, the change windows are open during times that have the least impact on your operations.

Maintenance Interruptions to Operations

With the virtualization of the modern compute infrastructure, new VMs can be created and deleted at a rapid pace. This allows for a highly resilient infrastructure. Modern cloud data centers are designed to resist almost any failure scenario. However, you are responsible for the architecture of your cloud deployment. If you do not design a highly available infrastructure using best practices and reference designs from the start, you may be adversely affected when performing maintenance.

In an ideal situation, you should have a design that allows for nonintrusive maintenance on different components. By implementing high availability and redundancy using failover, failback, and multiple availability zones, you can reduce interruptions to your operations when performing maintenance.

It is important to know what the impact of your scheduled maintenance is going to be and to plan accordingly. You may have to disable systems proactively or notify customers, suppliers, or other interested parties prior to the maintenance event.

Maintenance Automation Impact and Scope

Chapter 5, "Maintaining Cloud Operations," introduced scripting and some of the automation technologies such as Chef, Puppet, and Ansible. Automation is a huge asset when it comes to cloud maintenance. You can prepare for the maintenance work well ahead of time and have it staged in the automation systems that are configured to perform the operations automatically during the maintenance window. Automation makes it easier to ensure consistency in your maintenance operations.

Cloud dashboards allow for monitoring and sometimes configuring maintenance operations with the cloud provider. If you have regularly scheduled backups for your cloud storage volumes, you can configure the cloud provider to perform specific operations for you using its orchestration systems. When configuring the automation, you can define the maintenance window by day of the week and stop and start times.

Common Maintenance Automation Tasks

In this section, you'll learn about many of the tasks that must be performed during the ongoing operation of your cloud fleet of servers and associated systems. You'll learn about how to manage log files, manage storage, and disable accounts. Also, this section includes many networking-oriented subjects such as firewalls, DNS, access control, and security rules.

Log Files Archive and Clearing

Most computing, storage, and networking gear generates system log files detailing ongoing events that can range from highly critical to informational. Store these logs in a safe area where they can be retrieved and reviewed in case of a device failure, when you're troubleshooting an issue, or when you're creating baseline and capacity planning projects. A syslog server can act as the central repository of logging information. Utilities are available that can search these syslog files to correlate events and look for malicious activity, among other tasks.

Logging information from all of the devices being monitored and managed is sent to a central logging server and archived. By consolidating all the logs onto a logging server, you can easily review and audit them later. Centralized logging allows you to monitor for performance issues and perform baseline analysis. Logging information is also used for security issues, such as investigating a breach or an attempted breach. Logging analysis allows you to view suspicious activity and follow the trail using the consolidated logging information. Log files will collect network, security, server, storage, and application events. The more data that you can collect, the better view you'll get of your environment. A determination should be made as to what systems and applications are able to generate logging information and what level of detail is desired. Most end systems can be configured to provide detailed logging data to the central syslog server for analysis, with the trade-off being the need for additional CPU, storage, and network utilization. You must also decide whether the logging information should be encrypted during transmission and when on the storage systems, as well as whether the data should be stored in the cloud or at a remote location for security reasons. A lot of interesting applications have been developed to extract and analyze logging data. Big data applications can take a large amount of disconnected information and analyze trends and extract useful information about your systems, applications, and customers.

Another critical use of storing logging data is for regulatory compliance. It is your responsibility to comply with applicable regulations regarding the collection, analysis, and storage of logs. There may be a requirement for external audits to be performed based on the rules and regulations for your particular business. By retaining logs, you are better prepared if the requirement for an external audit ever arises. Each country and line of business will have different laws and regulations that will have to be understood and followed. It is often a good idea to involve your legal department in these issues when designing your logging solution.

Like many aspects of getting a cloud service up and running, the level and type of logging information must be defined and included in the service level agreement with the cloud service provider. Keep in mind that there will be logging data that must be collected both from areas under your responsibility and from areas controlled by your cloud service provider. It is also important that the format of the logging data be investigated to make sure that it is compatible with your logging and analysis applications.

Compressing Storage on Drives

Many organizations will include storage compression as part of their ongoing maintenance plans. The advantage of implementing compression on data at rest is that it can significantly reduce storage capacity requirements and, as such, reduce operating expenses since less storage space is required. Storage compression can compact the amount of physical storage space required to less than one-half the amount needed for uncompressed data.

Filesystem compression can be enabled to compress each individual file in a storage volume. This type of compression is best suited for long-term storage such as archival systems and not for operations that will require many read operations that necessitate that the data be constantly compressed and then decompressed, such as a database filesystem.

Compressing the complete storage array can be implemented by the storage vendors, and it is offered as a feature in the storage controllers and head ends. Storage array compression can operate at the block level below the filesystem.

Be aware that compression operations can decrease disk performance, and if you are planning on running a compression process on a previously uncompressed dataset, it should be scheduled to run during a maintenance window so as to not impact the disk I/O performance of regular operations.

Managing and Removing Inactive Accounts

Ongoing maintenance requires that accounts that are no longer used be removed or disabled. This is a best practice that reduces the surface area for a cyberattack.

Security service providers deliver account management as a standard offering and can do an inventory of users, groups, roles, federations, and permissions. Based on defined metrics, they can take administrative actions such as disabling or deleting inactive accounts.

Software products are available that automate the process search and actions on unused accounts. With a complete logging solution, a global search can be performed to determine when accounts were last used. Inactive accounts can then be dealt with accordingly.

Stale DNS Entries

In many cloud deployments, the DNS mappings from a device's domain name to its IP address can be dynamic as virtual systems are added and removed in the highly elastic environment of the cloud. Unfortunately, there are times when old DNS entries persist that point to nonexistent resources. Systems have been long removed, but their domain names and old IP address assignments are still configured in the DNS systems. Most of these are host, or "A," records that map a single host to a specific IP address.

Deleting stale DNS records can improve DNS performance and troubleshooting, so it's a good maintenance practice to review these mappings for consistency and relevancy. If they are stale, they should be removed as part of your ongoing cloud maintenance operations. Of course, an ounce of prevention is worth a pound of cure. If you're monitoring systems by domain name, you can find out pretty quickly when a DNS entry becomes stale.

Orphaned Resources

Orphaned resources are unused resources that are (usually inadvertently) left over from a service or process that no longer exists or is no longer needed. When you enable cloud-based resources such as servers, storage arrays, load balancers, content distribution, DNS, databases, or any other offerings, you may find it to be a challenge to monitor and manage all of these resources. When a service is no longer being used or was enabled for a short period of time, it is all too frequently the case that the services do not get terminated properly and remain active and chargeable even if they are not being used. For example, you may create a VM, use it for a few hours, then terminate it. But if you're not careful, the VM may leave behind a storage volume for which you'll continue to be billed for a long time after the VM is gone. It's crucial that you understand the dependencies that exist among your cloud resources so that you know what to check for. And, of course, you should review your cloud provider's billing console regularly for unexpected charges.

In other cases, different groups in a company may not be aware that there are inactive resources available in the cloud belonging to other groups that are being billed to the company. In this case, they may provision redundant resources and thereby increase costs.

With detailed knowledge of your operations, you can identify orphaned assets and either terminate them or redeploy them to active projects where they can be of use. Proper resource management can significantly reduce your cloud expenses and improve your company's bottom line.

Also, there are often underutilized resources that you are being billed for in your cloud deployment that can be downsized to reduce the number of billed elements. There may be VMs that have unused memory or processing power that you're paying for. This situation offers an opportunity to reduce costs by reducing the resources allocated to the VM. Other common orphaned resources include unattached storage volumes, unused databases, and idle load balancers or cache systems.

Monitoring systems can identify idle resources. Also, the cloud provider may offer a tool that uses automation to review your account and makes a series of recommendations on how to reduce your operational costs and improve your security posture. These systems generally do not make the actual changes but instead offer suggestions for you to implement a more efficient operation.

Outdated Firewall and Security Rules

As part of your ongoing maintenance of the cloud deployments, security should always be at the top of your maintenance list. Firewall rules are added as part of the normal change process as applications are added and the topology changes. The change management process typically focuses on bringing in the new rather than ringing out the old, so there's likely to be little attention on removing outdated, unneeded, or overly broad firewall policies. By performing regular reviews of your firewall rules, you can enhance your security posture and possibly even discover orphaned resources.

Over time, the number of firewall rules can grow very large and hard to administer. Rules can become obsolete, be duplicates of others, or conflict with each other. To ensure that compliance audits are successful, realize better performance, and ensure that the rules are effective, it is important that you clean up the rules on a regular basis. Rules can be cleaned either by a manual or an automated process that addresses the following areas:

- Analysis of the usage of each rule
- Analysis of traffic flows
- Duplicate rule identification
- Unused rule identification
- Overly broad and open rules
- Compliance test assessment suites
- Rule review and recertification
- Rule removal process

With a greater understanding of how your rules are being used, you are better able to manage and change the rules to meet your specific requirements and remove the rules that are no longer valid or pose a security risk. This process can be manual or automated.

Reclaiming Resources

Over time, as cloud resources are added and removed, it is common to find that many services are not completely removed or sit idle while you are being billed for them. If improperly configured, automation systems can remove some resources but leave others behind. Resources that are no longer being used may sit inactive or be abandoned. These idle systems can result in significant charges from your cloud provider over time, and by identifying and removing them, you can achieve significant cost reductions for your company.

Many cloud companies offer advisory services that use automation to locate unused resources and report them to you so that you can address them. Also, a manual process of inventory can be performed across all your accounts or departments to see whether there are unused resources that can be redeployed to other parts of your operations.

When deleting cloud resources, it is advantageous to educate yourself about what specifically gets removed and what remains. As with most technology systems, there are trade-offs and compromises that are taken into account with automation systems. These systems may not always do what you expect them to do, and being aware of what is not removed when deleting services can save money and keep your cloud configurations from getting cluttered with unused services.

Maintaining Access Control Lists

Maintenance of network and system access control is critical to maintaining a secure cloud infrastructure. ACL maintenance follows the same pattern as firewall rule maintenance that was discussed earlier. ACL entries accumulate over time and may not be reviewed for validity as they remain in the device configurations. It is important to review access control periodically and remove any policies that are no longer needed or that have become invalid.

A network ACL can allow or deny traffic into and out of a subnet. As servers are added and removed, and as new services are deployed, the network ACLs should be reviewed and updated as part of your ongoing cloud support operations.

Computer operating systems also have access control mechanisms that grant access rights to users for access to system objects such as storage volume directories and files, administrator rights, and so on.

Understanding your access control configuration will allow you to clean up any unused or overly permissive policies. This process can be either automated or performed manually, but it should be conducted on a regular schedule to allow for enhanced security and performance.

Summary

Disaster recovery is an important topic that addresses the survivability of an organization should an event occur that affects their IT infrastructure. You learned about cloud provider DR capabilities and key concepts such as restore and repair time objectives.

Preparing for a disaster requires extensive input and approval from your organization's leadership. Based on the business continuity plan, you learned how to create a disaster recovery approach that meets those needs. You learned about many of the technical issues that must be investigated when creating a complete DR plan, including dealing with WAN and ISP issues, scaling backup equipment, and keeping the backup configuration synchronized with the live data.

Hot, warm, and cold DR site architectures were introduced, and the pros and cons of each design were discussed. The chapter discussed other DR technical operations such as transferring data in the background, archiving data, and recognizing the value that third-party providers offer in DR planning and execution. Continuity of operations includes connectivity and the use of edge locations, backup hardware and software, and service level agreements.

Next you learned about the practice of performing ongoing maintenance operations on your cloud deployment and all the items that should be addressed. Maintenance windows, automation, and the tasks involved are a day-to-day responsibility of a Cloud+ professional.

Finally, you learned about some of the critical topic areas of ongoing maintenance such as managing logging files; compressing data; managing user accounts; dealing with stale DNS entries, orphaned services, and outdated security policies; and reclaiming idle resources.

Exam Essentials

Know the key concepts of disaster recovery. Know the DR responsibilities of the provider and of your company. Understand what an SLA is and how it defines responsibilities. Know that the RTO is the time it takes to restore operations after a disaster and that the RPO is the point in time that data is recovered and restored.

Know what business continuity planning is and the components to be considered. You may be asked about business continuity planning in a scenario that gives background information, and you have to identify what the question is looking for. Know that the business continuity plan is a corporate document that defines the ability of a company to survive a disaster and that it is used to create a disaster recovery plan to meet those objectives.

Understand the key components of ongoing maintenance. A maintenance plan includes scheduling and maintenance windows. Understand that automation and orchestration can assist in repeatable maintenance operations.

Explain disaster recovery (DR) designs. Study the DR models of hot site, warm site, and cold site and be able to distinguish the use cases for each one. Be able to identify the pros and cons of each approach.

Understand ongoing maintenance of different cloud services. The exam objectives require knowledge of certain ongoing maintenance tasks that you are expected to know and identify. These include working with log files, compressing data, dealing with inactive accounts, working with stale DNS, and dealing with outdated firewall and access control policies. Other maintenance topics that you can be expected to know relate to orphaned and unused resources and how to identify and reclaim them.

Written Lab

Fill in the blanks for the questions provided in the written lab. You can find the answers to the written labs in Appendix B.

1. To allow data to be moved to long-term storage off-site, a(n) ____________________ process is performed.
2. ____________________ as a service companies perform failover, testing, and restoration services.
3. ____________________ is the ability for an organization to continue operations and be able to deliver products and services after an event that disrupts its operations. It is the planning and preparation for a failure or outage and the steps for a business to recover quickly to an operational state.
4. A(n) ____________________ SLA will outline the fundamental issues of determining the business impact, performing a risk assessment, managing the risk, and planning for a disaster.
5. Security service providers offer account management as a standard offering and can do an inventory of accounts, groups, roles, federations, and two-factor accounts based on defined metrics. This is referred to as managing and removing ____________________ accounts.
6. ____________________ is the transfer and synchronization of data between multiple data centers.
7. The ____________________ is the amount of data that can be lost because of an outage, and the ____________________ is a measure of the amount of time a system can be offline during an outage.
8. By using a central server, you consolidate all of the ____________________ logs generated and have the ability to review and audit the collected data.
9. ____________________ are cloud-based services that are left over when a service terminates and are no longer needed or used.
10. Data systems such as databases or storage volumes can be deployed in multiple data centers for fault tolerance. Implementing a(n) ____________________ replication system will ensure that the data always remains synchronized.

Review Questions

The following questions are designed to test your understanding of this chapter's material. For more information on how to obtain additional questions, please see this book's Introduction. You can find the answers in Appendix A.

1. Data replication is often used to store copies of real-time data in remote zones. When there is a need to have the master data immediately updated, and then on the back-end update the remote zones, what type of replication would you recommend that your operations department configure?

   A. Synchronous

   B. Asynchronous

   C. Volume sync

   D. Mirroring

   E. RAID 5

2. Sharon has been directed to put together a disaster recovery (DR) plan based on directives from her company's executive management team. The company's core business is operating an e-commerce website selling winter apparel, with 85 percent of its revenue received during the holiday season. If there was a prolonged outage, it would put the company's ability to continue as a financially viable operation in peril. Sharon has been instructed to create a plan that will restore operations in the shortest amount of time possible. What DR model should she implement?

   A. Hot site

   B. Active/active

   C. Warm site

   D. Active/passive

   E. Cold site

   F. Rollover

3. Which disaster recovery metrics are used to create a measurable SLA that outlines when you can expect your systems to be back online and how much data loss you sustained after an outage? (Choose all that apply.)

   A. RSO

   B. RTO

   C. RPO

   D. DR

   E. VxRestore

4. These cloud facilities provide the ability to connect locally for fast, low-latency connections to the DR location. They can also store, or cache, data at these locations for very fast responses to local user requests.
   - **A.** Region
   - **B.** Edge location
   - **C.** Availability zone
   - **D.** Replication

5. Computer operating systems have mechanisms that grant rights to users for access to system objects like storage volume directories and files, administrator rights, and so on. What should you monitor to make sure that old or unused entries are deleted?
   - **A.** Stale cache
   - **B.** Access control
   - **C.** MFA
   - **D.** Dashboard

6. James has been directed by his employer's finance department that they cannot afford to lose any more than 30 minutes of data in case of a database failure or other catastrophic event. James has updated his corporate business continuity plan and has had his cloud provider update its SLA. What was the metric that was changed?
   - **A.** RSO
   - **B.** RPO
   - **C.** RTO
   - **D.** DBO

7. To meet regulatory requirements, Jill must store customer transaction records for seven years. The data will most likely never be accessed after the second year and can be stored offline to reduce storage costs. What type of storage operation can Jill implement to achieve her goal?
   - **A.** File transfer
   - **B.** Archive
   - **C.** Replication
   - **D.** Data store

8. Sharon is a network engineer for your firm and is investigating the WAN connection into the hot site. In the event of operations being moved to the backup location, she wants to make sure that the load capacity is available. What should she be most concerned about? (Choose two.)
   - **A.** Traffic normalization
   - **B.** Peak capacity
   - **C.** QOS
   - **D.** SLA
   - **E.** Packet loss and jitter
   - **F.** Bandwidth starvation

9. Cloud dashboards allow for monitoring and sometimes configuring maintenance operations with the cloud provider. If you have regularly scheduled backups for your cloud storage volumes, you can configure the cloud provider to perform specific operations for you using what back-end systems?
   A. Replication
   B. Automation
   C. Synchronous
   D. Block chain based
10. What service provides permit and deny policies that require regular review to delete unused entries?
    A. DNS
    B. DHCP
    C. Firewalls
    D. Active Directory
11. Christina has been pinging a new web server by its URL and getting strange and seemingly unexplainable responses from unrecognized systems. She recalls that the new web farm is on a reclaimed subnet that was no longer in use in their cloud server fleet. What would you recommend that she investigate to resolve the issue?
    A. DHCP
    B. Orphaned services
    C. Stale network access control lists
    D. DNS
12. During a disaster recovery switchover, what network services may need to be modified as part of a multisite failover to the backup site? (Choose all that apply.)
    A. RADIUS
    B. TACACS
    C. DHCP
    D. FTP
    E. DNS
    F. Active Directory
    G. None of the above
    H. All of the above

13. Mark has been reviewing disaster recovery planning, and after receiving direction from his company's board of directors, it has been determined that they can only withstand a maximum of 36 hours of downtime. Mark is updating his DR plan with this new metric. What part of the plan should he modify?

A. RSO
B. RPO
C. RTO
D. DBO

14. Jack is preparing to update his company's business continuity with details on its DR backup site. His plan is to have a facility ready with floor space, power, and cooling that has facilities for him to load in his server racks to restore service. What type of DR implementation is Jack deploying?

A. Hot site
B. Active/active
C. Warm site
D. Active/passive
E. Cold site
F. Rollover

15. Will is running his backup DR site in a DNS load-balancing rotation for testing. He needs to ensure that the database in the DR facility is updated in real time and current with the production replica in the primary data center. What type of updates should he define in his primary data center servers before enabling DNS load balancing?

A. Synchronous replication
B. Asynchronous replication
C. Volume sync
D. Mirroring
E. RAID 5

16. What DR location can be used to cache data close to your customer and ease access to your fleet of web servers?

A. Hot
B. Warm
C. Cold
D. Edge
E. Zone
F. Region

17. Jerry noticed on his WAN monitoring dashboard that there are peaks of traffic flow from the primary to his hot site. What two things might be taking place?
    - A. Synchronous replication
    - B. Asynchronous replication
    - C. File transfer
    - D. Continuity updates

18. Tom has been performing an ongoing inventory of his public cloud assets and has found a number of storage volumes, CPU allocations, VMs, and firewall instances that are not connected to any project and are not being used. On what services is Tom collecting data?
    - A. DNS
    - B. Stale services
    - C. Orphaned resources
    - D. Dashboard service

19. Hank is preparing a disaster recovery test drill in advance of the upcoming hurricane season along the Gulf of Mexico. His plan is to create a DR location in the Midwest and have a database server running at that location with a synchronously refreshed data replica. His DR plan calls for activating all other services in the event of a hurricane causing an outage at his primary data center. What model is Hank going to deploy to meet his requirements?
    - A. Hot site
    - B. Warm site
    - C. Cold site
    - D. Active/passive

20. Carl has been investigating stale records in his database that were added by other applications but never deleted or timed out after they were no longer in use. This mappings application is now causing issues with the server addressing and troubleshooting. What system is he looking at?
    - A. SNMP
    - B. DHCP
    - C. DNS
    - D. FTP

Chapter 7

Cloud Management

THE FOLLOWING COMPTIA CLOUD+ EXAM OBJECTIVES ARE COVERED IN THIS CHAPTER:

✓ **1.3 Explain the importance of high availability and scaling in cloud environments.**

- Oversubscription
  - Compute
  - Network
  - Storage
- Applications
- Avoid single points of failure
- Scalability
  - Auto-scaling
  - Horizontal scaling
  - Vertical scaling
  - Cloud bursting

✓ **2.3 Given a scenario, apply the appropriate OS and application security controls.**

- Policies
  - Password complexity
  - Account lockout
  - Application whitelisting
  - Software feature
  - User/group
- User permissions

✓ **3.1 Given a scenario, integrate components into a cloud solution.**

- Auto-scaling

✓ **4.1 Given a scenario, configure logging, monitoring, and alerting to maintain operational status.**

- Logging
  - Collectors
    - Simple network management protocol (SNMP)
    - Syslog
  - Analysis
  - Severity categorization
  - Audits
  - Types
    - Access/authentication
    - System
    - Application
  - Automation
  - Trending
- Monitoring
  - Baselines
  - Thresholds
  - Tagging
  - Log scrubbing
  - Performance monitoring
    - Application
    - Infrastructure components
  - Resource utilization
  - Availability
    - SLA-defined uptime requirements

    - Verification of continuous monitoring activities
    - Service management tool integration
- Alerting
    - Common messaging methods
    - Enable/disable alerts
        - Maintenance modes
    - Appropriate responses
    - Policies for categorizing and communicating alerts

✓ **4.2 Given a scenario, maintain efficient operation of a cloud environment.**

- Life-cycle management
    - Roadmaps
    - Old/current/new versions
    - Upgrading and migrating systems
    - Deprecations of end of life
- Change management
- Asset management
    - Configuration management database (CMDB)
- Impacts of process improvements on systems

✓ **4.3 Given a scenario, optimize cloud environments.**

- Right-sizing
    - Auto-scaling
    - Horizontal scaling
    - Vertical scaling
    - Cloud bursting

✓ **4.4 Given a scenario, apply proper automation and orchestration techniques.**

- Configuration management
    - Playbook

Cloud management involves making sure that your cloud deployment is optimized for your applications, meets performance agreements, is secure, has no faults or alarms, is configured correctly, and is collecting accounting data.

Many components and services come together under the umbrella of cloud management. In this chapter, you'll learn what cloud management is and how it is implemented. Traditional network management tools have been extended and adapted for cloud-based services, and at the same time, many new products and services have been introduced that specifically address this new and fast-growing market. In addition to the traditional information technology management providers, many investments have been made by startup companies that are developing products and services for the cloud.

The definition of network management is very broad, so let's drill down and look at the components of a complete network management solution. The basic architecture consists of one or more network management operation centers housing systems that monitor and collect information from the devices hosted in a private or public data center, as shown in Figure 7.1.

FIGURE 7.1 Basic network management topology

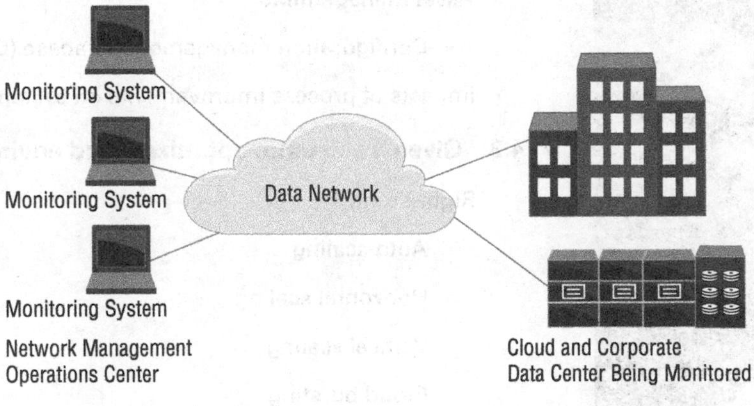

Cloud Metrics

A *metric* is a standard of measurement that defines the conditions and the rules for performing a measurement and for understanding the results of the measurement. To operate, monitor, manage, and troubleshoot your cloud operations effectively, you must gather cloud metrics in real time. *Cloud metrics* include different types of measurement information that can be collected from the many resources operating in the cloud.

To help you better understand cloud metrics, Table 7.1 lists examples of the different objects that can be recorded and logged as part of your cloud management operations. These represent just a small sample of the hundreds of objects available for measurement.

TABLE 7.1 Cloud metric examples

Metric	Description
Availability	Percentage of service uptime; total uptime vs. total time
Database utilization	The measurement of database activity usually measured in I/O requests per second
Horizontal server scalability	Ability to add additional servers to expand workload processing capability
Instance initialization time	The time required to start a new compute instance (VM)
Mean time between failure (MTBF)	The life expectancy of a hardware component; how long it is expected to operate before a failure
Mean time system recovery (MTSR)	The time for a resilient system to complete a recovery from a service failure
Mean time to repair (MTTR)	The time required to repair a damaged hardware component
Mean time to switchover (MTSO)	The time required from when a service failure occurs to when the backup system assumes operations
Network capacity	The available network capacity, usually measured by bandwidth
Outage time	The total time of a single outage, measured from when the outage began until it ended
Reliability	The measurement, usually as a percentage, of successful service operations compared to the total number of operations
Response time	The time to complete an operation
Server capacity	Server capacity usually measured as the total number of CPUs, CPU frequency, RAM, and storage capacity
Storage scalability	The amount of storage that can be added to increase capacity because of increased workloads
Storage total capacity	The measurement of storage device or volume capacity

TABLE 7.1 Cloud metric examples *(continued)*

Metric	Description
Task runtime	The time to run a task from the task request to task completion
Vertical server scalability	The ability to add resources to or expand the capacity of an individual server
Web server utilization	The measurement of load on a web server, usually measured in requests per second

With the collection of metrics and using that data to trigger orchestration systems, you can use thresholds to react to events at all layers of your cloud deployment. This allows you to be proactive in your cloud management operations.

Monitoring Your Deployment

The ability of your organization to monitor your cloud deployment is critical to your ongoing operational success in operating in the cloud. You must have visibility into your operations to be able to manage them effectively.

Cloud management requires detailed knowledge of your operations. The way that you acquire this information is by constantly monitoring your cloud services and making informed decisions based on the data collected. Your monitoring operations can be completely automated, and most services offer flexibility on selecting what metrics to monitor and at what granularity.

Baselines

In an earlier chapter, I discussed the importance of establishing baselines when you are determining the optimal size of the virtual machines required when migrating servers to the cloud. To get a baseline measurement of a cloud resource that you are using, you'll set a sampling interval that is not so short as to monopolize bandwidth, storage, and other resources, but also not so long of a sampling time window where the information becomes inaccurate. When you have your baseline established, you can then determine what deviations from this baseline are considered normal and what would require an investigation or a support incident.

For example, if CPU utilization on a database server is expected to run in the 70 percent range when averaged over a 10-minute interval, you can configure the application to create alerts when the server is averaging 95 percent CPU utilization. These values can be tailored to the requirements of your organization, of course. You can also use the monitoring and alerting functions of the application to determine the baseline and then use the baseline as your reference point to determine what is to be considered out of range. This is referred to as the *variance*. You can use baselines as a threshold to notify the network management or monitoring systems.

With help from performance monitoring software and services, you can use the collected data to provide trend analysis and capacity utilization information graphed over time. Historical data can be stored and used for future change management implementations. The network performance monitoring and management applications can also generate real-time data that can be stored for trend analysis.

Some network management tools have network discovery capabilities that can automatically document the cloud deployment's architecture and configurations. This feature can then use the baseline to dynamically track changes to the cloud over time.

Anomalies

Once you determine your baseline, you can use that as a reference to determine what an *anomaly* is—metrics that are either above or below your baseline. Being able to identify anomalies using cloud monitoring systems has many benefits. For example, you can use notification systems to alert systems and users of a critical issue, and automation and orchestration systems can act on reported anomalies and correct the issue, sometimes before they have an impact on services.

By analyzing metrics over time, you can predict future requirements and capacity needs. If a user's mailbox is reaching capacity, for example, the monitoring systems can be configured to add capacity before it fills up and rejects incoming emails. Other examples include network capacity issues or drops that are beyond your baseline references. A server's memory usage may be considered normal if it spikes to 75 percent of its available RAM for a few minutes. But if it stays at 75 percent for several hours, you can be notified and then take action on the anomaly.

Alert Methods

When the cloud monitoring applications detect an event that requires attention, the question becomes, "How do we let everyone know what is occurring with so many different devices, each with different interfaces?" In cloud systems, there is often a managed notification service that addresses these issues. Figure 7.2 shows an example of a notification system.

FIGURE 7.2 Cloud notification system

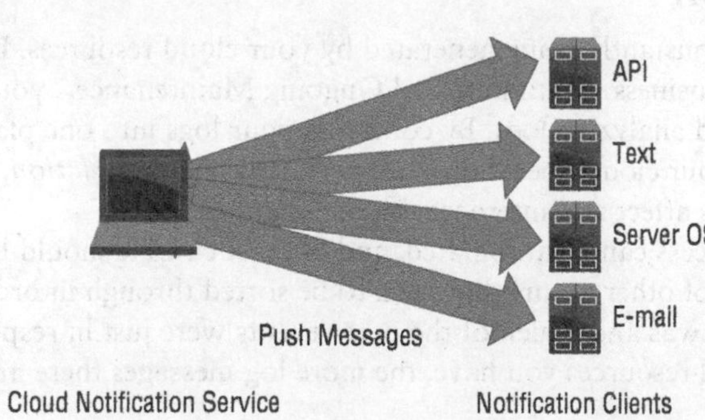

When the alarm is triggered, a notification can be sent, or published, to a notification service. The service can then pass the notification along to a variety of recipients called *subscribers*. A subscriber endpoint can be a text/SMS message, an email message, a push notification to a smartphone or desktop application, or even another cloud service. The notification service offers a scalable way to deliver an alert to many different devices that can act upon the received information. This type of notification system is called a *push service*, because it sends the events to the subscribed endpoints as they occur.

Alert Triggers

To create an alert, you must decide what metrics to monitor and what values fall enough outside of your baseline to trigger an alert. Alerts can also be generated in the case of a service outage or if an application is unresponsive. The cloud management interface will allow you to configure thresholds for alerting. The metrics that you can monitor include things like percent utilization, number of reads or writes, packet drops, and network latency.

You can reduce false positives by averaging the value of a metric over a period. For example, if you are monitoring the performance of your fleet of web servers, you may want to monitor the average CPU utilization of all servers over an 8-minute period. If the average is more than 90 percent for 8 minutes, it can trigger an alert. Such an alert can be used to add additional web servers automatically to your load-balanced deployment. In this case, avoiding false positives is especially important because you don't want to add unnecessary resources (and cost) in response to short bursts of high CPU utilization.

As your environment changes, it may be necessary to adjust the alert thresholds. What are initially finely tuned thresholds may become obsolete and lead to alerts that come too early or too late. If you perform an action—such as adding more servers—based on a premature alert, you risk spinning up new resources, and you'll be charged for these services even if they are not needed.

Variances in metrics aren't the only things that can trigger alerts. You can also configure alerts to occur in response to events. For example, you may want to know whenever someone terminates a VM. Terminating a VM is an event, and you can configure an alert in response to that.

Event Correlation

Logs and events are constantly being generated by your cloud resources. In Chapter 6, "Disaster Recovery, Business Continuity, and Ongoing Maintenance," you learned about collecting, storing, and analyzing logs. By collecting your logs into one place, you can get a complete picture of your cloud operations and perform *event correlation*, a process whereby you see how resources affect and interact with one another.

Of course, this process can be automated, and in most cases it should be. A single event can trigger a cascade of other events that need to be sorted through in order to determine what the trigger was and which of the other events were just in response to the main event. The more cloud resources you have, the more log messages there are to sort through and analyze.

For example, assume that someone in IT operations configured a network access control list (NACL) that blocked an application server from reaching a back-end database on your e-commerce site. This would probably trigger a lot of alarms that are outside your baseline metrics! You would be getting nonresponse alerts from the web servers trying to access the database, and the application servers would report timeouts from the database server. The database may even report that there had been zero table read or write operations, and so on. All of these alarms are written to the logging server and should be analyzed and reviewed in order to determine what is happening so that the root cause can be identified and the service restored.

Using event correlation, all of the events in the logging system will be scanned and processed to identify the root cause. In this case, the incorrectly inserted access control list statement that blocked the communications was identified by the correlation application as the root issue, and all of the other alarms resulted from this incorrect database deny rule.

As you can see from this example, event correlation is a valuable tool to have! It can be time-consuming and error-prone to sort through hundreds or thousands of log messages manually, trying to find that one event that caused the issue.

Forecasting Required Resources

After you have established your baselines, you can use this data to forecast what cloud resources you'll need. Accurate baselines are invaluable reference points for the ongoing management of your cloud operations. Any metric that you track can be analyzed for trends in resource utilization. Based on this data, you can proactively add or remove resources.

Major cloud providers can track metrics that you define and automatically add or remove capacity as needed in real time. This allows for a fast response to changes in cloud computing demands. For example, if queries against a database read replica begin to take too long, the cloud provider's orchestration system can dynamically provision an additional read replica to lighten the load. When the usage later decreases, the additional replica can be removed.

Upsizing and downsizing your cloud operations can also be a manual process that is tracked by the management systems monitoring your operations. When data is collected over a period, you can identify trends that allow for informed capacity forecasting. Based on the trending data, you can plan to add or remove resources as your needs require.

Event Collection Policies

When configuring your event collection requirements, the repetition required to define all the logging definitions for each device and enter them manually or add them to the automation systems, such as by scripts of orchestration systems, can be a large administrative task.

Many cloud configuration systems allow for policies to be defined and applied to objects. For example, a policy can be created to send a syslog message when a storage volume reaches 75 percent capacity. Once the policy has been created, it can be reused and applied to all the storage volumes as they are created or migrated. Event policies reduce the amount of management overhead and enforce consistency in your deployments.

Event Dissemination Policies

Logging systems can be surprisingly feature-rich given all the capabilities that have been added over the years. Policies, or rules, can be created to forward event information in a fan-out design to systems that may benefit from the data. Policies can be categorized into event families or types and dealt with differently. For example, a big data application may need to receive data about which countries are accessing specific files on your website and when. A dissemination policy can be created to forward the relative logging information to the big data application for analysis.

There will be a trade-off in the amount of information gathered compared to the associated costs that you'll incur from the provider and the management overhead of storing and analyzing the collected data. Although from a management and cost perspective it's easier to collect a minimal amount of data, keep in mind that regulations might require that you keep almost everything!

Cloud Support Agreements

When it comes to support, you get what you pay for. Cloud companies have a lot of variations and options in their support offerings. It is typical to offer a base Tier 1 offering free of charge that entitles the customer to basic email support, online forums, documentation, and limited response time commitments.

Beyond the basic free support options offered to all customers, the cloud providers have chargeable or premium offerings with higher support levels. Paid support plans may include guaranteed response times, enhanced and customized dashboards that give you the big picture of the status of your operations, and direct access to customer support engineers on the phone or via email. The premium services may also allow you to select service windows that meet your operational needs, such as Monday through Friday 8 a.m. to 5 p.m.; 24/7 plans; or customizable maintenance windows with different response time options based on the severity levels you are experiencing.

Standard Cloud Maintenance Responsibilities

The delineation of responsibilities for cloud resources will be detailed in the service level agreement (SLA). Cloud providers use a shared responsibility model where the cloud provider and customer share responsibility for managing the resource in question.

The responsibilities fall along the cloud service delivery model. For example, for IaaS systems, the cloud provider is responsible for all hardware infrastructure but not for anything higher up the stack, such as the operating system and applications for which you would be responsible. PaaS offerings have the cloud provider also taking on responsibility for the operating system, and you'll assume responsibility for any applications or services running on the operating system. With the SaaS approach, service providers have the greatest maintenance responsibilities because they also assume maintenance for the application and everything below, including the operating systems and all underlying infrastructures.

Configuration Management Applications and Tools

There are many tools for managing the cloud. *Configuration management* uses a central repository for storing, archiving, and tracking resource configurations. This is especially helpful for troubleshooting and regulatory compliance. For troubleshooting, you can consult the configuration management system to see what changes were implemented and, if necessary, reapply the correct configuration. Major cloud providers offer configuration management services as a separate feature at a nominal cost.

Change Management Processes

In Chapter 2, "Cloud Deployments," you learned about change management, the purpose of which is to minimize disruptions. Change management entails policies and procedures for changes, including recording the change, creating an implementation and backout plan, performing testing, getting approval, documenting the change, and validating that the change was successful. A post-change review can be added to the process if desired.

Change management usually begins with a request that includes the name of the requester, the reason for the change, and a description of the change and its expected result. A change request may include risks and required resources, such as a list of individuals responsible for the various aspects of the change, including the design, configuration, deployment, and validation steps.

Change Advisory Board

A critical piece of the change management process is a group commonly referred to as the *change advisory board (CAB)*. The change advisory board supports the change management team by reviewing, sequencing, and approving changes that have been requested and determining the priorities and adequate planning for all upcoming changes. The primary goal of the CAB is to manage risk and ensure that the changes are necessary and properly planned.

Generally, the change advisory board will meet with all parties that have submitted change requests for upcoming change windows. Each change request will be reviewed and discussed. It's the CAB's job to make sure that no conflicts exist among proposed changes. They approve the time windows and ensure that adequate resources are assigned to the change. If there are no issues, then the board will issue a *change approval*.

Change advisory boards advise change teams on guidelines and priorities, assess the changes, and determine the time and order in which changes are implemented. They may perform a postimplementation review to determine whether there can be any process improvements, or they may do a postmortem of a failed change.

Document Action and Backout Plans

All change requests may include a detailed plan on the steps to be taken to reverse or back out the changes and verify that all affected resources are returned to their pre-change state. The plan can include all CLI commands or web GUI input and the expected output. Remember, maintenance windows can be short, and your systems must be fully operational at the end of the allocated maintenance time. There will be no time to do any research. You must have everything documented before beginning the change.

The *configuration management database (CMDB)* is a family of applications designed to track inventory and configurations of your deployment. The CMDB can automate your change management steps in an archived online database. Many cloud providers offer applications that automatically back up and inventory your cloud resources. They can also allow you to add fields, such as change documentation and rollback, or backout, plans to the database.

If an actual CMDB system is not feasible, or if it is overkill for the size of your operations, a simple spreadsheet may be all that is required. Using a standard spreadsheet, you can record and track your actions taken and add columns as desired to add detail to your documentation. The key point is always to track and document your changes using whatever application works best for your operations.

Adding and Removing Cloud Resources

Over time, and as part of the ongoing operations of your cloud deployment, resources will be added and removed to tune and maintain your cloud presence. In this section, you'll learn about managing your resources.

Determining Usage Patterns

Usage patterns can be based on your collected metrics and baseline data. Also, a complete and up-to-date set of documentation can help in planning and understanding the details of your deployment and traffic flows. Cloud monitoring and management applications allow you to graph metrics over a defined timeline. Also, logging data can be viewed with analytics software to determine detailed usage patterns based on your requirements.

Bursting

Cloud bursting is a hybrid model in which you normally use on-premises resources but temporarily use public cloud processing during times of increased load. This is often an economical approach to accessing additional resources when required. When your on-premises resources are at capacity, the additional capacity of the public cloud can be used and billed for when it is needed. When activity returns to normal and the private data center can handle the workload, then the cloud resources can be deleted.

Migrating Between Cloud Providers

Is it possible to move workloads between different cloud providers? The answer is often a definite "maybe" or "it depends"! This requires some background research and engineering to pull off. Where there is commonality between service providers, there are also proprietary implementations that may prevent a simple migration between cloud providers. On a spectrum, IaaS resources are the easiest to migrate, whereas SaaS resources are the hardest.

With IaaS, most of the cloud operations are under your direct control, which gives you the most flexibility to migrate. With SaaS, however, the cloud provider controls the application, so they dictate your migration options. For example, migrating a hosted email service would require the provider to give you a way to export your existing mailboxes. Likewise, the provider to which you're migrating would have to provide a way to import those mailboxes. And that's not even considering possible version incompatibilities that might require you to perform additional steps. Fortunately, there are companies and software applications that specialize in migrations between cloud providers and that make sure all of the formats and configurations are compatible between the providers.

It's also important to review the financials involved in a migration to make sure that you do not have any long-term contractual commitments with the cloud provider you are migrating away from and are not forced to pay for stranded resources. Also, if you're migrating to an SaaS solution, check for potential issues caused by version mismatches.

Scaling Resources to Meet Requirements

Again, one of the primary benefits of the cloud is that cloud computing enables a utility business model that charges you only for the resources you consume. This model enables you to scale your cloud fleet to meet its current workload by adding and removing capacity as needed. This ability to scale yields financial savings, since you are no longer paying for resources and systems when they are not being used. In this section, you'll learn about some of the options available, and the techniques used, to scale resources to meet your current workloads.

Vertical and Horizontal Scaling

Adding or removing resources to meet demand is called *scaling*. To scale your cloud, you decide whether you need to scale up or scale out.

Scaling up, or *vertical scaling,* means increasing the capacity of your *existing* resources, such as adding resources like CPU power, storage space, or memory to a VM, as shown in Figure 7.3. Many applications, such as databases, will perform better after a system has been scaled vertically. For instance, a system that is CPU bound—its performance is most limited by the amount of processing power available to it—will perform better when scaling up with additional CPU cores. The same is true with applications that benefit from more RAM or network bandwidth. Keep in mind that vertical scaling usually involves downtime. If you want to add more RAM to a VM, for example, it will likely require, at the very least, an application restart.

Scaling out, or *horizontal scaling*, means adding *new* resources to handle a workload, as shown in Figure 7.4. To use horizontal scaling, your application must use a distributed architecture. An example of this is a fleet of web servers behind a load balancer. The load balancer keeps track of how many web servers are available, and it distributes the workload accordingly. Horizontal scaling is more reliable than vertical scaling because it doesn't require taking down resources.

FIGURE 7.3 Vertical scaling

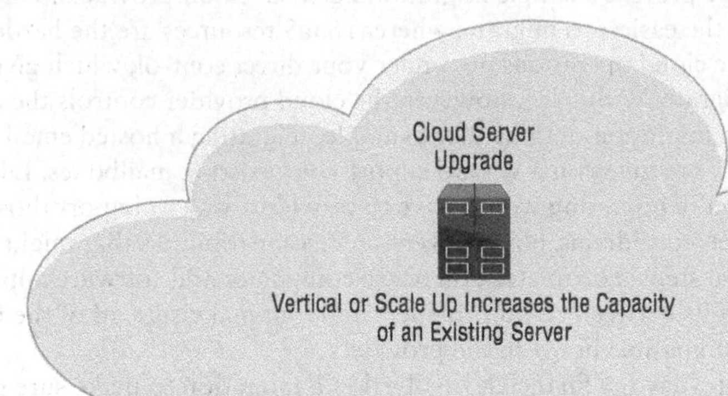
Cloud Server
Upgrade
Vertical or Scale Up Increases the Capacity
of an Existing Server

FIGURE 7.4 Horizontal scaling

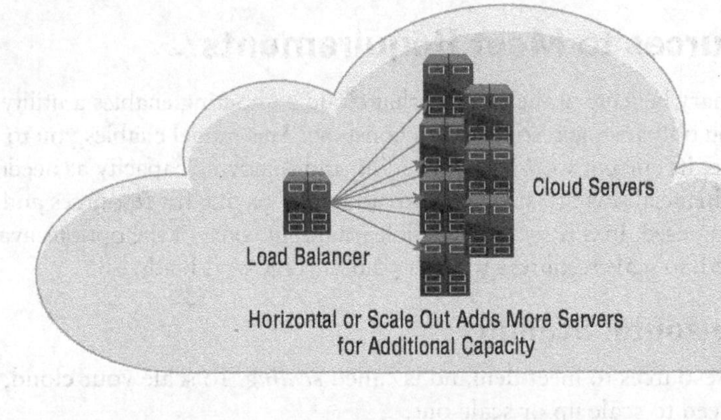
Cloud Servers
Load Balancer
Horizontal or Scale Out Adds More Servers
for Additional Capacity

It is important to check the cloud provider's offerings and what options it delivers when you are deciding whether to scale vertically or horizontally. The provider may offer better pricing options for multiple smaller systems than an equivalent larger system. The larger VM is a single management point as compared to multiple, horizontally scaled systems, but it is also a single point of failure. When deciding to use the horizontal approach, you must consider that you need to manage more systems, and the distributed workloads between the systems may cause some latency that is not found in a single larger server.

There is also a third option, referred to as *diagonal scaling*, which is a combination of scaling up to more powerful systems and scaling out by deploying more of these scaled-up systems. It is common to use horizontal scaling combined with load balancing on the Internet-facing web tier and vertical scaling for the back-end databases, since many database applications operate more efficiently on a single larger server than multiple small servers. Choosing the best approach usually comes down to each particular use case, the application capabilities, and the cloud provider's pricing structure.

Auto-Scaling

Cloud providers offer the ability to scale automatically—vertically or horizontally—using custom rules based on metrics. For example, suppose that you have a fleet of 20 web servers. You might want to have an auto-scaling policy that removes half of the servers if the average CPU utilization of the fleet remains below 50 percent for an hour. When the CPU utilization rises again, auto-scaling can scale vertically, adding more servers.

Community Cloud Scaling

A *community cloud* is a cloud where users with common interests or requirements access shared resources. These specialized cloud providers offer a wide array of different services and can be vastly different in their offerings and capabilities. As such, the ability to scale using a community cloud will be highly dependent on the capabilities of each individual community cloud provider.

However, it is helpful to remember that all clouds are, at their core, automated data centers controlled by software. So, if it is a community, public, or private cloud, the underlying capabilities are largely the same but may be different in scale and orchestration capabilities.

Scaling the Public Cloud

The pay-as-you-go business model of the public cloud is designed for large-scale deployments. Some of the larger public cloud providers can scale to thousands of servers on demand and offer many pricing options to meet your requirements. Public cloud utilities, applications, and orchestration systems are designed for elastic computing operations. These tools and features are used to differentiate themselves from their competitors and make scaling easy to implement for their customers.

Elasticity

The ability to dynamically add and remove resources on the fly is called *elasticity*. Although the cloud has a finite number of resources, those resources are so vast that, to the customer, the cloud appears as an unlimited pool of storage, compute, and networking. The elastic nature of the cloud allows cloud consumers to scale their resources up and down automatically in order to match their workload. With elastic computing, there no longer is any need to deploy servers and storage systems designed to handle peak loads—servers and systems that may otherwise sit idle during normal operations.

You can automatically expand as needed when the occasion arises, but that doesn't mean you have to. With more resources comes additional cost, and some organizations may want to cap their cloud costs by oversubscribing resources. Oversubscribing means provisioning just enough resources for a normal workload, rather than for peak workload. For example, you may provision just enough web servers to handle day-to-day traffic. But when a substantial traffic spike occurs that overwhelms the provisioned capacity, the servers become oversubscribed and performance will likely suffer. Oversubscription is a common strategy to limit costs, and it can be applied to compute, networking, and storage.

Extending the Scope of the Cloud

As an organization becomes more comfortable with the cloud, it may choose to deploy more resources there, perhaps even migrating data center resources. This is often referred to as *extending the scope* of the cloud deployment. Cloud providers are continually adding more SaaS offerings in the hope that organizations will migrate their in-house applications to cloud-managed services. For example, an organization that manages its own virtual desktop infrastructure (VDI)—complete with the servers needed to run it—might decide that it's worth using a cloud provider's VDI SaaS offering instead. This is an example of extending the scope of the cloud deployment—in this case, by reducing the scope of the on-premises deployment!

Understanding Application Life Cycles

All applications follow a basic pattern throughout their limited useful life. You deploy an application, upgrade it, perhaps migrate it, and eventually retire it. This is called the *application life cycle*. In this section, you'll learn about the complete cycle since you most certainly will work with it in your career.

The application life cycle can be broken down into the phases of deployments, upgrades, migrations, feature additions or deletions, replacements, and retirements.

Deployments

The deployment phase of the application life cycle includes determining the software requirements and performing testing, configuration, and validation. If the application isn't "off the shelf," this phase will also include coding.

Upgrades

As reviewed in Chapter 5, "Maintaining Cloud Operations," upgrades are a natural part of an application life cycle, and there are many different types of upgrades and patching that can occur. It is important to remember that software will most likely undertake many upgrade cycles over its lifetime, and each upgrade will need to be managed through the change management process.

Migrations

When a new application is brought online, there may be a need to migrate or move data from an older application or data store. Migrations need to be project-managed and controlled as part of both the life cycle and the change process. If the applications are significantly different, the format of the user data may have to be modified as part of the migration process.

Feature Additions or Deletions

An application will undergo upgrades and modifications over its lifetime. Some will be to resolve issues through the patching process, and others will be to add new features as they are released. Though less common, features can also be removed to save money by not paying for unused licenses.

Replacements

Applications will be replaced over time, and the process of project management to assist in replacing the existing application with a new or different approach must take place. This is a normal part of the life cycle process.

Retirements

Applications will, at some point, be removed after having their data migrated to a new system or being replaced. Though this is the end of the complete life cycle, it will most likely start over with the deployment of a replacement application.

Organizational Changes

Over time, there will be changes to your organization and its cloud computing requirements. Organizations constantly change as they grow and shrink in size, or as they enter and exit markets, and there may be legal or regulatory changes with which they must contend. There can also be mergers and acquisitions that can have a major impact on their IT and cloud operations.

With a pay-as-you-use-it model, you can design and deploy a test bed for the new compute operations and then tear it down when it is no longer needed. The cloud allows for a cost-effective way of testing new designs since no large capital expenditure is required to build a test site.

Mergers, Acquisitions, and Divestitures

Probably the most disruptive event that can happen to an organization—and its IT operations in particular—is that of a merger, acquisition, or spin-off of an operation. You should be prepared to work with new groups and departments to integrate or split off portions of your IT infrastructure. For example, in the case of a merger, duplicate applications could be consolidated. This is usually a large and sometimes complex undertaking, where attention to detail is your key to success. All interested parties must participate in this project management undertaking, and care must be taken to achieve success.

Cloud Service Requirement Changes

Cloud providers routinely add new services, occasionally with the intent of replacing old ones. As incentive to get you to move to the newer service, the provider may offer more competitive pricing. For example, a provider desiring to retire magnetic block storage might offer better pricing for SSD block storage. It's a good idea to stay abreast of new services, feature additions, pricing models, and trends in the cloud to see whether you can gain a competitive advantage and introduce efficiencies to save money on the new systems.

Regulatory and Law Changes

There are always going to be changes on the legal and regulatory landscape, and these can have a direct and long-lasting impact on your operations. This is especially true if you are in a regulated industry. But even if you're not, regulatory changes may require the cloud provider to make changes in their infrastructure, necessitating changes on your part. For example, suppose that you're using a load balancer to terminate HTTPS connections from customers, some of whom are using older browsers. If your cloud provider deprecates an outdated cipher that your customers are using, it could have a detrimental effect on their ability to connect. Cloud providers go to great lengths to make you aware of these changes in advance, but you have to be paying attention.

Managing Account Provisioning

Adding and removing accounts and changing permissions are part and parcel of the IT landscape. One of the most common occurrences is the addition of accounts for new employees or contractors. A request for a new account could come from anywhere, but it most commonly comes from human resources or a manager. Naturally, each account will need defined access to various resources. The account provisioning process can be manual or automated.

There may be multiple independent or federated identity systems where you'll need to create new accounts. For example, you may use Active Directory or another Lightweight Directory Access Protocol (LDAP) service for on-premises accounts, whereas you use a cloud provider's identity and access management (IAM) service for creating accounts with access to cloud resources. If these systems are separate and you need to add a new user with access to both on-premises and cloud resources, then you'll need to create two separate accounts. On the other hand, if your on-premises and cloud IAM systems are federated, you'll have to create only one account that can be used with both.

Account Identification

User accounts in the cloud will have different methods to identify them that may include a domain name; an incomprehensible, long number string; or a user-defined identification number. It is important that the root account manager for the account keep detailed records of each account for management and billing purposes. Also, it is common for a single corporation or entity to have many different account databases, with the same or multiple cloud companies, and it can become difficult to manage that many different accounts. To rectify this, some cloud providers can consolidate billing for a large number of accounts owned by a single organization.

Authentication

As you learned in Chapter 2, authentication is the process of determining the identity of a user. When you authenticate a user, you determine the identity of that user and can then permit or deny them access to cloud resources. Authenticating a user usually requires just a username and password but may include additional factors such as a token or a biometric. Authentication can also be done with just an access key identifier and a secret access key, and this is the typical way of programmatically authenticating when performing API calls.

Federations and Single Sign-On

You learned about federations and single single-on (SSO) in Chapter 2. A federation includes external user systems, primarily Active Directory, as a user repository for your cloud user accounts. The federated approach can eliminate the need to keep two sets of user account data, and it allows your cloud deployment to be accessed by other groups or companies that integrate with your user accounts using the federated approach.

In an SSO architecture, your users can authenticate just one time with the cloud and then access all the services to which they have rights without having to log in to each service individually. SSO allows you to centralize authentication systems into a single system and eases administration, since you do not have to manage multiple accounts for the same user. Directory systems using LDAP are an example of SSO systems where you log into the directory services just one time, and based on your rights, you can then access systems in the network without any additional login requirements. SSO eliminates the need to remember and input multiple username and password combinations, saving you time as you access different systems.

Authorization

After a user has been authenticated, the IAM system will determine their permissions using the *authorization process*. For example, database administrators can be given full access to manage a database application but be restricted from manipulating VMs.

Lockout Policies

A lockout policy can be applied to an account that defines the parameters that create a lockout event. It is most common to apply a lockout policy to failed login attempts. For example, you can define a policy where four failed login attempts in five minutes will disable an account for 30 minutes. A lockout policy will most likely be defined by your information security group, and you may be asked to create and apply the policy as part of your duties.

Password Complexity

Another policy that will most likely be defined by the IT security group is that of password complexity and reuse. Passwords that are too short or basic, or are in place for a long period of time, are security risks. The IT security group will most likely be the ones who dictate the complexity of the password and its life cycle. For example, a password may be required to be a nondictionary word that is eight or more characters in length and contain at least one uppercase letter and a special character. It is also typical to have a rotation policy that requires you to create a new password on a regular basis, such as every 30 days. To configure password complexity policies, the cloud configuration interface will have fields for these in the user or server login configuration dialog boxes.

Account Automation and Orchestration

Account provisioning can be done with automation systems that use the cloud provider's APIs. As discussed throughout this book, automation can reduce human error and reduce the time it takes to perform tasks that used to be routinely performed by hand.

User Account Creation

In organizations, the permissions a user has are generally determined by the user's job role. Rather than consulting a spreadsheet to determine a new user's permissions and then manually granting them, it is more efficient to write a script that simply asks for the new user's role and then automatically creates the user and assigns the permissions. Such a script can be run in seconds, reused over and over, and help prevent accidentally granting the wrong permissions.

This automated approach can be extended to reduce the need for human interaction even further. Instead of requiring a manual input for a user and role, the script could be reworked to pull this information from a database, text file, or spreadsheet. Even better, it could be automatically run on a schedule so that the only human input ever required is the file containing users' names and roles! As you can imagine, the possibilities can be extended even further, such as automatically creating email boxes, file shares, virtual desktops, and so on.

Resource-Based and User-Based Policies

One aspect of the cloud that strikes many as unexpected is that the permissions a user has aren't solely determined by the permissions assigned to the user's account. User-based policies are tied to the individual user and determine what resources the user has access to. These are typically what we think of when we talk about assigning permissions to users. For example, if a group has access to create new VMs and you assign a user to that group, then the user inherits the permissions to create a new VM. The policy is tied to the user.

Resource-based policies, on the other hand, are tied to the individual resource. For example, a file in an object storage bucket may have a resource-based policy that allows everyone read access. This is an example of a resource-based policy because it is tied to the resource rather than a user. You're likely to find resource-based policies where the users who need access to the resource are unknown or ambiguous.

It's important to understand how user-based and resource-based policies interact. Although this can vary by cloud provider, as a general rule, deny rules take precedence. For example, if a user-based policy grants a user permission to delete a bucket but the bucket's resource based policy explicitly denies that user such permission, then the user will in fact not be allowed to delete the bucket.

Removing Accounts

Part of a solid IT security operation is to remove unused accounts, policies, and resources. In Chapter 6, you learned about user account maintenance and the importance of tracking and removing accounts that will no longer be used. Management applications are available that can assist in the identification of accounts that need to be removed. Also, automation systems can be employed to automate the accounts flagged for removal.

Many organizations will simply disable an account for a period of time prior to deleting it. The ability to disable an account can be helpful in situations where the account will need to be reactivated at a future date and does not need to be deleted. Account disablement can be managed in the same manner as other account operations with a web front end or with the use of APIs for scripted and automated processes.

Summary

This chapter focused on the management operations of your cloud deployment. The subject of collecting monitoring and management data was covered. Once the data has been collected, a baseline can be determined by monitoring key data measurement points over a defined period. The baseline information can be used to determine future expansion and growth of the cloud. Also, if a system deviates too far from the baseline, a trigger can be created to alert that there may be a problem. You learned about notification systems that process the alerts and distribute them to users and systems using such channels as text, email, and API calls.

The chapter also went into detail on determining whether your resource allocations are correct and discussed the available options to add or remove capacity. Support agreements are critical for ongoing management of your cloud fleet. You learned about cloud providers' support structures and responsibilities.

Configuration and change management are ongoing cloud management tasks. In this chapter, you learned about backing up and recording your device configurations and what the change management process is, as well as the roles that the various groups and processes play in making sure that changes are implemented properly and that the risk of an error is minimized.

Your cloud fleet will most likely need to expand and contract as your needs change. You became familiar with usage patterns and how cloud bursting works and what its advantages are. Autoscaling systems allow you to add and remove resources based on measured loads and to automate your operations by taking advantage of the elasticity features of the virtualized cloud data center.

An important topic is application life-cycle management. You were introduced to the concepts of life-cycle management and the stages that are common as an application is designed and deployed through upgrades and ultimately retirement.

Cloud management will be driven by changing business requirements. Business disruptions, such as mergers, acquisitions, and spin-offs, all can have major impacts on cloud management. Other business-related topics include regulatory changes and how new laws may impact your operations and require that you make changes to meet new requirements.

The topic of user account management was revisited and expanded upon. You learned about identification and authentication, what a federated system is, and the advantages that can be gained by accessing user data by means of an external directory. User access control and permissions are defined to determine what systems a user or system can access and what actions they are allowed to perform on the system. Single sign-on, password management, user account creation, and disablement ended this chapter on cloud management.

Exam Essentials

Know what a metric is. A metric is a measurement of some property of a resource, such as CPU utilization or requests per second. By collecting metrics, you can determine trends in your usage. The exam may present a long, scenario-based question that can be solved by focusing on metrics and what they are used for.

Understand baselines and anomalies. A baseline is the range of metrics collected during normal operations, and values above or below the baseline are anomalies. You may encounter questions that test your ability to distinguish between these two terms.

Be able to explain alerting, methods, triggers, and notifications. When a metric falls outside a defined threshold, it can trigger an alert. You can configure a variety of responses to an alert, including notifications such as email or text messages. Particular events, such as terminating a VM, can also trigger alerts.

Understand cloud management support agreements and responsibilities. Cloud companies offer a basic support plan that is usually free of charge but limited in scope. Premium service agreements are offered with varying levels of support commitments. You may be given an example of an outage and asked whether the customer or cloud provider is responsible.

Know what change management and configuration management are. Configuration management is the tracking and documentation of ongoing changes to device configurations, including what changes were performed, by whom, and at what time. Change management is a complete process that monitors and manages all changes that are made to your cloud fleet. For the exam, understand the role of the change advisory board and the approvals documentation that are part of an effective change management plan.

Be able to identify when and how to scale cloud resources. You may be asked how and when to add or remove cloud computing capacity. Know the differences among cloud bursting, horizontal scaling, and vertical scaling. Also, be able to explain the limitations of each.

Understand the application life cycle. For the exam, you should be able to answer questions that outline the life of an application from its initial design, deployment, updates, migrations, feature changes, replacement, and finally retirement.

Know how organizational changes may impact cloud resources. Corporate mergers, acquisitions, spin-offs, legal, and regulatory changes can necessitate changes to your cloud resources. Even if your organization isn't directly affected by such changes, they may require your cloud provider to make changes that *do* affect you.

Understand user accounts. User account management includes authentication, authorization, federations, and single sign-on systems. Other topics that are fair game for the exam include account management such as new users, password complexity, policies, removal of old accounts, and permission settings. User accounts are an important part of ongoing cloud management, and you should expect several questions that test your knowledge of the topic.

Written Lab

Fill in the blanks for the questions provided in the written lab. You can find the answers to the written labs in Appendix B.

1. A(n) ________________ is a standard of measurement that defines the conditions and rules for performing the measurement and for understanding the results of a measurement.
2. Using metrics data to trigger ________________ systems, you can use thresholds to react to events at all layers of your cloud deployment.
3. Once Harry has determined what is considered to be a baseline during normal web server operations, he can use that as a reference to determine what is considered to be a(n) ________________ or a system that is reporting metrics that are either above or below his expectations.
4. If the event is deemed to be critical, alerts can be generated by configuring a(n) ________________.
5. As a general rule, the cloud providers will be responsible for the underlying ________________, and if it is not defined in the ________________, it will be your responsibility to maintain.
6. ________________ is the process of managing all aspects of the ongoing upgrades, repairs, and reconfigurations.
7. The management of a software application from the initial planning stages through to its retirement is referred to as ________________.
8. Users can be granted ________________ at the account level to perform a wide array of operations. The capability to manage cloud operations may allow the administrator to add, remove, or modify user accounts and the services that they are allowed to access.
9. Enforcing password ________________ may require a nondictionary word that is eight or more characters in length and that contains at least one uppercase letter and a special character.
10. All change request documents must include a detailed formal plan on the steps to be taken to implement, and if required, ________________ the changes.

Review Questions

The following questions are designed to test your understanding of this chapter's material. For more information on how to obtain additional questions, please see this book's Introduction. You can find the answers in Appendix A.

1. Carol is collecting information on objects to monitor in her community cloud deployment. She is interested in establishing a baseline to produce a trend analysis report. What are some objects that she could natively monitor? (Choose all that apply.)

   A. Availability

   B. Instance initialization time

   C. Task runtime

   D. Total storage capacity

   E. MTBF

   F. None of the above

   G. All of these

2. An organization wants to know what its normal day-to-day web hit count is so that it can plan for the upcoming holiday selling season. Jim's job is to measure the incoming web requests and graph them against delayed and missed connection counts. What type of dataset is Jim producing?

   A. Metric

   B. Variance

   C. Baseline

   D. Smoothing

3. Elaine works in IT security, and she is reviewing user count policies. She needs to strengthen passwords by enforcing a mandatory minimum of a nondictionary word that is six or more characters in length, contains at least one uppercase letter, and contains a special character. What is she defining?

   A. Object access

   B. User policy

   C. Complexity

   D. SSO

   E. Federation policy

   F. Firewall zone rules

4. Donald has been tasked by the IT security group in his company to prevent dictionary login attacks to the company's VMs running in a private cloud at a remote data center. You have been brought in to offer him advice to deter the random but steady login attacks. What would you recommend he enable to help prevent this type of cyberattack?

   A. Object

   B. SSO

   C. LDAP

   D. Lockout

   E. Access control list

5. Christina is configuring her public cloud object storage bucket for granular access from a new Linux VM. She wants to set the permissions on the storage system. What would you recommend?

   A. Access control list authorization

   B. Federations

   C. Permission-based

   D. SSO

6. Liza is reviewing the maintenance responsibilities between her company and its public cloud service provider. She notices that the cloud provider takes responsibility for the operating system, and she needs to assume responsibility for any applications or services running on the operating system. Under what type of service model is she operating?

   A. IaaS

   B. PaaS

   C. SaaS

   D. XaaS

7. Dawn has been working in the network operations center (NOC) and has been tasked with performing a root-cause analysis on a recent outage that affected the middle-tier web stack in a private cloud. She is looking at the log files and notices that there are more than 430 logs that were generated around the time the site failed. What function does Dawn need to perform to distill all of these log files into a meaningful report?

   A. Baseline

   B. Event analysis

   C. Event correlation

   D. Logging

8. To increase her organization's security posture, Allison is reviewing user accounts that access the fleet cloud resources. Allison notices that, although the summer interns have left to go back to school, their accounts are still active. She knows that they will return for the winter corporate announcements and new-product rollouts to assist in the project over winter break. What would you suggest Allison do with these accounts?

   A. Do nothing.
   B. Delete the accounts.
   C. Disable the accounts.
   D. Change the resource access definitions.
   E. Modify the confederation settings.
   F. Change the access control.

9. To make sure that all users can access only approved resources, Marie is auditing her public cloud identity systems. She wants to control specific access and operations. What is Marie defining?

   A. Federated access
   B. Resource-based policies
   C. User-based policies
   D. Access control lists

10. To promote consistent cloud monitoring and to reduce configuration overhead, Lisa has created a number of policies to obtain baseline data. What type of policies is Lisa creating?

    A. Collection
    B. Dissemination
    C. Notification
    D. Publishing

11. Matt is preparing for an upcoming promotion his company is offering during a major soccer game. He needs to determine his options to add capacity to his company's web server farm so that it can handle the anticipated additional workload. You are brought in to consult with him on his options. What do you recommend as possible solutions? (Choose three.)

    A. Vertical scaling
    B. Horizontal scaling
    C. Edge cache
    D. Cloud bursting
    E. Core elasticity

12. Bob is configuring an event notification service and notices that there are many different devices and services that can be subscribers to the notification system's published events queue. The notification services offer each event to be sent to a fan-out of multiple devices that can act upon the received information. What are examples of the notification server's receivers? (Choose all that apply.)

    A. A smartphone application
    B. Email
    C. APIs
    D. Service queues
    E. Text message
    F. All of these

13. Samantha has been monitoring her cloud web server dashboard, and she notices that the CPU utilization on her company's database servers has been consistently at more than 80 percent utilization. She checked her baselines and reported that 57 percent utilization is normal. What is she noticing?

    A. Deviation
    B. Variance
    C. Triggers
    D. Baseline imbalance

14. Mindy has a SQL database back end that runs on a multi-CPU instance that has reached 100 percent utilization. The database supports a single server. What options does she have to support the requirements of this database?

    A. Horizontal scaling
    B. Vertical scaling
    C. Pooling
    D. Bursting

15. What is the ability to dynamically add resources such as storage, CPUs, memory, and even servers?

    A. Bursting
    B. Pooling
    C. Elasticity
    D. Orchestration

16. Ethel is the network architect for a hybrid cloud operation and has interconnected her private cloud to a community cloud in another state. She is investigating using the community cloud to supplement her private cloud operations during end-of-month processing. What operation is she going to perform?

    A. Elasticity
    B. Bursting
    C. Vertical scaling
    D. Autoscaling

17. George and Wendy are working together as cloud engineers to combine two like systems into one. What type of activity would necessitate this? (Choose two.)
    - A. Merger
    - B. Acquisition
    - C. Divestiture
    - D. Bursting
    - E. SARBOX
    - F. HIPAA
18. Allison is preparing to modify a network access control list and add three firewall rules to her private cloud HR systems. She is planning on submitting a detailed plan to accomplish these tasks. What process is Allison following?
    - A. Cloud automation
    - B. Change advisory
    - C. Change management
    - D. Rollout
19. What does the application life cycle include?
    - A. Deployments
    - B. Upgrades
    - C. Migrations
    - D. Retirements
    - E. None of the above
    - F. All of the above
20. Dimitry has been tasked to develop a cross-cloud provider migration plan as part of his company's business continuity plan. As he assesses the feasibility of migrating applications from one public cloud provider to another, what does he find is the service model that has the most lock-ins and is the most complex to migrate?
    - A. IaaS
    - B. PaaS
    - C. SaaS
    - D. XaaS

Chapter 8: Cloud Management Baselines, Performance, and SLAs

THE FOLLOWING COMPTIA CLOUD+ EXAM OBJECTIVES ARE COVERED IN THIS CHAPTER:

✓ **1.2 Explain the factors that contribute to capacity planning.**

- System load
- Trend analysis
  - Baselines
  - Patterns
  - Anomalies
- Performance capacity planning

✓ **1.4 Given a scenario, analyze the solution design in support of the business requirements.**

- Requirement analysis
  - Software
  - Hardware
  - Integration
  - Budgetary
  - Compliance
  - Service-level agreement (SLA)
  - User and business needs
  - Security

- Network requirements
  - Sizing
  - Subnetting
  - Routing

✓ **3.1 Given a scenario, integrate components into a cloud solution.**

- Post-deployment validation

✓ **4.1 Given a scenario, configure logging, monitoring, and alerting to maintain operational status.**

- Monitoring
  - Availability
    - SLA-defined uptime requirements

✓ **4.2 Given a scenario, maintain efficient operation of a cloud environment.**

- Dashboard and reporting
  - Tagging
  - Costs
    - Chargebacks
    - Showbacks
  - Elasticity usage
  - Connectivity
  - Latency
  - Capacity
  - Incidents
  - Health
  - Overall utilization
  - Availability

✓ **1.3 Given a scenario, optimize cloud environments.**

- Right-sizing
  - Auto-scaling
  - Horizontal scaling
  - Vertical scaling
  - Cloud bursting
- Compute
  - CPUs
  - GPUs
  - Memory
  - Containers

In this chapter, you'll learn about the importance of measuring the performance of your cloud deployments and how to go about determining what you consider to be a normal operating condition. Once a good *baseline* is determined, then you can track operations and determine whether your services are operating outside of your desired parameters and take corrective actions if necessary. It is important that you collect actual measurements from your real-world operations and not estimate or simulate the baselines. This is done by analyzing the metrics of your cloud resources, more generically called *objects*. Specifically, you can collect metrics for various properties of your cloud resources. For example, the percentage of free storage space is one metric of a managed filesystem. As another example, minutes of uptime is a metric of a VM. By measuring and collecting such metrics during times when everything is operating normally, you can analyze metric trends to develop an idea of what normal looks like. You can then reasonably assume that if the trend begins to change significantly, it could indicate a problem. Hence, measuring, collecting, and studying the right metrics can give you insight into the overall health and performance of your cloud resources.

Baselines and performance *monitoring* are also used in capacity planning to determine whether you require additional cloud capacity based on usage and consumption information collected over time. For example, as connection counts increase on a web server farm, it is important to know if you need to add CPU, memory, or network capacity. With a solid baseline and trending data, you can effectively plan to add capacity before you experience performance issues.

Although cloud service providers detail performance guarantees for their services in the respective service level agreements (SLAs), it is your responsibility as the customer to monitor your systems to make sure that the provider is meeting those expectations. Monitoring is a great way to be able to hold your provider to their service guarantees.

Measuring Your Deployment Against the Baseline

Before you can determine whether your cloud resources—be they servers, storage, databases, load balancers, or any of the other many cloud services offered—are performing as expected, you must define your expectations! Let's begin this chapter by setting up your baselines so that you will know what is considered normal operations and what is out of your expectations.

Object Tracking for Baseline Validation

It's almost inevitable that you'll encounter performance issues in the cloud from time to time. But first, a little warning about terminology. The terms *objects*, *resources*, and *metrics* are often conflated. Any time you see the word object, it's important to look at the context to figure out what it means. In the context of monitoring, an *object* usually refers to a measurable property of some resource, like the CPU utilization of a VM. Regardless of the terminology, the concepts behind monitoring are pretty universal. A monitoring station receives metrics from various resources. You can then do with them whatever you want: record them, perform statistical analysis on them, generate alerts, and so on. Figure 8.1 shows how a monitoring station collects metrics from objects in the cloud.

FIGURE 8.1 Cloud object tracking

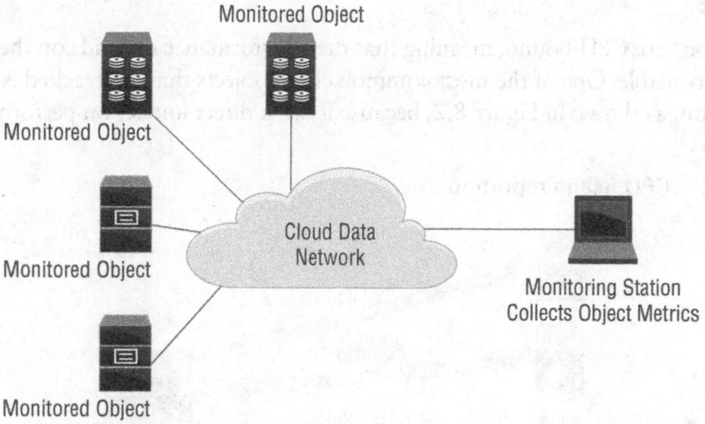

Before you can configure monitoring, you must decide what to measure and how often. If you are deploying a fleet of web servers, for example, then you may want to track average CPU utilization, memory usage, requests per second, and response times. It is important that you think this through and measure what you need, but not so much that you get flooded with data. How frequently you collect these metrics will determine how quickly you can identify and respond to a problem. Collecting a few metrics once an hour certainly won't overwhelm any monitoring system, but if a problem arises between measurements, you'll likely hear about it first from angry people rather than your monitoring system. On the other hand, taking measurements every 15 seconds increases the burden on both the measured resources and the system collecting the metrics. Not only that, you'll be picking up many short-lived but innocuous deviations from your baseline, and that creates extra work for you because you have to determine whether every intermittent spike or dip indicates a problem. Measure only what you need, and only as often as you need it. It's going to take some trial and error to figure that out.

The objective here is to get a detailed and comprehensive collection of data so that you can document what your performance requirements are. This allows you to scale your cloud fleet to the correct size so that you do not pay for capacity that is not required or have too little capacity that performance or response times suffer.

Application Versions

For proper baseline documentation, it is important that you make valid and meaningful comparisons between baselines. Part of this is making sure that you track the versions of applications, operating systems, and device drivers if needed. If there are significant performance differences between application versions, it may render your baselines invalid and require that you create a new, or updated, baseline measurement to account for the new version of your application.

CPU Usage

Many applications are CPU-bound, meaning that their performance depends on the amount of CPU resources available. One of the most common cloud objects that are tracked is the percentage of CPU utilization, as shown in Figure 8.2, because it has a direct impact on performance.

FIGURE 8.2 CPU usage reporting

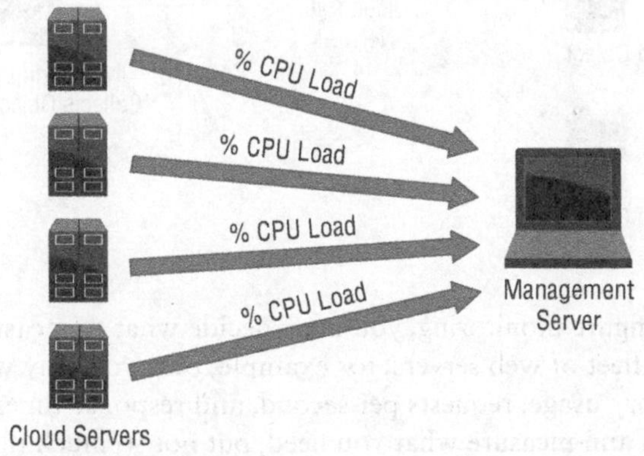

CPU usage can be tracked over time to identify trends, peak usage, and any anomalies that can provide invaluable information to you for troubleshooting and capacity planning.

Enabling the Audit Process

For regulatory or corporate compliance requirements, you may need to enable auditing of changes to your monitoring. Major cloud providers offer the ability to log and retain all such configuration changes. Although this level of detailed logging isn't unique to monitoring, monitoring is especially important to compliance because malicious hackers often try to thwart monitoring to cover their tracks. Having a record of if and when monitoring was disabled or reconfigured can be helpful in breach investigations.

Management Tool Compliance

The cloud providers will offer their own management tools and make accommodations for you to implement your own tools or those of a managed service provider. If there are compliance requirements for the various management tools, they will be outlined in the cloud provider's documentation as to what compliance requirements they meet. It is your responsibility to make sure that the chosen management tools meet what is required by applicable regulations.

Network Utilization

Network congestion can cause major performance degradation. High network utilization may cause dropped data packets, retransmissions, and poor response times. It is important that you consider network performance as a critical part of your metrics and benchmark process. Network performance measurements are common across all cloud service and deployment models and include the following metrics:

Capacity The end-to-end metric for maximum available network bandwidth. Capacity is a function of the cloud provider's connections to the Internet and other service providers. Although you'll have little or no control over it, you should track it for SLA compliance and troubleshooting purposes.

Jitter The variable latency or delay between source and destination. Excessive jitter will cause buffering and unpredictable performance for real-time traffic such as voice and video.

Latency The time for a packet to travel from source to destination. The impact of latency will vary by application, with time-sensitive applications such as voice and video being the most sensitive to high latency. Email and bulk file transfer applications are more tolerant of high latency.

Packet Loss The percentage or number of packets that are dropped in the network. Occasional packet loss is usually not a problem, but high packet loss leads to retransmissions and poor performance, particularly for TCP-based applications, which slow down the rate of transmission in response to dropped packets. Packet loss can have a noticeable effect on video and voice applications, such as dropped audio or jumpy frames, respectively. There are custom protocols in use that are designed for real-time communications that monitor network performance of the video or voice streams and adjust accordingly.

Patch Versions

As you learned in Chapter 7, "Cloud Management," keeping your cloud fleet of services patched is part of an ongoing cloud maintenance program. You can collect and record installed OS patch versions as part of your monitoring routine. You can also use scripts to collect and report application version information to keep track of what applications are installed on your VMs. Some cloud providers will offer instances or installable code that allows the VMs to collect local metrics and report them to a management server. This allows you to collect object data such as CPU and RAM utilization as well as look at the OS and installed application versions.

RAM Usage

Monitoring memory usage is one of the most critical objects to monitor and on which to collect baseline data. If memory utilization consistently approaches the amount of available memory on the server, you should address the problem before you take a performance hit. Adding RAM usually requires migrating to a larger VM instance and the associated downtime to perform the migration. The cloud providers offer a wide range of memory options to meet any compute requirement. Upgrading is straightforward and quick, but it requires a reboot.

Storage Utilization

Cloud storage systems offer a wide array of options and features from which you can select. By monitoring your storage usage, you can proactively allocate additional capacity or migrate stored data to lower life-cycle tiers to take advantage of lower-cost storage options. Keep in mind that cloud providers typically market their storage offerings as "unlimited," meaning that you'll practically never run out of space. You will, of course, have to pay for what you use, so monitoring how much "unlimited" storage you're using is a good idea.

Another important storage metric is I/O operations. I/O may be a billable metric, especially for SQL database deployments. Disk read and write objects can be defined and tracked as part of your storage system baselines.

Baseline Validation

Is your baseline actually realistic or valid? This can be a critical question since your operations will be measured against that benchmark. It had better be accurate! The best way to validate your baseline measurements is to collect them over a long period of time to smooth out isolated events or short-term variations. Also, if it is an e-commerce web server, for example, were the measurements taken during the busy holiday season or during a slow cycle? It may be helpful to compare your baselines against others that are in a similar operational state or use case. This can help to validate that your readings are what is expected and that there are no outlier measurements.

Compare and test all metrics collected, including CPU, network, memory, storage, and any custom metrics with all available data to ensure that your readings are in the range within which you would expect them to be. As time goes on, you'll achieve a stable set of operations that can be used to establish an accurate baseline.

Testing your deployment using simulations of load and application utilization can provide initial data on utilization rates to establish an initial baseline. After the testing runs, you can evaluate the data, make changes to any performance bottlenecks, and rerun the tests to validate the changes made.

After a system has been patched or upgraded, it is a best practice to run another validation to make sure that the post-upgrade performance metrics meet your baseline measurements. The best way to measure and document a baseline validation effectively during a system update or modification is to perform three benchmark validation tests:

- Pre-patch/pre-upgrade to get a snapshot of current baseline data
- Post-patch/post-upgrade to get performance data of the systems after modifications
- A comparison operation that measures the deltas between the pre- and post-reports

Applying Changes to the Cloud to Meet Baseline Requirements

In this section, you'll learn about meeting baselines. As part of your ongoing cloud maintenance plans, you'll be tracking your operations against your baselines and making adjustments as necessary. Some changes may be minor, whereas others will be disruptive and incur system downtime in some cases.

Performance Trending

Once you discover your baselines, you can continue to collect performance metrics and compare that data against your baseline, as shown in Figure 8.3. This comparison will give insight into trends such as incoming connections, CPU usage, and any other objects that you are tracking. You'll be interested to see the increase and decrease of usage during hourly, weekly, or monthly time windows.

FIGURE 8.3 Collecting trending data

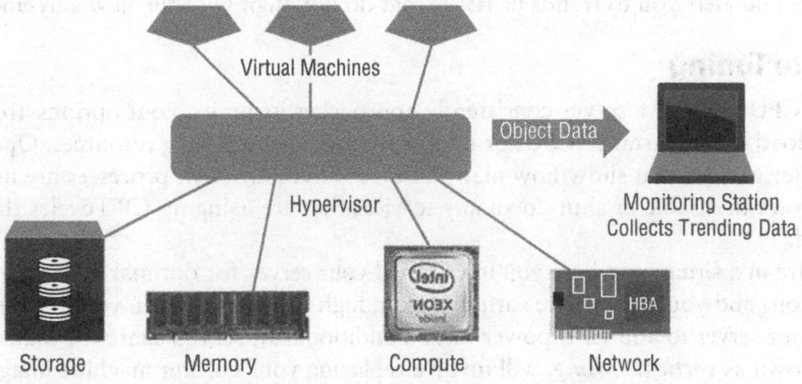

Trending data is crucial for planning resources to meet future demands. Trend reports let you see which services may need to be replaced or scaled. This allows you to manage your operations proactively and correctly scale services before they become a performance bottleneck.

Service Level Agreement Attainment

As discussed in Chapter 2, "Cloud Deployments," the SLA defines key performance indicators, which are the metrics selected to determine fulfillment of cloud provider performance guarantees. Objects to be tracked should align with the SLA metrics. By collecting actual data, you can compare it to the offered service levels outlined in the SLA and ensure that the guaranteed metrics are being met.

It is up to the cloud customer to track the SLA metrics to ensure that the guarantees are being met by the service provider. Effective monitoring allows you to accomplish this. However, raw data can be hard to interpret. Cloud management applications can process the collected data and present it in graphs and tables that present the collected statistics in an easy-to-interpret format. The management applications can also export the data in Excel format and PDF reports.

As your business objectives change over time, it may become necessary to renegotiate the SLA metrics that meet your new requirements. As part of your ongoing management processes, it is important to review the SLA on a regular schedule to make sure that the SLA meets your operational requirements. If the SLA of your current service doesn't meet your needs, you may have to upgrade to a different class or even a different service. In extreme cases, you might even have to rearchitect your cloud environment to achieve the levels of reliability that you require.

Review your baselines on a regular schedule and compare them to your SLA. Are they in alignment, and do they meet your current requirements? Are critical metrics missing? Based on this information, you can discuss your new SLA requirements with the cloud service provider and add, remove, or adjust as needed for your current needs. Once the new SLA has been agreed to and has taken effect, you can adjust your monitoring systems to measure compliance and alert you to trends or issues that do not align with the new agreement.

Compute Tuning

When the CPU usage of a server consistently approaches its limits, your options are either to lower the load on the instance CPUs or to add additional computing resources. Operating systems offer utilities that show how many CPU resources different processes are using. If possible, you can disable or shut down any services that are using up CPU cycles that are not needed.

If you are in a situation where you have tuned your server for optimal CPU resource consumptions and you are still are suffering from high CPU usage, then you may have to upgrade your server to add CPU power or add additional servers to share the load. The former, known as *vertical scaling*, will involve replacing your current machine image with that of a larger offering that has additional CPU capacity, such as higher clock speeds or more cores. Performing vertical scaling will involve some downtime to make the conversion. The latter option, *horizontal scaling*, involves adding extra compute capacity and doesn't require downtime.

Network Changes

When it comes to networking resources, you need to understand what you can control and what the cloud service provider controls. Many of the networking parameters are global to the cloud and out of your control. However, it is important to understand that making sure that the network performs inside your baseline and SLA is your responsibility.

Cloud companies do offer solutions for network-intensive requirements, such as high-performance computing. In high-performance computing applications, you place servers in the same subnet and availability zone to minimize network latency. You can use high-bandwidth network adapters that offer up to 100 Gbps of throughput. Cluster placement groups allow you to locate servers close together—in some cases even on the same host—to minimize network latency.

Storage Tuning

Baselines can be used to ensure that the storage systems you use in the cloud meet your performance requirements. You can monitor block storage systems for I/O utilization. Should there be excessive utilization, disk read/write performance will suffer and the application's performance will degrade. One solution may be to increase the bandwidth of the VM's storage adapter. Note that the adapters available will likely be limited by the VM class. For instance, you probably won't be able to select the bottom-of-the-line VM class and attach to it a top-of-the-line storage adapter.

Another potential option to improve storage performance is to select a storage class with better performance. Your cloud provider may let you select a guaranteed minimum number of I/O operations per second (IOPS). Keep in mind that the number of IOPS you can allocate is usually proportional to disk size. In other words, if you want better performance, you might have to pay for more storage capacity.

A related issue is database read/write replicas. If a database is highly utilized, a single database replica may be bandwidth-starved and become a performance bottleneck. This can be resolved by creating multiple read replicas on different storage volumes and balancing the server access across these replicas to distribute the load on the storage systems.

Service/Application Changes

Changing or upgrading services and applications may be required to add new capabilities and features or to stay compliant with regulations. If you are implementing an SaaS solution, then the cloud provider will be responsible for any changes made to the application. They will most often notify you that a change is being made in the form of an update announcing new features or a maintenance upgrade that will be implemented. Cloud providers are constantly upgrading applications such as database offerings and collaboration services, for example, and this is a benefit to you because you can take advantage of the new features and capabilities offered.

IaaS services, such as load balancers, firewalls, compute platforms, and block storage, also undergo frequent upgrades to keep pace with the competition and to add features. It's up to you to take advantage of these upgrades and changes, and cloud providers usually don't force them on you. For example, if you've been using magnetically backed block storage for several years, your provider is not likely to tear it away from you any time soon. However, as I said before, they may increase the price of outdated services to nudge you to newer offerings.

Changing Operations to Meet Expected Performance/Capacity Requirements

Now that you have a good overview of vertical and horizontal scaling, you'll dive deeper into the details of when and how to dynamically scale to meet changing requirements. It's worth repeating that you only need to be concerned with scaling with your IaaS and PaaS resources. The cloud provider is responsible for the performance of SaaS applications, and that includes scaling.

Vertical Scaling

Some applications, such as many types of databases, are not designed to scale horizontally. You'll need to upgrade to a larger machine image to increase resources for the application, as shown in Figure 8.4. The solution here is to configure monitoring metrics for critical server resources such as memory, storage, network and storage I/O, and CPU. As you learned, these metrics can be collected and analyzed by monitoring applications and triggers configured to scale the virtual machine to a large instance type to handle the presented workloads.

FIGURE 8.4 Vertical scaling

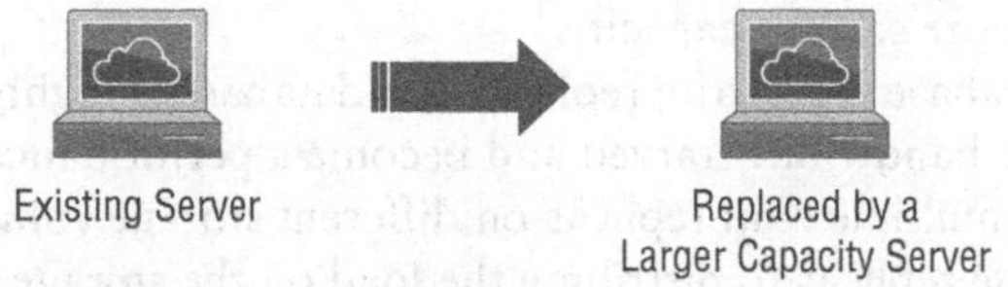

There are two ways to perform vertical scaling. One is to upgrade the machine in place, which involves shutting it down, upgrading to a more powerful VM class, and then restarting it. This process isn't destructive, and there's no need to migrate resources from one VM to another.

The second, and riskier way to scale vertically, is to create a new VM that has the horsepower you need. You then migrate resources from the original VM to the new VM. This will almost always include storage volumes and network adapters. Other operations involved in this method of vertical scaling may include reconfiguring applications and assigning the correct network ACLs and security groups to the new server. You're effectively replacing servers, so there will be downtime, and it might be extensive. When the new server replaces the older image, the IP address will move to the new machine so that any DNS records of application settings do not have to be modified.

Generally, you do not want to perform vertical scaling operations on a regular basis. The operations should be reserved for when it is absolutely required, and you plan on staying on that instance for a long period of time. This is because of the disruptive nature of the upgrade.

Horizontal Scaling

Horizontal scaling is the process of adding compute capacity by adding new servers to complement and share the load with existing ones. Horizontal scaling works well for distributed applications that can benefit from parallel processing, such as web servers, as shown in Figure 8.5. You keep your existing servers and add more to increase capacity.

FIGURE 8.5 Horizontal scaling

A common approach to scaling horizontally is to add or remove servers automatically, either in response to key metrics or based on expected load. Cloud providers offer this functionality as part of their orchestration management interface, and nearly universally all call it autoscaling. For example, you can monitor a fleet of web servers for CPU utilization, and if they all exceed 80 percent over a five-minute window, the autoscaling service will automatically launch more servers from a predefined image. You define the number of VMs to add as well as the class. The autoscaling service can also add the new machines to a load balancer group. You can set up alerting to be notified of the event for awareness. The autoscaling service can also be configured to terminate unneeded VMs and remove them from load balancer groups. Autoscaling services can also add and remove capacity on a schedule, which is useful when you have predictable times of peak load.

You can set limits on how many servers the autoscaling service can add or remove. For instance, you may always want to have at least three servers regardless of load. The autoscaling service will work to ensure that the number of running servers never falls below this minimum. Naturally, this requires the service to monitor the health of the VMs. If a server should fail for whatever reason, the autoscaling service will automatically replace it with another.

Cloud Accounting, Chargeback, and Reporting

Cloud management includes accounting mechanisms for measuring consumption, billing, and generating management reports. In this section, you'll learn about these nontechnical but important aspects of cloud operational management.

Company Policy Reporting

Companies will publish and manage IT policies. These policies cover a wide range of subjects, including, but not limited to, how cloud services are consumed and accounted for. To measure compliance effectively, you'll need to collect the required data and be able to process the information into effective reports.

Cloud providers are aware of policy reporting and offer services to assist you in collecting and presenting reports. These services are cloud-based and can be remarkably customizable. They are presented in a graphical format in a web browser dashboard. Also, the reports can be exported to Excel or PDF format, as shown in Figure 8.6.

FIGURE 8.6 Cloud reporting

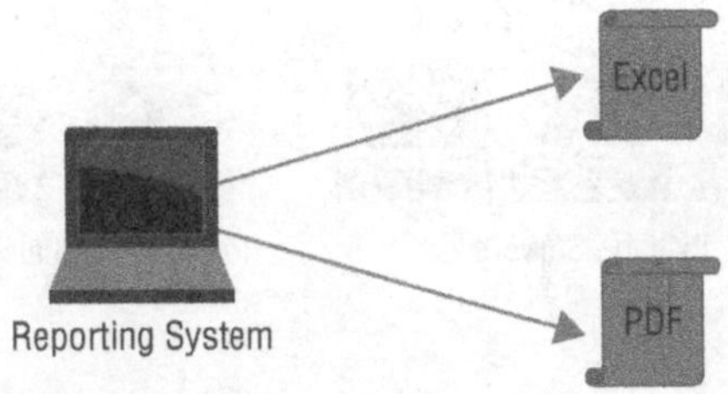

Reporting Based on SLAs

As you have learned throughout this chapter, one of the key reasons for collecting baselines is to measure them against your SLA in order to ensure compliance. Management services allow you to compare these two metrics and generate reports that can be used to analyze trends, identify problems, and store data for regulatory or corporate compliance purposes. These reports can be exported, as discussed earlier, in many different formats, including Excel and PDF documents.

Using the Cloud Dashboard

Cloud dashboards are incredibly useful and informative. It is common to display dashboards in operations centers or overhead in office environments to give an easy-to-read overview of operations. Dashboards are usually graphical and color-coded for quick notification of potential issues.

Dashboards are offered by the cloud providers, your internal monitoring and management applications, and any outside monitoring services with whom you have contracted. They allow you to define what you want to display and in what format. Dashboards are completely customizable and easy to configure. Once the dashboard has been defined, users with access rights can easily access them with a standard web browser.

Tags

Cloud providers offer the ability to assign custom tags to your cloud resources. A *tag* consists of a name and an optional value. For example, you can use tags to differentiate production and development servers by assigning each server an "Environment" tag with the corresponding "Production" or "Development" value. You can then use those tags to filter what you see in the dashboard.

Tags are useful for keeping track of resources that may not fit cleanly into only one category. Organizations typically tag resources according to multiple categories, such as automation, business, security, or technical. Some examples include tagging resources that are part of a particular automated process and tagging resources that belong to a particular business unit.

Costs

One of the most important metrics that you'll want to track is costs. Cloud providers offer the ability to see a breakdown of your costs by service, so you know exactly where your money is going. You can also use tags to help with cost accounting. For example, if you're tagging your development servers, you can filter your billing dashboard by that tag to see just what those servers are costing you.

Elasticity Usage

Elasticity is one of the great benefits that cloud computing offers. But with the possibility of elastic cloud resources comes elastic costs! It's therefore important to monitor your resource consumption and costs. Management applications can generate usage reports detailing consumption of elastic resources, such as object storage, autoscaling groups, and network data usage. As with the other reporting types, you can generate the reports in formats that meet your needs.

Connectivity

Corporate management and various departments in your company will always be interested in how their operations are being accessed and who is connecting to their cloud presence.

Reports and graphical presentations can be created to show connections over time, location, new or returning visitors, what was performed (did they buy anything on your e-commerce site?), and how long they were visiting. This is valuable data for sales, marketing, and accounting.

Latency

Poor performance can have an extremely negative effect on cloud operations. If an e-commerce site has high latency, many potential customers may give up and leave, causing lost revenue. Companies that rely on cloud-based services such as email, databases, or any of the other many benefits of cloud computing will suffer productivity declines as they sit and stare at a screen that is not responding.

Latency can come from many different sources, from a poorly written application to an operating system bug to a poor wireless connection on a client's laptop. Regardless of the cause, the result is frustrated employees and customers. Metrics, benchmarks, SLAs, and proactive maintenance all come together to keep latency low and performance high. Key latency metrics to monitor include storage, network, and application latency. Reports can show latency globally and drill down to individual services such as a web server's response and database read-write latency.

Capacity and Utilization

Capacity and utilization reporting can include a wide range of metrics including storage, CPU, RAM, network, and so on. These reports are helpful in managing usage trends and change requirements. Accounting will be interested to see that the capacity purchased is being used effectively. As with the other measurements, capacity reports are customizable and offered in a variety of formats.

Incident and Health Reports

Tracking support services and impairments will give you insight into the overall reliability of operations, and the collected data can be compared to your SLA to ensure compliance. Incidents can be defined by your company or the cloud provider as required. Incidents and health reports include trouble tickets opened, support engagements, and any event that causes degradation of your services.

Uptime and Downtime Reporting

A critical metric of any SLA is uptime. Both the cloud provider and your operations center should track uptime and identify the root cause of any outages. These reports can be analyzed to ensure that SLA metrics are being met and to see if you need to change your architecture to improve reliability.

Summary

This chapter focused on managing your cloud operations by establishing effective baselines, measuring performance, and understanding the importance of SLAs. Baselines establish the metrics that indicate normal operations. By measuring critical components and utilization, datasets can be created and measured over time to determine how your cloud components are being used. By comparing ongoing metrics with a well-established baseline, you can identify problems, determine whether resources need to be added or removed, determine whether SLAs are being honored, and understand usage trends.

Baselines are a collection of metrics that are gathered from cloud resources. Metrics include things like CPU usage, storage utilization, network throughput, and almost anything that can be quantified. Because baselines are developed over a relatively short period, they constantly need to be tracked as part of your ongoing operations. Baseline data allows you to analyze how your operations are performing, plan for growth, and generate reports for regularity or corporate compliance requirements.

You learned about how to add and remove capacity using vertical and horizontal scaling. You also learned how autoscaling can automate horizontal scaling, allowing you to achieve good performance while keeping costs in check.

You learned about collecting operational data to measure SLA compliance. SLAs may need to be adjusted as your business needs evolve, and this typically involves upgrading to a different service or class of service with a better SLA. Baselines may need to be modified to track new metrics included in the SLA.

Reports are used to show utilization, capacity, billing, SLA attainment, latency, incidents, and availability. Reporting is flexible with the management applications offered by cloud service providers and monitoring companies. They are highly customizable and can be tailored for your internal corporate audiences and for regulatory or compliance needs.

Dashboards are visual reporting of cloud objects and services. A dashboard can be created to display graphs and charts of what you deem to be important. Dashboards are often displayed in network operations centers and user browsers to display real-time cloud statistics.

Exam Essentials

Know what baselines are and how they are created. For the exam, you may be given long scenario questions that pertain to measuring a system to determine its normal operational state or the process of monitoring objects, such as CPU utilization, and you must be able to identify that the question concerns baselines.

Understand service level agreements and their purpose. SLAs are service provider documents that outline detailed performance metrics that the provider guarantees to meet for their customers. Items such as downtime, latency, compliance, and division of responsibilities are all included. The exam may detail what is included, and you'll be required to identify that it is the SLA that is being referred to in the question.

Know what objects and metrics are. Objects are anything that can be measured and on which data can be collected. Metrics are the actual data. You may be given a long scenario question that, for example, asks about a performance issue of a server and how data can be collected and analyzed to determine what the problem is.

Differentiate between reporting options. For the exam, know that there are many different types of reporting options available for management, marketing, accounting, and operations. Know that these may include policies, SLA attainment, elasticity, connectivity, latency, capacity and utilization, cost accounting, incidents, and availability. You may be asked to identify which reporting is being discussed in an exam question.

Be able to identify use cases for vertical and horizontal scaling. Given a scenario, you may be asked to identify a performance issue and determine what steps to take to remediate the problem. Vertical scaling is expanding the capacity of a server, whereas horizontal scaling is adding additional servers to your fleet. Read each question carefully to understand fully what the performance issue is and the application requirements to be able to identify if vertical or horizontal scaling is the correct solution.

Written Lab

Fill in the blanks for the questions provided in the written lab. You can find the answers to the written labs in Appendix B.

1. The ________________ measurements are used to detail resource usage under normal operations.
2. A(n) ________________ is data collected from an object.
3. Cloud components that data can be gathered from are referred to as ________________.
4. ________________ scaling is adding capacity by deploying additional servers.
5. Reducing swap file usage can be accomplished by adding extra ________________.
6. Network delays and slowdowns are an indication of high network ________________.
7. The ability of cloud resources to scale up and down is referred to as ________________.
8. The service provider outlines their performance guarantees in a(n) ________________ ________________.
9. ________________ is the process of replacing a single machine image with a larger, more powerful image.
10. For regulatory or corporate compliance requirements, you may be required to implement an ongoing ________________ process and retain the data for record retention requirements.

Review Questions

The following questions are designed to test your understanding of this chapter's material. For more information on how to obtain additional questions, please see this book's Introduction. You can find the answers in Appendix A.

1. When monitoring performance metrics on one of your servers, you notice that the server is utilizing 100 percent of the network bandwidth available to it. What modification could you make to the server that will most likely address the problem?
   - **A.** Add memory to the system.
   - **B.** Install a second network adapter.
   - **C.** Update the network adapter's firmware.
   - **D.** Install a second processor.
2. Which of the following is not a statistic that you would typically find in a server performance baseline?
   - **A.** CPU utilization
   - **B.** Disk transfer rate
   - **C.** Network transmissions speed
   - **D.** OS update history
   - **E.** Memory utilization
3. What type of scaling involves replacing an existing server with another that has more capabilities?
   - **A.** Horizontal
   - **B.** Round-robin
   - **C.** Elasticity
   - **D.** Autoscale
   - **E.** Vertical
4. Incident reports include which of the following? (Choose three.)
   - **A.** Trouble tickets
   - **B.** SLAs
   - **C.** Scaling
   - **D.** Support engagements
   - **E.** Outages
5. How can relational database read performance be improved? (Choose all that apply.)
   - **A.** Adding a read replica
   - **B.** Scaling vertically
   - **C.** Auto-sizing
   - **D.** Scoping horizontally

6. Cloud provider SLAs outline which of the following? (Choose two.)
   A. Device configuration
   B. DNS configurations
   C. Uptime
   D. Network performance
   E. Autocache
7. Reports are often provided to which interested parties? (Choose four.)
   A. Marketing
   B. Management
   C. Cloud provider operations
   D. Accounting
   E. Internal operation centers
   F. Customers
8. To collect metrics, you set up your management application to measure what?
   A. Database
   B. Server
   C. Hypervisor
   D. Objects
9. Where are reports generated?
   A. Hypervisor
   B. Databases
   C. Logging servers
   D. Cloud management and monitoring application
10. What is a visual representation of your current cloud operations?
    A. Operational matrix
    B. Management console
    C. Dashboard
    D. Health check
11. Upgrading to a newer operating system may require that you update what?
    A. SLA
    B. DNS
    C. Baseline
    D. VPC

12. Capacity and utilization reporting often contains data on which of the following objects? (Choose three.)
    - **A.** CPU
    - **B.** OS version
    - **C.** Volume tier
    - **D.** RAM
    - **E.** Network
13. Autoscaling can be configured to which of the following? (Choose four.)
    - **A.** Add capacity.
    - **B.** Configure time-of-day capacity.
    - **C.** Generate metric reports.
    - **D.** Remove capacity.
    - **E.** Maintain a minimum number of servers.
    - **F.** Track SLA objects.
    - **G.** Perform patch management.
14. Cloud-based reports can be generated in which formats? (Choose two.)
    - **A.** SQL
    - **B.** PDF
    - **C.** Python
    - **D.** JSON
    - **E.** Excel
15. What type of scaling involves adding servers to a pool?
    - **A.** Horizontal
    - **B.** Round-robin
    - **C.** Elasticity
    - **D.** Autoscale
    - **E.** Vertical
16. Carl has noticed a slowdown in the response times of his SQL database and has been tasked with investigating the root cause of the delays. He has decided to configure his monitoring application to gather additional data on what may be the cause of the delays. What are some of the objects on which you would recommend that he collect data? (Choose three.)
    - **A.** Read replica I/O
    - **B.** Load balancer latency
    - **C.** CPU
    - **D.** Network packet drops
    - **E.** Machine image
    - **F.** SLA

17. Object tracking can be helpful in identifying which of the following? (Choose three.)
   A. Resiliency
   B. Trends
   C. Metrics
   D. ACLs
   E. Peak usage
   F. Anomalies

18. Rebecca is writing a change management plan to increase the processing abilities of one of her middleware servers. What components can she upgrade to increase server performance? (Choose three.)
   A. CPU
   B. SLA
   C. RAM
   D. Network I/O
   E. ACL
   F. DNS

19. Object tracking should be aligned with which of the following?
   A. VPC
   B. SLA
   C. RDP
   D. JSON

20. Servers in high-performance computing clusters share which of the following? (Choose two.)
   A. Availability zone
   B. Group cache
   C. Identity group
   D. Hypervisor

Chapter 9

Troubleshooting

THE FOLLOWING COMPTIA CLOUD+ EXAM OBJECTIVES ARE COVERED IN THIS CHAPTER:

✓ **1.2 Explain the factors that contribute to capacity planning.**

- Requirements
  - Hardware
  - Software
- Standard templates
- Licensing
  - Per-user
  - Socket-based
  - Volume-based
  - Core-based
  - Subscription
- User density

✓ **2.6 Explain the importance of incident response procedures.**

- Preparation
  - Documentation
  - Call trees
  - Training
  - Tabletops
  - Documented incident types/categories
  - Roles and responsibilities
- Incident response procedures
  - Identification
    - Scope

  - Investigation
  - Containment, eradication, and recovery
    - Isolation
    - Evidence acquisition
    - Chain of custody
  - Post-incident and lessons learned
    - Root cause analysis

✓ **5.3 Given a scenario, troubleshoot deployment issues.**

- Connectivity issues
  - Cloud service provider (CSP) or Internet service provider (ISP) outages
- Performance degradation
  - Latency
- Configurations
  - Scripts
- Applications in containers
- Misconfigured templates
- Missing or incorrect tags
- Insufficient capacity
  - Scaling configurations
  - Compute
  - Storage
  - Bandwidth issues
  - Oversubscription
- Licensing issues
- Vendor-related issues
  - Migrations of vendors or platforms
  - Integration of vendors or platforms
  - API request limits
  - Cost or billing issues

✓ **5.5 Given a scenario, troubleshoot common performance issues.**

- Resource utilization
  - CPU
  - GPU
  - Memory
  - Storage
    - I/O
    - Capacity
  - Network bandwidth
  - Network latency
  - Replication
  - Scaling
- Application
  - Memory management
  - Service overload
- Incorrectly configured or failed load balancing

✓ **5.6 Given a scenario, troubleshoot automation or orchestration issues.**

- Account mismatches
- Change management failures
- Server name changes
- IP address changes
- Location changes
- Version/feature mismatch
- Automation tool incompatibility
  - Deprecated features
  - API version incompatibility
- Job validation issue
- Patching failure

Cloud computing can be complex! It is not uncommon to see a public cloud provider offering more than 100 different services. The combinations of all of these offerings are practically limitless. With this flexibility and sophistication comes the reality that there are a lot of things that can, and do, go wrong.

When your cloud resources fail or don't operate as they should, your ability to troubleshoot and resolve issues will be called upon. The process of troubleshooting is part art and part science. By understanding the details of your operations, referring to the proper documentation, and knowing how to use the tools and applications at your disposal, you can effectively troubleshoot and resolve any issues that you will encounter.

The objectives in this chapter cover common issues that you will be most likely to encounter as a Cloud+ professional. For this exam, you will be expected to identify them in scenario-based exam questions. This chapter builds on the knowledge that you have accumulated throughout this book, so knowledge of the many cloud services is expected before learning how to troubleshoot.

Incident Management

An *incident* is any event that threatens to interrupt your normal operations. In other words, an incident is anything an organization might find disruptive. Incident management boils down to a few steps: identify and categorize the incident, log it, prioritize it, respond to it, and finally, validate that the incident has been resolved. We'll begin with an overview of the incident management process and then cover some of the preparation that it takes to implement it.

Incident Types

Although cloud issues can appear to be specific to one service, they can span many different components and services in the cloud. To create some structure to troubleshooting, we have grouped some of the more common issues in this section. These broad categories act as pointers, or hints, to where a problem may reside. Also, when troubleshooting, eliminating these categories as the issue can help lead you to the source of the problem.

Automation

What could possibly go wrong with a fully automated system where just the click of an icon unleashes a host of cloud automation scripts? Well, many things can go wrong! Not only that, but automation often hides the components involved as well as their individual purposes, making troubleshooting more complex than it would be for a manual configuration where you're personally familiar with all the moving parts.

The ability to troubleshoot automation-related problems depends on whether you or another party—such as the cloud provider—control the process. If the automated systems are fully managed by the provider, then it is beyond your reach to troubleshoot the actual issue. However, when using these services, it is critical that you validate that the end result is what you'd expect. Look at your original deployment plan and what you configured in the deployment and compare that to your cloud resources. If there is a discrepancy, go back and review the relevant logs. It could very well be that the automation software did not work as expected, perhaps due to a human error, a bug, or an outage. Log files can be collected on all API calls to a device or service. These can offer valuable information on the success or failure of the scripts used. A well-written script can also validate the changes and roll back if there was a script failure. Monitoring dashboards can also be configured to monitor the results of the automated systems in a graphical manner. Since it is most likely that you do not have access to the underlying automation code, your only real option here is to open a trouble ticket with the cloud provider for investigation. Also, the frequently asked questions (FAQ) or support discussion forums may have additional information on the issue that you are troubleshooting.

If it was your organization that developed the automation applications, then you will have much greater flexibility in troubleshooting. Are there log files that were generated? Did the script fail before completion? Did an API call fail? By investigating the software and stepping through its execution, you or your development team should be able to identify the issue internally to your organization.

Cloud Interoperability

Interoperability between clouds, whether they be public, private, hybrid, or community, can expose a wide variety of issues that can trigger many hours of troubleshooting. Cloud interoperability issues should be well investigated by the architect teams prior to deployment. Cloud provider documentation and testing often provide best practices and validated configurations. There are many vendor papers published with best practices for interoperability. The support forums can be invaluable, as you may find discussions from other groups that are experiencing the same problems as you are and the results of others' troubleshooting. Also, the cloud companies often monitor or moderate these forums and can offer solutions to the issue you are experiencing. A good search engine and service provider documentation will go a long way toward resolving cloud interoperability issues. Search for validated or reference designs that detail tested configurations and compare them to your deployment.

As much as possible, you should investigate where the source of the issue is located. This can be done by investigating log files and monitoring systems. Effective dashboards will also be a huge help here. Once you have a good idea of where the problem is located, you can localize your investigation to that cloud provider. For example, if you want to move a virtual machine image from one cloud provider to another, all restrictions and caveats need to be identified to determine whether there are any interoperability issues that you may run into. To troubleshoot issues like this, investigate the possibility of changing the format of the image at the source when you create it to match the destination or to see whether there are image conversions or import services offered by the destination provider.

Interconnections

Your connections to the cloud can test your networking troubleshooting skills. Most cloud providers offer VPN connections from your offices or data centers to the cloud. These connections may drop and not reestablish or experience errors that cause retransmissions that degrade response times. The VPN console from the cloud company and the VPN system at your location can be investigated for status and log information that often points to the problem.

If the interconnection problems reside inside the cloud provider's infrastructure, such as connections between availability zones or regions, then you must rely on the cloud provider to resolve the issue. Cloud providers commonly post a health monitoring dashboard that offers a visual representation of any current problems they are experiencing.

Licensing

Licensing issues often manifest themselves as a sudden failure after everything has been working fine all year. After a quick investigation, you see in the log files that the application's license has expired!

The service model will determine how to start troubleshooting a licensing issue. As you learned, the IaaS and PaaS models allow you to install and run your own applications. Since you own the application, you are responsible for the licensing that allows you to use it.

With SaaS, the cloud provider is responsible for the application, and you pay for its use. As such, the SaaS provider is responsible for the software license, so the provider will manage all licensing-related issues.

You followed best practices and document how licensing is managed between your company and your application vendor, right? This will be extremely handy when troubleshooting licensing-related outages. There can be a remarkable level of complexity when licensing application software. The vendors offer a bewildering number of options, and no two companies are alike. Software licenses for cloud deployments may be different than the structure for the same application running in your private data center. One may base its license on the total number of users, named users, or concurrent connections. It is common to find licenses for each processor that is used or the number of cores. Additionally, licenses can also be based on actual usage measured by object monitoring.

License capacity can be measured in many ways, such as the number of users, total connections, named users, concurrent connections, or usage metrics. The license capacity responsibility is dependent on the service model. If it is an IaaS or a PaaS model, you will most likely be responsible for the licensing, and if it is an SaaS model, the cloud service provider will take care of all licensing issues. The bottom line is that you should track license consumption and keep ahead of capacity requirements.

TLS certificates, while not specifically licensing, also expire. This can be a catastrophic event because any service that relies on the certificate may fail. Keep track of all certificate expiration dates and renew them prior to expiration.

Networking

Networking issues were introduced in the "Interconnections" section. To expand on network-specific issues, you need to store your log files in a syslog server so that you can compare information across multiple network devices. Cloud dashboards or in-house management or monitoring systems collect networking object metrics and are invaluable in reporting network problems.

Troubleshooting networking issues can be from either the ground up or the top down. A ground-up approach starts with the link-level statistics. Are there errors on the link? Is the link "up" and communicating with the remote device? Check the physical and data-link layers where you can, and check routing tables to see whether there is a path to the remote network. `ping` is a common troubleshooting command that you can use to see whether the remote is reachable. Another troubleshooting command is `traceroute`, which follows a packet through the network from its source to the destination and can point to failures along the way. Check any access control lists or firewall rules that may be blocking traffic that you want to allow.

If you troubleshoot from the top down, you will start at the application and make sure that it is operational and able to communicate with the network stack. Work your way down from there until you verify that the data is reaching the network and being transmitted or whether there is a failure in the network stack.

Resource Contention and Starvation

As you learned in Chapter 8, "Cloud Management Baselines, Performance, and SLAs," a good baseline needs to be established so that you have solid data on what is normal. Once you have your baselines, you can monitor for resource contention issues, such as excessive CPU utilization, low memory, or saturated network bandwidth. A resource starvation issue will usually manifest itself as a slowdown in performance.

To monitor your resource usage, you can use a dashboard. Also, thresholds can be programmed to trigger alarms when, for example, CPU utilization exceeds 90 percent for five minutes.

Resolving contention and starvation issues usually comes down to throttling the application consuming the resource or adding capacity. If you're using autoscaling, you can often avoid resource contention issues altogether because the autoscaling service ensures that you have enough resources allocated to meet demand. However, if you can't scale horizontally, you may need to look into scaling vertically by upgrading your compute resources.

Service Outages

Companies often establish a "war room" where all the different groups that can assist in resolving the issue can congregate and collaborate. War rooms may also have video, audio, and collaboration links, with overhead displays to assist in troubleshooting. A service outage can include many different parts of your deployment, so you must be able to call in at a moment's notice the groups or individuals who are responsible. A good corporate response plan is needed in these cases.

Service outages can come from a wide variety of sources—some that are under your control and many that are not. If there is a power or carrier outage, you must rely on the provider to restore services. Storms or natural disasters can cause outages that may take time to restore. A good disaster recovery plan is essential because you may have to decide to fail over to your backup site if the outage is expected to last for an extended period of time.

Catastrophic outages in the cloud are rare, but they do occur. Public clouds are designed to be highly resilient to individual device failures. Should an availability zone fail in a cloud region, your applications can be designed to fail over automatically to the backup availability zone with a minimal loss of service.

Logging Incidents

You should have a centralized service desk where you log all incidents. Tracking all your incidents in one place makes it easier to correlate potentially related incidents, as well as to search for incidents and see trends that may be a sign of a larger issue.

Incident logs are often called *tickets*. The particulars of what you log in a ticket depend on your organization's policies, but they generally include the name and contact information of the person reporting the incident, a timestamp, and a description of the incident, including its categorization.

Prioritizing Incidents

Once you log an incident into a ticket, what do you do with it? The priority of an incident depends on the needs and wants of the organization. Some incidents, such as those that impact critical organizational functions, need to be addressed as soon as possible. Others, however, might safely wait for weeks before being addressed, or perhaps they may be ignored altogether.

Your organization must decide how it wants to prioritize incidents. A common approach is to classify incidents along two axes: impact and urgency. The *impact* or severity of an incident relates to how much damage the incident can cause if not addressed. For example, in a hospital setting, an incident that causes massive loss of patient data carries a high impact because it prevents the hospital from providing patient care and performing proper billing. These incidents have short- and long-term ripple effects, such as lost revenue and lawsuits.

The *urgency* of an incident deals with how quickly the incident must be resolved. Obviously, this is related to impact because high-impact incidents are by definition also urgent. However, the point of ranking incidents by urgency is to prevent relatively low-impact incidents from simply being logged and ignored. Sometimes a pattern of small incidents can indicate a looming larger problem.

To prioritize an incident correctly, you must understand the nature of the incident as well as its scope. This is easy to do for some incidents and difficult for others. For instance, in a company of 200 people, it's easy to quantify the scope of 50 users receiving a phishing email.

There may be more you don't know about, but you can safely say it's a potentially high-impact incident. On the other hand, if one user reports seeing a skull with crossbones flash across their screen for a split second, and nothing else seems amiss, then figuring out what sort of incident you may be dealing with will require some investigation. We'll cover the actual process of troubleshooting in the next chapter.

Preparation

The details of implementing an incident response process are well beyond the scope of the exam. Nevertheless, you should understand the components of the process and why they're important.

Documentation

It goes without saying that any procedures for dealing with incidents should be documented. Oftentimes people will develop their own undocumented workflows that they share with newcomers, and over time these procedures—which may work perfectly well—exist only in the minds of the people who perform them daily. In a small organization, this approach might work. However, if the organization sees sudden growth, perhaps due to an acquisition, then there may be an abrupt need to codify and share these procedures with others who don't have the benefit of context and thus might need a detailed lesson. Documentation is one of those things that seems useless until you need to use it!

Call Trees

When there's a high-impact incident that is likely to affect the ability of others to work, who do you call? Once again, in a small organization this may not be a concern. You just send an email out to a group of people and count on the recipients to forward the bad news along to anyone else who might need to know. But in a large organization, this approach can leave a lot of people uninformed. Perhaps a key executive checks their email only twice a day. Or perhaps the top salesperson is in a client meeting and has their phone on silent. This is where having a documented call tree can come in handy.

A *call tree*, or a phone tree, defines a hierarchy of who is responsible for informing who of high-impact incidents. The idea is that each person who receives a message of an incident is responsible for relaying the message to just a few people, each of whom relays the message to a few others, and so on. Despite the dated-sounding name, using a call tree doesn't necessarily mean calling people on the phone. It could involve sending emails, making an announcement over a public address system, broadcasting a pop-up message to everyone's computer, sending a text message, and so on.

Tabletops

A *tabletop* is a role-playing exercise wherein a group of people respond to a hypothetical incident. A tabletop exercise functions as a drill, but it also serves another equally important purpose: identifying problems with the incident response process. To illustrate, imagine that your workstation has been hijacked by ransomware. Your response could affect the entire organization, and you don't want to drop the ball. Who do you tell, and what other actions should you take? It goes without saying that you should isolate the computer to prevent the malware from spreading. But do you turn off your computer, or leave it on and just disconnect it from the network? The answer, of course, depends on your organization's procedures for incident response. More to the point, what *you* should do depends on your roles and responsibilities. It's quite common for organizations to define job duties vaguely so that it's unclear who's responsible for what. A tabletop exercise can clear up this ambiguity and give everyone valuable insight into how their roles and responsibilities on paper translate into practice.

One important discovery that may come from a tabletop exercise is how to handle incidents that may involve malware or hacking attempts. Because such incidents often call for the involvement of law enforcement to investigate, it's important to preserve evidence. Using the preceding example of your malware-infected computer, just powering off the computer may not be the best course of action because it could destroy in-memory evidence that could prove useful later. The preservation of evidence extends beyond just the affected device. Network logs and access logs may provide clues into where the malware came from and where it might be going. Preserving these logs and any other logs that might be relevant could be an important prerequisite to a successful investigation.

Documented Incident Types

Categorizing anything is tricky because most things fall into an infinite number of categories, so defining incident categories is really more of a subjective exercise. However, you may find it helpful to consider why people would want to categorize incidents in the first place. Understanding what incidents the help desk is spending most of its time on can alert management to potential issues. Suppose that they're getting a lot of calls about the phone system. Maybe users need more training on the system, or perhaps the system is just user unfriendly. Thus, using broad categories such as "Phone" and "Computer" can serve the purpose without leading the help desk into analysis paralysis or tempting them just to blindly pick a random category every time they log a ticket.

Templates

Templates are code that describes your cloud resources. Cloud providers and third-party automation systems can deploy and configure your resources from templates that you can create or customize. By using these templates, you can deploy and redeploy some or all your cloud resources with ease. This comes in especially handy if you find that starting fresh is easier than tracking down and trying to fix a problem. For example, if you have a database read replica that's not functioning properly, it may be easier just to destroy it and create a new one, rather than trying to troubleshoot the root cause.

Incidentally, it's a best practice to test and validate your templates every so often. A template may use API calls that have changed over time. You don't want to get caught with a nonfunctioning template when you need it most!

Time Synchronization

Cloud resources can be in many different time zones. It is desirable to collect logging (syslog) information in a central server for all your cloud objects. What happens if your devices all timestamp logging data in their local time zones? It's a huge mess. The *Network Time Protocol (NTP)* allows all devices to synchronize to a central clock. This ensures that all devices report the same times to allow for synchronization of logging information. It is important that you verify regularly that your cloud elements are synchronized with the NTP servers to prevent the drifting of device clocks. Cloud elements will have a command-line, API, or GUI interface that shows if there is time synchronization.

Workflow

Workflow services will often be a collaboration of many applications coordinated by a workflow application running in the cloud. *Workflow applications* track a process from start to finish and sequence the applications that are required to complete the process. There will be a management console for the cloud-based workflow applications that are offered under the SaaS model. You can track individual jobs and see where they are in the workflow process and whether there are any errors. Based on this information, you can troubleshoot or restart the workflow.

Troubleshooting Cloud Capacity Issues

In this section, you will learn about the limitations of the various cloud services, how to identify them, and what options are available to troubleshoot and resolve these types of issues. Any system, whether it be hardware or software, will have a limit to its ability to handle a workload. This is its *capacity*, which can be defined as the maximum amount that something can contain, or in the case of cloud resources, the maximum limit of any object or service that is supported.

Cloud capacity planning was covered in the previous chapter, and it is the process of monitoring your operations and adding resources prior to them becoming exhausted. If you do not plan and add resources in a proactive manner, then you will, at some point, run into resource starvation and performance issues. You will learn about the more common problems that you may find and how to troubleshoot them.

Capacity Boundaries in the Cloud

Every device or service will have a maximum threshold that, when exceeded, will fail, drop the requests, or slow down. Systems can, and do, get overloaded and often produce unpredictable results. It is a common practice for cloud providers to publish the performance statistics of their services that also include maximum supported metrics. A good baseline will show you your current capacity consumption and allow you to compare that to the maximum available. With this information, you can make informed decisions on managing your cloud operations.

You may have agreements with the cloud provider on the capacity level that you have purchased and included in your service level agreement (SLA). Should you approach the contracted capacity level, you can often purchase additional capacity and avoid any performance issues.

API Request Capacity

Application programming interface (API) requests are usually a metered and throttled resource in the cloud. You will be charged for the total number of requests over time and have a maximum available capacity. API performance is often measured in requests per second. For example, a cloud service such as a database requesting writes to a storage object may have an upper limit of 100 requests per second. When the database writes exceed 100 per second, throttling may occur, or additional charges could apply.

API requests are measured and can be tracked from baseline measurements to determine whether there is a variation. It may be as simple as adding to your contracted API capacity, or you may have to divide the requests across more than one interface.

To troubleshoot API issues, you will find it helpful to review your log files for any API-related errors or alerts. Also, monitoring applications can display actual compared to available API capacity.

Bandwidth

Network capacity starvation can lead to latency and degraded performance. Applications may time out and, for e-commerce sites, result in high customer dissatisfaction.

Network adapters are offered in a variety of speeds, ranging from a mere 1 Gbps to 100 Gbps and beyond. Network I/O is a measurable object whose metrics should be included in your baseline documentation. For applications that require high-speed and low-latency connections, it is best to locate all of your VMs in the same placement group and use high-speed adapters.

Bandwidth capacity between the cloud and the Internet can be a potential bottleneck. Public clouds will own this part of the network, including management and troubleshooting. If it is a private cloud, you may have greater control over bandwidth capacity and utilization. If so, it will be your responsibility to work with your network carriers to increase the speed of your existing connection or add additional circuits.

Cloud Batch Job Scheduling

Large cloud processing jobs can cause capacity issues in your cloud fleet. If you underestimate the amount of resources needed for a job, you may find that the job takes longer than expected, or you may need to acquire additional compute capacity on the spot. Once again, autoscaling can help you here.

Something to consider is that batch jobs may depend on relational databases, so running a job could put a strain on it and cause a chain reaction of performance issues. Make sure that your database server has enough capacity to handle jobs that involve heavy write activity. If your jobs are read-intensive, deploy enough read replicas to handle the load.

Compute Resources

When you create a VM in the cloud, you specify the speed of the CPU and the number of cores. Before migrating to the cloud, you should get a measurement of the processing power used prior to the migration. If it is a new deployment, you may have to rely on vendor documentation or what others have experienced.

Operating systems have utilities that monitor CPU utilization. This, of course, is a critical object to measure and track. With current measurements, deltas and trends can be determined from your baseline, and remediation can be performed before this becomes a serious issue.

In the event of CPU starvation, you have two options. One option is to reduce the load, either by throttling the application or by scaling horizontally (if possible) to distribute the load across more servers. The other option is to scale vertically, upgrading your server to a more powerful class. Because the latter will require some downtime, you'll have to suffer with poor performance temporarily until you can make the change.

Network Addressing

IP addressing is another area where capacity plays an important role. When you configure your cloud deployment, one of the configuration points is the size of the network subnets that are determined by the size of the classless interdomain routing (CIDR) block, which consists of an IP network and a subnet mask. For example, a common CIDR used on private networks is `192.168.0.0/16`. The smaller the subnet mask, the more IP addresses are available for use in the network. Hence, a CIDR of `10.0.0.0/24` would have fewer available addresses than `10.0.0.0/8`. Make sure that you specify a CIDR block that not only is large enough for current requirements but also allows for future growth.

Cloud providers generally require that you specify your CIDR block before deploying resources. Worse, you may not be able to change the CIDR block later on. The lesson here is to specify your subnets to have enough capacity that you will not exceed them in the future. If you ever need to change your CIDR block, it will likely mean redeploying many of your resources from scratch, or at the very least, reconfiguring all of them. Readdressing your devices is not anything you would ever care to do.

When designing and assigning your network addresses, be aware that there may be reserved addresses that you cannot use. Reserved addresses are for the default gateway, DNS servers, and NTP servers, and they usually are at the beginning of the block. For example, in the CIDR `10.0.0.0/8`, the address `10.0.0.1` would probably be reserved for the default gateway. Reserved addresses will be documented by the cloud provider.

Storage Capacity

One cloud resource that always seems to grow and grow is storage. Storage volume utilization can be tracked as a managed object, and triggers can be configured to alert operations at a predefined usage threshold. Managing storage capacity is a critical task. If a storage volume fills up, applications can fail, and data can be lost. Watch this closely! To resolve storage capacity problems, you can migrate the data to a larger volume, or if you have elastic storage volumes, increase the capacity.

Variance in Number of Users

When collecting data for your baselines and ongoing operations, the number of concurrent users is a useful metric to track. How you track this depends on the application. For a basic website, you may measure how many users are visiting your site over time and display valuable information on peaks and valleys of usage by the hour, day, and month. Site activity can, of course, be an important measurement for planning additional capacity. On the other hand, if users log into your application, then the number of concurrently logged-in users may be a better metric.

When you are troubleshooting cloud performance issues, the current number of users on the system can be an important indicator of load. When there are high user counts, you can track what parts of your deployment are most heavily used and track the load on all of the devices to see where the congestion points are. Also, tracking users and the variance from your baseline is critical to managing software license models based on user counts or usage volume. Many identity access control systems have maximum user hard limits that must be monitored and managed.

Troubleshooting Automation and Orchestration

This section covers automation and orchestration troubleshooting. You learned earlier in the chapter that oftentimes these systems are going to be out of your reach to troubleshoot and manage because they are controlled by the cloud service provider. If you are operating in a public cloud environment, your troubleshooting will be limited to that which falls under your division of shared responsibility. This includes the inputs—that is, the templates or individual configuration items to which the provider gives you access.

You can compare the input to the output of automation and orchestration systems to determine whether what you requested was what was delivered. Based on the results of your troubleshooting, you can either open a trouble ticket with the public cloud company or work internally with your development teams to troubleshoot the issue. Something to keep in mind is that if you are seeing a problem, chances are that many others are seeing it as well. Check the online support boards and discussion groups and participate in the resolution of the issue that you are troubleshooting.

Process and Workflow Issues

Many problems can be traced back to process, planning, implementation, and validation deficiencies. These issues tend to get worked out over time as you gain experience operating in a cloud environment. In the following sections, you will become familiar with some of the more common process and workflow issues.

Account Mismatch

Accounts include users and groups that are defined in the cloud management console. Once a user is defined, the user can be placed into a group of other users with the same job function, such as storage operators, or be assigned privileges directly. Should these privileges not match what is required for either the user or group of users to do their jobs, you may be called upon to troubleshoot the issue. You must determine what rights are needed. Are they valid rights for these users and groups to assume, and are they correctly defined in the identity and access console in the cloud? Since this can be a security issue, it is important that you make sure all the approvals are in place and then verify that the accounts are correctly configured for their intended roles.

Change Management Breakdowns

What happens when the server team schedules the installation of patches at the same time that the network team has scheduled downtime for critical network functions? Well, nothing happens for the server team unless the network is working. This is just one of many examples of the hidden complexities of the change management process. There are many dependencies, and they all must be investigated to make sure that one operation does not have a negative impact on other changes planned at the same time.

As you have already learned, change management requires a written plan that includes all contingencies as well as participating in change review meetings to discuss upcoming changes. During the change window, you must be prepared to react to anything that can go wrong. For example, the server team must be able to react if the network is down and cannot access the needed files. If the team is in the middle of upgrading the servers and the network goes down, there should be a contingency plan to roll back any of the changes if required. Afterward, action reports and reviews can be useful to discuss what went wrong, why, and what can be done to prevent a recurrence of the same issue.

DNS and Server Name Changes

DNS maps human-readable domain names to IP addresses. It's just like a phone directory that maps a person's easy-to-remember name to a less human-friendly phone number. So, for example, if you change a server's IP address or add a new load balancer to your deployment, it may require a change to DNS records.

Because most services are called by a domain name, you must define their DNS entries correctly. If you fail to make the correct DNS record changes, then the service will essentially become unreachable. Keep this in mind when troubleshooting connectivity issues, especially if there are timeouts or services that just never respond to connection requests.

The nslookup utility really comes in handy for troubleshooting DNS problems. It allows you to query a DNS server for specific records by entering the domain name and the DNS server replies with the IP address or an error message if there is no record. This allows you to see whether there is anything in the DNS server's database for that domain name or whether the information is inaccurate.

Version Incompatibility

With so many components being patched and upgraded, it is inevitable that there are going to be software compatibility issues. One moment everything is working fine, and then after the overnight changes, nothing seems to work. This issue can often be traced to version incompatibilities introduced by updates.

When these types of issues are reported, it is helpful to ask all the parties involved to see what was changed since the systems reporting the error were last operational. It can often be traced to a patch being applied or an application being upgraded. Did security credentials or requirements or network parameters change? Sometimes a solid review of your logging files will provide information on where and what the issue is.

IP Address Changes

Changing your IP addressing scheme requires careful planning and a thorough validation after the changes have been implemented. You just learned about the importance of keeping the DNS records up-to-date. In addition to DNS, you must verify that any access control lists that reference the old IP address be modified to reflect the new address. This is also the case for firewall rules and network routing tables. Also, the devices connected, such as servers or storage devices that have IP addresses assigned to their interfaces, will have to be reconfigured and tested. A carefully outlined change management plan will be invaluable in defining the steps required during such a project, including the testing and validation process and, if needed, how to back out.

Location Changes

Moving a deployment to another location can be completely transparent or a huge change management project. Most cloud providers have multiple availability zones in their cloud regions and can move services and servers automatically from one to the other should there be an outage. This level of resiliency is commonly automated in the SaaS model. In the IaaS and PaaS models, however, it's up to you to design for this flexibility. As always, the more money you spend, the more flexibility you can achieve. Having standby resources in another region makes it possible to switch operations from one region to another. On the other hand, if you're operating in only one region and need to move to a different one, then you can expect some downtime as you shut down services in one region and bring them up in another. These types of changes should be well planned and tested prior to implementing to make sure that all goes well.

Deployment Model Change

Possibly the most complex location change is migrating between service providers or deployment models. For example, moving from your company's internal data center to a public cloud's SaaS offering is a significant change. One of the advantages of the public cloud is the ability to turn up a test fleet of servers and then delete it when you are finished. You pay a minimal amount of money to build a test bed prior to deployment. You should take advantage of this flexibility and completely test your migration offline well in advance of making the changes. This approach allows you to plan fully and document location changes, helping to ensure a smooth transition.

Summary

This chapter covered troubleshooting and investigated many of the services and components that you may be called upon to troubleshoot.

Hundreds of services are available in the cloud, and most of them are interconnected, or interoperate, in a limitless number of combinations. To be effective in supporting and troubleshooting your cloud deployment, it is important that you have an in-depth knowledge of your systems, configuration repositories, diagrams, and extensive documentation. As you now know, this is a huge topic area—an entire bookshelf full of volumes discussing the subject could not completely cover it. What is expected is that you have an awareness of the main troubleshooting areas covered in this chapter and be able to identify the key points discussed on the exam.

Common cloud issues that may require troubleshooting include automation, interoperability, interconnections, software language support, licensing, networking, resource contention and starvation, outages, template issues, time synchronization, and workflows.

All of these issues (and more) will require that the Cloud+ professional understand what these systems are, what they do, and how to resolve issues as they arise. You were given an overview of each and learned how to troubleshoot each one. Many of the troubleshooting techniques are universal, so they can be applied to any cloud model of provider offerings. However, most cloud companies will offer their own interfaces and have different policies on what you can access and what is internal to the provider.

As your operations grow, it can be expected that what worked yesterday may not be sufficiently robust enough to work tomorrow. You learned about capacity issues and how to measure changes against your baselines. The capacity issues covered in this chapter include API request capacity, network bandwidth, batch job scheduling, compute resources, licensing, network address constraints, and making sure that your systems can handle the required number of users accessing the system.

When the baseline measurements are consistently exceeded, actions must be taken to ensure that your system has the resources needed to meet demand. How to determine where the capacity issues are using baseline comparisons and then adding resources to address the capacity shortage were outlined. There may be times when unexpected growth or unplanned expansions are going to need to be performed, and a solid understanding of these issues is necessary. This chapter discussed a basic plan on how to undertake cloud expansions.

Modern cloud systems are a marvel in their automation and orchestration capabilities. However, when automated systems fail or do not operate as expected, your job as a Cloud+ professional can get very interesting very quickly! You were given an overview of these software-based systems and what to look for in terms of performing basic troubleshooting. You will most certainly come across issues with automation tools that do not work well with the services that the automation systems are configuring. This chapter noted that automation and orchestration systems may be the responsibility of the cloud provider, and tips were given on how to proceed in these situations.

Cloud processes and workflows tend to get refined over time as you gain experience in your operations. Common topics include defining accounts to match your requirements, dealing with conflicts, and creating workflow sequences in the change management process. These are critical to understand and resolve in order to prevent a recurrence of the same issues. You learned about how to keep your DNS and server records up-to-date with changes such as IP address migrations.

Changes to your cloud fleet are a fact of life, and the change management process helps lessen any problems by undergoing a structured planning process. Some of the changes may include moving your cloud operations to a new location or having to change the network address scheme either to segment the network or to expand. These can be rather drastic changes, and proper planning, including how to validate the changes, was introduced in this chapter.

Exam Essentials

Know the key concepts of troubleshooting. Keep up-to-date documentation of your network, backups of current configurations, and current diagrams. You may be asked questions about planning for outages or basic troubleshooting preparedness and what records you should have available.

Know the basics of common problems that require troubleshooting. Although there are limitless issues that may require troubleshooting, for the exam be prepared for scenario-based questions that will ask you to select a specific service from multiple choices.

Explain capacity-related issues and how to identify and resolve them. The exam may quiz you on capacity starvation and verify that you know how to troubleshoot issues such as CPU, memory, network, licensing, API requests, or storage limitations and then how to resolve the problems once they have been identified.

Know how to identify and troubleshoot workflow issues. Workflows include account mismatches; failures in the change management process; and critical changes in IP, DNS, server names, or locations. The exam will present these topics as scenario questions, where you are expected to identify the underlying issues.

Understand automation and orchestration. You will be expected to know how to validate that the automation and orchestration systems perform as expected and how to troubleshoot any problems. You need to understand that these systems are often the responsibility of the service provider and that you will need to rely on them to perform any troubleshooting.

Written Lab

Fill in the blanks for the questions provided in the written lab. You can find the answers to the written labs in Appendix B.

1. _______________ are software representations of network systems.
2. _______________ _______________ _______________ allows all devices to synchronize to a central time service.
3. _______________ can be defined as the maximum amount that something can contain or support.
4. In the event of CPU capacity starvations, you can either _______________ _______________ or _______________.
5. Expansion planning can be unexpectedly challenged by _______________ and _______________.
6. DNS maps the _______________ _______________ to a(n) _______________ _______________.
7. After implementing a change, you should always _______________ that it is working as expected.
8. A centralized collection of device activity, known as _______________ _______________, assists in analyzing events during troubleshooting.
9. _______________ backups are valuable for quick restoration of a failed cloud service.
10. Proper network _______________ allow for a visual representation of your cloud deployment and facilitate troubleshooting.

Review Questions

The following questions are designed to test your understanding of this chapter's material. For more information on how to obtain additional questions, please see this book's introduction. You can find the answers in Appendix A.

1. Common cloud resources in your deployment that may saturate over time include which of the following? (Choose three.)
   - A. RAM
   - B. Power
   - C. CPU
   - D. Storage
   - E. Monitoring
   - F. IaaS
2. Connie has noticed an increase in the response time of the SQL database application that she runs in her IaaS deployment. When comparing current results against the baseline measurements that she recorded when the database was deployed, she verified that there has been a steady increase in the number of read requests. What should she focus her troubleshooting on?
   - A. Memory
   - B. CPU
   - C. Storage
   - D. Networking
3. What are recommended procedures to take when preparing an outage response plan? (Choose three.)
   - A. Configuration backups
   - B. SLA
   - C. Documentation
   - D. Diagrams
   - E. PaaS
4. Jeff has been monitoring resource usage increases in his web server farm. Based on trending data that he has collected, there will be regular requirements to increase CPU capacity for his web servers as usage increases. Jeff wants to use the automation capabilities of his private cloud to automatically use the orchestration software to add CPU cores as required. What can he implement to automate this?
   - A. Puppet
   - B. Chef
   - C. Docker
   - D. Autoscaling
   - E. SaaS
   - F. OpenStack
   - G. Resilient-scaling

5. Sharon posted a new software update to her company's popular smartphone application. After announcing the release, she has been monitoring her dashboard information and has noticed a large spike in activity. What cloud resource should she focus on?
   - **A.** CPU
   - **B.** Network bandwidth
   - **C.** RAM
   - **D.** API
   - **E.** Storage
6. Jim has added a new group of users to his IaaS-based NoSQL database. What license requirements does he need to investigate to ensure compliance? (Choose all that apply.)
   - **A.** Total connections
   - **B.** Named users
   - **C.** Current connections
   - **D.** Usage metrics
   - **E.** All of the above
7. Hank designed an application tier for his company's new e-commerce site. He decided on using an IP subnet that uses a /28 IPv4 subnet. He is planning for a maximum of 14 servers. You are brought in as a cloud architect to validate his design. What other devices may be on this subnet other than the servers that would also require IP address assignments? (Choose three.)
   - **A.** SLA
   - **B.** Default gateway
   - **C.** DNS
   - **D.** NTP
   - **E.** API
   - **F.** SNMP
8. Dale has been monitoring storage volume utilization and is writing a change request to add capacity. He has decided to automate the volume allocation size. What cloud feature can he take advantage of?
   - **A.** SaaS
   - **B.** API
   - **C.** Elasticity
   - **D.** OpenStack
9. Performance issues are measured by the load on a system. Which of the following should Jane be concerned about as she integrates her new marketing group into her PaaS cloud fleet?
   - **A.** APIs
   - **B.** Users
   - **C.** Cores
   - **D.** Licensing

10. Cloud capacity can be measured by comparing current usage to what?
   A. Orchestration
   B. Automation
   C. NTP
   D. Baseline
   E. APIs
11. SaaS orchestration systems are whose responsibility in the public cloud?
   A. Customer
   B. Provider
   C. Automation vendor
   D. DevOps
12. During a recent downtime window, the server team was applying patches to an application and the networking team was upgrading a router's interface to 10 Gbps. When the network was down for the upgrade, the server team complained that they could not download the needed software patches. During a post-downtime status meeting, it was determined which process should be modified to prevent this from happening in the future?
   A. Orchestration
   B. Automation
   C. Change management
   D. API calls
13. Jerry is expanding a public subnet in his company's e-commerce site. After performing the address change for all of his public-facing web servers, he tested connecting from a bastion host located offshore. He was unable to connect. What does he need to change to allow the remote site to connect to the web server?
   A. NTP
   B. STP
   C. DNS
   D. API
14. What are software representations of a cloud network?
   A. Automation
   B. Templates
   C. Orchestration
   D. APIs
15. What application tracks a process from start to finish?
   A. API
   B. NTP
   C. Workflow
   D. Orchestration

16. Capacity boundaries can cause which of the following? (Choose three.)
   A. Application failure
   B. Latency
   C. API abends
   D. Request drops
   E. Workflow loops
17. API request capacity is measured with what metric?
   A. Total lookups per second
   B. Connections per second
   C. Requests per second
   D. IOPS
18. Large batch processing jobs are common for which type of application?
   A. DNS
   B. NTP
   C. Databases
   D. Middleware
19. When configuring a machine image, what compute resources do you define? (Choose two.)
   A. Slots
   B. Cores
   C. Clock speed
   D. Threads
20. What determines the size of a group of servers in the same subnet?
   A. Default gateway
   B. DNS
   C. NTP
   D. CIDR block

Chapter 10

Troubleshooting Networking and Security Issues and Understanding Methodologies

THE FOLLOWING COMPTIA CLOUD+ EXAM OBJECTIVES ARE COVERED IN THIS CHAPTER:

✓ **5.1 Given a scenario, use the troubleshooting methodology to resolve cloud-related issues.**

- Always consider corporate policies, procedures, and impacts before implementing changes.

  1. Identify the problem
  2. Establish a theory of probable cause (question the obvious)
  3. Test the theory to determine cause
  4. Establish a plan of action to resolve the problem and implement the solution
  5. Verify full system functionality and, if applicable, implement preventive measures
  6. Document the findings, actions, and outcomes throughout the process

✓ **5.2 Given a scenario, troubleshoot security issues.**

- Privilege
  - Missing
  - Incomplete
  - Escalation
  - Keys

- Authentication
- Authorization
- Security groups
    - Network security groups
    - Directory security groups
- Keys and certificates
    - Expired
    - Revoked
    - Trust
    - Compromised
    - Misconfigured
- Misconfigured or misapplied policies
- Data security issues
    - Unencrypted data
    - Data breaches
    - Misclassification
    - Lack of encryption in protocols
    - Insecure ciphers
- Exposed endpoints
- Misconfigured or failed security appliances
    - IPS
    - IDS
    - NAC
    - WAF
- Unsupported protocols
- External/internal attacks

✓ **5.4 Given a scenario, troubleshoot connectivity issues.**

- Network security group misconfigurations
- Common networking configuration issues
- Network troubleshooting tools

In this final chapter, the focus will again be on networking, specifically the tools and techniques that you can use to identify and resolve network-related problems. In this chapter, you'll learn about some of the many tools that can be used to gather information and resolve networking problems. While networking is a topic area of its own, for the Cloud+ exam, you need to focus on the specific areas of networking that you will most likely encounter.

Security configurations and troubleshooting have become critical areas of concern for companies deploying services in the cloud. Throughout this book, I have discussed many different aspects of security. In this chapter, I will cover how to troubleshoot your security objects.

You will also learn about the processes of different troubleshooting approaches that will make you more effective as a Cloud+ professional.

Troubleshooting Cloud Networking Issues

Networking plays a critical role in the cloud, just as it does for any data center or corporate operation. When the network is not fully functional, all of the services connected to it may be degraded or fail. With networks being the lifeline of any corporation, it is critical that you be able to resolve network issues quickly and effectively.

Cloud providers will be responsible for the core network in their facilities. This includes the connections to the Internet and high-speed links that interconnect cloud zones and regions. The backbone switching and routing inside the data centers will also be managed by the cloud companies. The separation of responsibilities will be outlined in the service level agreement with associated uptime commitments.

Depending on the cloud services that you have implemented, you may be responsible for many aspects of the network, such as IP addressing, virtual private networks (VPNs), direct interconnections, static or dynamic routing, Domain Name System (DNS), and Dynamic Host Configuration Protocol (DHCP).

In the all too likely event of a network impairment or outage, you must be able to determine the origin of the problem and who has the ultimate responsibility for its resolution. In this section, you will learn about identifying issues as they arise.

Identifying the Common Networking Issues in the Cloud

A common networking issue covered on the exam is the IP addressing plan for your deployment. In addition to IP addressing, you must understand subnetting and routing.

Network latency is the time it takes for data to go from its source to its destination. Although some delay is inevitable, if the network latency becomes too great, you may experience application issues, such as long delays or timeout errors.

When a network becomes congested—that is, when the amount of data being sent exceeds the amount of available bandwidth, then some packets will be dropped. You may be able to configure quality of service (QoS) parameters to control which packets are dropped, effectively allowing for the prioritization of certain traffic types over others. This section covers QoS as required for the Cloud+ exam and as it pertains to cloud computing in general.

Network services such as DNS servers, firewalls, and proxies play an important role in a well-designed network. You will become familiar with these services and gain a basic understanding of how to troubleshoot them.

At the lower levels of the cloud network, configuration and troubleshooting of virtual local area network (VLAN), virtual extensible LANs (VXLAN), and Ethernet frame size may need to be addressed. You will be given a basic overview in this section so that you can be aware of the configurations of networks at the data-link layer.

Incorrect Subnet Issues

Application servers are commonly grouped together in the same IP subnets. By architecting the network in this manner, you ensure that the devices can send data directly to each other on the network and not have to traverse a router interface to a remote network. This decreases network latency and improves performance since all communications remain local.

By grouping servers together in the same subnets, you can craft efficient subnet-level firewall rules to restrict and permit what traffic is allowed to ingress and egress the subnet.

A 32-bit IP address contains two components. A variable portion of the leftmost bits identify the network address, and the remaining bits identify the individual hosts within the network or subnet. The addressing is flexible and can be adjusted using what is known as a *subnet mask*. The mask determines the total number of hosts in each subnet. Hosts use the subnet mask to determine whether a packet must traverse a gateway or router to reach its destination. Hence, all hosts in a subnet must be configured with the correct subnet mask or they may not be able to communicate with other devices.

Your documentation will contain your addressing scheme, show the subnets in use, and provide you with the correct subnet mask and address blocks. With this information, you can investigate the interface configurations and verify that the IP address, subnet mask, and default gateway are correct.

Incorrect IP Addressing

IP addressing is required for all devices connected to the network to be able to communicate. When deploying a new presence in the cloud, part of the engineering, design, and architecture process includes creating an IP address scheme. At implementation time, a validation test will verify that the addressing is configured correctly and is operational.

When IP addressing issues arise after a network has been deployed, troubleshooting should include asking whether there were any changes made recently. Change management logs and emails are good places to start. If any changes were made, investigate what was changed and whether that could have created the issues that you are troubleshooting.

If a network issue arises after an IP address change, you should verify that both the IP address and subnet mask are correct. Also, some addresses in the subnet will be reserved for networking services. This is especially true for the default gateway's IP address, which, by convention, is usually the lowest number in the range. The IP address range, subnet mask, and reserved IP addresses are integral parts of your documentation.

One of the more common addressing issues occurs when two devices on the same network are configured with the same address. Just think of the confusion if the same phone number were assigned to more than one person! A common symptom of duplicate IP assignments is intermittent loss of connectivity. Using the ping utility, verify that you are getting a 100 percent response rate from a host on the same subnet. If it is anything less, investigate a duplicate IP address issue. You can also look at the Address Resolution Protocol (ARP) table and see if a MAC address mapped to an IP address changes to another address. This indicates that an IP address is assigned to two or more devices.

Incorrect Default Gateways and Routing

The term *default gateway* can be misleading since a gateway is also called a *router*. But a *default gateway* is the IP address on the interface on the router on the local subnet that connects to the outside world. It gives computers on one network a path to other networks.

For example, a cloud web server that serves content to a client on the Internet will send the data to the default gateway router, which, in turn, forwards the data to the destination on the Internet.

Each device connected to the network must have knowledge of a gateway address to send data to the outside world. This is commonly called the *default gateway IP address*. Your network documentation should include this address.

When a device is sending data to the network, it first looks to see whether the destination IP address is within the subnet or outside of it. If the destination is within the subnet, the data is delivered directly to that device. However, if the reply is destined for a different subnet, the device will not have any knowledge of where it is, other than that it is not local. In this case, the packet is passed to the default gateway, or router, which, based on its routing tables, has knowledge of where to send the data.

When troubleshooting a networking scenario where you can use ping to connect to devices on the same subnet but are unable to connect to anything outside of the subnet, check the default gateway configuration on the local host and ping the default gateway's IP address. If you can ping the gateway and other hosts in the subnet, there is most likely a routing issue.

Network Infrastructure Troubleshooting

Generally, the cloud service provider is responsible for the hardware infrastructure in the cloud. For example, power, cooling, physical security, and all other facilities-related components are owned by the cloud provider. With this separation of responsibilities, all infrastructure will be managed by the cloud provider.

It is common for cloud providers to publish uptime and status reports on a browser-accessible dashboard. These dashboard services allow you to monitor the status of all facilities for alarms and will outline any current issues that the cloud provider may be experiencing.

Network Latency Troubleshooting

Network latency can be significant for time-sensitive applications such as voice and live video. For example, if voice traffic is delayed, it can be difficult for the two parties talking to communicate. When applications and storage data are transitioned to the cloud, they must be accessed remotely. This contributes to congested networks that lead to delays because packets must contend for limited network bandwidth. Network response time becomes critical, and the latency in the network when accessing the cloud is a critical factor in network performance.

Although electromagnetic energy can travel quickly, many factors can introduce network latency above and beyond simple congestion. When a wireless network is in play, latency can increase dramatically due to interference. There can also be other factors that introduce delay, such as compression. Quality-of-service policies may allow higher-priority frames to be forwarded and lower-priority frames to be buffered, which can also contribute to network latency. It's often impractical to figure out the exact path data takes through a network and what things might be introducing delay. It's therefore best to calculate the end-to-end latency as your primary measurement and not the latency of each individual device in the patch from the source to the destination. Many network management tools, as well as integrated test capabilities in the network gear, can track latency and even generate alerts if latency exceeds a predefined threshold. Figure 10.1 illustrates end-to-end latency.

FIGURE 10.1 Latency is an end-to-end network delay.

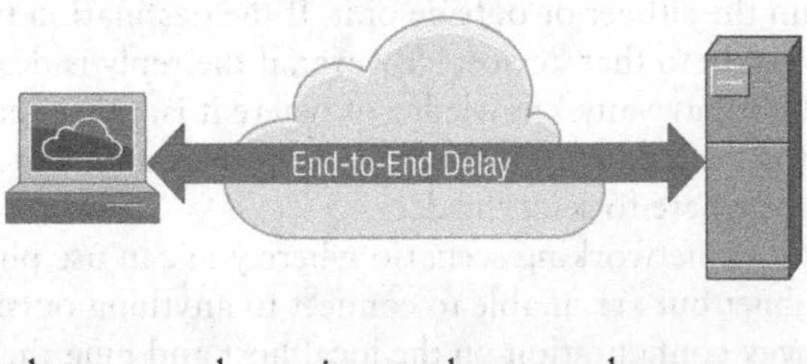

Cloud providers work to control, monitor, and manage latency to ensure that it does not affect applications or user experiences. However, outside the cloud data center on the Internet, latency can be a much larger issue and out of your area of control. With the increase in smartphones and mobile technology, latency can vary widely as you move from one cell tower to the next, for example.

Network monitoring systems and benchmarks will record standard latency and may also report current metrics. A simple ping test from the source device to the remote will report what the end-to-end delays are across the network from the source to the destination and back again, as part of its standard output.

Domain Name System

DNS servers may need regular configuration updates as hosts and devices are added to, and removed from, the network. Type A records that map a domain name to an IP address need to be changed every time a device's domain name or IP address is modified. Although many cloud providers offer DNS services, it is usually your responsibility to manage the day-to-day operations of DNS.

Troubleshooting DNS will consist of verifying that the current configuration of the DNS records matches the addressing in each server. If there is a mismatch, devices trying to reach a host in your cloud fleet by its domain name may be offered an incorrect IP address that causes the requesting device to contact the incorrect server. Use the nslookup or dig utility to query the DNS server and verify that it is returning accurate information for the record that you are troubleshooting. Also, to make sure that the DNS servers are reachable on the network, run a standard ping test. If the ping test fails, a traceroute to the server will show where along the path the traffic is stopping.

Quality of Service

Many different types of traffic are passing through your cloud data network. Not all of this traffic is created equally. Different types of applications have very different network requirements. Actions such as transferring files or sending an email message are not delay sensitive and have no issues with being buffered because of congestion as they traverse the network from source to destination. However, other types of traffic are susceptible to latency and *jitter*—variation in latency—across the network. Collaboration applications send voice and video over the same network as all other traffic. However, if voice is delayed or a videoconference is losing data and suffering long delays in the network, the quality will suffer and could ultimately cause the session to fail. The concept of quality of service addresses these issues.

Quality of service (QoS) is a general networking term for the ability of the network to provide differentiated services based on information in the Ethernet packet. For example, voice and video traffic are real time and delay sensitive. Some storage protocols suffer extremely poor performance in the face of packet loss. And although mail and file transfers are not sensitive to network delays, such delays can affect the speed of such transfers, something that might become an issue with replicating backup traffic. Using QoS, network devices can be configured to take the various application needs into consideration.

The IP header has a type-of-service field that specifies or marks the relative priority of the packet. Routers can be configured to treat packets according to these markings. They can also append or change such markings based on various criteria, such as the port numbers or IP addresses in the packet.

For the QoS markings to be effective, each device that the frame passes through must be configured to honor the QoS settings inside the frame, so the configuration can become complex. You can control QoS inside the data center but not over the Internet since the Internet backbone is beyond your administrative control. Also, if there is no network congestion, then QoS has no effect since there is ample bandwidth. However, when the links become saturated, then the QoS configurations can prioritize certain traffic flows over others.

For example, the long file transfers that take place during a backup can involve a large amount of data moving across the network, but it is not time-sensitive on the delivery. Also, when you send an email, you are probably not concerned if sending it takes 20 milliseconds versus 2 seconds. However, if you are on a voice call, a 2-second delay will be quite noticeable. Likewise, if you are meeting over a videoconference, jitter or latency in the network can cause video frames to freeze or drop. Although the popular notion of a "neutral network" that treats all traffic equally sounds nice, the reality is that it would put critical telemedicine traffic at the mercy of somebody's midnight movie streaming binge! Some traffic truly needs to be given priority during periods of inevitable congestion.

If there is sufficient network capacity, there is available bandwidth for all traffic types. However, when the network interconnections reach 100 percent traffic load, then QoS is needed to arbitrate which traffic flows will take priority over the others. In normal operations, traffic is forwarded on a first-come, first-served basis. QoS may be configured, but there is no current need to prioritize traffic until the network saturates.

You must also consider that the background control of the network, such as the routing protocols and the management applications, must command a high priority because if they are starved for bandwidth, the whole network could very well fail.

QoS can be configured on each step of the network that will define the priority of the traffic being sent across the network. There are many variations to QoS, and it can be a quite complex topic. Understand that each packet has information in its headers that you can use to make QoS decisions, and the network devices can be configured to act on this information and favor one type of traffic over another.

Maximum Transmission Units

The *maximum transmission unit (MTU)* is the maximum size in bytes of an Ethernet frame. Frames that are larger than the MTU are fragmented, or divided, into multiple frames to support the standard frame size. The standard MTU has traditionally been 1,518 bytes, and any Ethernet frame larger than the standard size is referred to as a *jumbo frame*.

It is often more efficient to use a larger Ethernet frame size than the standard Ethernet MTU inside the data center to reduce networking overhead. Jumbo frames allow for higher network performance by reducing the overhead in each Ethernet frame by using fewer but larger frames. Jumbo frames also reduce the number of times that a CPU will be interrupted to process Ethernet traffic since each jumbo frame can be up to six times as large as a standard frame.

Jumbo frames are now common in the cloud and enterprise data centers and are extensively used for storage over LAN technologies such as Internet Small Computer Systems Interface (iSCSI) and Fibre Channel over Ethernet. Modern data center switches will usually support jumbo frames up to 9,000 bytes. To support jumbo frames in the network, you will need to enable this feature on the switches, network interface cards (NICs), and any other devices in the data path.

To troubleshoot MTU issues, look at the interface statistics to see whether fragmentation is taking place. If the MTU of a frame is too large, a router interface may fragment it into smaller frames. This situation is not optimal, and you would have to verify that all devices in the source to destination path are configured for jumbo frames. The most common jumbo setting on network devices is 9,000 bytes, which is the standard frame size for storage traffic over the network.

Available Bandwidth

A network with insufficient bandwidth will experience high latency and lost packets, which may cause applications to fail or not work as expected. Many tools are available that you can use to measure network throughput. IPerf, for example, will give you a reading of the end-to-end network throughput from a source to a destination. Testing can also be as simple as downloading a large file, measuring the time that the download takes to complete, and calculating the network bandwidth. It is important to note that in a cloud data center, the core network will be architected with multiple high-speed links optimized for the traffic patterns commonly found in a data center. Also, network monitoring and management systems can alert the engineering staff if the links are saturated and additional bandwidth needs to be provisioned.

Validating Firewall and Proxy Configurations

After new firewall rules have been implemented, your change management plan will call for you to validate that the rule is operating as expected. Depending on the implementation, firewall rules may be processed in a top-down order. When there is a match, the rule is acted upon and further rule processing is stopped. Be aware that this order of operations can produce unexpected results. For instance, if you add the new rule at the bottom of the configuration that permits all Internet traffic to connect to a File Transfer Protocol (FTP) server on one of your public-facing cloud servers, check to see whether there is another rule above this preventing FTP access to your site that gets checked before your new rule. In this case, the deny rule would take precedence and the connection would be blocked. Because no more rule processing is done, your permit FTP rule will never be seen. The solution is to place the FTP permit higher in the search sequence than the deny rule. Enabling logging can provide invaluable troubleshooting information when troubleshooting a firewall, because the data provided in the logs will specify exactly what the firewall is processing and give details on the rules it referenced.

A proxy is a device that is inserted into the middle of a traffic flow and that terminates the connections in both directions and monitors the traffic between the source and the destination. Web proxies are commonly used in enterprise environments for content filtering. In the cloud and data center, reverse proxies are used to perform load balancing. When troubleshooting web proxy issues, make sure that the browser or client is not misconfigured for the proxy settings and that it has a valid IP address, subnet mask, and default gateway. Verify that the URL of the site you are trying to reach is not down and that there are no ongoing network issues that may be the root cause of the problem. Check the log files for the device performing the proxy function that may indicate if the issue is local to the server. Test from another computer on the same subnet and a different subnet that connects through the same proxy server. Verify whether the problems are consistent or intermittent. By gathering the background information of the proxy issue, you can then work to determine where the problem resides and develop a test and resolution plan.

VLAN and VXLAN Issues

Virtual LANs (VLANs) and virtual extensible LANs (VXLANs) are layer 2 segmentation standards that allow you to use shared network infrastructure to create isolated, independent virtual networks. VLANs have been a staple of office and data center networks for years. The IEEE 802.1Q standard, often referred to as Dot1Q, allows for 4,094 usable VLANs. 802.1Q works by inserting a header in the Ethernet frame that identifies the VLAN to which this frame belongs.

When hyperscale cloud computing arrived, it was clear that the standard VLAN limit of 4,094 was insufficient. Even if every customer used just one VLAN (hint: they use many), the limit would be only about 4,000 customers! To address the growing requirement for virtual networks, VXLAN was introduced.

VXLAN allows for millions of virtual networks. It encapsulates an Ethernet frame in an IP packet using User Datagram Protocol (UDP) as its transport. Another name for this is MAC-in-IP encapsulation (some call it MAC-in-UDP) because the layer 2 frame is untouched and wrapped in a normal IP/UDP packet. This allows virtual networks to span multiple availability zones and even regions. The VXLAN header is 8 bytes, or 64 bits. The VXLAN network identifier (VNI) uses 24 bits of that header and differentiates virtual networks, much like the VLAN ID distinguishes virtual LANs.

Automation, routing, and specialized monitoring systems track VLAN/VXLAN configurations and operations. It is important to know that a layer 2 VLAN will traditionally map to only one layer 3 IP subnet. When troubleshooting, make sure that these mappings are correct and that the links, or trunks that interconnect network switches have the VLANs configured on them to enable them to pass traffic on that VLAN from one switch to another.

VXLAN troubleshooting will almost always fall to the cloud provider since this is considered infrastructure. However, by analyzing log files, vendor monitoring applications, and command-line utilities, you can uncover the origin of the issue and begin troubleshooting.

Network Troubleshooting and Connectivity Tools

Cloud networks are usually not static. Rather, they change as new services, servers, and storage are added. In this section, you'll learn about some Windows and Linux tools commonly used to troubleshoot cloud networks. You can run these commands to test connectivity, resolve domain names, look at routing tables, log into remote devices, learn how the network interfaces are configured, determine the current status of these interfaces, and gather valuable troubleshooting information. Let's look at the most common and useful utilities for network troubleshooting.

ARP

The *Address Resolution Protocol (ARP)* maps an IP address to a MAC address. By using ARP, a device on the LAN can build a table of IP-to–MAC address bindings for every device in the LAN. For example, a workstation may need to communicate with a server at IP address 192.168.1.123. If it is in the same VLAN, the workstation will need to know the server's physical, or MAC, address to construct an Ethernet frame with accurate source (workstation) and destination (server) MAC addresses.

The workstation will broadcast an ARP request frame asking for the MAC address of the 192.168.1.123 server. All devices on the local LAN will receive the ARP request, but only the device that matches the 192.168.1.123 IP address will respond with its MAC address.

When each device on the segment receives the ARP packet, it will ask, "Who has IP address 192.168.1.123?" If the receiving device is configured with that address, it will reply with "That is my IP address, and my Ethernet MAC address is attached." Then communications can proceed because the device that sent the ARP packet now has all the information it needs to communicate with the remote device. Address resolution is constantly running in the background and rarely seen unless you have a packet sniffer attached to the network. To verify that the network or host you are logged into can see the remote device's IP/MAC address, check the ARP tables when troubleshooting.

The `arp` command will display information on the local ARP table, as shown in the following output from a Windows server:

```
C:\Users\todd>arp -a
Interface: 192.168.1.90 - 0xa
Internet Address      Physical Address      Type
192.168.1.1           d0-39-b3-4b-a9-83     dynamic
192.168.1.67          d8-25-22-77-cb-c6     dynamic
192.168.1.71          e4-98-d6-89-cc-b0     dynamic
192.168.1.75          f0-4f-7c-f1-92-e4     dynamic
192.168.1.77          00-20-00-72-4a-fa     dynamic
192.168.1.78          a8-86-dd-9a-9d-7a     dynamic
192.168.1.80          84-a4-66-c5-a7-02     dynamic
192.168.1.83          3c-a8-2a-a2-9c-7a     dynamic
192.168.1.89          00-10-75-44-1b-ad     dynamic
192.168.1.91          00-21-70-32-81-55     dynamic
192.168.1.96          fc-db-b3-c5-31-bc     dynamic
192.168.1.249         00-02-b9-f8-cd-c0     dynamic
192.168.1.250         00-24-dc-d1-16-00     dynamic
192.168.1.251         00-0d-65-49-87-00     dynamic
192.168.1.254         d0-39-b3-4b-a9-80     dynamic
192.168.1.255         ff-ff-ff-ff-ff-ff     static
224.0.0.5             01-00-5e-00-00-05     static
224.0.0.22            01-00-5e-00-00-16     static
224.0.0.253           01-00-5e-00-00-fd     static
```

ipconfig/ifconfig

`ipconfig` on Windows and `ifconfig` on Linux are commands used to verify and configure the local network interfaces. In the following example, this workstation is running both IPv4 and IPv6, and the addressing is provided in the command output. These commands' output can be expanded by using switches to obtain specific and detailed information. These are important troubleshooting tools to run to verify that the network interfaces are configured as expected.

```
C:\Users\todd>ipconfig
Windows IP Configuration
Ethernet adapter Local Area Connection:
Connection-specific DNS Suffix  . : attlocal.net
IPv6 Address. . . . . . . . . . . : 2602:306:8b80:2570::40
IPv6 Address. . . . . . . . . . . : 2602:306:8b80:2570:2d34:e50:95ef:1dcd Temporary
IPv6 Address. . . . . . . . . . . : 2602:306:8b80:2570:c84b:f814:a4ce:cfe1

Link-local IPv6 Address . . . . . . . . . : fe80::2d34:e50:95ef:1dcd%10
IPv4 Address. . . . . . . . . . . : 192.168.1.90
Subnet Mask . . . . . . . . . . . : 255.255.255.0
Default Gateway . . . . . . . . . : 192.168.1.1
```

`ifconfig` is the Linux command used to view and change network interface configurations:

```
host#ifconfig
eth0
Link encap:Ethernet
HWaddr 0B:55:65:DE:E9:23:F1
inet addr:192.168.28.10
Bcast:192.168.28.255
Mask:255.255.255.0
UP BROADCAST RUNNING MULTICAST  MTU:1500  Metric:1
RX packets:2472694671 errors:1 dropped:0 overruns:0 frame:0
TX packets:44641779 errors:0 dropped:0 overruns:0 carrier:0
collisions:0 txqueuelen:1000
RX bytes:1761467179 (1679.7 Mb)
TX bytes:2870928587 (2737.9 Mb)

Interrupt:28
```

Netstat

Netstat is a network statistics utility found on both Windows and Linux workstations and servers. You can use the `netstat` command when troubleshooting to see which protocols and ports an application is listening on, to view detailed protocol information, to see addresses used both locally and remotely, and to determine which state the TCP connections are currently in on the device. The basic `netstat` output is illustrated here:

```
C:\Users\todd>netstat
Active Connections
Proto  Local Address          Foreign Address                State
TCP    192.168.1.90:49546     8.18.25.62:https               ESTABLISHED
TCP    192.168.1.90:49550     unknown000d65498700:telnet     ESTABLISHED
TCP    192.168.1.90:49573     ec2-107-22-225-24:http         ESTABLISHED
TCP    192.168.1.90:49576     a-0001:https                   ESTABLISHED
TCP    192.168.1.90:49577     a-0001:https                   ESTABLISHED
TCP    192.168.1.90:49578     a-0001:https                   ESTABLISHED
TCP    192.168.1.90:58113     os-in-f188:5228                ESTABLISHED
```

There are many options for `netstat`, including the one shown next, where you're asking for TCP network statistics. By combining `netstat` options, you can get granular and detailed output like the following:

```
C:\Users\todd>netstat -ps
IPv4 Statistics
Packets Received                              = 559794
Received Header Errors                        = 0
Received Address Errors                       = 35694
Datagrams Forwarded                           = 0
Unknown Protocols Received                    = 0
Received Packets Discarded                    = 16057
Received Packets Delivered                    = 871906
Output Requests                               = 286165
Routing Discards                              = 0
Discarded Output Packets                      = 75730
Output Packet No Route                        = 0
Reassembly Required                           = 16241
Reassembly Successful                         = 8085
Reassembly Failures                           = 0
Datagrams Successfully Fragmented             = 0
Datagrams Failing Fragmentation               = 0
```

```
Fragments Created                    = 0

ICMPv4 Statistics
Received    Sent
Messages                           63761         31278
Errors                                 0             0
Destination Unreachable            63727         31242
Time Exceeded                         27             0
Parameter Problems                     0             0
Source Quenches                        0             0
Redirects                              0             0
Echo Replies                           7             0
Echos                                  0            36
Timestamps                             0             0
Timestamp Replies                      0             0
Address Masks                          0             0
Address Mask Replies                   0             0
Router Solicitations                   0             0
Router Advertisements                  0             0
Router Renumberings                    0             0

TCP Statistics for IPv4
Active Opens                    = 6293
Passive Opens                   = 88
Failed Connection Attempt       = 50
Reset Connections               = 360
Current Connections             = 1
Segments Received               = 109317
Segments Sent                   = 83586
Segments Retransmitted          = 2593

UDP Statistics for IPv4
Datagrams Received                = 176647
No Ports                          = 234005
Receive Errors                    = 1
Datagrams Sent                    = 156556
```

nslookup/dig

`nslookup` and `dig` are commands used to resolve hostnames to IP addresses using a DNS server. If you need to learn the IP address of a domain, use nslookup to resolve the DNS name to the IP address, as shown here:

```
C:\Users\todd>nslookup
 > 8.8.8.8
```

```
Server:  dsldevice.attlocal.net
Address:  192.168.1.254
Name:    google-public-dns-a.google.com
Address:  8.8.8.8
```

The `dig` command serves the same function. It queries a DNS system by giving a domain name and receives the corresponding IP address. Although `dig` has extensive command options, the basic command returns a remarkable amount of information, as shown here:

```
linux# dig www.google.com
; <> DiG 9.3.3rc2 <> www.google.com
; (1 server found)
;; global options: printcmd
;; Got answer:
;; ->>HEADER<;; flags: qr aa rd ra; QUERY: 1, ANSWER: 1, AUTHORITY: 3, ADDITIONAL: 3
;; QUESTION SECTION:
;www.google.com. IN A
;; ANSWER SECTION:
http://www.google.com/. 43200 IN A 200.99.187.2
;; AUTHORITY SECTION:
http://www.google.com/. 43200 IN NS ns2.google.com.
http://www.google.com/. 43200 IN NS ns3.google.com.
http://www.google.com/. 43200 IN NS ns1.google.com.
;; ADDITIONAL SECTION:
ns1.google.com. 43200 IN A 222.54.11.86
ns2.google.com. 43200 IN A 220.225.37.222
ns3.google.com. 43200 IN A 203.199.147.233
;; Query time: 1 msec
;; SERVER: 222.54.11.86#53(222.54.11.86)
;; WHEN: Wed Nov 18 18:31:12 2009
;; MSG SIZE rcvd: 152
[root@tipofthehat ~]#
```

Ping

Ping is part of the TCP/IP family of protocols; it is used to verify that a device is available and reachable on the network and to measure response latency. You can send a ping packet to a remote IP address and have it return, as shown in the following example. This will tell you that the IP stack and routing are configured correctly and that you can reach IP devices on both the local and remote networks. Ping is a fundamental and frequently used troubleshooting tool for verifying network connectivity. It is useful in verifying that the remote device is reachable and in determining if there is any packet loss from the source to the destination and back. Also, ping can help you spot unusually high latency.

```
C:\Users\todd>ping 8.8.8.8
Pinging 8.8.8.8 with 32 bytes of data:
Reply from 8.8.8.8: bytes=32 time=177ms TTL=53
Reply from 8.8.8.8: bytes=32 time=9ms TTL=53
Reply from 8.8.8.8: bytes=32 time=9ms TTL=53
Reply from 8.8.8.8: bytes=32 time=9ms TTL=53
Ping statistics for 8.8.8.8:
Packets: Sent = 4, Received = 4, Lost = 0 (0% loss),
Approximate round trip times in milli-seconds:
Minimum = 9ms, Maximum = 177ms, Average = 51ms
```

route

The route command shown in the following example can assist you in troubleshooting network reachability issues. Use this command when troubleshooting to look at a device's local routing tables.

```
C:\Users\todd>route print
===========================================================================
Interface List 10…00 1e 37 1e c1 60 ......Intel(R) 82566MM Gigabit Network Connection
===========================================================================
   IPv4 Route Table
===========================================================================
Active Routes:
Network Destination      Netmask          Gateway        Interface       Metric
0.0.0.0                  0.0.0.0          192.168.1.254  192.168.1.90    20
127.0.0.0                255.0.0.0        On-link        127.0.0.1       306
127.0.0.1                255.255.255.255  On-link        127.0.0.1       306
127.255.255.255          255.255.255.255  On-link        127.0.0.1       306
192.168.1.0              255.255.255.0    On-link        192.168.1.90    276
192.168.1.90             255.255.255.255  On-link        192.168.1.90    276
192.168.1.255            255.255.255.255  On-link        192.168.1.90    276
192.168.74.0             255.255.255.0    On-link        192.168.74.1    276
192.168.74.1             255.255.255.255  On-link        192.168.74.1    276
192.168.74.255           255.255.255.255  On-link        192.168.74.1    276
192.168.223.0            255.255.255.0    On-link        192.168.223.1   276
192.168.223.1            255.255.255.255  On-link        192.168.223.1   276
192.168.223.255          255.255.255.255  On-link        192.168.223.1   276
224.0.0.0                240.0.0.0        On-link        127.0.0.1       306
224.0.0.0                240.0.0.0        On-link        192.168.74.1    276
224.0.0.0                240.0.0.0        On-link        192.168.223.1   276
224.0.0.0                240.0.0.0        On-link        192.168.1.90    276
```

```
255.255.255.255          255.255.255.255  On-link        127.0.0.1     306
255.255.255.255          255.255.255.255  On-link        192.168.74.1  276
255.255.255.255          255.255.255.255  On-link        192.168.223.1 276
255.255.255.255          255.255.255.255  On-link        192.168.1.90  276
===========================================================================
Persistent Routes:
None
```

SSH

Secure Shell (SSH) is a secure replacement of the Telnet protocol, and it is used to access a command prompt or shell on remote devices. SSH and two other utilities built on top of it—Secure Copy Protocol (SCP) and Secure File Transfer Protocol (SFTP)—use TCP port 22. SSH is the de facto standard for accessing remote systems' command interfaces. Unlike Telnet, SSH provides encryption and authentication. With rare exceptions, you should use SSH and avoid using Telnet.

```
$ssh todd@192.168.1.23
```

Telnet

Telnet is a virtual terminal application that allows for command-line logins to a remote device. The Telnet application will allow you to log into remote servers or network gear in the cloud as if you are locally connected to your laptop or server.

Telnet is an industry-standard application, and though still used, it is not secure in that all commands, including your username and password, are sent over the network in the clear, unencrypted. Because of this, SSH has largely replaced Telnet. Here's an example of logging into a remotely located network switch using Telnet:

```
telnet 192.168.1.251
User Access Verification
Username: cloudplus
Password:
Core_rtr_a>
```

tcpdump

The `tcpdump` command allows a Linux system to capture or *sniff* packets on a network interface. `tcpdump` allows you to set up filters to select the traffic you are interested in capturing for monitoring or troubleshooting. Think of `tcpdump` as a command-line network analyzer.

```
$tcpdump -v -n
tcpdump: listening on eth0, link-type EN10MB (Ethernet), capture size 65535 bytes
16:43:13.058660 IP (tos 0x20, ttl 54, id 50249, offset 0, flags [DF], proto TCP
(6), length 40)
```

```
    64.41.140.209.5222 > 192.168.1.101.35783: Flags [.], cksum 0x6d32 (correct),
ack 1617156745, win 9648, length 0
16:43:13.214621 IP (tos 0x0, ttl 64, id 0, offset 0, flags [DF], proto ICMP (1),
length 84)
    192.168.1.101 > 173.194.36.6: ICMP echo request, id 19941, seq 1659, length 64
16:43:13.355334 IP (tos 0x20, ttl 54, id 48656, offset 0, flags [none], proto ICMP
(1), length 84)
    173.194.36.6 > 192.168.1.101: ICMP echo reply, id 19941, seq 1659, length 64
16:43:13.355719 IP (tos 0x0, ttl 64, id 0, offset 0, flags [DF], proto UDP
(17), length 71)
    192.168.1.101.22181 > 218.248.255.163.53: 28650+ PTR? 6.36.194.173.in-
addr.arpa. (43)
16:43:13.362941 IP (tos 0x0, ttl 251, id 63454, offset 0, flags [DF], proto
UDP (17), length 223)
    218.248.255.163.53 > 192.168.1.101.22181: 28650 1/4/2 6.36.194.173.in-
addr.arpa. PTR bom04s01-in-f6.1e100.net. (195)
16:43:13.880338 ARP, Ethernet (len 6), IPv4 (len 4), Request who-has 192.168.1.3
tell 192.168.1.101, length 28
16:43:14.215904 IP (tos 0x0, ttl 64, id 0, offset 0, flags [DF], proto ICMP (1),
length 84)
    192.168.1.101 > 173.194.36.6: ICMP echo request, id 19941, seq 1660,
length 64
```

tracert/traceroute

The tracert/traceroute commands are useful for network path troubleshooting. traceroute displays the route a packet takes to its destination. You can use it to determine whether routing is working as expected, and you might even be able to narrow down the location of a routing failure. In the following example, a traceroute command details the path that a packet takes to a destination on the Internet, along with the latency for each router hop. The traceroute command performs a reverse lookup of each IP address along the way and displays the corresponding DNS name, if applicable.

```
C:\Users\todd>tracert 8.8.8.8
Tracing route to google-public-dns-a.google.com [8.8.8.8] over a maximum of 30 hops:
1     1 ms     1 ms     1 ms  dsldevice.attlocal.net [192.168.1.254]
2   172 ms    49 ms     7 ms  108-218-244-1.lightspeed.austtx.sbcglobal.net
[108.218.244.1]
3     4 ms     5 ms     3 ms  71.149.77.70
4     5 ms     3 ms     3 ms  75.8.128.140
5     4 ms     5 ms     6 ms  12.81.225.241
6     9 ms     9 ms     9 ms  12.122.85.197
```

```
7    61 ms    59 ms    58 ms  206.121.120.66
8     9 ms     9 ms     9 ms  216.239.54.109
9    12 ms    11 ms    11 ms  72.14.234.145
10    11 ms     9 ms     9 ms  google-public-dns-a.google.com [8.8.8.8]
Trace complete
```

For Microsoft products, the command is `tracert`, and the `traceroute` command is used for Linux operating systems. The following is an example of `traceroute` with Linux:

```
$ traceroute google.com
traceroute to google.com (74.125.236.132), 30 hops max, 60 byte packets
1  118.26.54.19 (118.26.54.19)  89.174 ms  89.094 ms  89.054 ms
2  182.56.49.175 ( 182.56.49.175)  109.037 ms  108.994 ms  108.963 ms
3  16.178.22.165 (16.178.22.165)  108.937 ms  121.322 ms  121.300 ms
4  * 119.255.128.45 (119.255.128.45)  113.754 ms  113.692 ms
5  72.14.212.118 (72.14.212.118)  123.585 ms  123.558 ms  123.527 ms
6  72.14.232.202 (72.14.232.202)  123.499 ms  123.475 ms  143.523 ms
7  216.239.48.179 (216.239.48.179)  143.503 ms  95.106 ms  95.026 ms
8  bom03s02-in-f4.1e100.net (74.125.236.132)  94.980 ms  104.989 ms  104.954 ms
```

Remote Access Tools

When troubleshooting networks, it is not often that you will be directly in front of the equipment given that devices tend to be geographically dispersed and housed in secure locations. However, it is a common practice to connect to, log in, and access network devices remotely. Common approaches include remotely connecting to a terminal server in the data center and logging into devices or using a standard web browser for HTTP access since most devices now have web-based consoles. Windows-based systems can be managed with the remote desktop utilities. Command-line interfaces are prevalent in most servers, security, and network systems.

Console Port

Console ports are common in networking environments and are used to configure switches and routers from a command-line interface (CLI). Linux servers also use the console or serial ports for CLI access. In a data center, devices called *terminal servers* are deployed that have several serial ports, each cabled to a console port on a device that is being managed, as shown in Figure 10.2. This allows you to make an SSH or a Telnet connection to the terminal server and then use the serial interfaces to access the console ports on the devices you want to connect to. Also, a VM can use port redirections to connect to a physical serial port on the server for console connections.

FIGURE 10.2 Console port access

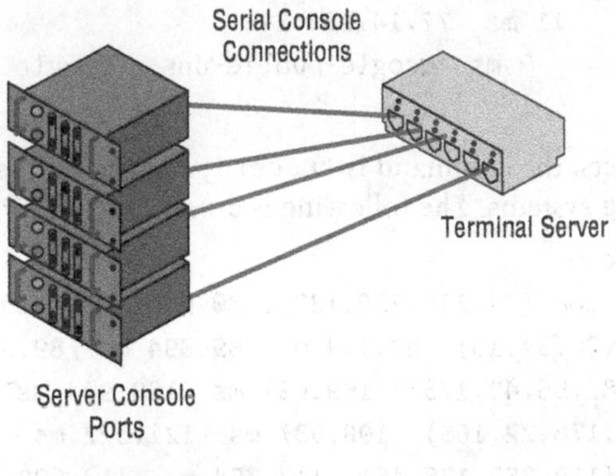

HTTP

Probably the most common and easiest way of managing remote devices is to use a standard web browser and access the remote device's web interface, as illustrated in Figure 10.3. When connected and authenticated, the web-based applications allow for a graphical interface that can be used to monitor and configure a device.

FIGURE 10.3 Console port access

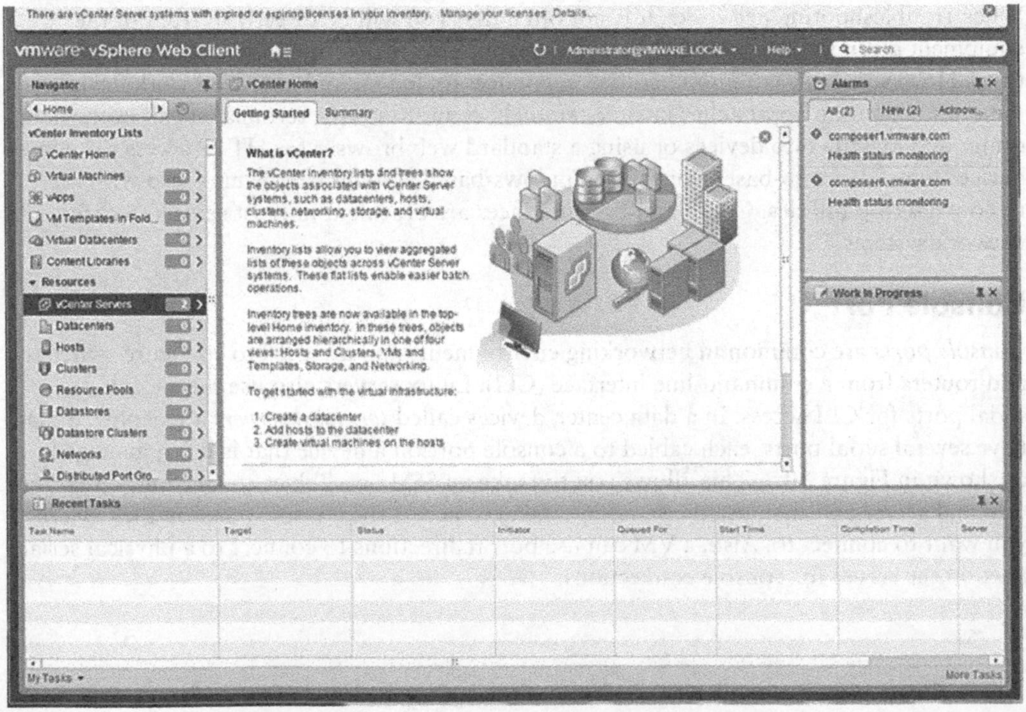

There has been a trend to move away from client applications that need to be installed on the local workstation and move everything to a web interface for ease of use. It is also common to use a web browser to connect to a hypervisor, virtual machine, or network device and then download and install the management application. HTTPS, which uses TCP port 443, is the suggested remote access protocol for web-based access since it is secure. The nonencrypted HTTP port 80 is rarely supported because of its lack of encryption and authentication.

RDP

The *Remote Desktop Protocol (RDP)* allows remote GUI access to Windows devices. Microsoft calls the application Remote Desktop Service and, in the past, has called it Terminal Services. RDP is a client-server application, which means RDP must be installed and running on both the server and the local workstation that you are using to access the cloud server. The desktop application comes preinstalled on most versions of Windows. Figure 10.4 shows a local computer running the RDP application to remotely access a Windows server running in the cloud.

FIGURE 10.4 Local computer running the RDP application to remotely access a cloud with a Windows server graphical interface

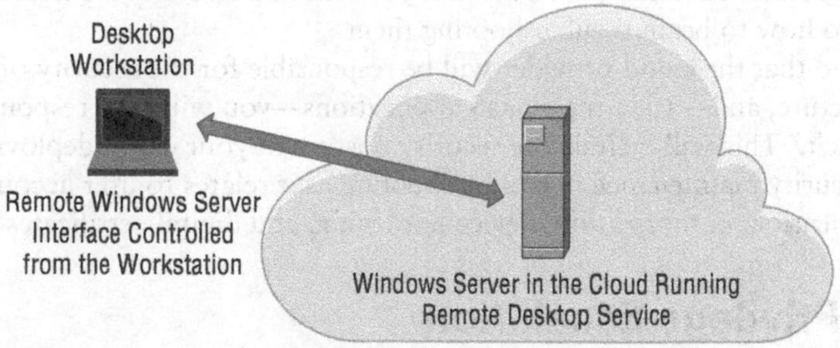

The RDP client will request the domain name or IP address of the remote server in the cloud and authentication credentials. Once connected, you will be presented with a standard Windows desktop of the remote server.

SSH

SSH is commonly used as a remote access utility for command-line access. The ability to support encryption and authentication and its widespread use across many different types of products and services makes it a popular application. To use SSH, the SSH service must be supported on the server or device in the cloud data center and enabled. This is pretty much standard on any Linux distribution, router, firewall, load balancer, or switch, and SSH can also be installed on Windows devices.

Many SSH clients are available on the market, both commercial software and free of charge in the public domain. The SSH client connects over the network using TCP port 22 over an encrypted connection, as shown in Figure 10.5. Once you are connected, you have a command-line interface to manage your cloud services. SSH is a common remote connection method used to configure network devices such as switches and routers.

FIGURE 10.5 Secure Shell–encrypted remote access

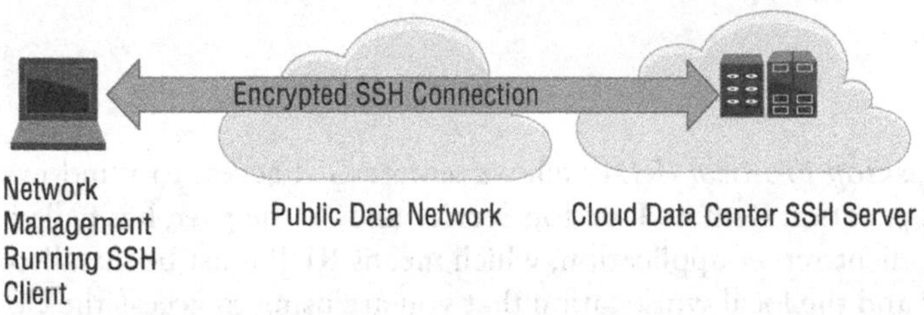

Troubleshooting Security Issues

In this section, you will learn about troubleshooting security-related issues in the cloud. I will discuss the most common problems that you will find as a cloud customer and give you insight into how to begin troubleshooting them.

Keep in mind that the cloud provider will be responsible for the security of the underlying infrastructure, and—aside from SaaS applications—you will take responsibility for the "top of the stack." This will include the security posture of your cloud deployments. You will learn about security maintenance in troubleshooting as it relates to user accounts, sign-on issues, authentication, authorization, device hardening, and digital certificates.

Account Privilege Escalation

Privilege escalation occurs when a user receives account privileges that they are not allowed to possess. A regular user of a computer would not normally be granted administrative access to install and remove software or reconfigure the system. If they were able to acquire permissions to do those things, that would be an example of privilege escalation. Privilege escalation can occur because of a bug, a design oversight, or delegating user account management to a person who is willing to change user account settings without gaining necessary approvals. Figure 10.6 illustrates the account privilege escalation pyramid.

To avoid potential privilege escalation problems, grant users only the privileges required for them to perform their duties. Also, make sure that operating system and application patches and antivirus definitions are up-to-date. Verify that the applications are running with the minimum privileges required for them to operate. Finally, make sure that you have configured security for mandatory access controls, as discussed in Chapter 3, "Security in the Cloud."

FIGURE 10.6 Account privilege escalation

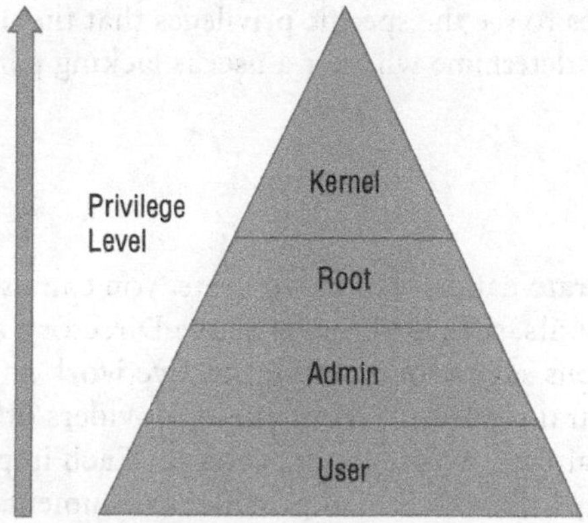

Network Access Issues

In order for you to access cloud resources, everything has to fall into place. Access control lists and firewalls must be configured to allow access. Often, for additional security, access is restricted to particular source IP address ranges such as your office. If you are not connecting a source IP address in the allowed list, you will be denied access. Many cloud providers have device-level security groups that block incoming traffic unless it is specifically configured to allow the connection.

Authentication

To review from Chapter 2, "Cloud Deployments," *authentication* is the process of identifying a user or device. Users and devices can be authenticated using a wide variety of methods, the most common being a username and password. Other methods include multifactor authentication (MFA) tokens and biometrics, such as fingerprint or iris scanners.

When troubleshooting authentication issues, the most valuable source of information will be in the logging files. When authentication fails, a log file will be generated, and information will be included on the reason for the failure. In addition to the obvious wrong password, other reasons for an authentication failure include disabled accounts and expired passwords. Also, if the user fails after the defined number of password attempts, most systems will lock the user out, and they will not be allowed to log in for a period of time.

Authorization

After a user is authenticated, the authorization process takes place wherein the user is granted privileges according to how their account is configured. It is common that when a user account is initially created, they are given few, if any, privileges. The systems administrator must grant access to each user by explicitly assigning authorizations to the user.

Access denied errors or the inability to perform certain tasks while being able to perform others could indicate an authorization problem. When you suspect an authorization failure, it's best to start with log files to see the specific privileges that the user has been granted or denied. From there you can determine whether a user is lacking particular privileges that they require.

Federations

Instead of managing a separate database of cloud users, you can use federations to allow your on-premises user accounts, such as those in Active Directory, also to be used to authenticate cloud users. Federations save a lot of administrative work and serve to consolidate user permissions into a central repository. Most cloud providers offer different options to connect the cloud to these already existing user accounts. Each implementation will be different, so you should closely follow the cloud provider's documentation. Once the federation connection is made, there should be monitoring and logging data available on the health of the connection. Federation involves mapping identities and permissions across different authentication systems, so when troubleshooting federation problems, you will most likely need to get your internal directory services team involved.

Certificate Configuration Issues

As discussed in Chapter 9, "Troubleshooting," it is important to make sure that TLS certificates are current and not expired. Keep track of all certificate expiration dates and renew them prior to expiration! When a certificate error pops up out of the blue, the most likely explanation is that it expired. Another possibility is that the domain name doesn't match one of the subject names on the certificate. Certificate mismatches frequently happen when a website's domain name changes.

Certificate management can be a complex and wide-ranging topic. In cloud computing, there are many different types of certificates and a variety of services offerings that range from your organization having complete control of the security certificates, to mixed offerings, to the cloud provider taking responsibility for certificate management.

Troubleshooting will be dependent on your key management plan. As usual, review log files, collect and distill the information that you have collected, and plan your approach to troubleshooting certificate issues. Oh, and check the expiration date!

Device-Hardening Settings

To prevent intrusions and hacks, all devices must be hardened from attacks. The hardening process can be rather extensive, and it is specific to the device or service. At a minimum, it's a good idea to follow the vendor or cloud provider's best practices on hardening each specific device or service. The best practices are usually published on the support websites or offered as whitepapers.

The trade-off of device hardening is that it breaks things and leads to more troubleshooting down the line. The hardening process by its nature restricts the capabilities of the device, so changes such as installing or upgrading an application are likely to require some after-the-fact changes to the hardening that has taken place. As a rule, the more you lock down a device, the more time you'll spend getting things to work. As always, security is a trade-off. Having good documentation as to what devices were hardened and how can go a long way in aiding your troubleshooting efforts.

External Attacks

It is common for cloud providers to provide first-level external attack protection since they control the cloud network resources. This will include denial-of-service and scanning attacks, to name a few. However, cloud providers cannot be responsible for preventing all attacks. Although outages caused by an attack are unlikely, you should be aware of the signs that might indicate one. Unusually high network traffic, errors, or failed login attempts could indicate an attack. This is where having good baselines can come in handy. Also, various application firewalls have the intelligence to recognize an attack and take measures to block and mitigate them. Your cloud provider may also offer the ability to report and block the source of the attack before it ever reaches your resources, potentially saving you lots of money!

Internal Attacks

Social engineering is the most predominant internal attack where someone is tricked into providing credentials or holding a door open into a secure data center, for example. Training seems to be ongoing to educate the workforce on common tracks to obtain information or access using social engineering. Use common sense and always be a bit suspicious if someone asks you to do something that you do not feel comfortable with or that seems out of the ordinary.

Devices can be deployed inside the security perimeter and can be configured to capture data, scan the network, or masquerade as another system. Most cloud provider security operations will shut down a device that is doing a port scan of their infrastructure. Cloud systems monitor for intrusion detection and prevention, taking the needed actions to mitigate the threat.

Maintain Sufficient Security Controls and Processes

The cloud provider will most certainly have a dedicated security department that encompasses not only security from a technology standpoint but also physical security. However, the security of your cloud resources is ultimately your responsibility. It's impossible to become hacker-proof, but you should do due diligence to avoid breaches and to keep in front of those who want to damage you or your company's reputation.

The security landscape is ever changing. As part of your ongoing operations management practice, your cloud team should regularly evaluate the security of your cloud resources to determine whether they're vulnerable to novel attacks.

The concept of least privilege is important as it grants security permissions for only what is required. Division of duties is common where there is no one single person who has end-to-end access responsibility. With the division of duties, a single individual cannot take control because there is a second person who has access to a critical part of the cloud that the other does not possess but needs to complete the role.

Network Access Tunneling and Encryption

Data sent across a network unencrypted is susceptible to interception and modification by an attacker. Encrypting data in transit is always a good idea, and when using a public network such as the Internet for transport, strong encryption is absolutely necessary. The standard approach to encrypting all traffic between your cloud and on-premises environment is to use a VPN, and cloud providers offer managed VPN services to facilitate this. Because a VPN connection is essentially a network connection, the same problems can arise with it as in any other network. Routing problems, incorrect access control entries, and dropped VPN connections can all present complex troubleshooting challenges. It's standard to have redundant VPN connections to different availability zones in order to ensure continuous connectivity.

When using a VPN isn't feasible—between your cloud resources and a customer, for example—you can achieve encryption by using secure application protocols. HTTPS, SSH, SFTP, and SCP are examples of protocols that are secure out-of-the-box and appropriate for transmitting sensitive information over public networks.

Troubleshooting Methodology

Problems can come about in many ways, including configuration errors, software bugs, hardware failure, malicious attacks, or overloaded resources, just to name a few.

Troubleshooting is the process of diagnosing the cause of an impairment and resolving the issue. All troubleshooting begins with comparing what *is* occurring with what *should* be occurring. The troubleshooting process includes the following:

- Identifying the problem
- Establishing a theory
- Testing the theory
- Establishing and implementing a plan of resolution
- Verifying the resolution
- Documenting the cause and resolution

To troubleshoot effectively, it's usually best to follow a methodical approach. Sometimes, a methodical approach isn't necessary. If you've seen a particular problem before and recognize it easily, it would be a waste of time to walk through a process just to arrive at an answer that you already know. But with complex or unfamiliar issues, following a strict approach can save you time and frustration and prevent confusion. Haphazardly trying different fixes and hoping that one of them works could end up creating additional problems. It also makes it hard to provide feedback and document steps to prevent the issue from recurring in the future. A structured approach allows you to reduce duplicate troubleshooting steps, and it ensures that you do not skip any steps and are able to effectively update others about the potential issues that you have eliminated and what still needs to be investigated.

Identifying the Problem

As I said, all troubleshooting begins with comparing what *is* occurring with what *should* be occurring. It bears repeating because one of the most common mistakes when troubleshooting is failing to articulate the problem clearly. When multiple users report what appears to be a common problem, their descriptions can vary widely and include irrelevant or just plain wrong information. Trouble reports may leave out important information because they reflect a user's perception at a certain point in time. Your responsibility is to define the problem clearly, and this requires determining what data is valid and relevant to the problem at hand.

Collecting relevant data isn't always easy. In larger organizations, different divisions, or as they are sometimes called, silos, are responsible for different portions of the IT infrastructure. You may need some information about a database, for example, and have no idea who the database administrators are or even where they are! During a major incident, an organization may set up a "war room" where these groups can collaborate on troubleshooting and share information that they normally wouldn't. But with smaller issues, you'll probably have to make some effort to track down the parties who can provide you with the information that you seek. Correlating user reports with available logs and metrics can often provide some helpful insights. But again, in a large organization, just getting this information can be a chore.

Establishing a Theory

After identifying the problem, the next step is to establish a theory of probable cause. This is where the bulk of your troubleshooting time will likely be spent. Simply gathering data often leads to more questions and thus the need to gather more data. When gathering information to identify a problem or to establish a theory, you must decide where to start. To reiterate an earlier point, if you already have a good idea of where the source of the problem lies, you don't need to waste time following every step of a formal process. But if you're facing multiple likely possibilities, you should methodically proceed through each one to arrive at the best one.

The most common methods are top-down, bottom-up, and divide-and-conquer. The *top-down approach* refers to the seven-layer Open Systems Interconnection (OSI) networking model. You begin at the highest layer, the application layer, and work your way down the stack into the lower layers of routing, addressing, and physical connectivity. Using utilities such as ping, traceroute, and others, you can work your way down the stack, as shown in Figure 10.7.

FIGURE 10.7 Top-down troubleshooting approach

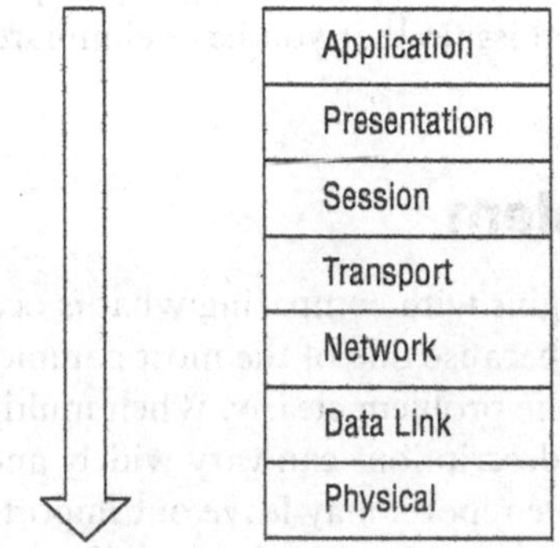

Reversing the preceding approach gives you the *bottom-up approach*, as shown in Figure 10.8. When dealing with widespread issues, this approach may be more prudent because the upper layers of the OSI model are dependent on the lower layers, and thus a problem at the lower layers is likely to have a broader impact.

FIGURE 10.8 Bottom-up troubleshooting approach

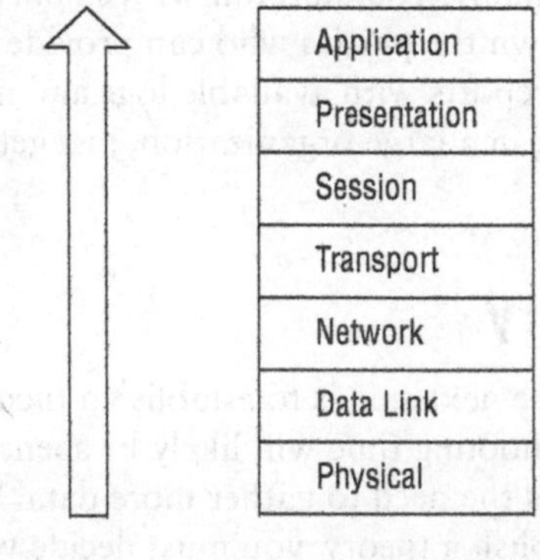

Divide-and-conquer is a variation of top-down and bottom-up troubleshooting approaches, where you start in the middle of the OSI model, say at the network layer, and based on your testing results, work either up the stack or down, as shown in Figure 10.9.

FIGURE 10.9 Divide-and-conquer troubleshooting approach

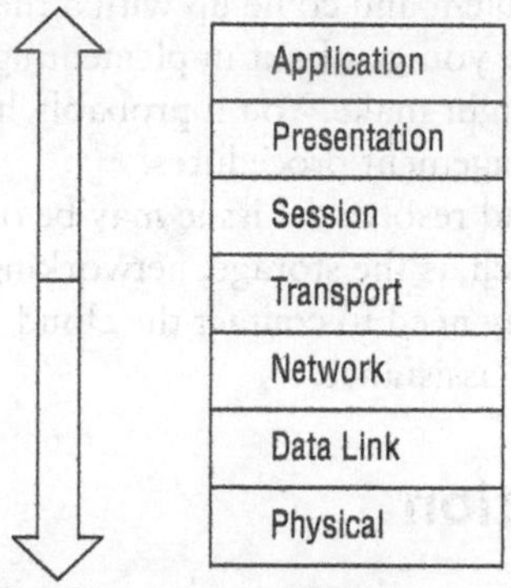

Regardless of the method that you use, your diagnostic efforts may involve looking at multiple devices, multiplying the time it will take to formulate a theory. To save time, it may be helpful to narrow your search to just a handful of likely suspects. An effective way to do this is by using the *follow-the-path approach* to locate the approximate point of failure. Utilities such as ping and traceroute will be helpful when implementing this approach. Also, if you're tracking changes, configuration comparisons may offer clues as to whether a change caused the issue under investigation and what devices were affected by the change.

Understanding the dependencies that exist is crucial at this juncture. For example, if a particular application is unusually slow to respond, knowing what factors affect the application's responsiveness can and should guide the development of your theory. Look for evidence that eliminates areas that could have been part of the issue. If the application depends on a database but the database seems to be operating normally and other applications that use the same database are functioning with no problem, then you can probably rule the database out of your troubleshooting. You may have to follow different threads before arriving at a plausible explanation. Did I mention that establishing a theory would be the most time-consuming part of your troubleshooting?

Testing the Theory

After you've come up with a theory and convinced yourself that it's right, the next step is to test it. Of course, often the only way to test your theory is to make a change that will probably affect an important system and might even cause an outage. If you have a test environment or lab, now's a good time to make use of it. Using your theory as a guide, attempt to re-create the problem in your controlled test environment. If you can re-create the problem, you're probably on to something. And if you're able to resolve the problem in your lab, then you have a de facto plan of action that you can apply to the real problem.

But testing your theory in a controlled setting isn't always feasible, nor will it necessarily give you accurate results because a lab environment never exactly mirrors a production environment. Sometimes, safely testing your theory is a luxury that you simply can't afford. Instead, you have to test in production, and for that you need a plan.

Creating and Implementing a Plan of Action

After you have identified the problem and come up with a theory, the next step is to craft a plan to resolve the problem. How you go about implementing your plan will look uncannily like any other change that you might make. You'll probably have to go through your organization's (emergency) change management procedures.

The actions required to test and resolve the issue may be out of your area of control, and working with different groups such as the storage, networking, or virtualization teams may be required. Additionally, you may need to contact the cloud vendor's support group and open a troubleshooting ticket for assistance.

Verifying the Resolution

Because changes often occur when users have gone home, verifying the resolution might not happen immediately after you implement the proposed fix. Once again, you may have to call on the people who originally reported the problem to determine whether it's been fixed. And if the problem is one that shows up only intermittently—say when a user runs a once-a-month process—then you may be waiting a long time for confirmation that your theory was right!

Documenting the Ordeal

Memories fade and people move around organizations. Thus, it's important to document your findings and actions while everything is still fresh in your mind. If you resolved the issue, you'll have a record that you or others can use later should the problem reoccur. And documentation doesn't have to be formal or lengthy. Simply communicating to the appropriate parties the cause and resolution by updating a status dashboard or sending an email might be sufficient.

If you made configuration changes as part of the resolution, the documentation should include backing up the working configurations. If you made any changes to a device configuration, add what was changed and why the change was made to resolve the issue in your documentation and then back up the actual configuration to a server as an archive.

Summary

In this chapter, you learned about some of the common networking issues that you will find in the field, including IP addressing issues such as subnetting, routing, and gateway configurations. This chapter discussed troubleshooting DNS, QoS, VLAN, VXLAN, firewall configurations, network latency, MTU, and proxies.

Many utilities are available for both the Windows and the Linux operating systems that are invaluable aids in troubleshooting networking problems. The primary commands are `ping`, `tracert/traceroute`, `telnet`, `netstat`, `nslookup/dig`, `ipconfig/ifconfig`, `route`, `arp`, and `tcpdump`. I discussed use cases and showed the text output to help you understand how to use these critical tools when troubleshooting network problems.

Troubleshooting account issues is common, so you learned about what to look for when working on sign-on, authentication, authorization, and confederation problems. Privilege escalation and role changes were also included in this section.

Troubleshooting security issues includes dealing with certificates, encrypted communications, security hardening, and physical facility access; keeping your security technologies up-to-date by following new developments; and assessing your security posture to new offerings on the market.

The chapter ended with a general overview of troubleshooting and some of the various models you can use, such as top-down, bottom-up, and divide-and-conquer. You then learned about additional processes to follow for effective and timely resolution of issues.

A troubleshooting methodology includes identifying the problem, collecting information, and establishing a theory. You then establish and execute a plan of action to test the theory, hopefully resolving the problem in the process. Finally, you should document the findings, actions, and outcomes.

Exam Essentials

Know the various network connectivity issues and how to troubleshoot them. Common network issues on which you can expect to be tested include IP addressing such as misconfigured subnet masks, default gateways, routing, and DNS. Know at a basic level what QoS is and the symptoms of network saturation. Given a problem, be able to identify the most likely root cause. For example, being able to connect to a remote site by its IP address but not by its domain name suggests a DNS problem.

Know how to identify networking issues. Be able to identify and perform basic troubleshooting of network connectivity failures. This can include using command-line troubleshooting tools, investigating log files, and monitoring systems to gather information on the reported issue. There may be a long scenario where you are given a large amount of detail, and you should be able to discard what does not apply and select from the answers given the core processes to identify the problem.

Be able to diagnose user account issues. You may see questions on the exam with a description of a user not being able to access the cloud and a brief explanation of the symptoms. You need to be able to distill the problem to common user issues such as account lockouts, authentication and authorization problems, and account federation problems.

Describe the process of identifying certificate problems. Know that security certificates have expiration dates and that you need to renew them prior to that time. Certificates must also match the domain name(s) that they're used with. Certificate management can be a fully managed cloud service or handled internally by your organization. You may be asked what steps to take when troubleshooting a certificate problem and to identify the correct answer offered given the scenario.

Identify types of attacks. You may be given an example of an attack, and you should be able to identify whether it is originating internally or externally. Also, know the distinct signs of denial-of-service and social engineering attacks.

Explain remote access technologies and uses. Know how to access cloud resources. The Remote Desktop Protocol is commonly used for administering Windows servers. Remote command-line access uses the Secure Shell protocol because it is encrypted and more secure than Telnet. Console ports are used for command-line serial port access for remote configuration and monitoring. Many devices offer a web-based configuration interface that can be accessed using the HTTPS protocol, much like accessing websites on the Internet.

Summarize the various approaches to troubleshooting. Troubleshooting methods include top-down, bottom-up, and divide and conquer.

Know how to use a troubleshooting methodology. You may be presented with a question where a description is given of a troubleshooting step and you are asked to identify which step in the troubleshooting process is being used. Examples are identifying the problem, establishing a probable theory of the cause, testing the theory, establishing a plan of action to resolve the problem, and implementing the solution. The final step is documenting the findings, actions, and outcomes.

Written Lab

Fill in the blanks for the questions provided in the written lab. You can find the answers to the written labs in Appendix B.

1. When a network becomes saturated, ________________ can be implemented to define priorities.
2. An Ethernet frame larger than the standard size is a(n) ________________ frame.
3. A(n) ________________ is a device that is inserted into the middle of a traffic flow, terminates connections in both directions, and monitors traffic between the source and the destination.
4. ________________ can be used to create more than 16 million isolated virtual networks.
5. The ________________ network utility is found in both Windows and Linux operating systems and can be used to show open network connections.
6. Both the ________________ and ________________ utilities query a DNS server.
7. When the cloud issue has been resolved, the final step in the troubleshooting process is to create ________________.
8. After you have identified and articulated the issue, the next step is to ________________.
9. Social engineering is a(n) ________________ attack where someone is tricked into providing credentials or holding a door open into a secure data center, for example.
10. ________________ occurs when a user receives account privileges that they are not allowed to possess.

Review Questions

The following questions are designed to test your understanding of this chapter's material. You can find the answers to the questions in Appendix A. For more information on how to obtain additional questions, please see this book's Introduction.

1. Cari is researching various remote access options to access her Linux servers in a public cloud. She has been asked to provide a standardized and secure solution that protects against snooping. As a Cloud+ architect, you have been asked to assist. What protocol would you advise Cari to implement?

   A. RDP

   B. Telnet

   C. IPsec

   D. SSH

   E. Terminal server

2. Kevin is troubleshooting a DNS issue and wants to look at DNS frames being sent and received from his network adapter card on a web server. What command would he use to collect the traces?

   A. `dig`

   B. `netstat`

   C. `tcpdump`

   D. `nslookup`

3. An intern at your company is asking about the mappings between the layer 2 MAC address and the gateway router. He wants to verify that the VM has the correct network mapping information. Which command would you tell him to use to gather this information?

   A. `dig`

   B. `ipconfig`

   C. `arp`

   D. `netstat`

4. Sharon is unable to reach her Linux-based web server hosted in the Singapore zone of the cloud. She is located in Austin, Texas. What command can she use to see where packet loss might be occurring?

   A. `traceroute`

   B. `ipconfig`

   C. `arp`

   D. `netstat`

   E. `ping`

   F. `tcpdump`

   G. `route print`

5. Eric is documenting different methods that his remote operations center can use to access the Calgary fleet of servers operating in a community cloud. Which of the following are *not* viable methods? (Choose two.)

   A. RDP

   B. Telnet

   C. IDS/IPS

   D. Terminal server

   E. DNS

   F. HTTP

6. Allison is in the process of migrating away from locally installed monitoring applications. What approach should she used instead?

   A. Java

   B. CSS

   C. Web

   D. RDP

   E. SSH

7. Mark's remote disaster recovery location follows the warm site model. To configure the network switches, routers, and firewalls remotely, Mark will need serial port access from his company's operations center. He has 14 serial ports currently, but he needs to be prepared for any unplanned expansion requirements during a disaster recover cutover. What device would you recommend that Mark implement at the warm site?

   A. RDP

   B. Telnet

   C. IPsec

   D. SSH

   E. Terminal server

8. Imani manages user accounts for her company's cloud presence. She has a trouble ticket open with Jill to assist her in accessing an SSD storage volume in the San Paulo region of the public cloud. What kind of user issue is she investigating?

   A. Authentication

   B. Authorization

   C. Federation

   D. SSO

9. Shaun is getting alarms from the public cloud's application load balancer about security failures. Harold reviews his problem resolution documentation to investigate, and there have been no troubles reported in the past year. The load balancer has been configured to offload port 443 web traffic from the back-end fleet of web servers. As a Cloud+ consultant brought in to assist, you decide which of the following should be the focus of the investigation?

   A. HTTPS
   B. Certificates
   C. IPsec
   D. RDP
   E. `ssldump`
   F. `netstat`

10. Multiple users are complaining that they cannot access a cloud-based collaboration system. The operations center has been investigating and has, so far, verified that the MFA applications are operational. What user system are they troubleshooting?

   A. Authentication
   B. Authorization
   C. Federation
   D. SSO

11. Your organization's back-end fleet of web servers is intermittently failing load balancer health checks and dropping out of the pool. You are involved in troubleshooting and begin your investigation by making sure that the web application is operational. What approach are you undertaking?

   A. Top-down
   B. Bottom-up
   C. Divide-and-conquer
   D. Evaluation
   E. Validation

12. Your web servers have lost communications to the SQL back-end database on your e-commerce public website. You are assisting in resolving the problem. After reviewing the log files and the monitoring system, you suspect that it may be a network-related issue. You devise a series of tests that starts with checking the server's connection to the database. What troubleshooting approach are you implementing?

   A. Top-down
   B. Bottom-up
   C. Divide-and-conquer
   D. Evaluation
   E. Validation

13. A middleware application running in the cloud is reporting session drops in its log files. You need to resolve the issue quickly and get the server back online. You decide to run `ping` and `traceroute` tests on the server as your first line of troubleshooting. What approach are you using?

    A. Top-down

    B. Bottom-up

    C. Divide-and-conquer

    D. Evaluation

    E. Validation

14. What are valid troubleshooting steps? (Choose all that apply.)

    A. Gather information

    B. Identify the issue

    C. Reboot everything

    D. Create a plan of action

    E. Test and verify

15. Cloud providers are responsible for the security of which of the following? (Choose all that apply.)

    A. Building

    B. Device

    C. Infrastructure

    D. VPNs

    E. User accounts

16. Kelly has picked up a trouble ticket that shows the connection between the Toledo field office and the Detroit cloud edge location has dropped. She confirms that it is a secure Internet-based access solution. What type of connection is this?

    A. Direct peering

    B. IDS

    C. VPN

    D. AES-256

    E. RDP

17. Nick is setting up a new fleet of IIS web servers in his IaaS e-commerce site. The company has elected to use a hybrid approach and desires graphical connections to the Windows bastion hosts. What traffic must he permit through the external-facing firewall to the host?

    A. SSH

    B. RDP

    C. DNS

    D. IPS

18. Jill logs into her NoSQL database server residing in a private subnet on a public cloud. She needs to verify IP connectivity with the application tier. What command can she use as a quick connectivity test?

    A. `arproute`

    B. `netstat`

    C. `tcpdump`

    D. `ping`

19. After deploying a new public website, your validation steps ask you to check the domain name–to–IP address mappings. What utility can you use for validation? (Choose two.)

    A. RDP

    B. dig

    C. SSH

    D. nslookup

    E. IPsec

    F. IPS

20. Donna logged into her cloud bastion host by making an SSH connection from her desktop. She uses the Linux host to connect to other systems in the private cloud. She needs to add an access control list rule to allow the bastion server to access a new subnet. Donna needs the source IP address of her host. What command can she run on the server to collect this information?

    A. `curl /localhost/metadata/global/interface`

    B. `ipconfig`

    C. `ifconfig`

    D. `netstat`

Appendix A

Answers to Review Questions

Chapter 1: Introducing Cloud Computing Configurations and Deployments

1. A. Infrastructure as a service (IaaS) gives you complete control of the operating system.
2. C. Resource pooling is the allocation of compute resources into a group or pool; these pools are then made available to a multitenant cloud environment.
3. A, C, D. Elements and objects are examples of devices and systems in the cloud. In this question, the elements are CPU, memory, and storage.
4. C. Pooled virtual resources include memory, storage, networking, and CPU. Security is a concept and not a physical resource that can be pooled.
5. B, D. One of the prime advantages of cloud-based computing and the automation and virtualization it offers in the background is the ability to leverage the rapid provisioning of virtual resources to allow for on-demand computing.
6. A, B, E. Elasticity, on-demand-computing, and pay-as-you-grow are all examples of being able to expand cloud compute resources as your needs require.
7. B. The interconnection of multiple cloud providers is referred to as a hybrid cloud.
8. C. A virtual switch is a virtual resource that's associated with one or more physical network interfaces on the host. VMs can connect to a virtual switch to connect to each other or to an external network.
9. B. The pay-as-you-grow cloud characteristic allows billing for only the services used.
10. A. It is best practice to split operations into different and isolated sections of the cloud for testing and isolation.
11. D. On-demand cloud computing allows the consumer to add and change resources dynamically with the use of an online portal.
12. C. Software as a Service offers cloud-managed applications as well as the underlying platform and infrastructure support.
13. A, E. Network delays, storage input/output performance, swap file usage, and the ability to scale are all examples of cloud performance components. Firewalls and encryption are security components, IaaS is a service model, and memory pooling is not relevant to the question.
14. A. Cloud operators segment their operations into regions for customer proximity, regulatory compliance, and resiliency.
15. A, B, D. Prior to performing a cloud migration, baseline measurements, a determination of capacity requirements, and complete documentation are all requirements for success.

16. C. The shared responsibility model outlines for which services and portions of the cloud operations the cloud consumer and provider are responsible.

17. C. Penetration testing is the process of trying to exploit vulnerabilities that exist in your infrastructure.

18. B, C. Community clouds are offered for a specific community of interest and shared by companies with similar requirements for regulatory compliance, security, or policy. Because in the SaaS model the cloud provider fully manages the app, they're responsible for the ongoing maintenance of it.

19. B. Orchestration platforms automate the provisioning of cloud services and often include a self-service dashboard that allows the consumer to manage and deploy cloud services with a web browser. The automation used by cloud providers allows for fast deployment of new services and applications.

20. B. Platform as a Service offers computing hardware, storage, networking, and the operating systems but not the application software.

Chapter 2: Cloud Deployments

1. C. A private cloud is used exclusively by a single organization.

2. D. A community cloud is used by companies with similar needs such as medical or financial services.

3. D. Multifactor authentication systems use a token generator as something that you have and a PIN/password as something you know.

4. B. With asynchronous replication, there will be a delay as the data is copied to the backup site and provides eventual consistency as it uses a store-and-forward design. The backup storage array is normally several transactions behind the primary.

5. C, D. When migrating stored data to the cloud, the two available options are online and offline.

6. B. When migrating a server that is running on bare metal to a hypervisor-based system, you would be performing a physical-to-virtual migration.

7. C, E, G. HTTPS, SSH, and FTPS all provide encrypted transmission of data.

8. B. Obfuscation is a technique to make information difficult to understand. One example of obfuscation is using random strings for usernames instead of obvious names like "admin."

9. D. A storage area network (SAN) is a high-speed network dedicated to storage transfers across a shared network. Block access is not a networking technology. Zoning is for restricting LUNs in a SAN, and VMFS is a VMware filesystem.

10. C. Authentication is the term used to describe the process of determining the identity of a user or device.

11. A, C, E. Application programming interfaces (APIs), command-line interfaces (CLI), and GUI-based interfaces are all commonly used tools to migrate, monitor, manage, and troubleshoot cloud-based resources.

12. B, D, F. A virtual machine will consume virtualized resources including virtual RAM, virtual CPUs, and memory pools.

13. C. Tiering is the process of defining the storage needs of the cloud customer and aligning them with the cloud provider's offerings. RAID is a hardware storage family of redundancy types. Multipathing is a redundant SAN technique, and policies are not related to the question.

14. B. RAID combines physical disks for redundancy and performance. Multipathing is a redundancy SAN design, masking is a LUN access process, and tiering is a storage hierarchy technique.

15. D. RAID 5 has parity information that is striped across multiple drives, which allows the drive array to be rebuilt if a single drive in the array fails. The other options do not have parity data.

16. B. The service level agreement (SLA) outlines specific metrics and the minimum performance provided by the cloud provider.

17. C. Storage area networks support block-based storage.

18. B. Identity systems using federations allow multiple organizations to use the same data for identification when accessing the networks or resources of everyone in the group.

19. B, D. Both migration WAN bandwidth and compatible VM file formats are critical to a successful migration.

20. D. Intrusion detection systems monitor network traffic for malicious activity and generate reports and alerts. Intrusion prevention takes this a step further and actively attempts to shut down the intrusion as it is happening.

Chapter 3: Security in the Cloud

1. B. The Platform as a Service model offers operating system security provided by the service provider.

2. B, C. Logging into a system is referred to as authentication, and the use of a password and a token to log in describes two-factor authentication.

3. C. The question outlines the function of a role-based access control approach.

4. C. Service Organization Controls 3 reports are for public disclosure of financial controls and security reporting.

5. B. The National Institute of Standards and Technology (NIST) FIPS 140-2 publication coordinates the requirements and standards for cryptography modules.

6. B. The Department of Defense Information Assurance Certification and Accreditation Process (DIACAP) is the process for computer systems IT security. DIACAP compliance is required to be certified to meet the U.S. Department of Defense security requirements for contractors.

7. B. The Health Insurance Portability and Accountability Act defines the standards for protecting medical data, and it is mandatory for Mary's requirements.

8. A, B, E. Hardening web servers, self-hosted databases, and on-premises DHCP servers are the responsibility of the customer. The cloud provider is responsible for hardening managed services, such as elastic filesystems.

9. A. The mandatory access control approach is often found in high-security environments where access to sensitive data needs to be highly controlled. Using the mandatory access control approach, a user will authenticate, or log into, a system. Based on the user's identity and security levels of the individual, access rights will be determined by comparing that data against the security properties of the system being accessed.

10. B. The Federal Risk and Authorization Management Program is a U.S. federal government program that outlines the standards for a security assessment, authorization, and continuous monitoring for cloud products and services.

11. B. The company's security policy outlines all aspects of your cloud security posture.

12. B. Two-factor authentication includes something that you have (in this case, a card) and something that you know (a PIN).

13. C. Advanced Encryption Standard is a symmetrical block cipher that has options to use three lengths, including 128, 192, and 256 bits. AES 256 is a very secure standard, and it would take an extremely long time and a lot of processing power to come even close to breaking the code. AES has been approved and adopted by many governments, including the United States and Canada, to encrypt sensitive data. AES has also been adopted as a standard by the National Institute of Standards and Technology.

14. B, C. Lightweight Directory Access Protocol and Active Directory are two technologies that enable SSO access to cloud resources.

15. B. A reverse proxy sits at the edge of a network and intercepts incoming requests and then proxies the request to the server. A reverse proxy is in a perfect position to perform load balancing.

16. A. Multifactor uses temporarily issued numerical tokens that must be entered at the time of user authentication.

17. C. Transport Layer Security (TLS) provides an encrypted session between the client and the server. To secure websites, it's a part of the Hypertext Transfer Protocol Secure (HTTPS) protocol.

18. C. Many IPsec implementations are found in routers and firewalls within VPNs, application security, and network security to provide a secure connection over an insecure network such as the Internet.

19. A, B, D, F. Securing user accounts and policies include installing antivirus software, disabling unused servers, implementing host-based firewall services, and shutting down all default user accounts.

20. B. Single sign-on allows a user to log in one time and be granted access to multiple systems without having to authenticate to each one individually.

Chapter 4: Implementing Cloud Security

1. A, C, D. Cloud segmentation is the process of dividing up your cloud deployment into sections that allow for granular security. Common segments include compute, network, and storage. APIs, JSON, and XML are used in automation.

2. B, D. One-time numerical tokens are generated on keyfob hardware devices and smartphone soft-token applications.

3. C. Applying security applications on a virtual server will cause an increase in CPU usage.

4. C. Automation of cloud deployments was instrumental in the growth of cloud-based services.

5. B, D. Storage systems and database applications both can store data at rest, so Carl must ensure that these services properly encrypt the data. VPNs deal with data in transit, whereas client encryption falls outside of the purview of the cloud.

6. C. A dashboard is a graphical portal that provides updates and an overview of operations.

7. C. Ultimately the responsibility for data in the cloud belongs to the organization that owns the data.

8. C. Orchestration systems automate cloud operations. Some examples are Chef, Puppet, and Kubernetes.

9. A, B, C, E. All of these cloud services have APIs that can be accessed for creation, configuration, and monitoring using standard RESTful APIs.

10. E. A host-based intrusion detection system will allow Jim to apply intrusion protection to a specific virtual machine.

11. D. Multifactor authentication services use a token that is generated on a schedule and can be a numerical value. The other options are not cloud services.

12. C. An application programming interface (API) offers programmatic access, control, and configuration of a device between different and discrete software components.

13. B, C, E, F. All compliance requirements should be integrated into the complete lifecycle of a project. including the design, planning, implementation, and validation phases of the project.

14. A, B. Extensible Markup Language (XML) and JavaScript Object Notation (JSON) provide a flexible way to describe data, create information formats, and electronically share structured data among computing systems. Both are lightweight data-interchange formats that are easily readable for computing systems to parse and generate.

15. C. Intrusion prevention systems will monitor for malicious activity and actively take countermeasures to eliminate or reduce the effects of the intrusion.

16. B. TLS is the most common encryption protocol for web-based applications. MD5 is a hash algorithm. IPsec is used for encrypting VPN connections, not HTTP connections.

17. C, D. Temporary storage volumes that are only in existence when the VM is deployed are referred to as ephemeral or nondurable storage.

18. B. It is considered a best practice to group compute resources into like segments and apply security to the segment.

19. B. The command-line interface is a text-based interface to most network services that allows for remote and local configurations.

20. C. Based on the information given, the description is for a GUI management application.

Chapter 5: Maintaining Cloud Operations

1. A. Full backups offer the advantage of a complete and up-to-date copy of your data in one operation. They have the disadvantage of taking a long time to perform because all the data in a storage system must be copied instead of just the modified data from the last backup.

2. C, D. Cloud configuration front ends as well as automation systems using scripting or API calls can shut down and restart virtual machines as required. Both restarts and shutdowns may be performed because of a code upgrade, troubleshooting, or other needs. The shutdown and restart processes can be monitored through the management systems and dashboards that are offered by the cloud provider. If they do not respond, these systems can be configured to generate an alarm.

3. A, C, E. Common patch management offerings are Chef, Puppet, and Ansible.

4. B. A patch is a piece of software that is intended to update an application, operating system, or any other software-based system to fix or improve its operations. Generally, patches are synonymous with fixes for security vulnerabilities or any other type of operational bug.

5. C. Cloning takes the master image and clones it to be used as another separate and independent VM. Important components of a server are changed to prevent address conflicts. These include the UUID and MAC addresses of the cloned server.

6. B. A snapshot is a file-based image of the current state of a VM, including the complete set of operating systems and all the applications that are stored on it. The snapshot will record the data on the disk, its current state, and the VM's configuration at that instant in time. Snapshots can be created while the VM is in operation and are used as a record of that VM's state. They can function as a backup that you can restore from later.

7. A. Many corporate and most regulatory requirements will specify that the backup data must be located at a separate data center from the origin data center and that the two must be geographically away from each other. Many cloud providers interconnect their data centers into regions and availability zones using high-speed, directly connected fiber networks that allow large backup sets to traverse the data network between the data centers and that make remote backups feasible.

8. C. A version update is the process of replacing a software product with a newer version of the same product. Version updates can add new features, bring the system up-to-date, provide a rollup of all previous patches, and improve the product.

9. B. Workflow automation defines a structured process for a series of actions that should be taken to complete a process. With cloud-based workflow services, special workflow applications are offered as a managed service that creates a defined sequence of events, or workflow, with each procedure tracked and passed to the next process in the workflow.

10. C. The main function of orchestration systems is to combine and execute the multiple tasks that must be completed to accomplish an operation. These tasks are combined into a workflow that defines the order of events and steps needed to complete the operation. The orchestration system uses software systems and processes to carry out the workflow.

11. A, D. Placing a system into maintenance mode and disabling system alerts ensure that the management systems will not alert on false positives when a system undergoing regular maintenance does not respond when polled by management systems, and it will not send out unsolicited alarms because of the maintenance being performed.

12. A. A hotfix is a software update type that is intended to fix an immediate and specific problem with a quick release procedure.

13. C. Online backup storage is a system that can be accessed at any time without the requirement for a network administrator to mount the media into a storage system. Online is the most common storage design, and backups offer an always-available method to store and retrieve the data.

14. C. A cluster is a group of tightly coupled systems designed for high availability and that still operate if one or more nodes is offline.

15. B, C, E. Infrastructure that is part of the infrastructure-as-a-service (IaaS) service provider's area of responsibility includes load balancers, hypervisors, and routers. A virtual machine, database, or email server would be the responsibility of the customer.

16. B. A rolling configuration will sequentially upgrade the web servers without causing a complete outage and would meet the requirements outlined in the question.

17. D. The manager is requesting data on the results of the quality assurance testing on the release. Rollout is a patch deployment process, and both automation and orchestration systems are used to install the patch.

18. C. Blue-green is a software deployment methodology that uses two configurations for production that are identical to each other. These deployments can alternate between each other, with one being active and the other being inactive.

19. C. Incremental backups are operations based on the change of the source data since the last incremental backup was performed. Incremental backups can be run, for example, on a nightly basis and capture the changes that were made since the previous backup was run the night before. This allows for an efficient backup operation since only the changes in the past 24 hours are stored on the backup media. Incremental backups are much less time- and resource-consuming than a full backup and are used to complement them.

20. D. Offline storage requires the administrator to make the data available by inserting a tape or other media into a storage system for retrieval. Offline storage can be transported to remote storage facilities or stored in vaults for protection.

Chapter 6: Disaster Recovery, Business Continuity, and Ongoing Maintenance

1. B. Asynchronous replication is when data is written to the primary first, and then later a copy is written to the remote site on a scheduled arrangement or after a delay.

2. A. The hot site model is the most viable option given the requirements. A hot site is a fully functional backup site that can assume operations immediately should the primary location fail or go offline.

3. B, C. The restore point and restore time objectives are the measurements for data lost and the time needed to get back online after an outage.

4. B. Edge locations are not complete cloud data centers. They are cloud connection points located in major cities and offer the benefits outlined in the question.

5. B. Access control systems are used to grant users object access in an operating system. For ongoing maintenance and best security practices, it is important to delete old and unused access control policies.

6. B. The restore point objective is the point in time at which data can be recovered. James had to update the RPO metric.

7. B. Moving inactive data or data that is no longer being used to a separate storage facility for long-term storage is referred to as archiving. It can be more cost-effective to store archived data in less expensive storage systems and still allow the cloud consumer access to that data for backup and retrieval as needed.

8. B, F. The backup site's network connections must be engineered to accept the expected traffic load and prevent bandwidth starvation.

9. B. Automation systems are back-end processes for front-end systems such as dashboards or catalogs.

10. C. Firewalls contain a list of policies, or rules, that either permit or deny traffic. Over time, as the environment changes, it is a best practice to review the firewall rules and remove or modify any rules that are obsolete or unused.

11. D. Stale or out-of-date domain name entries may point to servers that are no longer in use.

12. H. It is important to review all of your network services to address any changes required when implementing a disaster recovery plan.

13. C. The recovery time objective is the amount of time a system can be offline during a disaster. It is the amount of time it takes to get a service online and available after a failure.

14. E. A cold site is a backup data center provisioned to take over operations in the event of a primary data center failure, but the servers and infrastructure are not deployed or operational until needed.

15. A. Synchronous replication offerings write data to both the primary storage system and the replica simultaneously to ensure that the remote data is current with local replicas.

16. D. Cloud edge locations are often used for proximity services at remote locations that provide data caching locally and offloads the need for calls to the web server fleet.

17. A, B. Synchronous and asynchronous replication are ongoing file synchronization processes.

18. C. Orphaned resources are left over when a service terminates and they are no longer needed or used.

19. B. A warm site approach to recovering from a primary data center outage is when the remote backup of the site is offline except for critical data storage, which is usually a database. The warm site will host an operational database server that is in sync with the database server at the primary data center and is sometimes referred to as the candlelight or pilot light design.

20. C. DNS records can be modified by external operations and can map domain names to IP addresses. There you will find occurrences of DNS entries not being deleted and becoming stale over time.

Chapter 7: Cloud Management

1. G. All of the options listed are valid metrics for establishing a baseline.

2. C. The establishment of average usage over time is the data that gets collected for a baseline report.

3. C. Password complexity defines password length, if it is a nondictionary word, and if uppercase/lowercase or special characters are required.
4. D. A lockout policy can be applied to an account that defines the parameters that create a lockup event. It is most common to apply a lockout policy to failed login attempts. For example, you can define a policy where four failed login attempts in five minutes will disable an account for 30 minutes. A lockout policy will most likely be defined by your information security group, and you may be asked to create and apply the policy as part of your duties.
5. A. Access control systems are user configurations that grant roles and duties to users or groups of users and also to systems such as VMs, applications, and storage volumes. For example, database administrators can be given full access to manage a database application but be restricted from performing VM or storage operations.
6. B. With the platform-as-a-service (PaaS) model, the cloud provider will maintain the operating system and all supporting infrastructure.
7. C. The process of taking a large amount of event data and comparing the logs to determine the sequence of events is referred to as event correlation.
8. C. The ability to disable an account can be helpful in situations where the account will need to be reactivated at a future date and does not need to be deleted. Account disablement can be managed in the same manner as other account operations, with a web front end or with the use of APIs for scripted and automated processes.
9. C. User-based policies are tied to a user and define what permissions a user has. Contrast these with resource-based policies, which are tied to a particular resource.
10. A. Once the collection policy has been created, it can be reused and applied to other objects as they are created or migrated. Event collection policies reduce the amount of management overhead and enforce consistency in your deployments.
11. A, B, D. Cloud computing operates with a utility business model that charges you only for the resources that you consume. This model enables you to scale your cloud fleet to meet its current workload and be able to add and remove capacity as needed. There are many options for using elasticity to scale cloud operations, including vertical and horizontal scaling and bursting.
12. F. All of the answers offered are valid event notification service receivers.
13. B. The measurement of the difference between a current reading and the baseline value is referred to as the variance.
14. B. Scaling up, or vertical scaling, will add resources such as CPU instances or more RAM. When you scale up, you are basically increasing your compute, network, or storage capabilities.
15. C. Cloud automation systems offer the ability to dynamically add and remove resources as needed; this is referred to as elasticity.
16. B. Cloud bursting allows for adding capacity from another cloud service during times when additional compute resources are needed.

17. A, B. Mergers and acquisitions may necessitate combining two cloud operations into one single system. You should be prepared to work with new groups and departments to look at how the other company's cloud deployment is architected and what options are available to integrate them. Applications may be duplicated, and there could be efficiencies gained by integrating them.

18. C. Change management includes recording the change, planning for the change, testing the documentation, getting approvals, evaluating, validating, writing instructions for backing out the change if needed, and doing post-change review if desired.

19. F. Managing the life cycle of an application will include deployments, upgrades, migrations, feature additions and deletions, replacements, and retirements.

20. C. The higher up the services stack you go, from IaaS to SaaS, the more difficult it will be to migrate. With infrastructure as a service (IaaS), most of the cloud operations are under your direct control, which gives you the most flexibility to migrate. However, if the cloud provider controls the application, you may not have many options to migrate.

Chapter 8: Cloud Management Baselines, Performance, and SLAs

1. B. If a server is using all of its network bandwidth, then the most logical solution is to add more. You can do this by installing a second network adapter and connecting it to a different subnet. The other solutions could conceivably address the problem, but success is less likely.

2. D. Performance baselines characterize hardware performance, so the OS update history would be of little or no use for future comparisons. A server baseline typically consists of CPU, memory, disk, and network performance statistics.

3. E. Vertical scaling is the process of upgrading or replacing a server with one that has greater capabilities.

4. A, D, E. Incident reports include events such as opening trouble tickets and contacting customer support and outages. Scaling and service level agreements are not considered impairments.

5. A, B. Most databases are designed to scale vertically. They can also be scaled (not scoped) horizontally by adding a read replica.

6. C, D. Service level agreements outline performance and availability commitments and not configurations.

7. A, B, D, E. Cloud reporting is intended for internal corporate groups such as marketing, management, accounting, and operations.

8. D. Objects are queried to gather metric data.

9. D. Cloud reports are formatted collections of data contained in the management or monitoring applications.

10. C. A dashboard is a configurable graphical representation of current operational data.

11. C. After performing a major system upgrade, you should collect new baseline data as the overall system performance has changed.

12. A, D, E. CPU, RAM, and network utilization are all important objects to manage for capacity and utilization tracking. Storage volume tiers and OS versions do not apply to this scenario.

13. A, B, D, E. Autoscaling allows for adding and removing cloud compute capacity, providing capacity changes based on the time of day, and maintaining a minimum number of VMs. Report generation and SLA object tracking are not autoscaling functions.

14. B, E. Both Excel and PDF are the most common reporting formats. The other database, programming, and scripting options are not applicable to report generation.

15. A. Horizontal scaling is the process of adding extra servers for increased capacity. Round-robin is a load-balancing metric and does not apply. Elasticity is the ability to add and remove resources. Autoscaling is the automated process of adding and removing capacity. Vertical scaling is expanding a server.

16. A, C, D. Databases return data from read operations and are a critical performance metric. CPU saturation could cause a slowdown as well as network issues such as packet loss.

17. B, E, F. Trends, usage, and deficiencies are all management report outputs that can be identified using object tracking.

18. A, C, D. Server performance can be increased by adding more CPU processing, memory, and network capacity. SLA, ACL, and DNS are not related to increasing server capacity.

19. B. Tracking object performance data should match with the guaranteed levels outlined in the service level agreement.

20. A, D. High-performance computing relies on the servers being in close proximity to reduce network and storage latency. Being in the same availability zone and on the same hypervisor accomplishes this. There is no such thing as a group cache.

Chapter 9: Troubleshooting

1. A, C, D. Resources such as the amount of RAM needed, CPU cycles, and storage capacity are common systems that may become saturated as your cloud compute requirements grow.

2. C. Database read and write requests utilize storage I/O and should be the focus for troubleshooting.

3. A, C, D. When troubleshooting, it is helpful to have access to configurations, documentation, and diagrams to provide information on your cloud deployment.

4. D. Cloud autoscaling can dynamically add server capacity based on loading.

5. B. A large number of users downloading a new application would cause an increase in network bandwidth usage.

6. E. Any of these answers would be correct depending on his licensing agreement with the database provider.

7. B, C, D. In addition to the web servers, IP addresses may be required for the NTP and DNS services and the default gateway.

8. C. Elasticity allows for cloud services to expand and contract based on actual usage and would be applicable to increasing storage capacity.

9. B. When troubleshooting cloud performance issues, the current number of users on the system can be an important indicator of load. When there are high user counts, you can track what parts of your deployment are most heavily used and track the load on all of the devices to see where the congestion points are.

10. D. A baseline measurement is used as a reference to determine cloud capacity increases and decreases.

11. B. The cloud service provider owns its automation and orchestration systems, and they cannot be directly accessed by the customer.

12. C. The change management process would need to be modified to prevent one change from affecting another that is taking place simultaneously.

13. C. The Domain Name System records need to be changed to reflect the new IP address mapped to the domain name.

14. B. Templates are software definitions of a cloud network and are used for automated deployments.

15. C. Workflow applications track a process from start to finish and sequence the applications that are required to complete the process.

16. A, B, D. Symptoms of reaching the capacity boundary of a service include application failures, increased latency, and request drops.

17. C. The common measurement for an API is requests per second.

18. C. It is common for batch processing to be performed on database applications.

19. B, C. The total number of CPU cores and clock speed are common parameters to define when configuring a machine image.

20. D. The CIDR block determines the size of a subnet.

Chapter 10: Troubleshooting Networking and Security Issues and Understanding Methodologies

1. D. SSH is the encrypted replacement of the Telnet protocol, and it is used to access remote devices using a command-line interface. RDP is a Windows graphical interface. Telnet does not offer encryption, and terminal servers offer serial port access but may or may not support encrypted network access.

2. C. `tcpdump` allows a Linux system to capture live network traffic, and it is useful in monitoring and troubleshooting. Sometimes called sniffing, `tcpdump` allows you to set up filters to select the traffic that you are interested in capturing for troubleshooting. Think of `tcpdump` as a command-line network analyzer. `dig` and `nslookup` show DNS resolution but do not display the actual packets going across the wire. `netstat` shows connection information and is not DNS related.

3. C. ARP is the protocol that maps an IP address to a MAC address on a local network. The mappings can be seen with the `arp` command. `dig` is used for DNS resolution, `ipconfig` shows the network adapter parameters, and `netstat` shows connections.

4. A. The `traceroute` (Linux) or `tracert` (Windows) command is useful for network path troubleshooting. It shows the routed path that a packet of data takes from source to destination. You can use it to determine whether routing is working as expected or whether there is a route failure in the path. The other options are incorrect since they do not provide network path data.

5. C, E. Common remote access tools include RDP, SSH, and terminal servers. IDSs/IPSs are for intrusion detection, and DNS is for domain name–to–IP address mappings and is not a utility for remote access.

6. C. Of the options given, the web approach does not require any local application installations and offers a graphical systems management interface.

7. E. In a data center, terminal servers are deployed and have several serial ports, each cabled to a console port on a device that is being managed. This allows Mark to make an SSH or a Telnet connection to the terminal server and then use the serial interfaces to access the console ports on the devices to which you want to connect. The other options given do not provide serial port connections.

8. B. The question is asking about being able to access a specific cloud service. This would concern Jill having authorization to access the storage volume. Authentication and SSO are login systems and not rights to services. A federation links user databases.

9. B. The question shows that the load balancer is terminating SSL/TLS traffic from the web. SSL certificates have expiration dates, and so as part of the troubleshooting approach, security certificate expirations need to be investigated. The other options do not accomplish this requirement.

10. A. Logging into systems is referred to as authentication. Also, the question references multifactor authentication (MFA) as part of the system. Authorization is the accessing of services after the authentication process, federations interconnect external user accounts to the cloud, and single sign-on (SSO) allows a user to authenticate one time to access all resources in the cloud.

11. A. The top-down approach references the OSI model; it starts at the application layer and works downward until the problem is identified. The application is checked first, and if that is operational, you continue to work down the network stack until you identify the problem.

12. B. The bottom-up approach starts at the lowest level of the ISO model with the physical network connections, such as cabling, and works upward by investigating VLANs, IP addressing, and so on, until the issue is located.

13. C. The divide-and-conquer troubleshooting approach starts in the middle of the OSI networking stack and, depending on the results, directs future tests. In this case, the troubleshooter began at the network layer, which is in the middle of the OSI model. This is the divide-and-conquer approach.

14. A, B, D, E. All of the answers except "reboot everything" are valid troubleshooting steps.

15. A, B, C. Building, device, and infrastructure security are all the responsibility of the cloud provider. The provider may implement measures such as having nondescript facilities, video surveillance, and biometric access.

16. C. A secure Internet-based connection would be a VPN.

17. B. The Windows Remote Desktop Protocol allows for remote connections to a Windows graphical user desktop.

18. D. The `ping` command verifies end-to-end IP connectivity and is the correct answer. The other options either do not apply, such as `tcpdump` and `netstat`, or are not valid commands, such as `arproute`.

19. B, D. Nslookup is a Windows command-line utility for resolving domain names to IP addressing. The Linux equivalent is the dig utility. The other options are not valid for the solution required in the question.

20. C. The Linux command `ifconfig` will display all network-related configuration information for that computer and is the correct answer. `ipconfig` is the Windows equivalent, and it is not relevant to this question. `netstat` and the query string are not applicable to the question.

Appendix B

Answers to Written Labs

Chapter 1: Introducing Cloud Computing Configurations and Deployments

1. Software
2. Infrastructure
3. Platform
4. Ubiquitous access
5. Virtualization
6. A dedicated private connection
7. Replication
8. Load balancer
9. SSH, RDP
10. Baselines

Chapter 2: Cloud Deployments

1. Memory ballooning
2. Storage area network
3. Fault tolerance
4. Synchronous replication
5. Virtual-to-virtual
6. Application portability
7. Federations
8. Load balancer
9. Benchmark
10. Intrusion prevention system

Chapter 3: Security in the Cloud

1. Know, have
2. Security policy
3. Discretionary access
4. Single sign-on
5. Cipher
6. Automation
7. Object
8. Shared
9. Public key infrastructure
10. Software as a service

Chapter 4: Implementing Cloud Security

1. Data classification
2. Segmentation
3. At rest
4. Know, have
5. Automation
6. API
7. Graphical user interface
8. Intrusion prevention systems
9. CPU
10. Automation

Chapter 5: Maintaining Cloud Operations

1. Blue-green
2. Rolling update
3. Rollback

4. Snapshots, cloning
5. Backup target
6. Replicas
7. Hotfix
8. Differential backup
9. System alerts
10. Backup window

Chapter 6: Disaster Recovery, Business Continuity, and Ongoing Maintenance

1. Archiving
2. Disaster recovery
3. Business continuity
4. Disaster recovery
5. Inactive
6. Replication
7. RPO, RTO
8. System
9. Orphaned resources
10. Synchronous

Chapter 7: Cloud Management

1. Metric
2. Orchestration
3. Anomaly
4. Trigger
5. Infrastructure, SLA
6. Change management
7. Life cycle management
8. Permissions
9. Complexity
10. Back out

Chapter 8: Cloud Management Baselines, Performance, and SLAs

1. Baseline
2. Metric
3. Objects
4. Horizontal
5. Memory
6. Latency
7. Resiliency
8. Service level agreement
9. Vertical scaling
10. Auditing

Chapter 9: Troubleshooting

1. Templates
2. Network Time Protocol
3. Capacity
4. Reduce load, add capacity
5. Mergers, acquisitions
6. Domain name, IP address
7. Validate
8. Log files
9. Configuration
10. Diagrams

Chapter 10: Troubleshooting Networking and Security Issues and Understanding Methodologies

1. QoS
2. Jumbo
3. Proxy
4. VXLAN
5. netstat
6. dig, nslookup
7. Documentation
8. Create a theory of probable cause
9. Internal
10. Privilege escalation

Index

A

B

C

D

E

F

G

H

I

J

L

M

N

Q

R

S

T

U

V

W

Z